A STILL AND QUIET CONSCIENCE

A STILL AND QUIET CONSCIENCE

The Archbishop Who Challenged a Pope,
a President, and a Church

John A. McCoy

ORBIS BOOKS
Maryknoll, New York 10545

ORBIS BOOKS
Maryknoll, New York 10545

Fathers and Brothers
MARYKNOLL™

Fifth Printing, January 2016

Founded in 1970, Orbis Books endeavors to publish works that enlighten the mind, nourish the spirit, and challenge the conscience. The publishing arm of the Maryknoll Fathers and Brothers, Orbis seeks to explore the global dimensions of the Christian faith and mission, to invite dialogue with diverse cultures and religious traditions, and to serve the cause of reconciliation and peace. The books published reflect the views of their authors and do not represent the official position of the Maryknoll Society. To learn more about Maryknoll and Orbis Books, please visit our website at www.maryknollsociety.org.

McCoy, John A.
    A still and quiet conscience : the archbishop who challenged a pope, a president, and a church / John A. McCoy.
        pages cm
    Includes bibliographical references and index.
    ISBN 978-1-62698-117-1 (pbk.)
    1. Hunthausen, Raymond G. 2. Bishops—United States—Bishops—Biography. 3. Catholic Church—United States—Bishops—Biography. 4. Catholic Church I. Title.
    BX4705.H855M33 2015
    282.092—dc23
    [B]
                                                          2014042163

To my late mother, Marian E. McCoy, for her love of a church that gave meaning to this life and a path to eternal life.

To my wife, Karen Chesledon McCoy, for her love of God in spite of a church that stumbles, falls, and loses its way.

"I feel within me a peace above all earthly dignities,
a still and quiet conscience."

—William Shakespeare, *Henry VIII*

CONTENTS

PROLOGUE

An archival photo dominates the front page of the special October 11, 2012, edition of *The Catholic Northwest Progress* commemorating the fiftieth anniversary of the momentous Second Vatican Council. The photo, taken in St. Peter's Square in Rome in 1965, pictures then–Seattle Archbishop Thomas A. Connolly with five seminarians. Smiling in varying degrees, the six men stand abreast and look directly at the camera.

Connolly, at the photo's center, wears a white surplice with billowy sleeves over his purple cassock and has a purple biretta on his head. The seminarians wear buttoned black cassocks with Roman collars. The photo caption identifies Connolly and two of the five seminarians but the other three, presumably because they later left the priesthood, are anonymous, their names erased from history much as *Pravda* expunged fallen Soviet leaders.

This special Vatican II edition of *The Progress,* the official publication of the Catholic Archdiocese of Seattle, does a curious job of recalling the most significant event in the Roman Catholic Church in the past five hundred years. Some twenty-eight hundred bishops from all over the world came to St. Peter's Basilica for four sessions from 1962 to 1965 to address the challenges the modern world presented to the church. They produced sixteen documents, dealing with issues such as liturgy, divine revelation, church governance, ecumenism, religious liberty, education, and nuclear war. In doing so, they laid the foundation for a dramatically different kind of church.

The Progress devotes much of its Council edition to quoting Connolly, who died in 1991. It chose to reprint excerpts from the first-person accounts that he typed out on his portable Olivetti and wired home from Rome fifty years earlier. The late archbishop's reports are supplemented with a Catholic News Service story about key theologians at the Council, a boxed list of actions and documents related to Vatican II, and another CNS news story quoting Cardinal William Levada, Rome's doctrinal chief under Pope Benedict XVI. Levada describes the Council as "doctrinal in principle" and bemoans confusion and misunderstandings about its interpretation.

Halfway down page thirteen of this special edition is a photo of an elderly, white-haired man dressed in a black clerical suit and Roman collar. He is seated in an empty cathedral pew in front of a newly blessed shrine to Pope John XXIII, the convener of the Council. The photo caption identifies the man as Archbishop Emeritus Raymond G. Hunthausen.

In fact, at the time *The Progress* went to press, Hunthausen, archbishop of Seattle from 1975 to 1991, was the only surviving American bishop who participated in all four sessions of the Council. He was visiting Seattle and was of sound mind and spirit. Yet there is no interview or article nor are there quotes from him on how the Second Vatican Council changed his life, the archdiocese, or the Catholic Church. There is no reporting about Hunthausen's wholehearted implementation of the reforms of Vatican II and how he endeavored to create an inclusive, caring, and relevant church. No mention of that at all.

Yet Hunthausen was the quintessential Vatican II bishop. "Born again" as a result of his experience of the Council, he returned home with a vision of church in which all its members—in fact, all people of good will—worked together to build the kingdom of God in this world. It would be a church that flung open its doors and welcomed and embraced the world—women, gays, the divorced, the remarried, doubters, and unbelievers as well as the poor, suffering, and oppressed. It would be a church that addressed the preeminent moral issues of the day—war, peace, justice, human dignity, and human life. It would be a church that worked collegially, reaching decisions by consensus, and sharing responsibility for the decisions it made.

But it was a church that was not to be. From the time of his election in 1978, Pope John Paul II, assisted and succeeded by his doctrinal watchdog, Cardinal Joseph Ratzinger (later Pope Benedict XVI), halted and reversed the reforming spirit of the Council. Perhaps nowhere was this played out more dramatically than in Seattle where John Paul found himself faced with an archbishop whose conscience and understanding of the Council caused him to challenge U.S. President Ronald Reagan, a Vatican ally, over the issue of nuclear arms.

Hunthausen's tax protest against nuclear weapons marked a pivotal point in the history of the U.S. Catholic Church. His prophetic voice was stifled as John Paul made common cause with the Reagan administration against the Soviet Union. Meanwhile, the U.S. bishops, their ranks filled with John Paul appointees, fled from Council reform, forsook collegiality, and bowed to Vatican authority. Rome made Hunthausen its sacrificial victim. He was investigated, humiliated, and pressured from office so that the U.S. bishops would understand that the pope reigns supreme.

The U.S. bishops' capitulation to Roman absolutism had dire consequences. Because of John Paul's indifference, the bishops repeatedly failed to address the scandal of clerical sex abuse, destroying much of their integrity in the process. They lost themselves in polarizing culture wars over abortion, same-sex marriage, and health care coverage of contraception. The prophetic teaching role they had exercised in Hunthausen's time—when their pastoral letters on peace and the economy set a moral standard for the nation—was long gone.

As a life-long Catholic and resident of western Washington, I likely met Archbishop Hunthausen at some church event not too long after his appointment to Seattle in 1975. My wife suggests I don't recall the occasion because Hunthausen is "refreshingly normal," and thus unremarkable. What riveted my attention was the speech he gave in June 1981 at the annual regional meeting of Lutheran pastors in Tacoma. Hunthausen described the nuclear-armed Trident submarine as the "Auschwitz of Puget Sound" and suggested that people withhold their federal income tax to protest nuclear arms. The reaction to his speech was explosive.

At the time, I was working on the city desk of the *Seattle Post-Intelligencer*, the morning newspaper. I remember the city editor reading the wire story of Hunthausen's talk, looking up incredulously, and exclaiming to me, "McCoy, who is this guy?"

Over the next few years, I was one of several *P-I* reporters who interviewed Hunthausen on various occasions—at peace rallies outside the Bangor base, during the attempted blockade against the first Trident submarine, and when the FBI acknowledged keeping a secret file on him. The media interviews covered a host of topics: abortion, euthanasia, homosexuality, the role of women in the church, AIDS, sanctuary for Central American refugees, clergy sexual abuse, and his own ordeal with Rome.

In 1989, I became public affairs director for the Seattle archdiocese. As such I was the chief spokesman for the archbishop, a job my seven-year-old daughter described "as talking to people the pope can't be bothered with." I also had editorial oversight of *The Progress*. I held the position through Hunthausen's retirement and the first four years of the administration of Archbishop Thomas J. Murphy, who succeeded him.

While at the archdiocese, I began doing interviews and taking notes with the intention of writing a biography of Hunthausen. Neither he nor Murphy was very keen on the idea. Murphy feared such a project could cause further troubles with Rome. Hunthausen simply didn't want any more attention. After he retired, however, he agreed to talk about his life.

I interviewed him, all six of his siblings, childhood friends, priest and bishop colleagues, members of his diocesan staffs in Helena and Seattle, supporters, critics, and advocates and activists for the causes of peace and a more inclusive and loving church. I stored all this interview material along with notes and news stories on an old Macintosh computer. I had good intentions to write the book when the time came. But it never did.

More than twenty years went by. I raised a family, pursued my career in communications, and eventually retired from full-time work. I remained a practicing Catholic but a conflicted one. I love the sacraments, the eucharistic meal of consecrated bread and wine, and the parish community striving to be the Body of Christ. I can be moved to tears by a magnificent liturgy, a splendid homily, or a glorious celebration of God's word in prayer and song. Such moments are truly transcendent.

But at the same time, I have been embarrassed and mortified by church leaders who have gotten things so wrong. Priests who scolded their congregations for consorting with Protestants or for countenancing same-sex relationships. Bishops who covered up for pedophile clergy and transferred them from one unsuspecting parish to the next. Prelates who reduced Catholic teaching to one all-encompassing issue—abortion—and barred pro-choice politicians, including the president of the United States, from speaking at their institutions or receiving communion in their churches. Church leaders who acted as autocratic monarchs with little concern for transparency or accountability to the very people they were called to serve.

Under John Paul II and Benedict XVI, we became a church that censured, excluded, and punished to protect what was defined as universal Catholic truth. I abhorred Benedict's notion that for the sake of the truth, it would be better if the church dwindled to a small, faithful, and orthodox remnant.

Such an idea presumes that doctrine is unchanging. Yet Vatican II recognized that doctrine evolves and develops in its encounter with the world. How could a church that once justified slavery and called Jews "Christ-killers" hold that its teachings on marriage, sexuality, ordination, or any issue—save Christ's divinity, love, and promise of eternal life—are immutable and unchangeable?

Since Hunthausen's time, the Catholic Church in the United States has suffered a great loss in credibility and the departure of nearly a third of its membership. I watched as my family and friends drifted away from the church. Some left angry. Some left disappointed. But most left despairing of a church they found irrelevant, unable or unwilling to engage with the central issues of their lives. I look around at Mass on Sunday mornings. Nearly half the pews are empty. My fellow worshipers look like me—old, gray, and cognizant of the fact that the next life is not that far away.

And then along came Francis. I don't know where Pope Francis will ultimately lead the church. But I am encouraged. He reminds me in many ways of Hunthausen. He's humble, kind, compassionate, plain spoken, and unpretentious. He has a Vatican II vision of church, of a church that is inclusive, loving, and transformative, of a church with a heart for the poor and the oppressed. He wants bishops who love poverty and simplicity, who are so close to the people that they smell like sheep.

The hope occasioned by Francis caused me to revisit the book project I had abandoned two decades earlier. I pulled out the old Macintosh computer, plugged it in, and it fired up. There on the hard drive were all the Hunthausen files. As I began reading them, I realized that the story of the archbishop's remarkable life remains a compelling one. And, in light of Francis, a much more relevant one because here was an unlikely leader who showed the way to a church that might have been. A church that could still be.

At its core, this is a story about a man struggling with God's will for him. Hunthausen, Pope Francis, you, and I engage in that same struggle. We try to make sense of our lives. Those of us who believe in Christ seek God's guidance, using our conscience to find the way.

Archbishop Hunthausen prayed long and hard in his struggle to understand what God wanted of him and the church. He had his doubts and he had his sorrows. But he also experienced God's joy, peace, and love. This is the story of his life journey as best I can tell it.

John A. McCoy
Seattle, Washington

1

TRIDENT

*We have grasped the mystery of the atom
and rejected the Sermon on the Mount.*
—General Omar Bradley

It was not what they had expected to hear.

Some of them had arrived at mid-morning on this soggy August Sunday in 1982. They'd each made a dollar donation to the Klallam Tribe to park their cars on Indian land. And then they had traipsed out with their signs, banners, and picnic lunches onto the grassy isthmus of Point Julia. By early afternoon when the peace rally opposing the Trident submarine was supposed to start, there were more than sixty-five hundred of them.

On the mucky, tidal flats of Puget Sound the rally organizers had erected a stage, a rickety wooden platform built on stilts. The ten-foot-tall structure faced the crowd and the beach, beyond which the land rose abruptly to steep hillsides of fir and cedar trees. Behind the stage were the open waters of Hood Canal where the *USS Ohio*, the first Trident submarine and the world's deadliest nuclear weapon, was to arrive within the week. An oversize banner tacked to the stage's crossbeams proclaimed: "Resist Trident. Celebrate Hope."

On the other side of Hood Canal, in the sheltered waters of Oak Bay, forty peace activists watched and waited with the small boats they planned to sail or row into the path of the mammoth submarine. They envisioned a David vs. Goliath battle that would slow or halt the *Ohio* and call the world's attention to the folly of nuclear arms.

At Point Julia, the rally organizers had miscalculated the time of the ebb tide, which resulted in a half-hour delay until the amplifiers and the sound system could be safely connected. No worries; the crowd was patient and the mood was festive. It was a heterogeneous group of all ages and social classes, of children, grandparents, peace activists, and curious bystanders. They were teachers, nurses, nuns, veterans, environmentalists, pacifists, school kids, and radicals. They spread blankets and tarps along the gravelly shoreline and made themselves as comfortable as possible on this unseasonably cool and drizzly summer afternoon. Some wore bright yellow buttons that read: "Resist Trident."

A contingent of Japanese Buddhist monks chanted and beat drums. They had propped up photographs showing the death and destruction caused by the atomic bombs dropped at Hiroshima and Nagasaki in 1945. Three Benedictine nuns from the St. Placid Priory in Lacey unfurled a hand-stitched cloth banner that read: "We All Grow Better in a Peaceful World."

People of faith were everywhere: Catholic parishioners from Olympia, Mennonites from south Seattle, a Methodist minister, a Nestorian Orthodox priest, a Native American shaman, and the head of the United Church of Christ in Washington and Northern Idaho. The Catholic Youth Organization had rented buses to transport foot passengers from the ferry landings at Winslow and Kingston. $1.50 round-trip. A disabled Baptist woman motored to the rally grounds in a battery-powered wheelchair.

But you didn't have to be a believer to be there. A young couple identified themselves as "Atheists Against Trident."

"The religious community doesn't have a monopoly on morality," the young woman said.

Sure enough, there were members of Greenpeace, the Revolutionary Communist Party, Veterans for Peace, and the Union of Concerned Educators. A conga line of demonstrators wove through the crowd lofting giant paper mache puppets of President Ronald Reagan, Soviet leader Yuri Andropov, and military bigwigs from both nations. More than a hundred "peacekeepers," assigned to answer questions, maintain order, and point out the parking and the port-a-potties, circulated through the crowd. But they had little to do. The mood was mellow, almost joyful.

Point Julia was an unlikely site for the huge anti-Trident rally. The organizers wanted a location on the Canal as near as possible to the giant Navy base at Bangor where the submarine would dock. But they were hard pressed to find one. Kitsap and Jefferson Counties, the two jurisdictions bordering the Canal, refused to issue permits to use their parks. Other properties were either too small or the property owners were leery of offending their neighbors or the Navy. The rally organizers went to the Klallam tribal council but were rebuffed.

Then, as time was running out, a member of the tribal baseball team phoned with an offer. He said he could persuade the tribal elders to approve use of Indian land for the peace rally if the ball team could operate a food concession stand there. The team needed money for uniforms. The rally organizers agreed to the deal and the ball-player convinced the tribal council. The largest ever anti-Trident rally was on.

Point Julia affords a clear view of all maritime traffic—including surfaced submarines—coming into Hood Canal through Admiralty Inlet from the Straits of Juan de Fuca, the international waterway that separates the United States from Canada. The point, which juts out into tiny Port Gamble Bay, is just a few miles north of the Bangor base.

Once the tide was far enough out to lay the power cords, the peace rally got under way. It felt like a folk festival. Musicians, dancers, and singers mounted the stage to perform. Employing familiar melodies, they sang parodies with lyrics about Reagan, the Trident, and the madness of the arms race. The crowd joined in, linking arms and swaying to the rhythm of the music.

An hour into the program, Archbishop Raymond G. Hunthausen was announced. As he crossed the wooden platform and approached the microphone to speak, the crowd jumped to its feet and roared its approval. The standing ovation continued for nearly a minute.

"It's Hunthausen," a woman cried enthusiastically.

The archbishop, embarrassed by such rock-star adulation, nodded sheepishly, hoping to quiet the crowd. An introvert, he had no love for public speaking. By temperament and good grace he was a listener, not a talker. Now here he was before a lustily cheering crowd that wanted an oration.

He knew that what he planned to say would likely disappoint them. He was going to tell them to love their enemies. He was going to offer a blessing for the officers and sailors on the *Ohio*, the submarine that would barrel into Hood Canal four days later, flicking the little flotilla of peace boats off its back like a mighty Moby Dick.

Wearing black clerical garb and a Roman collar, Hunthausen stood tentatively at the microphone. A wet wind ruffled his receding gray hair and left raindrops on his balding scalp. Of average height, with a broad forehead, blue eyes, and a prominent nose, there was nothing out of the ordinary about him. Hiding his discomfort, he peered through large, black-framed bifocals at his prepared text. As a hush fell over the crowd as he began to read.

"We come together today to pray for the officers and crew of the submarine *Ohio* and to ask God's blessing upon these men," Hunthausen said. "We pray because we want these men to know that we respect their dedication; we esteem and love them."

These men are not our enemies, he continued. They are fellow Americans. They are fellow Christians and people of other faiths. In fact, the archbishop went on, they are like us, and see themselves as working for peace. No, we don't agree with their methods, Hunthausen conceded, but we have the greatest respect for their dedication to our shared goal of peace on earth.

The stilled crowd remained silent, mulling over what the archbishop was saying. A breeze blew a chill into the afternoon.

Hunthausen continued to read his text. Each of us, he suggested, possesses only a part of the truth. Consequently, we need to "be willing to work with compassion to understand the truth shown to us by the 'other side.'" We must hear each other out, listening to each other in a spirit of love and forgiveness, he said. May we be slow to criticize and condemn, honest in our disagreement, courteous in our conversation, and always respectful to one another as children of God.

"We are all—Navy and peace people—caught up in the same system," he said. "We all struggle to do the best we can to live according to our beliefs."

Hunthausen acknowledged that the imminent peace blockade of the Trident would be a confrontation. Yet, it is to be a nonviolent confrontation, a gentle confrontation, he said. "It is not done with an attitude of antagonism, but with a respect and love for the people on board the *Ohio*."

"And so, my friends, we pray," he concluded, looking out at the thousands gathered before him. "Heavenly Father, we beg your pardon for any way in which we may have wronged or offended them. We wish to be their brothers and sisters in the cause of peace."

The applause that followed Hunthausen's blessing was restrained, much less enthusiastic than the standing ovation earlier. The archbishop hadn't wanted to displease the crowd but he felt that he had to say something different. He had to try to bridge the chasm that separated the Navy and its supporters from the peace activists and theirs. He knew that many of his flock, the half million Catholics who lived in western Washington, were either opposed to or outright indignant about his stand on nuclear weapons. Many thought him naïve or impractical. They wanted him to stick to religion and stay out of politics. What did the Trident submarine have to do with the Gospel?

As the archbishop stepped back down onto the mudflats of Point Julia, a news reporter accosted him. Why would you bless the *Ohio*? she asked.

"The Gospel tells us to," he replied.

There were certainly plenty of other people prepared to bless the *Ohio*. Just down the Canal at the Bangor base, the Navy was planning a gala welcome for the submarine. Top naval officers, public dignitaries, and the sailors' families would jam the pier while a brass band played "Anchors Aweigh." A huge banner had been prepared. It read: "Welcome Ohio. Peace Thru Trident." The Navy League in conjunction with the Central Kitsap Chamber of Commerce was planning a reception and a picnic for the *Ohio*'s officers, crewmembers and families. In the nearby towns of Poulsbo, Silverdale, and Bremerton, merchants were offering special "*Ohio*" discounts to sailors. The mayor of Bremerton was planning to give the submarine's crew the keys to the city.

Catholics were also enthusiastic about the Trident. A group calling itself "Roman Catholic Laity for Truth" bought two prominent ads in the *Bremerton Sun* welcoming the submarine. The ads suggested that bishops who speak out about nuclear disarmament are heretics and communist dupes.

Local reaction to the peace activists was largely chilly and suspicious, if not outright hostile. At Oak Bay Park, where the anti-Trident protesters were camped in anticipation of the *Ohio*'s arrival, a group of some forty locals set up an impromptu counter-encampment. They sat back, drank from a keg of beer and played high-volume rock music to drown out the folk songs coming from the other side of the beach. They strung a large banner from the roofs of several outhouses. The banner depicted a huge nuclear submarine with its cavernous jaws crunching and devouring the "Pacific Peacemaker," the flagship of the protesters' mosquito fleet.

The day before Archbishop Hunthausen spoke at Point Julia the Federal Aviation Administration announced the closure of air space over the northern part of Hood Canal. The U.S. Coast Guard closed off eighteen miles of the Canal and was imposing a one-thousand-yard, moving security zone around the *Ohio* when it arrived in Puget Sound waters. Those who invaded this prohibited air or sea space were subject to ten-year jail terms and $10,000 fines. Several church leaders, including Hunthausen, challenged the restriction on constitutional grounds. In a compromise, a federal judge upheld the controlled zone around the submarine but allowed the protesters the use of two small bays on the Canal for peace vigils: Oak Bay on the west and Port Gamble Bay on the east.

By the day of the peace rally at Point Julia, everyone knew the *Ohio* would appear in Hood Canal within the week. Hunthausen, the state's two other Catholic bishops, the area leaders of six Protestant denominations, and a Seattle rabbi planned to "witness" the *Ohio*'s arrival by conducting a prayer vigil in a boat just outside the restricted zone. Father Harvey McIntyre, the jovial, gregarious priest who headed Catholic advocacy efforts with the state legislature, offered his boat, the fifty-two-foot *Heather Queen*. The thirty-year-old cabin cruiser, which doubled as McIntyre's home and office, was docked at Shilshole Bay Marina in Seattle. But with sufficient notice of the *Ohio*'s appearance,

McIntyre figured he could round up his crew of religious leaders and speed to the mouth of the Canal within two hours.

From the vantage point of the twenty-first century, it's hard to imagine the overwhelming fear of nuclear war that gripped the world in the early 1980s. Today communism is dead and the Soviet Union is gone. America is the only superpower. Only the United States has the capability and the overwhelming firepower to incinerate the planet many times over. Its Trident submarines, silent, stealthy, and all-but-forgotten in the depths of the oceans, still have their missiles aimed and ready to launch on command. Within twenty-five minutes of pressing the button, their warheads can strike even the most remote corners of the planet, unleashing nuclear destruction. With the end of the Cold War, however, fear of nuclear annihilation has faded from public consciousness.

It was very different in 1982, the year the first Trident submarine arrived at Bangor. Doomsday seemed very close. Arms talks with the Soviets had broken down. The Reagan administration, preaching "peace through strength," had embarked on the biggest nuclear arms buildup in history. The USSR was responding in kind, beefing up its already superior ballistic missile numbers with yet more missiles. There was serious talk of first strikes with tactical or "surgical" nuclear weapons. Anxiety and apprehension stalked the land.

Nearly forty books on nuclear war came out in 1982, dealing with everything from the impossibility of recovering from a nuclear attack to the prospect of concluding a non-proliferation treaty. The most compelling and widely read account was titled "The Fate of the Earth," a three-part series of articles by Jonathan Schell that ran in the *New Yorker* in February and later became a book. Schell challenged readers to confront the unthinkable: the destruction of humanity and the end of civilization.

The American public not only read about nuclear war, they watched it. There were new documentaries about the atomic bombings of Hiroshima and Nagasaki. More than one hundred million Americans saw *Testament* and *The Day After*, movies about the devastating effects of a nuclear attack on small town America.

In *Testament*, the town survives the immediate blast but its inhabitants slowly and inexorably succumb to radiation poisoning. First the infants die, and then the children, until the cemetery is filled and bodies are burned on a pyre. There is no water, no electricity, and, worst of all, no word from elsewhere. The sky gradually grows darker and fills with dust. In the midst of this devastation, the mother, in a deeply touching performance by Jane Alexander, sustains the family's hope as she sees all their dreams disappear and die. Watching the film, the movie critic Roger Ebert cried.

The Day After, a powerfully graphic TV movie of nuclear annihilation, tells the story of the days leading up to and following a nuclear strike. The telltale black mushroom cloud of destruction appears in the sky. But the people of Lawrence, Kansas, try to go on with their daily lives. As radioactive fallout and starvation close in, the people realize there is no future. The movie ends with two old men embracing and waiting to die.

Hunthausen shared the general anxiety as the United States and the Soviet Union stepped closer to the precipice of nuclear war. He'd seen the movies and read the stories. He'd watched a video produced by Physicians for Social Responsibility about the effects of a single atomic warhead hitting a major metropolitan area like Seattle. The video explained that within a thousandth of a second of the detonation of the bomb, a fireball would form spreading more than two miles in all directions. Temperatures would hit twenty million degrees Fahrenheit, hotter than the surface of the sun. Everything under the fireball—people, buildings, cars, trees, the crust of the earth itself—would be vaporized. Human beings would simply disappear, reduced to smoke and fine ash. At a distance of four miles, the blast would generate winds up to six hundred miles per hour, picking up and hurling people and objects at lethal velocities. At a distance of six miles, the heat would remain so intense that it would melt automobiles, and at ten miles, it would level wood and masonry buildings and make steel skeletons of concrete structures.

Radioactive fallout, most of it in the form of ash, would begin to drop almost immediately, with levels of radiation rising quickly to many times the deadly dose. As the fallout reached twenty miles—the distance from Seattle to Bangor—an intense heat would burn wood, paper, cloth, and flesh. Hundreds of thousands of fires would coalesce into a giant firestorm, covering over eight hundred square miles and consuming all the oxygen. Every living thing would die.

Beyond the firestorm itself, the destruction would continue. Hundreds of thousands of people, if not millions, would be crushed, gored, burned, and blinded. Most would die alone and in great pain. Of those who managed to survive, many would expire of cold or lack of shelter or food. Or they might be killed by an epidemic or overexposure to sunlight because of the depleted ozone layer. Or they might be murdered by others seeking food.

Hunthausen's ecclesial jurisdiction was one of the most militarized regions in the nation. Per capita military spending in Washington was double the national average, making the state especially beholden to the armed forces for jobs and economic development. There were Boeing aircraft plants in Seattle, Everett, and Renton. There was a huge U.S. Army base at Fort Lewis and a U.S. Air Force base just south of Tacoma. There were Navy installations in Everett, on Whidbey Island and the Kitsap Peninsula. And now, on his watch, the Navy was planning to make Bangor the home of the world's most lethal nuclear weapons system.

The Navy picked Bangor for the Trident because the deep, cold, clear waters of Hood Canal are ideal for large vessels, especially those that travel under water. An eighty-mile long saltwater inlet, the Canal provides easy access to the Pacific Ocean. With its bunkers, warehouses, offices, machine shops, housing, roads, and other facilities, the Bangor base sprawls over seven thousand acres of mostly green forests surrounded by a chain link fence topped with barbed wire. The base is close to the Puget Sound Naval Shipyard in Bremerton and the Naval Underwater Warfare Center in nearby Keyport.

Aside from its geographic advantages, Bangor is situated in a Navy-friendly community. When the Navy announced in 1973 that it had chosen Bangor as the homeport for the Trident submarines, the *Bremerton Sun* described the reaction as "almost universal satisfaction." The newspaper estimated that Trident would bring $7.5 million a month in new wages to the area. Ten thousand people would work at the base to support a fleet of eight Trident submarines and bunkers housing sixteen hundred nuclear warheads.

The Trident owes its existence to Admiral Hyman Rickover, a persistent, abrasive, gnomish man regarded as the father of the nuclear Navy. In the late 1950s, Rickover led the research team that figured out how to put a nuclear reactor in a submarine hull and then load the submarine with nuclear missiles. His success in creating a mobile, underwater missile system gave the United States the most effective limb of its three-legged nuclear defense strategy. It now had aircraft capable of dropping or firing nuclear bombs, intercontinental ballistic missiles capable of launching them from land-based silos, and virtually undetectable submarines capable of firing multiple nuclear ballistic missiles from almost anywhere in the world's oceans.

The U.S. nuclear defense strategy is based on two premises: (1) eliminating the possibility that an enemy could destroy all of the nation's nuclear forces in a first-strike attack and (2) thereby creating a credible threat of a second strike in which the United States would hit back and inflict massive destruction and loss on the attacking power. This strategy of "nuclear deterrence" is based on the belief that "mutually assured destruction" (MAD) deters nuclear war.

As the Cold War intensified in the 1960s and 1970s, the United States enlarged its nuclear policy by announcing that it would use "tactical nuclear weapons" to deter a conventional Soviet attack in Europe. Successive U.S. administrations pushed Admiral Rickover to develop a next-generation submarine with nuclear missiles capable of scoring direct hits on Soviet launch sites. The new Trident missiles would be able to strike with pinpoint accuracy and high blast power.

On April 7, 1979, Annie Glenn, the astronaut's wife, smacked a bottle of champagne on the bow of the *USS Ohio* and it slid out of its birth in Groton, Connecticut, and into Long Island Sound. It still had a year and a half of sea trials and test missile firings before commissioning and stationing at Bangor.

Rickover was forced to retire eight months before the *Ohio* arrived at Bangor. With retirement, the father of the nuclear Navy had second thoughts about the role he had played in developing the world's most deadly weapons system. He feared that mankind would destroy itself with nuclear arms.

"I'm not proud of what I've done," he confessed to a congressional committee, adding that he would like to sink the nuclear ships to which he had dedicated his life.

The Trident submarine, Rickover's last creation, is a behemoth. At 560 feet, if stood on end, it is taller than Seattle's Space Needle. It weighs 18,750 tons. The eighteen Tridents now in operation—each built at a cost of $3 billion—are able to remain submerged for long periods without surfacing and cruise under water at speeds up to twenty-five knots. Their underwater invisibility, speed, and secure communications systems make them almost impossible to find or destroy. Two crews, each with fifteen officers and 140 enlisted men, are assigned to each Trident. The crews spend alternating periods of seventy days at sea, closed off from the world.

The Trident submarine carries twenty-four Trident II missiles, each equipped with 8 warheads for a total of 192 warheads on board each vessel. The Trident II missile travels at 250 miles a minute and can land within three hundred feet of targets up to six thousand miles away. Each warhead packs six times the destructive power of the atomic bomb dropped at Hiroshima. The Navy has boasted that the *USS Ohio* alone "has more explosive power than what was fired by all the world's navies in all the wars in history."

In his first year as archbishop of Seattle, Hunthausen received a letter from James W. Douglass, a Catholic theologian, author, and conscientious objector, who was completing a book titled *Resistance and Contemplation: The Way of Liberation*. In this book and in an earlier one called *The Non-Violent Cross: A Theology of Revolution and Peace*, Douglass argued that Jesus was a pacifist and that the way to follow

Jesus was to pick up and carry his nonviolent cross. Jesus turned the other cheek when they hit him. Jesus prayed silently when they mocked, beat, and spat upon him. And Jesus willingly offered up his life when they crucified him.

In his writings, Douglass offered the nonviolent examples of Mahatma Gandhi, Thomas Merton, Martin Luther King Jr., Dorothy Day, and others. He disputed Catholic "just-war theory," contending that an honest and entirely orthodox reading of scripture rejects all violence whatsoever.

Catholic just-war theory originated with Augustine, the fourth-century theologian and father of the church, and was refined by Thomas Aquinas, the medieval scholastic philosopher and theologian. The theory holds that war is justified if it meets these conditions: (1) the decision to go to war is made by a legitimate authority; (2) the war is fought for a just cause; (3) war is the last resort; (4) the war has a reasonable chance of success; (5) the good achieved by the war outweighs the evil that will result from it; and (6) the war is waged in accordance with international law.

Douglass argued that the nuclear age makes just-war theory obsolete. How could the overwhelming obliteration of a nuclear attack ever be just, proportional, or achieve a greater good? Post-Hiroshima, he wrote, there are just two choices: the nonviolent path to disarmament or the violent path to nuclear holocaust.

In his letter, Douglass told Hunthausen about the Pacific Life Community, a largely faith-based group organized to oppose the development and deployment of the Trident submarine. Hunthausen wrote back, expressed his support, and enclosed a small contribution. It was the first contact between the populist theologian and the new archbishop, a contact that would ultimately lead to making Hunthausen a hero to the peace movement and a lightning rod to the Reagan administration and the Vatican.

Douglass, an intense, quiet-spoken man with boundless energy and perseverance, had graduated from Santa Clara University, a Jesuit institution, in philosophy and English, and then completed a master's degree in theology at Notre Dame. Despite his philosophy and theology studies, he was not an immediate convert to pacifism. He served six months in the U.S. Army and later in the Army Reserve. By the early 1960s, however, he was studying theology again, this time with the Jesuits in Rome, where he witnessed some of the Second Vatican Council. He then embarked on a career as a theology and religion professor, first at a small Catholic college in Louisville, Kentucky, and later at the University of Hawaii.

In Hawaii, he took up civil disobedience. He encouraged young men subject to military induction to burn their draft cards and refuse active duty in Vietnam. In 1972, Douglass and several others broke into the Hickam Air Force Base at Pearl Harbor and poured blood over secret military files. The trespassers were arrested and booked in jail. But the federal case against them for illegal entry and destruction of government property fell apart when the Air Force would not produce the top-secret files.

By 1974, Douglass and his wife, Shelley, were living with extended family in Hedley, British Columbia, a remote mining town in the Canadian province's vast interior. One day, Robert Aldridge, a Lockheed engineer on the design team for the Trident missile, arrived at their doorstep. He told them he had resigned from his job because his conscience was tormenting him. He had become convinced that the Trident missile was a first-strike weapon. It had maneuverable warheads that could zero-in on targets with pinpoint accuracy, which gave it a big advantage over the blunderbuss Soviet missiles with their huge blast power but more limited aim. The Trident, Aldridge argued, was meant for taking out Soviet missile silos and underground command posts. These are first-strike targets, he insisted.

Aldridge told the Douglasses that Trident would escalate the arms race with the Soviets and move the world a giant step closer to nuclear annihilation. With less sophisticated anti–submarine warfare equipment, the Soviets would be forced to adopt a hair-trigger, launch-on-warning policy, he said. They would fire as soon as they saw a missile-like blip on the radar screen. Moreover, if the Soviets regarded Trident as a first-strike weapon, they might be tempted to launch a preemptive attack before the new missile system became operational. Doomsday was indeed looming on the horizon.

The room went silent when Aldridge stopped speaking. The Douglasses asked what they could do. The former engineer pulled out a map of Puget Sound, highlighted Hood Canal, and drew a line of the submarine's path to Bangor. He circled the base and noted the Explosives Handling Wharf where the nuclear missiles would be loaded onto the submarine.

In January 1975, the Douglasses and fourteen other Canadians and Americans had founded the Pacific Life Community (PLC), a motley group of radical Christians, Quakers, feminists, and Catholic Workers. A summary of their initial meeting noted that "almost the only thing we had in common was our concern with the nuclear arms race and our hopes for peaceful social change." In language that would later be embraced by Hunthausen, they said they also wanted to confront "the Trident within" themselves by rooting out the personal violence in their own lives.

The PLC believed that repeated protests at the Bangor base could attract sufficient media attention to wake up Americans to the destructive evil of the Trident. During its initial year, the PLC staged more than a dozen demonstrations at the Navy base. They leafleted sailors and civilian workers going in and out. They used wire cutters to break through the fence and knelt in prayer until guards arrested them. They rowed boats or swam to the base's protected shore. When they jumped the fence with gardening tools and planted a vegetable garden, the story appeared in news reports across the country.

After receiving the letter and contribution from Hunthausen, Douglass wrote from Canada and asked if he could visit the archbishop in Seattle. Hunthausen agreed, inviting the peace activist to meet with him in his living quarters at the seminary. It was September 1976, two months before the U.S. presidential election in which Jimmy Carter faced Gerald Ford. Douglass was planning to join a thirty-day public fast in Washington, DC, to bring attention to the arms issue and ask both candidates to renounce any first use of nuclear weapons.

He and Hunthausen talked in the archbishop's small, sparsely furnished room at the back of the seminary building. After relating how he had come to understand nonviolence as fundamental to Christ's message, Douglass discussed why he had poured blood on military files and why he had cut through the fence at Bangor and been arrested. He explained the first-strike potential of the Trident submarine system and how it was pushing mankind to the brink of nuclear obliteration. Douglass gave Hunthausen a copy of the statement put out by the "International Fast for Peace." Subsisting on water only, he and others would conduct their thirty-day fast while praying in front of the White House, the Pentagon, the Russian embassy, the Republican and Democratic campaign headquarters, and at other locations in the nation's capital.

The archbishop listened intently but expressed no immediate opinion. He told Douglass he would pray for those who would be fasting and ponder over what he had heard. Douglass and his passion for the cause of peace impressed him.

Within days of his conversation with Douglass, the archbishop read an article in *U.S. Catholic* magazine by Father Richard McSorley, SJ, a Georgetown University professor active in the peace and civil rights movement. The article was titled "It's a Sin to Build a Nuclear Weapon." McSorley had been captured during World War II by Japanese forces in the Philippines and had spent much of the war in an internment camp. The experience had made him an ardent pacifist.

In the *U.S. Catholic* article, McSorley argued that the taproot of violence in America was the country's willingness to use nuclear weapons. Once we entertain the possibility of obliterating the world, he wrote, all other evil is minor by comparison. McSorley concluded that any hope of improving public morality is doomed to failure until we squarely face the question of our consent to use nuclear weapons.

"If I intend to use nuclear weapons in massive retaliation," McSorley wrote, "I have already committed massive murder in my heart."

Two weeks into his fast, Douglass phoned Hunthausen from Washington and asked what the archbishop had decided to do. They discussed the McSorley article. The archbishop told Douglass that he had prayed over the nuclear arms issue and reflected on what Trident meant for the world and the archdiocese. In mid-October 1976, while Douglass was still fasting, Hunthausen wrote an open letter to the priests of the archdiocese. It was his first public statement on what he saw as a moral obligation to promote peace by opposing nuclear weapons, especially the Trident.

In typical Hunthausen fashion, he told his "dear brothers in Christ" that he would have preferred to have spoken with them in person, heard their feedback, and given the matter further reflection. But time is short, he wrote, and the issue critical. He told them about meeting Douglass, whom he described as "a serious and Christian gentleman." He explained how Douglass and others were engaged in thirty days of prayer and fasting in hopes the presidential candidates would reject nuclear weapons. He said their cause deserved his encouragement and cooperation.

"As a teacher and preacher of Christ's Gospel message of peace," he wrote, "I have a deep conviction that silence and inaction at this time is nothing less than the betrayal of the charge given to preach the Gospel."

Hunthausen went on to quote from the McSorley article. He referred to *Gaudium et Spes,* the Vatican II document on the importance of the church engaging with the modern world. And then he closed the letter by encouraging his priests to comment, pray, and, if they chose to do so, by sharing his letter with their parishioners. We need to take the sign of Christ's peace outside the church, he concluded, "and into the open forum of public opinion and action."

The next time Hunthausen saw Jim Douglass, the peace activist was in the King County Jail in downtown Seattle. Douglass and his wife, Shelley, had been tried, convicted, and sentenced to ninety days in jail for breaking through the security fence at Bangor. The judge had declined to allow Douglass to make a sentencing statement so Douglass had refused to move from the courtroom. Jail guards had carried him to his cell where he began another water-only fast. Two weeks into his fast, five federal marshals burst into his cell, strapped him into a wheelchair, and rolled him to an empty room. He had his first visitor: Hunthausen. It was the first of several jail visits that the archbishop made to see the Douglasses and other PLC members imprisoned for trespassing at Bangor.

On Christmas Eve 1976, Hunthausen went to Harborview Hospital, the big public hospital just down the street from St. James Cathedral, to give Douglass communion. Weak and emaciated from fasting, Douglass had been transferred to a hospital bed, an armed guard at his side. The eucharistic bread broke his fast. That same day, *The Catholic Northwest Progress* printed a letter from Douglass in which he juxtaposed the power of nonviolence that Christ's birth had brought to the world against "the total darkness of self-destruction represented by Trident."

Hunthausen admired Douglass. This was a man who, because of the strength of his faith, had abandoned a comfortable career in academia, embraced voluntary poverty, and subjected himself to multiple arrests and imprisonment. The archbishop found the anti–nuclear arms arguments advanced by Douglass, McSorley, and other peace activists logical and convincing. Surely nuclear holocaust was the biggest of all evils. Destroy God's creation and there is no life. Nothing. If Trident is indeed a first-strike weapon, aren't we upping the ante with the Soviets and hurrying the day of ultimate destruction? How should we confront the prospect of a nuclear Armageddon?

Hunthausen rolled the questions over and over again in his mind: What is my moral obligation? What should I do as a follower of Jesus Christ? What is my responsibility as the leader of a local church whose territory will soon include the world's most lethal weapon?

While the archbishop pondered the questions, the protests against Trident intensified. The Church Council of Greater Seattle organized a Trident Concern Week, which culminated in an ecumenical prayer service at St. Patrick's Church on Seattle's Capitol Hill. Hunthausen told a standing-room-only crowd how he was still haunted by his seminary memories of Hiroshima.

In December 1977, the Douglasses and seven other PLC members each contributed $100 toward a down payment on a small wood house on 3.8 acres of land. The property, which ran smack up against 330 feet of the Bangor security fence, was ideally located for the anti-Trident campaign. They raised the rest of the $14,000 down payment in six weeks, renamed themselves Ground Zero, and took possession of what they called the Ground Zero Center for Non-Violent Action. On Labor Day weekend 1978, Jim and Shelley Douglass and their seven-year-old son, Tom, moved in.

Soon afterward, Hunthausen came by for a visit. He brought Tom a chronometer, a clock-like nautical instrument that he had had as a boy. While Tom puzzled over the gift, his parents and the archbishop talked about nonviolence, civil disobedience, and the faith questions raised by nuclear weapons. They were fond of the writings of Thomas Merton, the Trappist monk, poet, and author whose contemplative approach to life sought to infuse the secular with the spiritual. Merton emphasized the practice of nonviolence in word, thought, and action as a way to transform oneself and the world.

Over the next several years, Hunthausen would make numerous visits to Ground Zero. He showed up at his first Bangor demonstration on Sunday, May 21, 1978. Nearly five thousand demonstrators, waving signs and banners, linked arms and paraded past the main entrance to the base. It was the biggest anti-Trident crowd until the peace blockade rally that would take place at Point Julia four years later. Nearly three hundred protesters vaulted over the security fence and were arrested.

Hunthausen, inconspicuous in his tan raincoat and flat wool cap, stood silently in the crowd. He had not been asked to speak and had no official role at the event. In fact, he had passed unnoticed until a church employee spotted him and pointed him out to a reporter. The reporter asked the archbishop why he was here.

"Yes, I'm here," Hunthausen acknowledged. "I'm here out of my own personal conviction on the matter. I'm not here as the archbishop; I'm here as me."

By the following year, Hunthausen was ready to speak out publicly at an anti-Trident demonstration at Bangor. On a chilly, overcast Sunday in late October 1979, some two thousand demonstrators including the Douglasses and many other Catholic religious and laypeople clustered at the gate to protest and pray. Jesuit Father Jack Morris, a childhood friend of the archbishop, celebrated a late afternoon Mass on a patch of grass just north of the base entrance. A young couple from Tacoma had their baby baptized.

While speaking to the protesters, the archbishop acknowledged that he had struggled with his decision to join the demonstration. He knew that some people saw his participation as unpatriotic.

"I love my country and I love the human family," he said. "These weapons are destined to destroy us as a human family. While I may be criticized, I think that to not do something is to open myself to deeper criticism."

After Hunthausen spoke, more than a hundred people, including six priests, two nuns, and Jim Douglass, were arrested for climbing over the Bangor fence and trespassing on government property. Douglass, who scaled a second fence into the high-security area, was arrested twice. He was later tried and sentenced to two six-month prison terms.

Hunthausen watched as the Rev. William Cate, the head of the Church Council of Greater Seattle, and his wife, Jan, scrambled through the chain-link fence and onto the base. The Cates were quickly handcuffed and escorted to the detention bus. He wondered if he should have been with them.

He struggled to separate his personal convictions from his responsibilities as archbishop. The church consecrates bishops to teach, to lead, and to ensure the spiritual welfare of the faithful. As successors of Christ's apostles, bishops are meant to be exemplars of the Christian life and shepherds to the people. It is not a nine-to-five job. Hunthausen felt as strongly about the evil of nuclear weapons as the Cates, the Douglasses, the priests, nuns, laypeople, and other activists who were being arrested and jailed for climbing the fence. He understood the rationale for civil disobedience and agreed with it. But, given his role, was it right for him?

He asked God for a sign that he was on the right path. He didn't expect a dramatic revelation like St. Paul being struck off his horse on the road to Damascus. Rather, like the prophet Elijah, he listened for the small, still whisper of God's voice. It might come through another person, or a book, or an event—something totally unexpected. "The Spirit doesn't necessarily hit you over the head," he said.

Hunthausen pondered the idea of civil disobedience. Going to jail on the strength of his convictions might make a powerful statement about nuclear arms, but it would also take him away from his ministry obligations. Gradually he sensed that climbing the fence or sitting on the base's railroad tracks was not what he was called to do. Rather, he was called to do something else, to engage in a form of civil disobedience, the symbolism of which would strike at the heart of the false god of nuclear arms: tax resistance.

The archbishop's condemnation of Trident and his increasing participation in protest activities did not sit well with some of his flock. Letters began to appear in *The Progress* calling Hunthausen irresponsible, naïve, and foolish. A retired rear admiral from Bellevue wrote a public letter to the archbishop disputing the archbishop's contention that Trident is an aggressive "first-strike" weapon. Rear Admiral J. A. Jaap, a Catholic who had served as a commander in the Navy's nuclear operations division, argued that Trident was a necessary deterrent to Soviet attack. Jaap applauded Hunthausen for backing nuclear disarmament talks but warned that "to lower our guard in advance could be fatal."

The Wanderer, the ultra-orthodox national Catholic weekly, repeatedly lambasted Hunthausen for what it regarded as a host of illicit practices involving the Mass and the sacraments. The attacks referenced the archbishop's peace activities in a dismissive and hostile tone. *The Wanderer* would play a significant role in undermining

Hunthausen's credibility in Rome and spurring a Vatican investigation of his ministry.

A number of pastors responded to Hunthausen's activism by inviting the archbishop to face their puzzled and sometimes hostile parishioners. Hunthausen appeared at parish councils, study workshops, religious education conferences, and other forums throughout the archdiocese.

"I went with some misgiving," he recalled, "because I knew that my position and my presentation, well, they weren't going to be accepted."

Things got hot at Holy Trinity Church in Bremerton, just up the road from the naval shipyard and a short commute from Bangor. Some parishioners worked for the Navy. The parish council had decided to open up the discussion to the community, so the church hall was packed and Father Joe Erny, the pastor, was nervous. Hunthausen began by showing a short peace video about the arms race and the Trident. Then he explained how he had come to oppose the Trident because he rejected the doctrine of strategic deterrence. He said he agreed with McSorley that if we intended to use nuclear bombs in mass retaliation, we were already intending to commit mass murder in our hearts.

As Erny retreated to the side, Hunthausen was bombarded with aggressive questions: Are we supposed to lie down and let the Russians take over? What about the communist menace? Why don't you stick with religion and stay out of politics?

Hunthausen looked intently at each of his questioners and listened. He offered no rebuttal to their arguments. He simply said that he was trying to apply the message of the Gospel as best he could to what he thought was the most pressing issue of the day—the very real possibility of nuclear genocide.

Surprisingly, several rose to thank him for coming. We don't agree with you, they said, but we're glad you came.

"These are the kinds of things we need to talk about in honesty and charity," the archbishop said in reply. "Thank you. You've given me something more to think about."

Even some of Hunthausen's staff was discomfited by his peace activism. They questioned whether Jim Douglass had exercised a disproportionate influence on the archbishop's thinking. Despite his mild-mannered demeanor, Douglass could be intemperate in his choice of words. Some wondered if Hunthausen's nuclear arms speeches, whose first drafts were often written by Douglass, reflected the archbishop or the veteran peace activist.

Father Peter Chirico, Hunthausen's theological advisor, was apprehensive about Douglass. "Unlike the archbishop, Jim Douglass was infallibly sure that he was right," said Chirico, who also drafted speeches for Hunthausen. "I don't like people like that. The archbishop would never say I'm absolutely sure. He'd say: This is the way I feel."

Chirico held a doctorate in theology from the Gregorian University in Rome, wrote for numerous theological journals, and was internationally recognized as an expert on Catholic doctrine, papal infallibility, and the application of Christian morality. A thin, animated man, slightly hunched at the shoulders, he wore his steel-grey hair in a long flattop and spoke with a native Brooklyn accent. He delighted in pondering an issue, examining the arguments pro and con, and separating what was essential church teaching from what was "prudential judgment" or cultural accretion.

Chirico believed that just-war theory was still applicable in the nuclear age. But, since Catholic teaching upholds the primacy of an informed conscience in moral decision-making, he respected the right of the archbishop and others to make up their own minds on the nuclear issue.

"Even if you've got an erroneous conscience," Chirico said, "you've got to follow it. No one in some central bureau can tell you what to do."

He and Hunthausen were close. They discussed the issues frequently, over dinner at the cathedral rectory and on long walks through downtown Seattle.

George Weigel, another Hunthausen advisor, was disturbed by what he regarded as Douglass's utopian pacifism and misinterpretation of Catholic thought on war and peace. A Catholic layman, Weigel taught theology at St. Thomas Seminary, where Chirico also taught, and in 1977 became scholar-in-residence at the World Without War Council of Greater Seattle. Weigel took the position that the path to peace was through enforceable, negotiated arms agreements. He abhorred the idea of unilateral disarmament as a means of de-escalating the nuclear arms race.

Weigel left the council in 1984 and found residence with a number of conservative institutes back East where he wrote prolifically on Catholic issues. An astute apologist for the Vatican, he became the official biographer in English of Pope John Paul II, writing two tomes on the Polish pontiff along with other scholarly works on Catholicism. Acerbic and academic with an air that did not suffer fools lightly, Weigel had no hesitation in castigating Catholics—including Jim Douglass and Archbishop Hunthausen—whom he believed had strayed from orthodoxy.

The Progress published regular columns by Douglass and Weigel, offering its readers a diversity of Catholic opinion rarely found in a diocesan newspaper. (In fact, Weigel noted that never once did the archbishop, the paper's official publisher, ever seek to change or influence anything he wrote.) Among other things, Weigel called Hunthausen and "the peace bishops" confused, misguided, isolationist, divisive, and unfaithful to established Catholic tradition.

He put much of the blame on Douglass, whom he described as a counterculture Catholic and lobbyist for pacifism. He contended that Douglass's theology was influenced by Eastern mystics, revolutionaries, feminists, and New Age eccentrics. Weigel was particularly disdainful of the daylong Catholic retreat that the Douglasses led at their Ground Zero property one rainy Saturday in January 1982. The archdiocesan Justice and Peace Center had invited him, the archbishop, chancery staff, and Catholic leaders from throughout western Washington to come together to pray and reflect on the nuclear arms issue. The speakers included a Hiroshima survivor.

The group of about a hundred assembled in an unfinished geodesic dome. Weigel recalled the dim light, a creaking electric generator, and a big golden statue of the Buddha before whom were placed burning joss sticks and a basket of fragrant oranges. Rainwater fell through the leaky roof onto Hunthausen's head as he read an opening blessing from scripture. According to Weigel, the Douglasses then told the gathering that the purpose of the retreat was not to think about the arms race or a Catholic moral response, but rather to "get in touch with our feelings." On the ferry ride back to Seattle, Weigel encountered Father William Sullivan SJ, the president of Seattle University. Weigel said Sullivan was staring into a plastic cup of beer and musing about how the church had invested a half a million dollars in his education. And now, Sullivan said, he was being told not to think but to get in touch with his feelings.

Whatever Weigel and Sullivan may have thought about their feelings, the Douglasses viewed the rainy January day under the dome as a success. They had engaged key Catholic leaders, some of whom began participating actively in the anti-Trident campaign and many more who took the message back to their offices and parishes.

At forums and gatherings in church basements and school halls, Hunthausen began identifying himself as a "nuclear pacifist" and calling for unilateral disarmament. He conceded that many regarded his proposal that the United States should begin disarming in hopes that the Soviets would reciprocate as naïve, simplistic, and off the wall.

"But it would be even more naïve to think that we can continue a nuclear-arms race and not have it lead to a devastating nuclear war," he insisted.

There was no bilateral alternative, he noted. The SALT II talks had been abandoned and both sides continued to deploy more nuclear arms. So why not a unilateral initiative? The point, the archbishop said, was to take a step toward arms reduction, then another and another, even if the Soviets did not. After all, our faith and trust is in God, not our nuclear stockpile, he said. We can't say we put our trust in you, Lord, and then add that it's nice to have nuclear weapons around.

Hunthausen's critics found his arguments unconvincing. Disarming could encourage a nuclear attack by showing weakness and vulnerability, they contended. The archbishop was failing to deal with the realpolitik of the world. Unilateral disarmament was surrender. His Christian critics accused him of cherry picking scripture and ignoring the bellicose God of the Old Testament.

The archbishop admitted that unilateral disarmament could result in suffering and death at the hands of an occupying power. But what is the greater evil, he asked: to kill or to be killed?

In his 1980 Christmas message, the archbishop proposed that Catholics set aside Mondays for fasting and special prayer about the violence in our lives. He linked the "major evil" of abortion with the evil of an "out of control" arms race, noting that both destroy the preciousness of human life.

Early in the new year, the Rev. A. G. "Kip" Fjellman, the regional Lutheran bishop, invited Hunthausen to be the keynote speaker at the annual June meeting of the church's Pacific Northwest Synod at Pacific Lutheran University. The archbishop accepted. He liked Fjellman, whom he knew well from the informal Thursday breakfast meetings of church executives at the Lutheran church on Seattle's Phinney Ridge. Hunthausen had shared with the half dozen denominational leaders his struggle with the nuclear arms issue.

Shortly after accepting Fjellman's invitation, the archbishop received a phone call from Douglass, who had just been released from a federal prison in California. Hunthausen told Douglass that he would be speaking to six hundred Lutheran pastors and lay ministers gathered for their annual convention in Tacoma. They expected him to talk about a faith response to the nuclear arms race. He would title his address "Faith and Disarmament." In thinking about what he might say, the archbishop mentioned that he was especially concerned that his taxes were helping pay for weapons that could end the world.

"What if I refused to pay those taxes?" he asked Douglass. "What about that?"

Chirico wrote the first draft of Hunthausen's speech a couple of weeks before the Lutheran synod meeting. The archbishop had the draft with him when he and other denominational executives met at St. Thomas Seminary for a day of reflection on war and peace. The main presenters were Weigel and Charlie Meconis, a former priest, pacifist and anti-nuke activist who directed the Seattle Religious Peace Action Coalition. In his presentation, Meconis broached the subject of tax resistance as a form of civil disobedience against nuclear weapons spending. Hunthausen listened but said nothing. When the day was over, he asked Meconis if he could give him a lift to a nearby auto repair shop where the archbishop's Oldsmobile was being repaired. Meconis obliged and the two talked about tax resistance. Hunthausen was impressed by Meconis's willingness to risk fines, seized wages, and imprisonment rather than have some of his tax dollars pay for nuclear weapons.

"I felt the same way," the archbishop recalled. After listening to Meconis, Hunthausen decided his speech needed to be bolder and more challenging. He met with Douglass who rewrote parts of it, using stronger language and some bold metaphors. The final draft ended with the archbishop urging the people of the state to consider withholding 50 percent of their income tax in "resistance to nuclear murder and suicide."

Two days before he was scheduled to speak at Pacific Lutheran University, Hunthausen showed the draft to Father Michael G. Ryan, his chancellor and chief confidante.

Ryan read the draft speech with a growing look of shock on his face. "You're not going to give that," he told his boss. "You're not going to say that."

Surely, Ryan suggested, there was a middle way, a more moderate method of stopping the arms race than calling for a tax revolt. Think how divisive and polarizing this will be, he told the archbishop. It could bring about anarchy. Please consider some alternatives.

Hunthausen listened, said little, and took Ryan's arguments under consideration. The very fact that his most trusted advisor was so alarmed gave him pause. On the other hand, he felt very strongly that this was what he was called to do.

A day later, he went back to Ryan and told him, "I am going to give this talk, Mike. Yes, I am."

"Okay," Ryan replied. "But we need to gear up in terms of public relations. This is going to be a huge thing—front page news."

"Oh, come on, Mike," the archbishop replied. "Really?"

2

TAX PROTEST

*Our lives begin and end
the day we become silent about things that matter.*
—Martin Luther King Jr.

On the evening of Friday, June 12, 1981, Archbishop Hunthausen stepped up to the podium at Pacific Lutheran University's Olson Auditorium and delivered a twenty-five-hundred-word address that reverberated around the world. A Catholic archbishop, a citizen of the United States, the country that regards itself as the global champion of freedom and democracy, he invited all Americans—especially his fellow Christians—to revolt against their government's investment in nuclear arms by refusing to pay their federal income tax.

Calmly reading from his prepared text, Hunthausen explained how he had come to this decision. He recalled his deep shock when he saw the news about Hiroshima in 1945. He told the assembly about reading McSorley and then realizing that his own archdiocese would be home to the Trident, the most deadly weapons system ever made.

"We must take special responsibility for what is in our own backyard," he said. "I say with deep consciousness of these words that Trident is the Auschwitz of Puget Sound."

He described the nuclear arms race as leading to a cataclysmic final act of violence—"a demonic reversal of the Creator's power of giving life." Politics by itself, he said, is powerless to overcome the evil of nuclear weapons. We need faith in the God who gives and sustains life.

Hunthausen invoked the Gospel call to peacemaking, noting that those called to be peacemakers would be persecuted, much as Christ was persecuted. He quoted from Mark's Gospel: "For anyone who wants to save one's own life will lose it; but anyone who loses one's life for my sake, and for the sake of the Gospel, will save it."

22

Expanding on that Gospel passage, the archbishop urged his listeners to take up the cross of Christ in the nuclear age. Jesus' rejection of the sword and acceptance of the cross is the Gospel's statement of unilateral disarmament, he said. Our security lies not in the idol of nuclear weapons but in a loving, caring God.

How might we take up the cross of nonviolence? Hunthausen asked. How might we halt the senseless slide toward nuclear annihilation?

Writing political leaders and taking part in demonstrations, protests, and peace campaigns is all well and good, he said. "[But] I would like to share a vision of still another action." Hunthausen then suggested that a sizable number of people in Washington State—five hundred thousand maybe—refuse to pay the 50 percent of their taxes that goes toward military spending and thus use the IRS Form 1040 to vote for life.

"The teaching of Jesus tells us to render to a nuclear-armed Caesar what the Caesar deserves—tax resistance," he said.

The archbishop then candidly acknowledged that he was not yet refusing to pay his taxes. He conceded that there would never be large numbers of tax resisters unless people like him were willing to stop paying for war. He said he was sharing the vision as part of his own struggle of how best to apply the Gospel of peace.

The archdiocese was not prepared for the deluge of media calls that flooded in when the chancery opened the following Monday morning. The speech had created a stream of inquiries, local and national, from newspapers, magazines, radio, and television. It occasioned calls and letters from Catholics and others from throughout the archdiocese and the nation.

Marilyn Maddeford, the petite, unflappable personal secretary to the archbishop, was caught flat-footed by her boss's call for a taxpayer revolt.

"His support for the anti-nuclear movement has always been very vocal," she told the *Seattle Post-Intelligencer*, "but he hadn't told anybody what his plans were."

Once they got over their initial shock, Seattle's church leaders rallied to the archbishop's support. The church council and the state association of churches began circulating a petition praising Hunthausen's "courageous stand" and asking the public to take his proposal seriously. Even so, with the exception of Bill Cate, the Seattle church council president and a fellow Bangor protester, no faith leaders were ready to endorse civil disobedience by refusing to pay their taxes.

Nor were any of the state's political leaders. A spokeswoman for U.S. Senator Slade Gorton said the Republican lawmaker "just can't imagine why the archbishop would be advocating something that's illegal." U.S. Representative Tom Foley, the Democratic Speaker of House and the only Catholic in the state's congressional delegation, shared the archbishop's concern about nuclear weapons but questioned his suggested method of protest. Even U.S. Representative Mike Lowry, a vociferous critic of nuclear weapons spending, said he couldn't support civil disobedience.

In a CBS Radio commentary, Dan Rather noted that Hunthausen did not say "what Roman Catholic archbishops usually are expected to say—certain pieties about peace and good will." Instead, Rather continued, Hunthausen denounced nuclear arms as "demonic weapons which threaten all life on Earth" and called for a tax protest. The CBS newsman described the archbishop as "an establishment figure" giving new fire to the movement to rid the world of nukes.

A few Catholic bishops wrote personal notes of support to Hunthausen.

"Be assured that at least some of your brothers in the episcopacy share your position," wrote Bishop Walter Sullivan, of Richmond, Virginia, who, like Hunthausen, would later be investigated by the Vatican.

Bishop Peter Gerety, of Newark, New Jersey, wrote, "This little note is to tell you how much I admire your guts."

Hunthausen received a more formal letter from Father Thomas C. Kelly, general secretary of the national bishops' conference. Kelly wrote that he respected the integrity of the archbishop's tax resistance, and then warned, "other members of our Conference, of course, will have different expressions of their desire for peace."

McSorley, the Georgetown Jesuit, sent a postcard urging Hunthausen to begin lobbying efforts on the U.S. bishops' planned pastoral letter on war and peace.

Helen Caldicott, the Australian doctor who headed Physicians for Social Responsibility, wrote to tell Hunthausen that she was using excerpts from his "Faith and Disarmament" address in her own speeches all over the world. If more church people like you come out, she said, "humanity will be able to stop this crazy arms race."

Caldicott, who devoted her life to opposing nuclear weapons, and Hunthausen later crossed paths in Minneapolis where the archbishop was speaking at a large conference of religious educators. The two had lunch together. During the course of their meal, the Australian physician told the archbishop that he ought to run for president.

"President of what?" he asked.

"President of the United States," she replied.

Hunthausen received letters of support from peace activists, authors, environmentalists, and the heads of numerous religious orders and faith groups. He was especially touched by the invitation he received from his niece, Cindy Stergar, to participate in the Helena Diocese Youth Convention. Cindy remarked that she had ordered some "I Love Hunthausen" buttons since her grandmother, the archbishop's mom, was now wearing one. "You are doing a great job," she wrote. "Thanks Dutch!"

The chancery mailbag also contained criticism. A few letters called Hunthausen names, labeling him a "communist," "a Russian stooge," and "a traitor."

An officer on the USS Ohio, scheduled to arrive at Bangor within months, strongly objected to the archbishop's comparing the Trident to Auschwitz. "I have been a practicing Catholic for twenty-eight years," he wrote. "Am I also a member of the SS?"

Eight Polish-American Catholics from Seattle signed a joint letter noting that the Polish pope had told Catholic clergy to stay out of politics.

Nearly two dozen Catholics wrote letters or returned solicitation cards from the annual Catholic appeal saying they would withhold their pledge in protest of the archbishop's withholding his taxes. Charles M. Pigott, a multi-millionaire donor who had long supported Catholic institutions, copied Hunthausen on a letter to his pastor. Pigott told his pastor that he would not contribute to the archdiocesan fund and would urge his fellow Catholics to withhold their contributions because of the archbishop's stand.

Hunthausen wrote back to Pigott: "As to your decision to withhold your support from our annual Stewardship appeal, I would simply want you to know that this is a decision which you must make in all good conscience, as must your friends."

Despite such opposition, the 1981 appeal surpassed its $1.95 million goal within two weeks of its start, and the number of donors increased by more than four thousand over the previous year.

Along with the letters and calls, Hunthausen was inundated with speaking invitations. They came from churches, peace organizations, and colleges and universities around the world.

William Sloane Coffin Jr., the Yale chaplain and anti-war activist, asked the archbishop to participate in a fall conference called "Reverse the Arms Race" at the historic Riverside Church on Manhattan's west side. At the conference, participants would be encouraged to come forward to sign a pledge to refuse to pay half their income tax. The conference speakers, including Coffin, Caldicott, and other well-known peace activists, planned to go to Washington, DC, afterward to meet with President Reagan.

Hunthausen declined this invitation as he did most of the others. "My primary responsibility remains the shepherding and leading of this large and far-flung archdiocese," he wrote Coffin. "Consequently, I have decided to confine my efforts on behalf of the peace and disarmament issue, as well as I can, to efforts that I will be able to carry out here."

After Hunthausen's speech at Pacific Lutheran University, more U.S. Catholic bishops followed his example in denouncing the arms race and rejecting the doctrine of nuclear deterrence. Five dozen of the nearly three hundred active bishops signed petitions supporting a freeze on nuclear weapons. A few endorsed unilateral disarmament, but no others said they would withhold their taxes in protest.

At least one, Bishop Leroy P. Matthiesen of Amarillo, Texas, questioned whether Christians should work in the nuclear arms industry. At a plant in his diocese, workers were assembling the warheads for the Trident missile. Matthiesen urged them to consider the implications of what they were doing. He suggested that they find jobs that "would contribute to life rather than destroy it." A howl of protest erupted. But the Catholic bishops of Texas stood behind Matthiesen, noting that his stand was consistent with the teachings of the church on nuclear weapons. Catholics ought to get out of the nuclear weapons business.

The Amarillo bishop later joined Hunthausen and Douglass at a Ground Zero retreat along the railroad tracks that carried the warhead-laden "White Train" into the Bangor base. Out of the retreat came a public letter signed by Hunthausen, Matthiesen, and eight other bishops through whose dioceses the nuclear weapons trains passed on their way to Bangor. The letter called on people of faith to stand along the tracks on Pentecost Sunday "in prayerful witness to the alternative power of divine love and nonviolent action."

As he drove his Olds around the archdiocese to preside at Masses, confirmations, and other religious ceremonies, Hunthausen ruminated on whether he should take the next step. Should he do what he had encouraged others to do—withhold his taxes in protest of nuclear weapons? At first, he thought that his suggestion of withholding taxes would create a stir for a couple of days and then disappear. After all, the real issue was nuclear weapons, not what method you took to draw attention to them. He soon realized he was very wrong.

One of the letters he received in response to his Pacific Lutheran University speech was from an attorney who advised him not to ask people to take an action that he was not prepared to take himself. Then Jim French, a popular talk show host on Seattle's KIRO Radio, phoned him to ask if he was ready to withhold half of his federal income tax. No, the archbishop replied.

"So," French concluded, "what you're really saying is: Don't do what I do, do what I say?"

French's comment got under the archbishop's skin. He realized he had to make a decision.

So when Jean Enersen, the evening news co-anchor at Seattle's KING-TV, asked him on air if he'd made up his mind yet about tax resistance, he blurted out, "Yes, I have. I'm going to do it."

In the studio wings, Maury Sheridan, the ever-cautious archdiocesan communications director, rolled his eyes and moaned.

"I didn't know you were going to say that," he told the archbishop afterward. "We should have drawn up a statement, released it to the press and published it in *The Progress*."

"Well, Maury," Hunthausen replied, "she asked me the question and I figured I'm going to answer it honestly. So I did."

The communications office quickly issued a press release announcing that Hunthausen would withhold half of his 1981 income tax to protest "our nation's continuing involvement in the race for nuclear-arms supremacy." He would give to charity what he was withholding from federal taxes on his $10,000 annual salary.

Along with the press release was Hunthausen's letter to the Catholics of western Washington. He addressed it: "Dear People of God."

He began by explaining that he felt compelled to speak out against the nuclear arms race because it pushes the world toward nuclear war and diverts immense resources from helping the needy. As Christians committed to peacemaking, he wrote, we must find ways to reverse the nuclear-arms buildup. His way, he had decided, would be to withhold half of his federal income tax.

Hunthausen acknowledged that some would agree with him but that many "conscientious" people would not. His tax protest was just one strategy for drawing attention to the destructiveness of the arms race, he wrote. He welcomed ideas on other practical, nonviolent ways of addressing the matter, especially from his fellow bishops who had begun work on an important pastoral letter, a teaching document on war and peace. He recognized that many people could not follow his example because it could put their families or their jobs at risk.

"I prefer that each individual come to his or her own decision on what should be done to meet the nuclear-arms challenge," he wrote. "I believe that the present issue is as serious as any the world has faced. The very existence of humanity is at stake."

Hunthausen noted that there is a higher authority than the laws of man: God's law. "There may even be times when disobedience (to civil law) may be an obligation of conscience," he wrote. "I am saying by my action that in conscience I cannot support or acquiesce in a nuclear-arms buildup which I consider a grave moral evil."

The archbishop said he hoped that his action would awaken those who hadn't questioned the arms race, stir those who disagreed with him to find a better way than more weapons, and encourage all people of goodwill to pursue the path of peace.

"I cannot make your decision for you," he wrote in closing. "I can and do challenge you to make a decision."

Hunthausen said he was ready to face the possible consequences of his tax protest, including the IRS garnishing his wages and even sending him to jail. He considered that prospect unlikely.

"My withholding hardly constitutes a serious threat to the defense budget," he said.

On the eve of the federal income tax deadline, Hunthausen made it official. At a Seattle Press Club luncheon, he told the media that he was refusing to pay about $500, approximately half of his federal tax obligation.

The *Seattle Times* was not impressed. "Withholding taxes is a crude and ineffective way to change government policy," it editorialized. "Its final effect would be anarchy."

The day after he publicly announced his tax protest, Hunthausen was in South Bend, Indiana, to speak to students at Notre Dame, the country's paramount Catholic university. A huge crowd crammed into the school's Memorial Library auditorium to hear him speak. The archbishop explained his decision to withhold part of his income taxes "as one small way I have chosen to find my way back to the cross of Christ." He described American preparations for nuclear war as "the global crucifixion of Jesus." He challenged the students to study the issue, discuss it, pray and fast, and then make their own decisions.

At the request of Bishop John Cummins of Oakland, California, Hunthausen reluctantly agreed to be part of a panel discussion on nuclear weapons at the Pacific School of Religion in Berkeley in mid-February 1982. He got there and felt totally out of his league. The other panelist on the anti-nuke side was Robert McAfee Brown, the prominent Presbyterian theologian, civil rights and peace activist, and a

Protestant observer at Vatican II. The two panelists on the pro-nuke side were both physicists from the nearby Livermore Weapons Research Laboratory. One of them was the Nobel laureate who had invented the laser.

Hunthausen was invited to speak first, followed by a physicist, who would be followed by Brown and then the other physicist. Each had fifteen minutes to speak.

The archbishop did not present a point-by-point argument disputing what the physicists might say. Instead, he spoke very simply from the heart. He said that as someone trying to follow Jesus, he found it impossible to support weapons of mass destruction. He offered a couple of Bible quotations and sat down. End of speech. Elapsed time: four minutes.

According to Brown, Hunthausen's approach totally unnerved the physicist who was scheduled to speak next. Brown guessed that the fellow had been prepared to deal with a fiery dialectic by a prince of the church, rather than a simple declaration of faith. The physicist, sitting next to Brown, seemed unable to get up. Finally, Brown whispered to him that it was his turn. He fumbled with his papers and then, turning to Brown in utter helplessness, whispered back, "You go ahead." Brown did. The physicist recovered enough to speak fourth and last, but his heart was not in it. He had been reduced to silence, Brown concluded, not by brilliant oratory, but by an unassuming, "believing Christian."

For the most part, Hunthausen found himself speaking to friendly audiences terrified by the thought of nuclear war. The Nuclear Weapons Freeze Campaign, a national effort to halt the production and deployment of nuclear weapons, had captured the public's attention. Initiated in 1980 by Randall Forsberg, a disarmament researcher, the campaign was based on a straightforward proposition to both the United States and the Soviet Union: Stop. It gained traction after the U.S. Senate failed to ratify the SALT II arms control agreement that had been negotiated with the Soviets. Not only were many Americans even more anxious, they were also fed up with the vast sums the Reagan administration was diverting from human needs to pay for a huge military buildup.

Senators Mark Hatfield, a Republican from Oregon, and Ted Kennedy, a Democrat from Massachusetts, introduced a resolution calling for an immediate, bilateral freeze on nuclear weapons. But the resolution stalled in Congress. President Reagan said there could be no freeze until the United States achieved weapons parity with the Soviets, a virtually impossible goal since parity was so difficult to define. Reagan held to his position of "peace through strength," including the strength of the nation's nuclear arsenal. Congress went along, approving the president's 1982 defense budget by a wide margin.

On Ash Wednesday 1982, Hunthausen gave a Lenten homily about peace at St. James Cathedral. He recounted the child's story of a mouse who asks a dove about the weight of a snowflake.

"Nothing more than nothing," the dove replies. So the mouse tells the dove how he had rested on a fir branch, counting the snowflakes until their number was in the millions. And then, with the settling of just one more flake, the branch suddenly cracked and fell to the ground. Such was the weight of nothing.

"Perhaps," the archbishop told the congregation, "there is only one more person's voice lacking for peace to come about in the world."

A poll conducted in April 1982 found that 75 percent of Seattle residents supported a nuclear freeze. Three-quarters of them also thought the Puget Sound area would be a likely target of a Soviet attack in a nuclear war.

On Good Friday, Hunthausen was at Ground Zero to bless the eleven pilgrims, including Father Morris, his childhood friend, who were beginning a 6,500-mile walk from Bangor to Bethlehem. Hundreds had come to see them off. The pilgrimage would trek across America, picking up others along the way, cross the Atlantic, hike through Europe, and arrive in Bethlehem on Christmas Day. Hunthausen began the march with them, walking the six miles to St. Olaf's Church in Poulsbo, exchanging greetings with friends and strangers along the way.

Meanwhile, civic, academic, business, and religious leaders announced "Target Seattle," a nine-day extravaganza of workshops, speakers, films, and other activities scheduled for late September 1982. The purpose of the event was to discuss how to prevent nuclear war. Besides Hunthausen, the speakers included Dr. Jonas Salk, Helen Caldicott, environmentalist David Brower, Watergate special prosecutor Archibald Cox, and Ambassador Edward Rowny, the chief U.S. negotiator at the U.S.–Soviet arms talks in Geneva. Questioning the arms race, remarked the corporate executive chairing the group's finance committee, "is no longer a suspect activity."

The Reagan administration did not welcome such questioning. It feared that the peace movement, bolstered by tax-resisting church leaders like Hunthausen, would undermine public support for nuclear weapons and cause Congress to slash the defense budget.

John F. Lehman, Jr., the U.S. secretary of the Navy, was presiding over a projected $1 trillion expansion of the Navy, with the Trident submarine at the core of a planned fleet of six hundred vessels. Hand-picked by Reagan, the feisty and impetuous ex-naval aviator was a consummate Washington insider with sufficient clout to force Admiral Rickover's retirement. A Catholic, Lehman kept track of church statements on nuclear war and was alarmed by the growing opposition of some Catholic bishops to nuclear deterrence. He was convinced that the United States could fight and win a nuclear war.

The Navy secretary seethed when he learned that Hunthausen had called Trident "the Auschwitz of Puget Sound." He struck back. At a Sunday service in March 1982, in the Chapel of the Four Chaplains at Temple University in his hometown of Philadelphia, Lehman lashed out at the Seattle archbishop with anger and venom.

He characterized Hunthausen's remark about the Trident "as particularly tasteless," adding that "such an ignorant and repugnant statement illustrates how far the abuse of clerical power has been taken by a few religious leaders."

The Navy secretary went on to deplore the archbishop's advocacy of unilateral disarmament. "The evil seen in the lifetimes (of religious spokesmen like Hunthausen) would pale beside the evil that our unilateral disarmament would inevitably produce in this country and throughout the world."

Lehman charged that Hunthausen and other Catholic advocates of unilateral disarmament "have not understood the clear words of the pope." Moreover, he warned, these "uninformed and overly idealistic religious leaders" were jeopardizing national security by undermining U.S. military strength. "This fashionable pacifism we see and hear today cannot and will not lead to peace."

The following morning a bold black headline ran across the front page of the Seattle Post-Intelligencer: "Chief of Navy Rips Bishop for Nuclear Stand."

Hunthausen issued a brief response from his office at the chancery. He said he respected the right of the Navy secretary to disagree with him, but he rejected Lehman's notion that a bishop may not speak out on the moral aspect of public questions.

"This is to misunderstand the long Roman Catholic tradition," he said. "Religion is not to be locked up in the sacristy."

Lehman and other members of the Reagan administration feared that the Seattle archbishop was becoming the symbolic head of a growing, faith-based peace movement that could scuttle the Trident and jeopardize the next generation of nuclear weapons. Their worst fear was that Hunthausen's influence might persuade the U.S. bishops to write a pastoral letter that rejected nuclear deterrence and even embraced unilateral disarmament. If the leaders of the nation's largest and most powerful church did that, what effect would it have on the nation?

On the afternoon of June 9, 1982, Vice Admiral J. D. Williams, the top Navy commander in the Pacific Northwest, appeared at the chancery in Seattle. Arriving early for his appointment with the archbishop, he sat in the waiting room attired in full dress blue uniform with gold buttons, sleeve stripes, and shoulder boards. His blue visor cap was decorated with gold insignia and braid. His driver waited in the car.

Williams was the naval officer with primary responsibility for the safe arrival of the Trident that summer. Working with the regional Coast Guard commander, he was determined to see the *Ohio* dock at its Bangor berth without incident or injury. For its part, the Coast Guard would ensure that it had sufficient vessels and personnel to safeguard the passage of the Trident and ward off or detain any protesters who got too close to the giant submarine. It had ninety-nine boats assigned to patrol Hood Canal and adjacent waters.

Hunthausen, seemingly nonplussed about a rear admiral in his office, received Williams at the scheduled two o'clock hour. The admiral quickly got to the point. He asked the archbishop to call off the protesters and stop the blockade. In effect, he said, get your troops to stand down.

"The Trident doesn't stop like a car with brakes," Williams explained to the archbishop. "It may not be able to stop in time to prevent injury to the demonstrators."

The archbishop listened attentively. He said he understood the danger involved. He offered no rebuttal to what the admiral had said and made no promises.

He was so cordial that Williams left the half-hour meeting thinking that he had changed the archbishop's mind about the blockade. The admiral conceded, however, that Hunthausen never said he would do anything.

And, in fact, the archbishop did nothing to impede the blockade.

Admiral Williams wasn't the only high-level government official to try to bend Hunthausen's ear. Edward Rowny, Reagan's chief weapons negotiator and a Catholic, phoned Hunthausen's office out of the blue one day and asked to speak to the archbishop. Hunthausen wasn't in at the time. When the archbishop got the message later, he was baffled. "What on earth could this be about?" he asked Maddeford, his secretary. She called Rowny back seeking more information. But to no avail. A conversation between the two never occurred.

Another feeler from the Reagan team came through Father Matthew Naumes, who worked on the archbishop's staff as judicial vicar for the marriage tribunal. A Benedictine priest and past president of St. Martin's College, Naumes had connections with Republican philanthropists and fundraisers. Shortly after Hunthausen suggested a tax protest, Naumes got a phone call from an official in the Reagan administration asking him to help arrange a meeting between the archbishop and Raymond Donovan, Reagan's secretary of labor. Donovan, also a Catholic, had once studied for the priesthood. The official proposed that Donovan and the archbishop have a private lunch at a neutral location in Seattle so that the labor secretary could hear Hunthausen's concerns and convey them to the president.

Naumes took the proposal to the archbishop. "Why would I do that?" Hunthausen asked. "What would I say?" So Naumes called the official back and told him the archbishop wasn't interested.

Dealing with the supplications of the Reagan administration, the demands of the media, and the adulation of peace activists wore on Hunthausen. He had never sought to get involved in all this. He would have preferred to quietly slip away. That became increasingly difficult because now people recognized him everywhere, even on his occasional hikes up nearby Tiger Mountain.

One day a pastor from Whidbey Island brought a group of Catholic school children to Seattle to see the cathedral. They were assembling in a very orderly fashion, lining up in rows on the sidewalk in front of the chancery building. Naumes sauntered past them and into the building where he found Hunthausen preparing to leave his office.

Naumes jokingly told the archbishop, "Hey, there's a crowd out there. It's small now but it's bound to grow."

A look of panic crossed Hunthausen's face. "Oh, my God," he said. "I left my car right out front so I can't use the back exit. I guess I'll have to face them."

The archbishop squared his shoulders, steeled himself, and strode out the front door. A chorus of young voices greeted him: "Good morning, Father."

Out on Hood Canal, Ground Zero and other peace groups continued their planning to blockade the USS Ohio. On the summer day it finally appeared in the Canal, they would launch a flotilla of canoes, rowboats, rubber rafts, and outboards and encircle the submarine, forcing it to slow down or stop, thus dramatizing the world's desire to halt the nuclear arms race and eliminate nuclear arms. The peace activists saw themselves as Davids, flinging their little boats against the enormous bulk of a Goliath submarine.

On August 11, 1982, anticipating the *Ohio*'s imminent arrival, Hunthausen and the other religious leaders boarded the *Heather Queen*, motored out into the waters of Admiralty Inlet, and anchored just outside the Coast Guard security zone to conduct a prayer vigil. They were twelve hours too soon. When the sleek, black hull of the submarine loomed into sight at dawn on August 12, the *Heather Queen* was moored back at the marina in Seattle. Hunthausen, honoring a previous commitment, was in Spokane for an annual conference of Native American Catholics.

Consequently, he did not see the protesters spring into action. At the sight of the *Ohio*, they donned wetsuits, ran to their small boats and paddled, rowed, or motored toward the submarine. The *Pacific Peacemaker* and the *Lizard of Woz*, the peace blockade's two large sailboats, assembled their crews and headed directly for the *Ohio*. The Coast Guard used its fast cutters and patrol boats to surround the demonstrators and bottle them up in Oak Bay. When the *Lizard* refused to halt, Coast Guardsmen opened up with high-pressure water hoses, knocking wooden rowboats off the *Lizard*'s deck and scattering protesters into the frigid water. A Coast Guard cutter approached the *Peacemaker* and ordered it to cut its engines. Rifle-carrying Guardsmen then boarded the boat and began handcuffing those on board. Meanwhile, other Coast Guard vessels went after the other protest boats. They snagged the canoes, dinghies, and rubber rafts with grappling hooks and pike poles and doused the occupants with blasts from water cannons.

Jim Douglass, Lutheran pastor Jon Nelson, his seventy-nine-year-old mother, Ruth, and two others were in one of the small boats previously tethered to the *Peacemaker*. They called their little vessel *The Plowshares*, a reference to Isaiah's injunction "to beat swords into plowshares and spears into pruning hooks." They'd managed to jump into the boat, untie it from the *Peacemaker*, and head toward the submarine. A Coast Guard cutter quickly pursued them, came alongside and halted *The Plowshares*. One of the Guardsmen leaned over the cutter's guard rail with a water cannon, aimed and was about to fire when Ruth Nelson's voice rang out: "Not in my America, young man, not in my America." He put the hose down.

In a comic moment for the protesters, a pint-sized peace boat with three aboard and a strong outboard engine zipped through the cordon of Coast Guard vessels, circled the *Ohio* once and was aiming to do another loop when the Coast Guard managed to clip its gas line. For a moment, the little boat floated helplessly as helicopters circled overhead, churning the water into a furious froth. One of the two women aboard repaired the fuel line by jamming the two severed ends together. The skipper, a retired schoolteacher, pulled the engine cord and the motor roared to life. Evading Coast Guard patrol boats, the little boat sped away unmolested.

Of the scores of protesters who participated in the actual blockade, only Douglass, Jon and Ruth Nelson, the tax resister Charlie Meconis, the skippers of the two big blockade boats, and eight others were arrested and charged. All charges were dropped a week later.

No American Catholic Church document has ever generated as much attention as the U.S. Catholic bishops' 1983 pastoral letter, "The Challenge of Peace." The widely distributed peace pastoral was a cover story in *Newsweek* and *Time* and the topic of countless articles, editorials, and columns around the nation. The *Boston Globe* called it "revolutionary," former national security advisor McGeorge Bundy hailed it as a "landmark," and George Kennan, the foremost authority on U.S.–Soviet relations and former ambassador to Moscow, described it as "the most profound and searching inquiry [into nuclear ethics] yet conducted by any responsible collective body." The Reagan administration considered the letter's moral criticism of nuclear weapons such a threat that it went to some length to influence the final outcome.

The bishops' letter, 175 pages long and highly nuanced, was the result of more than two years of consultation with ethicists, moral theologians, weapons experts, the Vatican, foreign bishops, and high-ranking members of the Carter and Reagan administrations. Approved by a lopsided vote of 238 to 9 at the U.S. bishops' meeting in May 1983, the peace pastoral upheld traditional Catholic "just-war theory" but with some clear applications for the nuclear age. It said that:

- Direct targeting of civilian population centers, even in retaliation for a nuclear attack, is morally wrong. Thus, no Hiroshima, no Nagasaki, ever.
- There is no justification for initiating a nuclear attack.
- Bilateral, verifiable agreements to halt the testing, production, and deployment of new nuclear weapons systems (including the Trident) should begin immediately.
- Possession of nuclear weapons as a deterrence to attack may be temporarily justified as long as urgent efforts are under way to reduce and eventually eliminate nuclear arms.

- Pacifism and unilateral disarmament, while commendable,
  pose risks for protecting a nation's security.

The bishops' letter was unprecedented not only because of what it said but because of how it had come about. The peace pastoral was the result of an open and very public process. Vatican II had created and inspired national bishops' conferences to exercise authority on national issues, albeit under the watchful eye of Rome. The peace pastoral marked the high-water point in the exercise of authority by the U.S. bishops, but only up to a certain point. Before the final vote on the letter, Pope John Paul II intervened to influence the process and ensure that the ultimate document was to his liking.

The letter, like the documents of Vatican II, was unique in its appeal to reason and conscience. The ominous, authoritarian tone of most church edicts was left behind. The U.S. bishops wanted Catholics and other Americans to reflect on what they regarded as the most pressing issue of the day. Examine the morality of nuclear war, they wrote, consider what we have said, and then follow your conscience in making decisions that further the cause of peace.

Archbishop Hunthausen's involvement with the peace pastoral began in 1980. He joined with Auxiliary Bishop Thomas Gumbleton, of Detroit, and fifty other bishops who were members of Pax Christi, the Catholic peace group, to put the issue of nuclear arms on the conference meeting agenda. At the time, Gumbleton was the best-known peace activist in the conference and the prime mover in pushing the bishops to oppose the Vietnam War. Committed, fearless, and principled, he roomed at the YMCA rather than stay at the swanky hotels where the bishops held their annual meetings.

"The Mayflower," he joked, "doesn't have a swimming pool."

Gumbleton, Hunthausen, and the other Pax Christi bishops argued that the United States was sliding toward nuclear war, and the church ought to exercise its moral authority and say something about it. The conference leadership agreed. Archbishop Joseph Bernardin, then of Cincinnati, was named to head an ad hoc five-member committee that would produce a draft statement for debate at the bishops' meeting in November 1982.

Later named archbishop of Chicago and ultimately a cardinal, Bernardin was an urbane, patient, and skillful diplomat known for his deft ability to create consensus. Slender and prematurely bald, he had a thoughtful, judicious manner that gave comfort to others. He was extremely self-disciplined, beginning each day with an hour of private prayer. Years later, when the Vatican needed a trusted troubleshooter to resolve the mess it had made trying to discipline Hunthausen, the job went to Bernardin. He is perhaps best remembered for describing Catholic moral teaching as a "consistent ethic of life from conception to natural death," and thus a "seamless garment," a reference to the cloth Christ wore at the crucifixion.

Bernardin knew the U.S. bishops were on safe ground in denouncing nuclear weapons. Vatican II had called nuclear war a crime against God and humanity that "merits unequivocal and unhesitating condemnation." The Council had described the arms race as "an utterly treacherous trap for humanity and one that ensnares the poor to an intolerable degree." Pope Paul VI in his 1965 address to the United Nations had pleaded, "No more war. War never again!" And in February 1981, just a few months before Hunthausen's comparison of Trident to Auschwitz, John Paul II spoke at the Peace Memorial Park in Hiroshima and decried nuclear weapons as a threat to the entire planet.

What was more challenging for the bishops, Bernardin realized, had to do with the questions around nuclear deterrence and unilateral disarmament, the questions that Hunthausen and "the peace bishops" were raising. If it is morally wrong to use nuclear weapons, how can it be permissible to possess them with the threat of using them? Does just-war theory apply in the nuclear age? Should the bishops endorse nuclear pacifism? Should they urge the nation to put its trust in God by beginning to disarm regardless of what the Soviets did?

Bernardin was well aware of the diversity of opinion among the bishops. Consequently, he balanced his committee by naming Gumbleton, the Pax Christi bishop, Auxiliary Bishop John O'Connor, a former military chaplain in charge of the U.S. church's ministry to the armed forces, and two well-regarded moderates.

O'Connor, a favorite of the Vatican and popular with the Reagan administration, would soon be named archbishop and then cardinal in New York City. Later he would join Bernardin and San Francisco Archbishop John Quinn on the Vatican-appointed three-member commission charged with resolving the Hunthausen affair. Tall and talkative with black, slick-backed hair, O'Connor was a force to be reckoned with. He sorely tested Bernardin's mettle and the committee's patience by introducing amendment after amendment and threatening to resign when he didn't get his way. Among other things, his amendments sought to justify deterrence and leave the door open for "tactical nuclear warfare."

At the committee's first meeting in July 1981, Bernardin set one firm ground rule: under no circumstances would the committee support unilateral disarmament. A political realist, Bernardin knew that advocating unilateral disarmament would divide the conference and distress the Vatican. He continually urged the committee, especially in writing the third and final draft, to move "back toward the center." The prohibition on unilateral disarmament, however, did not prevent Hunthausen and other bishops from discussing it, nor from submitting amendments advocating for it.

As a result, the second draft of the pastoral presented at the bishops' November 1982 meeting was a firm, tough-minded document that tried to merge the just-war tradition with the case for nuclear pacifism. With a few notable exceptions, the bishops wanted strong language and more specifics, including condemnation of the MX and Trident missiles as first-strike weapons. The peace bishops, in particular, had asked for more emphasis on pacifism by referencing the nonviolent example of Christ. Other bishops had argued that justification of nuclear deterrence, even in the short term, amounted to an end-justifies-the-means approach to moral theology. Still others had recommended that the pastoral endorse the nuclear freeze campaign.

As usual, the bishops met in Washington, DC. The draft pastoral with its condemnation of first-strike weapons and criticism of the Reagan arms buildup had put the media spotlight on their proceedings at the Capitol Hilton.

On the opening day of the meeting, the *Wall Street Journal* ran a long op-ed by Navy Secretary Lehman alleging that the bishops' recommendations "could lead directly to immoral consequences." The anti-feminist Phyllis Schlafly showed up in the hotel lobby with a counter-pastoral denouncing communist, neo-pagan governments. Father Morris and other members of the Bethlehem Peace Pilgrimage including Father George Zabelka, the repentant priest who had served as chaplain to the U.S. airmen who dropped the A-bomb on Hiroshima, were on the scene as well.

Inside the meeting room, Bernardin introduced the pastoral letter, then invited five specifically chosen bishops to comment. The five were picked as representatives of key constituencies in the conference and ranged from hawks to doves. Positioned in alphabetical order, Hunthausen would go third. Although he had attended U.S. bishops' meetings for twenty years, it was the first time he would speak to the full body. He was tense and uncomfortable. Clutching his prepared text, he waited nervously as Cardinal Terence Cooke of New York led off.

Cooke said the pastoral ought to pay more tribute to the military and better acknowledge the reality of the communist threat.

Archbishop Philip Hannan, of New Orleans, a former military chaplain, spoke next. The pastoral had so many defects, he said, that it ought to be scrapped. One of a handful of bishops to vote against the final version, Hannan thought the pastoral undermined the U.S.

moral obligation to defend itself and Western Europe. Moreover, he argued, issuing the pastoral would undercut the Reagan administration's arms control efforts and create division among Catholics and their fellow Americans.

In a parting shot, Hannan declared, "If we had gone by this in World War II, we would never have won."

Hunthausen spoke next. He placed his text on the podium and paused as if to let the air clear after Hannan. He had had input on his speech from Jim Douglass, Father Chirico, Charlie Meconis, and Father William Greytak, his friend and colleague from Carroll College in Montana. But, in the end, the words were his and he had agonized over them.

"My brother bishops," he began, his voice soft and calm. "Christ calls us to proclaim his Gospel . . . in the way we judge will best reach the hearts of men and women in our day."

After thanking Bernardin and his committee for their work, Hunthausen praised the draft document for restoring the legitimacy of pacifism to the center of the Catholic tradition. He applauded the rejection of limited nuclear war, the condemnation of first use of nuclear arms, and the denunciation of first-strike weapons. He was pleased the draft included a well-grounded theological reflection, support for a nuclear weapons freeze, and more emphasis on disarmament initiatives.

Then he hesitated for a moment before taking up what he viewed as the pastoral's shortcomings. If God is the ultimate source of our solace and safety, he asked, how can we make nuclear weapons the absolute basis for our security? Nuclear deterrence is idolatry, he said. It's a false doctrine that is the continuing cause of the arms race. It's a false doctrine that assumes hostility and separation are of the essence in international relations. It's a false doctrine that rejects forgiveness and reconciliation with God and one another. "I find that profoundly anti-Christian," he said.

Hunthausen then broached the subject of unilateral disarmament, Bernardin's taboo topic. Quoting directly from the words of the draft pastoral, he read, "in all of his life and ministry, Jesus refused to defend himself with force or violence."

"In our pastoral," he continued, "we [should] call on our people and our government to begin to lay down our nuclear arms now, regardless of what others do. To many this is foolishness, but to us in our proclamation of the Gospel, it is the cross, the power of Christ, who is the savior of the world."

The power of Christ's cross, Hunthausen said, is the power that confounds the power of the world. It is free from corruption, accessible to all, and endures forever.

With a look of relief on his face, he was done. He had said what he wanted to say and stepped down from the podium. The room broke out in applause, louder and longer than for any of the other four bishops who spoke. While few were prepared to back Hunthausen on unilateral disarmament or tax resistance, they respected the humble, prayerful way in which he had arrived at his convictions. As Hunthausen returned to his seat, Bishop Francis Quinn, of Sacramento, a supporter of unilateral disarmament, reached out, squeezed the archbishop's arm, and playfully whispered in his ear, "What's the big idea talking about Jesus and the Gospel?"

Cardinal John Krol, of Philadelphia, spoke after Hunthausen. He supported the pastoral but he also wanted more language about the Soviet threat and the legitimate right to self-defense. Archbishop John Quinn spoke last. He argued that the letter needed better criteria for defining when nuclear deterrence is acceptable.

At the end of the session, the conference leadership conducted a straw poll on how the bishops felt about the draft letter. More than two-thirds of them said they were in "basic agreement" with the document. With those encouraging results, the bishops voted to take up final approval of the peace pastoral at a special May 1983 meeting in Chicago.

Before the bishops got to Chicago, however, Rome intervened. The Vatican summoned Bernardin and three other conference executives to Rome for a two-day secret consultation in January 1983. The Americans met with Cardinal Joseph Ratzinger, the head of the office on doctrine, Cardinal Agostino Casaroli, the Vatican secretary of state, and bishop leaders from six Western European nations. The European bishops, particularly the Germans, were unhappy with the draft pastoral. They welcomed U.S. nuclear missiles as a protection against Soviet invasion and felt the letter underestimated the communist threat and caved in to pacifism.

Ratzinger and Casaroli, the pope's top lieutenants, were concerned that the Americans had gone off in directions the universal church was unwilling or unprepared to go. John Paul II, they said, had the same concerns.

While the Polish pope had vociferously denounced the arms race, he had never condemned nuclear deterrence. Nor had he ever proposed unilateral disarmament. The Vatican was particularly perturbed by the draft pastoral's treatment of pacifism as equivalent to and equally important as just war.

"There is only one Catholic tradition: the just-war theory," Casaroli bluntly told the Americans. While an individual could choose to be a pacifist, a government has a moral obligation to protect its citizens from aggression, even to the point of going to war, he said.

Chastened, Bernardin and the other Americans went home and revised the second draft, rewriting the text along the lines demanded by Rome. To be sure, the document still condemned the arms buildup, nuclear war, and the first-strike use of nuclear weapons. But it also gave conditional support for nuclear deterrence. It subordinated pacifism, affirming the superiority of just-war theory. And it regarded unilateral disarmament, while biblical and visionary, as unrealistic and unworkable.

When the U.S. bishops gathered in Chicago in early May 1983, Bernardin told them about the January consultation with the Vatican and the pope's concerns with the letter. The bishops could not take a position inconsistent with or in advance of Rome, he warned them. He then successfully pushed through the revised final draft of the pastoral.

Bishops are duty bound to display unanimity even on matters of prudential judgment lest breaking ranks damage their credibility and confuse the faithful. Consequently, virtually all of the peace bishops, including Hunthausen and Gumbleton, voted for the final version of the pastoral, even though it was not what they wanted.

Hunthausen felt caught between his conscience and his loyalty to his brother bishops and Rome. Why were they unwilling to ask the "People of God" to accept the risk that he felt the Gospel demanded? Wasn't Christ saying take up the cross, throw away your nuclear weapons and, in your vulnerability, discover your humanity? That's what he believed in his heart. But in his mind he kept questioning himself: Why were so many other bishops unconvinced? Who was he to say that the Vatican was wrong? Certainly, there was much that was good in the pastoral.

In the end, Hunthausen regarded his vote as "conditional approval" in hopes that the bishops' conference might take a stronger stand in the future. It was an illusory hope. Overruled by the Vatican, the bishops never touched the subject again.

In the May general meeting itself, Hunthausen did not speak from the podium or the floor. His mind was elsewhere. During a coffee break, Archbishop Pio Laghi, the papal delegate to the United States, pulled Hunthausen aside. He informed him that the Holy See would like to visit the Seattle archdiocese.

Shrewd, polished, and charming, Laghi was the career Vatican diplomat charged with managing Rome's sensitive relations with the U.S. administration and the American church. His earlier assignments had included postings in Palestine, India, and Argentina, where he regularly played tennis with one of the leaders of the military junta during that country's "Dirty War." Beneath his charm, critics saw a crafty opportunist who used his Roman education and connections to advance the pope's agenda.

Hunthausen thought Laghi acted nervous and unprepared when he approached him at the coffee break. It seemed like he needed to share some information but didn't quite know how to do it. They had little history together, having exchanging no more than pleasantries in the past. So, at first, Hunthausen didn't know how to take the papal delegate's news of a Vatican visit to Seattle.

"I naively felt, great, that's wonderful," he recalled. "And then when I found out what an apostolic visitation was all about, I wondered: What in the world?"

Increasingly troubled and perplexed, Hunthausen tried to phone Laghi at the hotel the next day. But the papal delegate had returned to Washington, DC. Hunthausen called again and was told that Laghi was in Rome.

Hunthausen returned to Seattle with a sense of dread. He heard nothing more from Laghi for several weeks. And then, out of the blue, he got a call from the papal delegate informing him that Archbishop James A. Hickey, a veteran prelate and theologian who had dutifully followed orders to quash dissent in his own Washington, DC, diocese, was coming to Seattle to investigate him.

MONTANA YOUTH

The first duty of love is to listen.
—Paul Tillich

One would be hard pressed to imagine a place more remote and more removed from the world of Vatican politics and ecclesial power than Anaconda, Montana, the hometown of Raymond G. Hunthausen. There was little in the small, blue-collar mining town nestled in a high Rocky Mountain valley that would suggest that one of its sons would grow up to become an archbishop and a lightning rod in the Roman Catholic Church.

Founded in 1883, six years before Montana became a state, Anaconda was a workers' town. It owed its existence to the nearby supply of water and timber used to smelt the ore from Butte, a rival town that sat atop a mother lode of copper. For nearly a century, what Butte mined, Anaconda melted. It was the "Smelter City," its monument the 585-foot-tall illuminated smokestack that soared above the fiery melting pots below.

The Anaconda Copper Mining Company, which grew to be one of the largest mining operations in the world, dominated the Anaconda of the future archbishop's early life. Until its closure and collapse in 1980, the company operated the biggest smelting operation on the planet. In the glory years, it ran Anaconda, employing more than twenty-five hundred workers from a population of less than twenty thousand. It built and maintained the city's water supply, its electricity, and the streetcars that ran from the workers' homes to the smelter. It paved the streets and provided land for churches and social clubs. And it constructed the grand, neo-classical courthouse at the top of Main Street.

The company hoped its paternal beneficence would ensure a grateful community and a compliant work force. Not so. Anaconda was a union town and had to survive several long and bitter strikes.

It was also a town of immigrants, most of them Catholic. They were Irish, Italian, Polish, Croatian, and German. The three Anaconda parishes of the time—St. Peter, St. Paul, and St. Joseph—were full for Sunday Masses and drew crowds for novenas, mission speakers, Holy Week liturgies, marriages, and funerals.

The birth of Raymond Hunthausen, the first-born child of Anthony and Edna Hunthausen, on August 21, 1921, was treated like a religious event. On that hot August afternoon, Edna knew that she was going into labor as the contractions came closer together. She had made all the necessary arrangements and nearby St. Anne's Hospital was ready to receive her. Her husband Anthony, however, was not quite ready to go. He was in his work clothes. He changed into a suit and tie so he would be appropriately dressed when he met his new son.

The young couple picked the name "Raymond" for their baby boy simply because they liked it. His middle name would be Gerhardt, after his paternal grandfather.

Raymond, soon to be nicknamed "Dutch," was the first of seven children born to Anthony and Edna Hunthausen. Marie was born in 1923, Tony in 1926, Jack in 1927, Edna in 1929, Art in 1931, and Jeanne in 1934.

Anthony Hunthausen, a Missouri farm boy on a wanderer's trip west in the summer of 1910 had happened to stop in Anaconda. He got a job at the smelter and fell in love with Edna Marie Tuschscherer, the daughter of the local brewery owner. The couple married at St. Paul's Church, an old brick and stone structure in the heart of Anaconda's business district, on Columbus Day 1920. He was twenty-eight; she was twenty-seven.

Anthony stood more than six feet tall and weighed nearly 220 pounds. He was a strong, imposing, handsome man with a full head of dark brown hair and an extrovert's enjoyment of people. After serving in the U.S. Army Air Force in World War I, he became proprietor of his father-in-law's grocery. He also sold insurance and real estate.

Anthony delighted in children, a love inherited by his oldest son. As kids stood in the store mesmerized by the candy counter, he would sneak up behind them, grab them around the waist, and growl like a grizzly bear: "Grrrrr."

"He was brilliant at relating to people," recalled Art, the youngest son. "He knew everybody. In those days, people bought groceries from you because they liked you."

Intelligent and jovial with an infectious laugh, Anthony retained the rural humor he'd acquired as a farm boy. He especially liked telling jokes on himself. He claimed that he ate so much wild rabbit as a kid that when a dog barked, he'd run under the porch. There were limits to Anthony's joke telling, however. He didn't like ridicule or sarcasm or poking fun at another's expense. Dutch recalled the time his dad was told a joke belittling Harry Truman. No sign of amusement crossed his father's face. He later told his son that we don't know the burdens and responsibilities that others bear and we ought not criticize them. Dutch applied the lesson to his own life.

Anthony was especially active in the Kiwanis Club, which elected him district governor for Montana. The family has a picture of him speaking to a group of five hundred Kiwanis at their national convention in Atlantic City, New Jersey.

"I remember how proud I was of him," Dutch recalled. "But I could feel his anxiety because he didn't have much education."

Anthony thought of himself as a fortunate man whose lucky number was seven. He was one of seven children; so was Edna. The two of them had seven children. And the phone number at the grocery store was simply "7."

While Anthony was a faithful churchgoer, he was not particularly pious or devout. He didn't talk about religion. He didn't read the Bible outside of Mass nor did he regularly recite the rosary. He kept the grocery story open on Sunday afternoons. He practiced rather than preached his faith. He carried many customers on credit, especially during the Depression, knowing there was little likelihood they could ever pay.

When Anthony had heart trouble later in life, doctors told him he should stop laughing and telling stories because the laughter was going to kill him. On June 24, 1957, it did. His heart gave out. The funeral procession from St. Peter's Church was one of the longest ever witnessed in Anaconda.

Edna Marie Hunthausen was the fifth child of an enterprising businessman who, looking for investment opportunities, moved his family west from Wisconsin in 1901. Adam Tuschscherer found a brewery for sale in Anaconda, purchased it, and produced an ale called "Old Fashioned." He eventually acquired or helped his relatives and in-laws acquire other enterprises—a bottling works, a warehouse, a dry goods store, an icehouse, a drug store, and a gas station. He also sold insurance, dealt in real estate, and built homes. Though comfortable, Edna's family was not especially wealthy. Prohibition closed the brewery and the Depression crippled her father's business enterprises.

Edna loved music and had a fine voice. Accompanied on the piano by one of her sisters, she overcame her timidity enough to sing publicly. After graduating from Anaconda High School, she lived at home and worked for her father as a bookkeeper until she married Anthony Hunthausen.

A strikingly attractive woman with a warm smile, Edna was nearly a foot shorter than her husband. But what she lacked in stature she more than made up for in determination and discipline. She ran the Hunthausen household. At all times, she knew where her husband and her children were. In later years, when she had dozens of grandchildren, the family jokingly called her "The General." She mustered the troops and gave the orders.

She didn't wear her rank easily, however. Like her oldest son, she was a shy introvert, more comfortable standing back than charging forward. Edna prepared the big meal at midday so that Anthony could work uninterrupted in the evening at the store. Family and friends were always welcome. Because the Hunthausens lived on a corner, some kids used the house as a way station and a shortcut to the store. In the front door and out the back.

"People would drop in, come in without ringing the bell and she'd welcome them," said Art, the sixth of the seven Hunthausen children. "Father would come in with a group of people and say, 'Let's eat.'"

Early in their marriage, Anthony and Edna Hunthausen lived in a small wood frame house connected to the grocery store at 321 West Park Avenue. But the little house couldn't accommodate the growing family. In 1927, with the arrival of Jack, the fourth child, the Hunthausen family moved into a new house that Edna's father had built on the corner lot at 701 West Third Street. Three generations of Hunthausens occupied the two-story stucco house, painted white with red window shutters and a glass-enclosed front porch, for the next ninety years. A sign in the upstairs hallway summarized the family creed. It read: "God sees you and He loves you."

Anthony and Edna lived agreeably with their differences. Anthony's need for fraternizing tired Edna at times. Dutch recalled her saying to her husband's many invitations, "Oh my goodness, we've got to do that again?" But after her initial reluctance, she'd get dressed to go out and end up enjoying herself. Dutch became the same way.

The couple was not demonstrably affectionate with each other or their children. Edna and Anthony came from practical, no-nonsense German-American homes where kissing was private, emotions were held in check, and only kind thoughts were spoken.

"There was no gossip in our family," said Marie, who like her older brother has the habit of listening carefully. "Mother and Dad just didn't approve of that. They never talked about other people's problems."

In disciplining their children, Edna and Anthony favored reason over the rod. "If we did something wrong, they'd sit us down, point out what was wrong, and ask if we had learned something from it," Marie explained. "Our punishment, more or less, was thinking about what we had done. We would feel pretty bad about it because we dearly loved them and we realized that we had hurt them."

Edna Hunthausen outlived her husband by more than twenty-five years. She spent the last third of her life as the matriarch of a family that would include thirty-seven grandchildren, twenty-four in-laws, and twenty-five great grandchildren at the time of her death in April 1983. Every other August, the family gathered for a four-day reunion at Legendary Lodge, a church summer camp on Salmon Lake in the Montana Rockies.

When Edna was dying at the hospital in Helena, all seven of her children gathered at her bedside. They clustered around and began telling stories about her. Dutch went first. The storytelling would later adjourn to brother Tony's house where it would go on until four in the morning because some of the siblings were telling stories that the others had never heard before.

In the end, they agreed that the best story was not a story at all. It was their mother's parting words. Serene and radiant in her hospital bed, Edna looked around the room at her children and said, "Thank you for being such great kids. And don't ever stop having family reunions."

Dutch Hunthausen's earliest memories are blurred snapshots from the family's trips, first by train, then by car, back to Missouri to see his dad's parents and relatives. There is a photo from an early trip of four generations of Hunthausen men: great-grandfather, grandfather, father, and four-year-old Dutch wearing a baseball uniform.

Despite his shy and reticent nature, Dutch was a child capable of making mischief. In Anaconda, a laundry man picked up dirty clothes and delivered clean ones in a cart pulled by a single horse. At lunchtime, he left the horse and cart at the curb, securing them with a leather strap attached to a metal weight that he tossed on the ground. One day Dutch picked up the weight and threw it into the laundry wagon. The startled horse took right off. Dutch bolted home in fright while the neighbors pursued the horse down Park Avenue.

Another time he was wandering the block on a hot summer afternoon when he came across a little girl running through a sprinkler. He joined her. The two of them got soaking wet and decided to take off their clothes. So there they were, boy and girl, cavorting nude in a sprinkler.

"Some women came by, saw us naked, and made some very dis-approving remarks," said Dutch, laughing at the memory. "They frightened me to death so I ran home buck naked. I wasn't about to deal with those ladies."

Ed Dolan, one of nine children of Irish immigrant parents who lived a block from the Hunthausens, first encountered Dutch as a towheaded kid jumping off the roof of a house under construction. Dolan was amazed by the little kid's pluck and soon joined him in leaping off the roof. The two became life-long friends.

In those days, every kid in Anaconda seemed to have a nickname. It was one way of distinguishing kids from others with the same last name. So if you were a Sullivan or a Kelly, you might be nicknamed Pinky, Curly, or Butch. There were even other kids called "Dutch," like the girl who married Skinny Francisco.

"Hunthausen" is, in fact, German, not Dutch. It means "a place where the hound dwells," a "dog house." The episcopal coat of arms that Dutch later took as a bishop depicts a large hound running in front of a medieval castle topped with a cross.

Dolan, a slight man with lively green eyes, a mischievous laugh, and a bedside manner befitting his many years as a physician, ex-plained that Anacondans conflated "Dutch" with "Deutsch," and thus "Dutch" became an affectionate term for a likeable German.

"We never called him anything but Dutch," Dolan said, "and fi-nally his folks started calling him Dutch too."

Dutch himself had a different story about the origin of his nick-name. He said that Dolan's older brother, Bobby, named him after a college football star. Even as a six-year-old, Dutch was a confident, competitive player with sure hands and quick feet. So Bobby Dolan began calling him "The Flying Dutchman," after John Wesley "Dutch" Kitzmiller who played at the University of Oregon in the late-1920s and was later inducted into the College Football Hall of Fame.

In the fall of 1927, Dutch Hunthausen started first grade at St. Paul's, the parish grade school five blocks from home. The two-story, red brick school building had eight classrooms on the first floor, one for each grade, with thirty to forty children in each class. An auditorium occupied the second floor, and behind the school there were separate playgrounds for boys and girls. The Ursuline Sisters, a religious order dedicated to teaching children, staffed St. Paul's and lived in the handsome brick convent next door.

Dutch enjoyed school. Motivated and conscientious, he found that the classwork came easily to him. He received good grades and made new friends. His childhood friend, Owen Greenough, has a photograph of Dutch and his friends from that time. Dutch, a solidly built boy with a wavy shock of blond hair, wears a plaid shirt. He has an impish smile on his face.

Also in the photo are Ed Dolan, Jimmy Kelly, and Dutch's cousin, Jack Sugrue. The three boys, Owen, and Dutch called themselves "The Third Street Gang." They played together year round. Baseball in the summer, football in the fall, and basketball, ice skating, and tobogganing during Anaconda's long, cold winter.

"Dutchie had a great deal of athletic ability," said Greenough. "But he didn't make a big show of it. And he was fearless. Anything with a little thrill to it delighted him."

Greenough, the son of a locomotive engineer, grew up a block away from the Hunthausens. A nostalgic man with blue eyes, a firm jaw, and ruddy complexion, Greenough, like Dolan, graduated from Anaconda High School and Creighton University. While Dolan went on to medical school, Greenough became an accountant, moved to Seattle, and retired after a long career at Boeing.

The Third Street Gang and their pals spent much of the summer in Washoe Park, the complex of fields, gardens, and picnic areas built by the Anaconda Company.

"We'd go there with our rubber band guns, choose sides, and fight it out," Dolan recalled. "Once the rubber hit you, you were done."

Sometimes the gang strolled along the top of the wooden flume that carried water to the smelter. The flume crossed gullies and ravines and cut across hillsides, making it a natural walkway through the countryside. In the winter, the boys walked it with their dogs, knocking giant icicles off its barrel-like sides. At the smelter itself, they slipped in and grabbed some of the twelve-foot bamboo poles used to shake ore off the chains in the rail cars.

The poles were great for vaulting into a sand pile in the empty lot next to Grandpa Tuschscherer's brewery. One time when Dutch was vaulting, he fell hard and knocked himself out. The other kids stood frozen in shock. "He's dead," pronounced brother Tony. Grandpa suddenly appeared, picked Dutch up, and carried him into the brewery where he revived.

With his father's encouragement, Dutch began playing golf as a six-year-old, carrying and selecting his dad's clubs. The game became a lifelong passion, and he soon shot at par or better. Brother Art recalled a time when the two of them were playing the course outside Anaconda. Art pulled out a seven-iron, teed up, and remarked, "If I could just get the ball on the green."

Dutch, with a look of disapproval, replied, "That could be part of your problem, Art. You're supposed to aim for the pin."

In the lower grades, Dutch worked after school in his dad's grocery store. He stocked shelves, sorted potatoes and onions, and rinsed out pop bottles. He had a bicycle with a big front basket for groceries and was paid four cents a delivery. During Prohibition, when Grandpa's brewery was forced to convert to soft drinks, Dutch helped bottle Orange Crush. He clambered up to the top of the large stone mixing vats with a huge wooden paddle and stirred the liquid mixture until he could stir no more.

In roughly two-year intervals, Dutch's siblings followed him to St. Paul's School. First Marie, then Tony, then Jack. By the time sister Edna Ruth began first grade, Dutch, eight years older, was in high school. As the oldest child, he was respected and admired by his younger siblings.

Childhood was not all rosy for Dutch Hunthausen. He had scarlet fever, the chicken pox, and his share of broken bones. He had worries and fears about kids who might bully or take advantage of him. He witnessed more than a few fights that started over someone taunting someone else over something trivial. Punches and blows followed the taunts until faces ran red with blood and teeth were knocked loose.

The Anaconda street fights left a lasting impression on the future archbishop. What was the point? Might did not make right, and violence only begat more violence. It was a lesson he would apply in his life work.

When Dutch was in the upper grades, an eighth-grade boy was killed—not in street violence, but in a hunting accident. The gun misfired and the boy died immediately.

"I remember how those with him, including a classmate of mine, brought him back down the hill and how they were honored and the boy mourned," Dutch recalled. "It left a desolate feeling in me. It was hard to accept death in someone my own age."

In the fall of 1935, Dutch enrolled at St. Peter's High School, which counted a mere 120 students for all four grades in the red brick building next to the church at Fourth and Alder. Given its small enrollment, St. Peter's played in Montana's Class B sports league, which meant that students with even modest athletic ability could make the team. So Dutch, who stood just five feet and weighed a meager ninety pounds as a fourteen-year-old freshman, was able to shine. By his junior year, a foot taller and fifty pounds heavier, he played quarterback and took St. Peter's football team on to win the state high school Class B championship.

But the athletic feat that Ed Dolan remembered best occurred at a baseball game. Dutch was playing shortstop for Anaconda's American Legion Team, the biggest baseball show in town. Butte, then the largest city in the state, was a baseball powerhouse and perennial champion because it had several high schools from which to draw the best players. Anaconda had just two schools—the public high school and little St. Peter's.

The summer Dutch turned sixteen, Anaconda faced Butte in the American Legion regional playoff. It was late in the game and Anaconda was losing. Dutch came up to bat.

"There's two of our guys on base and Dutchie drives the ball," Dolan excitedly recalled more than fifty years later. "And I swear it went four hundred and some odd feet, way, way over the center-fielder's head. I'd never seen a ball hit that hard by a kid in my life. Dutchie trotted around the bases and the Anaconda Legion won the game. I was in the stands screaming: 'This is our guy. This is our guy.' I ran home and told his mother and father. And they laughed."

At St. Peter's, the nuns often asked Dutch to do presentations or give talks, such as welcoming the bishop when he visited the school or speaking to social clubs about the school's service projects. It was difficult for him. When he had to speak his face flamed scarlet "like a scorched tomato."

"I was almost frightened by it, by this public exposure," he recalled. "Yet when faced with a reasonable set of arguments, I'd say, 'Well, all right, I'll try it.'"

The sisters encouraged Dutch to think about religious life. In grade school, the parish priest had visited the classroom regularly and asked: How many of you are going to be priests? And the boys would raise their hands. How many of you are going to be sisters? And the girls would raise their hands. But Dutch had never raised his.

Talk of priesthood made him uncomfortable. The thought of committing his whole life to Christ and sacrificing the possibility of marriage and family was more than he could imagine. He enjoyed dating and dancing and the summer parties of boys and girls at the lodge on Echo Lake, just west of Anaconda.

A great boon to Dutch's social life was access to the family car, a 1930 Nash sedan. He had started driving at fourteen, when his mother propped him up on pillows so he could see over the steering wheel. They drove around Anaconda and sometimes ventured over to Columbia Gardens, an amusement park on the outskirts of Butte that featured dancing and exotic horses from Italy. Once he was in high school, Dutch was permitted to drive on his own.

Intelligent, athletic, and good-looking, Dutch was attractive to girls. And he was very attracted to them. Yet he felt awkward and nervous in their company. He was self-conscious and blushed easily. He envied those friends who were so free and casual with the opposite sex. Given his athleticism, he figured he should be a good dancer. But he was very hesitant to dance.

"I didn't like the fact that I couldn't be more myself," he recalled.

Dutch's most serious girlfriend was Madge Owens, whom he dated during the last two years of high school and the first two years of college.

Dutch, Ed Dolan, and Owen Greenough regularly visited the Owens's home in Anaconda, particularly during the holidays. The Owens were a large, close-knit family, Welsh Protestants with their own rituals and customs.

Dolan fondly remembered a New Year's Eve gathering when Madge, her parents, siblings, and other relatives were gathered around the hearth in the family's cramped living room. At midnight, one of the older boys went outside to fetch a lump of coal. He brought it back and handed it to his mother who gave him a shot of whiskey in return. He knocked back the whiskey and poured a shot for the others. They drank, and then joined hands to sing "Auld Lang Syne." And then they danced.

On another evening at the Owens house, Dutch and his two friends were sitting in the small living room with the family. Dolan recalled how "the old granddad got a little bit oiled, stood up and said, 'I wanna man that kin sing.'"

Dutch, pointing at Dolan, said, "There he is. That guy there. He's taken lessons."

The old granddad sized up Dolan and looked dubious. "I don wanna man that's taken lessons," he said. "I wanna man that kin sing."

Sheepishly, Dolan rose and sang, belting out a version of "Danny Boy" that brought tears to the eyes of the old granddad.

For at least a couple of years Dutch and Madge Owens were on a path that would lead to marriage.

Asked years later if it was love, Dutch sighed. "I don't know," he said. "I don't think so. I think love is that sense of being inseparable from the other. I've never had that feeling toward anyone although I fully know that it can happen." He said he has witnessed that special feeling in the marriages of his siblings and their children, that wonderful place where joy, fulfillment, and life come together.

In the spring of 1939, Dutch Hunthausen graduated first among the boys and third overall in his senior class of thirty-six students at St. Peter's High School. In response to a request from the admissions office of Carroll College in Helena, his teachers compiled a "personality rating" for him. They gave Dutch 8 out of 10 points on intellectual ability and on aptitude, initiative, leadership and social skills. They rated him "9" on emotional control and "10" on integrity.

Carroll College, the only Catholic school of higher education in western Montana and then open only to boys, offered Dutch an unsolicited $200 honors scholarship for being the highest-ranking boy in his graduating class. But Dutch wasn't interested.

He, his cousin Jack Sugrue, and Owen Greenough had more immediate plans. For graduation, Sugrue's parents had given him a new '39 Plymouth coupe with a rumble seat. The threesome planned to drive it to California and back. Dutch and Greenough had never been south of Salt Lake.

"Coming out of Montana, it was a big thing for us to be turned loose on our own," recalled Greenough, relishing the memory of that epic journey. "Our lives were like silver dollars."

They left Anaconda in early August, each of them with about $85 in their pockets. In Salt Lake, they saw Artie Shaw and his band play outdoors at Salt Air, then headed southwest to the Grand Canyon, Las Vegas, and Los Angeles. They stayed in motels or overnighted with relatives, particularly in Los Angeles, where Sugrue had cousins. They swam in the ocean at Huntington Beach, where a lifeguard had to rescue Greenough from an undertow, and then drove on to San Francisco, where they took in the World's Fair on Treasure Island. In northern California, they motored through the Redwoods and when they got to Seattle they crossed Lake Washington on the newly opened Floating Bridge. By the end of the month, they were back home in Anaconda, which suddenly seemed very small.

Dutch was still undecided about where to go to college. He had given some thought to Montana State, where he might pursue science and perhaps become a chemical engineer. He also considered Notre Dame. The priest at St. Peter's and his dad encouraged him to reconsider Carroll. But his dad added that he would support Dutch at any school he chose, including Notre Dame. Ultimately, it was a former Notre Dame football player who clinched the deal, not for Notre Dame, but for Carroll.

Ed Simonich, a six-foot-two, 240-pound star halfback at Notre Dame, was Carroll's new head football coach. He sought out Dutch and assured him that, as an experienced high school tailback, he was a natural fit for the backfield that Siminich envisioned at Carroll.

"I felt, well, I've got a place where people would like me to go," Dutch recalled. "So I'll go."

Carroll College, where Dutch registered for classes in the fall of 1939, was no Notre Dame. The Catholic school in the state's capital city was tiny, with only 125 full-time students when Dutch started. The school struggled to stay open, nearly closing during World War I, and later surviving the Second World War by inviting a naval officers' training program to share its buildings and campus.

The Most Rev. John Patrick Carroll, the second bishop of the Diocese of Helena, founded the school in 1909 on fifty acres of donated land a short walk from Last Chance Gulch, the main street in Helena. He had raised enough funds from a mine trust, fraternal groups, and the railroad tycoon James J. Hill to build St. Charles Hall, the imposing, five-story brick building that sits atop the highest point in the city. Carroll named the school Mount Saint Charles College after St. Charles Borromeo, a sixteenth-century cardinal archbishop of Milan and a church reformer.

He declared that the college's purpose was "to give the young men of Montana a thorough, liberal education which will fit them for leadership in any vocation they may choose and at the same time so surround them with a religious atmosphere that they will ever follow conscience as their king." When Bishop Carroll died in 1925, the college's board of trustees renamed the school in his honor.

Besides its Catholic heritage, Carroll College had at least one other thing in common with Notre Dame: a fervor for football. Among the Catholic high school boys recruited from all over Montana by Coach Simonich were Dutch and Jack McCarvel, who had played quarterback at Anaconda High School. "Bobcat" McCarvel, who later became a lawyer and a judge, was Dutch's backfield teammate and roommate in St. Charles Hall.

Assessing his thirty-man roster, Siminich told the Helena Lions Club that the 1939 squad averaged less than 165 pounds. "They're small," he conceded, "so our strategy will be founded on deception." *The Helena Record Herald* ran pictures of players in full uniform, including one of Dutch bent forward in a running position, clutching the football to his stomach. He weighed exactly 165 pounds.

Simonich started two freshmen: Dutch Hunthausen at left halfback and Bobcat McCarvel at right end. For the 1940 season, he moved McCarvel to quarterback. Consequently the two Anaconda sophomores ran the backfield. After an initial non-conference loss in Idaho, the Saints won all their games and earned the Montana Collegiate Conference football title with Dutch as the team captain. The *Record Herald* excitedly described him as "the Anaconda mighty mite" who does "the brainwork in the Saint backfield" and is "the team's most consistent yardage machine."

Dutch played more than football. He was a starting guard on Carroll's varsity basketball squad, shortstop on the baseball team, and a member of the golf team. But football was his favorite.

"I realized that the sport of football was a natural for me," he reminisced. "That's where my athletic talents were. I could pass; I could punt; and I got to know how to really manage a backfield."

But Dutch's football career had an abrupt ending. In the last game of his sophomore year, he leaped to recover a fumble, hit hard, and dislocated his right elbow. The dislocated bone never properly healed, leaving him with a vulnerable right arm. Thereafter his football play was limited to kicking punts and field goals.

There was further bad news for Carroll football, however. With the Japanese attack on Pearl Harbor in December 1941, the United States went to war and colleges cut back on athletics in support of the war effort. After winning all its games that season, Carroll College suspended football.

On campus, Dutch and McCarvel settled into Room 307 of St. Charles Hall and enjoyed the camaraderie of the dorm. At an all-boys school, there was a fair bit of smoking, drinking, and hijinks despite the priest monitors who patrolled the halls.

With the advent of the war, Father Emmet Riley, the college president, instituted a physical education program to prepare his charges for service to the country. Students rose at 6 AM for a half hour of calisthenics in the gym before proceeding to chapel for the 7:05 AM Mass.

Dutch made time for calisthenics and Mass as well as sports, academics, and a busy social life. Most of the girls he knew, including Madge Owens, were back in Anaconda or Butte or off to college elsewhere. Nonetheless, he managed to find dates for the Harvest Ball, the proms, and the other dance events sponsored by Carroll. On occasion, he served on the date committee, lining up unattached students with partners for the dances.

Dutch came to Carroll thinking he might pursue science or engineering. Intrigued by the experimental lab work in a physics course he took sophomore year, he wanted to declare physics as his major. But Carroll offered no advanced physics classes, so he majored in chemistry instead.

In the spring of his sophomore year, he was one of eight Carroll students to enroll in the school's new civil aeronautics program. It included eighty hours of ground school and thirty-five hours of instruction in the air and, because of the daytime academic schedule, was taught mostly at night. Dutch loved flying the biplanes at the nearby airfield. He and the flight instructor sat in tandem seats, taking turns working the stick throttle. He dreamed of doing aerial acrobatics.

"I'd see these double-winged planes over the valley, doing all these spins and dives," he said, imitating the mmmmah drone of a small plane engine, "and that's what I wanted to do."

With World War II under way, Dutch figured that the pilot training would give him an automatic slot in the Army Air Force. "That wouldn't have been a bad thing for me," he said.

Dutch's fantasies of being a military pilot and a married man waned under the influence of Father Bernard Topel, a math and physics professor at Carroll and also the diocesan vocations director. Topel was to became Dutch's spiritual mentor and confessor for the next forty years. Dutch would later say that, next to his parents and the grace of God, Topel exercised the biggest influence on his life.

Scholarly and extremely self-disciplined, Topel had a thoughtful wisdom that awed the eighteen-year-old college freshman. Of average height and build, he wore heavy-framed glasses that gave his long, oval face an attentive, inquisitive look. He was an excellent listener. As a younger man, he was not at all reluctant to impose his rigorous convictions on others. But as he grew older, he mellowed and let go. His beliefs remained firm but the righteousness subsided, replaced by an accepting kindness, a self-deprecating humor, and a mirthful joy.

The Montana-born son of German-speaking immigrants, Topel had studied at Carroll, completed seminary in Montreal, earned a master's degree in education from Catholic University, a master's in mathematics from Harvard, and a doctoral degree in math from Notre Dame. After earning his doctorate, he taught for two years at Notre Dame, but the diocese needed him back in Helena. So he returned to Carroll where he taught math for nearly twenty years.

Topel was a brilliant theoretical mathematician with an intuitive ability to grasp even the most challenging problems. In scientific circles, even Albert Einstein was aware of him. "There are very few people who understand my theory of relativity," the famous physicist once said. "And one of them is a young priest out of Montana."

Nearly everyone, including Topel, was surprised when he was appointed bishop of Spokane in 1955. "I thought I was the least prepared man to become bishop ever," Topel said.

Nonetheless, he became an able administrator who led the Spokane diocese in developing social projects such as homes for unwed mothers, housing for the elderly, and a new model of retreat house providing spiritual direction for priests, nuns, and laypeople. He sold the bishop's seventeen-room brick mansion, his gem-studded crozier, and his gold pectoral cross and gave the profits to charity. He moved into a dingy, four-room frame house that he bought for $4,000 in a rundown, inner-city neighborhood. He refused to draw a church salary and gave much of his Social Security income to the poor. He wore second-hand clothes and grew his own food—beans, peas, potatoes, squash and other vegetables—in a backyard garden.

I met Bishop Topel in 1977 when I was covering religion for the *Walla Walla Union-Bulletin*. The bishop's voluntary poverty had attracted media attention from around the country. So I asked him if this was the way of the church.

Yes, he replied, contending that if Catholics lived like St. Francis of Assisi the church would be gaining believers rather than losing them.

"Simplified living is essential for the good of the church," he told me, foretelling what Pope Francis would say years later. "Those of us who should be giving leadership in following Christ's teaching have not been living the message of Christ. We water it down. The salt has lost its savor."

Topel retired as bishop of Spokane in 1978. He subsequently was diagnosed with Alzheimer's disease and moved into a nursing facility staffed by the Providence Sisters. Hunthausen visited regularly, but his mentor in his last years no longer recognized him. Topel died at age eighty-three in October 1986, three weeks before the Hunthausen case forced a showdown with the Vatican at the U.S. bishops' national meeting.

At Carroll, Topel modeled the ascetic life for which he would later become well known. He denied himself meals, movies, possessions, even the thrill of listening to a Notre Dame football game on a Saturday afternoon. He spent much time at prayer in the school chapel and was in great demand as a retreat leader.

Some, including Dutch's little sister, Edna Ruth, found him too strict and out of touch with the real world. They thought he pushed too hard in encouraging young men and women to consider vocations to religious life.

Edna remembered Topel coming to the family home in Anaconda one time looking for her older brother. She was sixteen and wearing bright fuchsia lipstick.

"I saw his car out front and I hollered out the window: Dutch isn't here!" she recalled. "And my mother said, 'You don't do that. You go out the back door and you go to the car and tell him.'"

So Edna went out to the car to tell Topel that her brother wasn't home. Topel saw the bright red lipstick on her face and ordered her to get back in the house and remove it immediately.

Enraged, Edna ran back inside and demanded of her mother, "Who does he think he is? My dad doesn't talk to me like that. Dutch doesn't talk to me like that."

Her mother asked Edna to sit down and calm herself. "Father Topel doesn't know what it's like to be a sixteen-year-old girl," she explained. "Don't let him get to you."

Four years later, Edna would join the Sisters of Charity, eventually accepting a pastoral assignment at the lone Catholic parish on the dusty, cold, windswept Blackfeet Indian Reservation in northern Montana. In that disheartening place, those she served dealt with the deadliest issues—extreme poverty, unemployment, alcoholism, domestic violence, and cultural disintegration. There was no tougher assignment.

Topel captivated Dutch, and the two soon became close friends.

"He didn't hesitate to talk about God. That was discomforting and at times embarrassing for me," Dutch recalled. "But he wanted to know what I was doing with my life and where my life was going. He didn't mince any words."

At Carroll, Dutch saw Topel once a week for confession and spiritual guidance. Topel suggested he read the spiritual classics, the devotional writings of Thomas à Kempis, St. John of the Cross, St. Teresa of Avila, and others. Then they talked about what he had read.

In their discussions, Topel kept emphasizing one point: You should want to do what God wants you to do.

Dutch had no problem accepting that. "That made eminently good sense to me," he said. "That's the only way one ought to live."

His question was: How do I find out what God wants of me?

Discovering God's will for his life became Dutch's biggest challenge. During one of their conversations, Topel asked Dutch if God might want him to be a priest. Dutch replied that he didn't know one way or the other. So Topel suggested that since Dutch didn't know, he should avoid making decisions that would close the door on priesthood. Being open to serious consideration of religious life, he proposed, could mean leaving aside activities like sports, dating, and airplane flying. It could also mean taking on other activities like studying theology and philosophy or practicing contemplative prayer.

Dutch didn't feel any pressure from Topel. "He wasn't forcing me," Dutch said. "He was just saying: Keep your options open. And that's about what I did."

Under Topel's guidance, Dutch decided to add philosophy, Latin, and church history to his course load of science and math during his junior year at Carroll. That way if he did decide to pursue priesthood, he would meet the basic course requirements for the seminary. At the same time, he figured that if God was calling him to a life of priestly celibacy, he needed to stop dating, dancing, and going to movies.

Dutch found that extremely difficult. He was attracted to marriage and family. He was fond of women. He was enthralled by the romance of the movies. Yet he also felt that perhaps he was being called to abandon this to serve God. The sadness and longing for an intimate, loving relationship with a life partner didn't go away however.

"I would respect it and live with it and admire it in other people all my life," Dutch said. "Yes, I very much missed having a special person with whom to share my life. But God seemed to want something else of me."

Because Dutch associated priesthood with celibacy, he knew that he would not be a husband or a father. He realized that the love he felt for others would be shared in a very different way as a pastor to a broader community. Was that enough? Could he find the joy in ministry that was found in a good marriage? He was willing to try.

It was tough for Dutch to give up the active social life he was enjoying at Carroll. As president of the junior class, he was expected to lead the first dance at the annual Junior-Senior Dinner Dance in April 1942. *The Prospector,* the student newspaper, called it "the highlight of the spring social season." Dinner was at the Montana Club with music and dancing afterward in the club's Rathskeller Room. Jack McCarvel, Dutch's roommate and master of ceremonies, would deliver "a beautiful and stirring" speech on patriotism.

Despite pressure from McCarvel and his friends, Dutch decided not to go.

"I can still remember the night of the ball," he recalled fifty years later. "I decided I would just get out of the dormitory and I went way down to the athletic field and walked around for a couple of hours until all the guys were gone." The night was chilly and clear with stars and the first quarter of a new moon lit Montana's unending big sky. So marvelous and wondrous was God's creation.

Around the time of the Junior-Senior Dinner Dance, Dutch went to Anaconda to talk with Madge Owens, his girlfriend, and Ed Dolan, his close friend. Dolan remembered the night well. The three of them and a couple of other friends went to Butte to have a late dinner. Dutch, who had use of the family's Chrysler, drove everyone home afterward—including Madge, who had seemed to know something Dolan didn't. Finally only the two boys were left in the car. It was nearly 3 AM and Dutch was driving aimlessly around town, saying nothing.

"I knew that he was going to tell me something profound," Dolan recalled. "He rarely poured his heart out and I knew he was trying to feel me out about what I thought of him going to the seminary. So, finally, I said to him: Are you going into the priesthood?"

"Well," Dutch responded. "It's worth a chance."

Dutch told Dolan that he wasn't certain he had a vocation to be a priest. He said he would love to be happily married with a wife, kids. and a family home. And he worried that he might start the seminary, then decide to leave and have to come back to Anaconda as an embarrassing failure.

Reassuringly, Dolan said, "You got to do what you got to do."

"Yeah, I know," Dutch sighed.

After talking with Dolan, Dutch knew that he had to tell other friends and family members about his decision. He told his dad on the third hole of the municipal golf course in Helena. Anthony Hunthausen, who had come to town to play a round with his son, had asked Dutch what he planned to do after graduation. With the war going on, Anthony suggested that perhaps he should enter the officers' training program now available at Carroll.

"Dad," Dutch told him, "I'm probably going to do something else."

Dutch explained that he felt he might have a call to priesthood and was planning to enter the seminary.

His father, overcome with emotion, said, "I'm thrilled. I'm all for you."

Nearly four years later, as Dutch prepared to take the final step toward ordination, Anthony Hunthausen wrote his son recalling that afternoon conversation on the golf course.

"Sure I was thrilled," he wrote, "so thrilled that, on many occasions since, my Adam's apple became unruly in glad remembrance of your lofty aspirations.... It was a great decision to make, and we here at home are ever thankful."

Dutch Hunthausen graduated cum laude with a degree in chemistry from Carroll College on May 23, 1943. Helena Bishop Joseph Gilmore, whom Hunthausen would succeed nineteen years later, conferred degrees on seventeen graduating seniors following a baccalaureate Mass at St. Helena's Cathedral. Dutch, the class president, also received the president's gold medal for oratory as a result of his winning speech at the Carroll Oratorical Contest in April. His address was titled "Our

Ally Russia." To complete his chemistry degree, he wrote a senior thesis titled "Electromotive Force Measurements with Acetamide as a Solvent" and graduated with the second highest grade point average in his class.

His college achievements occurred during the time when the nation was increasingly absorbed by the Second World War. Even in the mountainous confines of western Montana, the war was close at hand. Coach Simonich, an athletic director deprived of a football team, recruited students to construct a "commando training trail" of tunnels, walls, barricades, and pits on the northeast slope of the campus. Students were drilled on air raids, blackouts, first aid, and fire prevention.

There would be no further military training for Dutch, however. He was granted a deferment from military service so that he could attend St. Edward Seminary near Seattle. Six weeks after graduating from Carroll, he and three other seminarians from the Helena diocese boarded the train to Seattle. They got off at the King Street Station and caught a bus to the seminary, whose 366-forested acres bordered the northeast end of Lake Washington.

Bishop Edward John O'Dea, Seattle's third bishop, had founded the seminary in 1930, using his personal inheritance to purchase the land on the wooded hill overlooking the lake. He built a four-story Romanesque structure of pastel brick and white marble arches that would house both minor (high school) and major (college and graduate) seminarians.

He engaged the Sulpician Fathers, an order dedicated to the education of diocesan priests, as faculty, and the Little Sisters of St. Joseph of Montreal as kitchen and domestic help. Seminary tuition, full room and board were $425 a year when Hunthausen arrived in 1943.

In its catalogue, St. Edward's described itself as a "house of study" and "a school of spiritual life and Christian perfection." Its aim was to lead "young men to sturdy manhood while developing within them priestly souls accustomed to prayer, sacrifice and action."

In the major seminary, where Dutch and the other Carroll grads were enrolled, students wore black cassocks, Roman collars, and black birettas. "Clothes other than black will not be tolerated," the catalogue decreed. Parents and relatives were allowed to visit between 1 and 4 PM on the third Sunday of the month.

Dutch accepted the seminary regimen but never enjoyed it like he had relished living in St. Charles Hall at Carroll. There were so many rules, requirements, and prohibitions. Wartime restrictions made things worse. The seminary administration didn't want its charges out and about lest people ask why these healthy young men weren't subject to the draft. So nearly two hundred seminarians—three dozen of them from the diocese of Helena—were confined to the grounds.

The day began with a mandatory wake-up call, followed by morning prayer, then a half-hour breakfast consumed in silence before the first class began. A two-hour recreation period came after lunch, then more classes and dinner. Evenings were reserved for studying. A 9:30 PM bell signaled a half hour of free time for a short walk or a cigarette break. After night prayers the "Grand Silence" began and continued until the dawn's wake-up bell.

"Bud" Sullivan, who a few months earlier was writing a column for the Carroll College *Prospector*, hated the seminary. He reeled off a list of grievances: You couldn't talk above the first step on the first floor. You couldn't visit anybody's room. You had one day a week off—Wednesday. You had to check in and check out. You had to go to certain restaurants and dare not approach a bar.

Sullivan, Dutch, and the others who had already graduated from college found it trying to be treated as "diaps" ("diapers"), as they called the high-school seminarians. A buoyant, blue-eyed Irish-American with a delightful chuckle, Sullivan said he and Dutch were pleased that the war condensed their seminary educations from four to three years by requiring them to attend classes during the summers.

"I couldn't have stood four years," said Sullivan, laughing.

Since he already had a college degree, Dutch plunged immediately into theology studies at St. Edward's. He took courses in scripture, canon law, homiletics, church history, pastoral theology, liturgy, dogma, and moral theology (the latter two courses in Latin). Still, he felt ill prepared for priesthood.

"What did all this mean?' he asked afterward. "It was all book learning. We didn't have any practice. We didn't go out to parishes—hardly at all."

At the seminary, Dutch was cut off from the outside world, from family and friends. Occasionally, a friend from Anaconda or Carroll days would manage a Sunday afternoon visit. Because of the war, many showed up in military uniform and some were captains of PT boats or pilots of P-38s. Dutch was envious.

"There was such a gap between their lives and mine," he recalled. "At the seminary it was so unreal."

Dutch's seminary curriculum, heavy on theology and philosophy, did not touch on the subject of human sexuality, an issue that would bring the Catholic Church to its knees in sex scandals a half-century later. Other than cautioning against "particular friendships," a euphemism for homosexuality, the priest professors at St. Edward's made little or no mention of sex. There was not even much talk about priestly celibacy.

"If we had discussed celibacy," Dutch said, "we could have explored what it really means and what relationships mean. It would have made for a lot healthier growth."

Aside from study and prayer, the seminarians occupied themselves with sports, choir, drama, talent shows, and an occasional swim in Lake Washington. Dutch was much less involved in extracurricular activities at the seminary than he had been at Carroll. Indeed, the *Harvester,* a quarterly published by St. Edward's seminarians, contained but two mentions of Dutch from 1943 to 1946. It noted his ordination in 1946 and praised his work in helping build a floral garden with a fishpond for the Sisters of St. Joseph in 1944.

"Ray Hunthausen, a human bulldozer, literally leveled the ground as he hewed down massive trees, rooted up deep-seated stumps, and cleared away the debris," the *Harvester* reported.

As his days at the seminary dragged by, Dutch found himself increasingly apprehensive about ordination. "Every day in the seminary was a day of pain for me—every day," he recalled, "because I knew I had the option of opting out."

At least ten times, Dutch began writing letters to Topel. Typically, they'd start off: "All this [at the seminary] is good. But at the same time, I'm not sure that I'm happy. I'm not sure that this is where I'm supposed to be. I feel a tug and attraction to married life and family. I'm distracted by all my friends in the military. I could still be a pilot . . ."

But he never completed nor sent one of them. He already knew Topel's answer: Go another day. Delay until tomorrow. Wait until it's clear what you're supposed to do. Until you have a strong feeling, until it's clear, just do the best you can and abide by what the Lord is saying to you.

So Dutch waited. During his final year at St. Edward's the time came for him to be ordained a subdeacon, a major step on the path to priesthood. His ordination would require him to commit himself to celibacy and service to the church. But he was still unsure.

"I could go this way or I could go that way," he recalled. "I had no stronger awareness of where God wanted me to go than I ever had."

But he heard nothing telling him "no." So he took the step, made the commitment, and was ordained a subdeacon.

"When I made that step, all of that doubt left me," Dutch said. "I never again had a sense of indecision on that matter. It was a great grace. Kind of like, here I am, I'm not sure what's going to be but God will take care of me. Finally, I was at peace."

Once Dutch made the decision for priesthood, he never looked back. "I never doubted it was what I was supposed to do," he said. "How can you be happier than to somehow have that sense that this is what God wants of you?"

As Dutch prepared for final ordination to Catholic priesthood, the Second World War took a dramatic turn and abruptly ended. On August 6, 1945, the United States dropped an atomic bomb on Hiroshima, Japan. Three days later, it dropped a second A-bomb on Nagasaki. With Germany defeated in Europe, Japan agreed to an unconditional surrender.

Word of the A-bomb attacks and the subsequent pictures of the devastation shocked and horrified the twenty-three-year-old seminarian. Dutch saw news photos of a deranged mother looking for her burned child, of an elderly man, delirious and suicidal, running back into the nuclear firestorm, and of another man, naked and bleeding, holding his eyeball in his hand. And he saw pictures of relief workers collecting the dead—their bodies burnt, mangled, and irradiated—lying in a spectral landscape of blackened rivers and the charred, skeletal remains of demolished buildings.

The horror of Hiroshima and Nagasaki lodged in his brain. "I remember how profoundly saddened I was," he said. "I could just not fathom a bomb so destructive that it would annihilate that many people in an instant without any reference to who they were or why they were being killed. From that moment on, I could never accept the bomb."

He was horrified that the United States, the country he loved, had resorted to nuclear obliteration.

"Why couldn't we have warned them?" he asked. "Why couldn't we have dropped the bomb in the Pacific to show them? Why did we have to drop it on people?"

With the A-bomb ending the war, the seminary rector asked students to gather in the chapel to sing a *Te Deum*, a traditional hymn of praise. While other seminarians assembled in the pews, Hunthausen slipped off into the woods and mourned. The ghastly killing at Hiroshima and Nagasaki sank into his soul and festered there, nagging at his conscience.

Dutch became Father Raymond G. Hunthausen, ordained a priest of the Roman Catholic Church for the Diocese of Helena, Montana, on Saturday, June 1, 1946. Bishop Gilmore conducted four ordinations that day, one in Missoula, and the other three at St. Paul's Church, the Hunthausen family parish in Anaconda. Normally, all four ordinations would have occurred at the cathedral in Helena. But because gas rationing was still in effect, the bishop decided to economize. The *Montana Standard*, Butte's daily newspaper, proclaimed that it was "the first time in the history of the diocese that ordination ceremonies had taken place in the Smelter City."

Hunthausen's parents, siblings, grandparents, aunts, uncles, their children and friends attended the ordination ceremony as well as the first Mass that the newly ordained priest celebrated the following Monday at St. Paul's. Father Topel and Ed Dolan, now a practicing physician in Anaconda, were there too. Brother Jack, a seminarian, served as master of ceremonies. Little sister Edna, a junior in high school, was resplendent in a new dress, thinking how cute she looked. Marie, the second-born child, and her husband, Pat Walsh, were carrying their infant son, the first of the next generation of Hunthausen children.

The new Father Hunthausen was humbled and intimidated. "I was in shock in a sense," he said, recalling an event he described as etched in his memory. "There aren't many professions where in an instant you move from insignificance to the person on the pedestal. ...I certainly felt honored but I also felt inadequate and ill prepared to do all that I felt people expected me to be able to do."

Following the Monday Mass, participants adjourned for a reception at the Hunthausen family home. Overwhelmed by the number of people who showed up, Hunthausen recruited Dr. Dolan to stand with him on the front porch and help him identify and greet the guests. "I can still hear Ed whispering to me, 'This is Mr. and Mrs. So and So coming up the steps,'" he recalled.

Dolan remembered how happy the occasion was with Anthony Hunthausen grand and eloquent and taking it all in stride and Edna Hunthausen warm and welcoming and bustling about. One of Edna's sisters presented her nephew with the ordination gift of a new Dodge sedan. Watching his childhood friend, Dolan saw more in Hunthausen than the new priest saw in himself. He saw a man whose whole concept of life had shifted, who seemed more committed, more dedicated to the idea that God had something in store for him.

With ordination, Hunthausen thought he would now be assigned as the parish priest he had prepared to be. But God and Bishop Gilmore had other plans.

4

PRIEST, COACH, AND COLLEGE PRESIDENT

There is no greatness where there is not simplicity,
goodness, and truth.
—Leo Tolstoy

Three months after his ordination, Father Raymond G. Hunthausen received a one-sentence letter from Bishop Gilmore, his boss and the religious leader responsible for shepherding the Catholic flock in western Montana.

Gilmore was also an Anacondan and had graduated from St. Peter's grade school twenty-eight years before Hunthausen. He received his seminary training at Carroll and in Rome, where he completed a doctorate in sacred theology at the age of twenty-two. In fact, he was so young that awarding the degree required a special dispensation from the pope. A classics scholar with an encyclopedic knowledge of the church, Gilmore could tell jokes in Latin. Following ordination, he was assigned to Carroll to teach Latin and English and direct athletics. He then served as diocesan chancellor before his appointment as bishop. Intellectual and cosmopolitan, Gilmore was a humble yet formal man. Popular with his priests, he enjoyed a drink or two with them in the evening and loved an erudite conversation.

On August 30, 1946, Gilmore wrote Hunthausen, "I hereby assign you to the faculty of Carroll College and request that you report for duty at the beginning of the Fall Term, Sept. 10, 1946." That was it. No discussion. No possible alternatives. So, after filling in for a vacationing priest in Anaconda, Hunthausen was now returning to his alma mater as a chemistry and math professor. He hadn't looked at a science book since graduating from Carroll three years earlier.

"I worked harder than I probably ever did in my life," Hunthausen recalled. "I was learning with the kids. All the things they'd stumble over, I'd stumbled over the night before."

Father Topel helped him with the freshman math course. And Dr. Edward "Doc" Neuman, the chair of the chemistry department and the college's vice president, assisted with freshman inorganic chemistry. When the summer of 1947 arrived, Bishop Gilmore sent Hunthausen to St. Louis University for some graduate cramming. Hunthausen took courses in organic chemistry and upper division math. He took courses for the next three summers, first at Catholic University, and then at Fordham. Finally, in 1952, Gilmore allowed him to spend the school year at Notre Dame, where he was awarded an MS in chemistry in 1953.

Hunthausen returned to Carroll for the 1953–54 school year as a fully degreed chemistry and math professor and acquired two additional jobs: athletic director and dean of men.

Carroll's enrollment had doubled to more than five hundred students since his graduation a decade earlier. But with exception of the nursing program—housed across town at St. Peter's Hospital—the school remained all boys. Or, at least, all male. Some of the boys were men, veterans of World War II and the Korean War.

Carroll continued to be a very traditional, rule-bound school typical of American Catholic institutions of higher learning in the mid-twentieth century. Catholic education was insular and self-protective, a reaction against a predominantly white Protestant culture that tended to view Catholics as ethnic immigrants and closet papists whose patriotism was just a bit suspect. The Catholic response was to safeguard the faith while proclaiming love of God and country. With the election of John F. Kennedy, the first Catholic president, and the social revolution of the 1960s, the defensive parochialism began to fade away. Catholics became part of the American mainstream.

Catholic schools were expected to function *in loco parentis*, taking on the legal and mentoring responsibilities of parents. Carroll took this role very seriously. Because most of its faculty, staff, and students lived on campus—principally in St. Charles Hall—the instruction and formation of Catholic young men was unceasing. The college motto was and remains: *Non schola, sed vitae*—"We do not learn for school, but for life."

Guido Bugni, whom Hunthausen recruited as a student, football player, and later a faculty member, described Carroll as a big family poured into one big building.

"Say you're doing your homework in your room and you get stuck," he explained. "Where do you go? Up to the teacher's room and pretty soon everybody else who's stuck on that problem is up there too."

At the time, eighteen of Carroll's thirty-seven faculty members were resident priests who exercised a disproportionate influence on campus life. In his role as dean of men, Hunthausen was responsible for maintaining an academic and moral environment that would promote the formation of upstanding Catholic men. That meant order and rules.

"Dutch made them toe the line," recalled Father Humphrey Courtney, the wizened, chain-smoking classics professor who, like Hunthausen, lived alongside the students in St. Charles Hall. "He was very much a Topelian in terms of discipline."

Courtney, who described himself as very comfortable with the "monarchical church," endorsed Hunthausen's tough-guy approach. If students got rowdy, they were told to shut up and get back in their rooms.

Hunthausen was the assistant dean of men when Joe Harrington lived in the dorm. Harrington graduated in 1952, entered the priesthood, earned a PhD in biology from Catholic University, and, with the exception of a five-year interval as college president, taught science at Carroll for the rest of his career. Tidy, gentle, with large ears and pale blue eyes, Harrington was known as "blast-off Joe," for his oft-spoke need to "blast off" as class time approached.

At St. Charles Hall, Hunthausen was strict and stern, often issuing orders in a military-like manner. If a student asked why he should do something, Hunthausen responded, "You don't need to know why. You just do what you're told."

Although he never used physical force, Hunthausen acted like he might. Harrington remembered a kid who would scream out maliciously in the middle of the night just to wake everybody up. Hunthausen quickly put an end to that.

"If I find out who's screaming," he told the dorm residents, "I'll shove a potato down his throat." Harrington said there was just enough menace in the dean's voice to suggest he might really do it.

The dorm rules were clear. No booze or girls were allowed in the building. Card playing was forbidden during study time. Leaving campus at any hour required permission and checking in upon return. By 10 PM on school nights, all students were expected to be in their rooms and ready for bed. The dean and assistant dean checked the rooms at 10:45 PM and again at midnight. On Friday and Saturday nights, students with permission could stay out to midnight. Those who violated the rules were confined to campus, or, in the case of serious infractions, called before a disciplinary board that could expel them from school.

Despite the firm rules, Hunthausen tolerated innocent pranks, horseplay, and the minor infractions that made dorm life fun. One evening, under cover of a power outage that had plunged St. Charles

Hall into darkness, he slipped down the hallway, armed with a flashlight and two water pistols, and fired away at every student he encountered. Water fights were frequent. They'd start with water guns, then cups of water and soon buckets of water hurled across the terrazzo floors.

Pranks went back and forth. On occasion, students would remove the doorknob to Hunthausen's room so he couldn't get in or out. Then he'd take the doorknob off the room of one of the culprits. He got angry only once when someone removed all the doorknobs on the dorm rooms and absconded with them.

Like Harrington, William Greytak lived in the dorm when Hunthausen was assistant dean. Greytak graduated from Carroll in 1952, entered the priesthood, studied theology at the University of Louvain in Belgium, and earned a PhD in European history. Back at Carroll, however, he was asked to teach Spanish, which he didn't know, and succeed Hunthausen as dean of men. A jovial man with a keen intellect and an ample double chin, Greytak played handball with Hunthausen, and the two talked frequently about how to improve campus life at Carroll.

Greytak took a somewhat more relaxed approach to student discipline. He felt foolish making demands of some students, especially war veterans who were older than he was. Sometimes he looked the other way. So, in fact, did Hunthausen.

Despite the prohibition against card playing in the rooms, Greytak and several other students were playing hearts one time when Hunthausen happened by and asked if he could join them. Sure, they said. After a couple of hours of play, they were all hungry. So they took up a collection to buy hamburgers. Hunthausen contributed and suggested to one of the boys that he go get them. After the boy departed on his errand, one of the others said, "You shouldn't have sent him."

"Why not?" Hunthausen asked.

"He's campused," they replied.

In June 1956, Bishop Gilmore gave Hunthausen an additional responsibility. He appointed him to succeed Topel, who'd left to be bishop of Spokane, as the diocesan vocations director. Young men considering a vocation to priesthood lived in a designated area on the fourth floor of St. Charles Hall and would later be housed in the new Borromeo Hall, which was to function as the de facto diocesan seminary. The priesthood candidates took a heavier load of theology and philosophy courses along with their regular classes. After his appointment,

Hunthausen moved in with the "Borromeans" and sought to provide the spiritual direction that Topel had given him.

Father Emmett O'Neill, a political science professor and self-described "liberal, half-ass scholar," lived a few doors down from Hunthausen. He remembered the vocations director as "a lovable, likeable kind of guy who was very, very conservative." O'Neill, who was also campus pastor, encouraged Hunthausen to adapt the liturgy for college students.

"He wasn't all that eager to do that," O'Neill recalled. "That's why it was great to see what happened to him later as a result of the Vatican Council."

John Gagliardi, who would later achieve coaching greatness at St. John's University in Minnesota, coached virtually everything at Carroll when Hunthausen began teaching in the autumn of 1946. Gagliardi, like Hunthausen, was just starting his career, but he already had a playing philosophy that was the antithesis of standard college football. His football program had no weight lifting, no wind sprints, no calisthenics, no blocking dummies, and no whistles. In practices, which were limited to ninety minutes, Gagliardi prohibited tackling lest someone get hurt. Instead, he stressed learning the plays, being at the right spot to block, make a tackle, and throw or receive a pass. A slender man with wiry black hair and a sly sense of humor, Gagliardi had more wins (489) and had coached more seasons (sixty-four) than any coach in U.S. college football history when he retired from St. John's in 2012.

Gagliardi recruited the priest professor as his assistant coach for football and basketball, and enlisted his help with baseball, track, and golf. In football, Hunthausen coached the backfield. Football fans became accustomed to seeing the assistant coach, dressed in black clericals and a Roman collar, pacing the sidelines with Gagliardi. The young priest smoked in those days and to soothe his nerves without resorting to another cigarette, he'd scrape a handful of snow off the frozen turf and stuff it in his mouth. You couldn't miss him in the annual team photos—the unhelmeted guy in formal black attire among the purple and gold suited players.

Hunthausen liked coaching even more than playing. He considered it a special form of teaching and took it very seriously. He was delighted to see a player master a new skill and then go out and apply it. He loved the camaraderie and the solidarity that developed as team members discarded their individual selfishness and came together to work for the greater good. He felt a tremendous responsibility as a coach.

"A coach has a brief moment in time," he recalled long afterward, "just a few weeks or maybe a couple of months to use that special influence. It's a privilege, a real privilege, and it was unlike any other experience in my life."

After the 1952 football season, Gagliardi told Carroll's president, Father R. Vincent Kavanagh, that he was accepting a position to coach football at St. John's. Kavanagh asked whom he would recommend to replace him at Carroll. Gagliardi replied: Father Hunthausen.

Kavanagh paused. Hunthausen already had a heavy teaching load and numerous other campus responsibilities. Moreover, there was the propriety of a priest being the college's head football coach.

Gagliardi persisted. "He's just a workhorse. He can handle it."

With the support of Carroll's athletic board, Kavanagh asked Hunthausen to coach football and, like Gagliardi, also be athletic director. Reluctant as ever, Hunthausen told Kavanagh, "There's something wrong here but if you think I can do it and if you want me to do it, I'll try."

So with the 1953–54 school year, Hunthausen was professor of chemistry and math, dean of men, dorm supervisor, athletic director, and head coach for football, basketball, baseball, track, and golf. His sports responsibilities included lining up games with other schools, establishing an equipment and travel budget, determining minimum guarantees for ticket sales, recruiting and training players, and, at least in Carroll's case, constructing a football field. Nonetheless, he said, "It was a great life."

Hunthausen wanted Carroll to have a suitable athletic field, a replacement for the rocks and tumbleweeds of old Scullon Field. So in the late summer of 1953 the new football coach enlisted players, students, and Frank Sabados, the plumber who passed for the college engineer, to help him enlarge and improve old Scullon. Sabados had no fingers beyond the knuckles, the result of frostbite during a bout with the bottle. But he was an able worker and a crafty operator.

Hunthausen was equally disabled. He had ruptured the Achilles tendon on his left foot in a pickup basketball game at Notre Dame the previous winter and snapped it again in the spring. Consequently, he was on crutches through the summer and into the football season. Nonetheless, he, Sabados, and their crew began the field project. Hunthausen found irrigation pipe at a government surplus store. He convinced Helena Sand and Gravel Company to donate a power shovel and a friendly contractor to provide a grader and trucks for hauling topsoil on the weekend. He and Sabados concentrated on installing the underground pipe for the sprinkler system. Discarding his crutches and working with a pick and shovel on his hands and knees, Hunthausen aligned the pipe while Sabados tied it into the city water system. Years later Hunthausen learned that Sabados never told the city about the hookup. Consequently, the new Carroll field thrived on pirated water.

Hunthausen took great pride in that field. The following summer he was down admiring the turf one evening when he noticed that one of the sprinklers, a huge overhead metal contraption, was spinning crazily. So he ducked down, crawled underneath the whirring arms of the sprinkler and attempted to grab one of them. He missed and, absentmindedly, brought his head up. The sprinkler arm caught him full in the face, ripping away flesh, gouging his eyes, and covering him in blood. Blinded, Hunthausen managed to crawl away but could not open his eyes. Eventually his vision returned. The force of the sprinkler arm destroyed 80 percent of the sympathetic nervous system in his right eye. The pupil of that eye would be dilated ever afterward.

Over his four years as head coach and athletic director at Carroll, Father Hunthausen was just as successful as Coach Gagliardi. His teams won eight conference championships, including three in football and two in basketball. As a result, Hunthausen was inducted into the National Association of Intercollegiate Athletics (NAIA) Hall of Fame in 1966. A telegram from Montana's U.S. Senator Mike Mansfield congratulated him "for such an honor which I am sure is rarely awarded to members of the religious community."

In 1954 and again in 1955, the Fighting Saints won places in the NAIA regional basketball playoffs in Bozeman. It was an unlikely appearance by a little school that offered no athletic scholarships and whose coach doubled as a priest and chemistry professor. Both years the Saints were eliminated. In 1955, they lost the NAIA opener to the College of Idaho, which started a lanky six-foot-five freshman forward who scored forty-four points against them. The frosh was Elgin Baylor. Three years later Baylor took Seattle University to the NCAA championship game and went on to become one of the all-time greatest players in the NBA.

Winning games wasn't easy for Carroll. With just five hundred students, the talent pool was neither big nor deep. Hunthausen coached a varsity basketball team that often traveled with as few as seven players. Consequently, some of them played the entire game, running up and down the court in a fast break offense no matter how exhausted they were. His pre-game and half-time pep talks were always the same—positive, encouraging, asking the players how they thought they could best solve a defense problem or deal with an offensive threat. Should we double-team that guy? Go man to man and break up the zone? Although he was a fierce competitor, he never yelled or screamed or stomped out on the court. After all, he was dressed as a priest.

Losing was tough, especially against archrivals like Montana Western. The Saints 1955 team, with Hunthausen coaching from the end of the bench, was fifteen points behind late in the final quarter on their opponents' home court in Dillon. There was no way Carroll was going to win. The hometown crowd was on its feet, delighted with the prospect of defeating the defending conference champion. With the Bulldogs already over 90 points, the crowd was roaring for 100. "One hundred! One hundred!" came the deafening chant from the stands.

Hunthausen called a time out. His players, beaten and dejected, slouched back to the bench. Hunthausen said to them, "Let's face it, guys, we aren't going to win this game. So you want to have some fun?"

They glared at him like he was crazy. "I know we're not supposed to give up until the buzzer sounds and all the rest of it," he explained. "But hear what the crowd wants—100 points. Why don't we stall and not give it to them?"

So the Saints went back into the game and stalled, lobbing the ball back and forth to each other, taking their sweet time bringing the ball down court. The crowd was furious. It booed and hollered. And then the Bulldogs fell apart, so frustrated by the Saints' stall that Carroll outscored them in the final minutes. And the Bulldogs didn't reach 100.

"The stall changed the whole demeanor of the game," Hunthausen recalled, laughing. "Our kids went back out on the court with the sense of, by golly, we can do something about this. And they did."

Traveling to away games, especially during Montana's bitter fall and winter weather, was an ordeal. Because fewer small colleges played football, the Saints' team traveled widely, engaging opponents in Idaho, Washington, Wyoming, Utah, and South Dakota. The trip to Rapid City to play football against the South Dakota School of Mines was a four-day affair with an overnight each way at motels in Miles City and Billings. Usually Hunthausen, Claude Weaver, the Carroll grad and insurance salesman who was his coaching assistant, and a few seniors drove their own cars and carried other players. But the South Dakota trip was by bus.

On one occasion, the bus came to a fork in the highway with two possible routes. Coach Hunthausen suggested they take the "scenic route" through the Black Hills. So the bus, loaded with football players, coaches, the manager and all their gear, began winding through

South Dakota's famous western hills. At one point, the road became so steep that the players had to get off to lighten the load. At another point, the bus had to squeeze through a narrow tunnel bored through a mountainside. There was so little clearance that the players stopped to take photos that made it appear like the rocky hillside was giving birth to a bus.

Hunthausen remembered that 1953 football game in Rapid City with particular fondness. At halftime, the Saints were trailing 19 to 12 against a bigger team with many of its players on athletic scholarships. He gave the usual pep talk, noting that he had overheard one of their opponents remark that the Saints weren't that bad, considering that none of them had free rides.

"You can play ball with these guys," he told them. "It's obvious you can."

In the second half, the Saints went out and tied the game at 25-25. Back and forth the contest went, with good football played by both sides. The Saints scored a final touchdown and went ahead 31-25 with four minutes to play. Somehow the Hardrockers managed a touchdown of their own, tying the game at 31-31 with just eight seconds left. The home team lined up to kick the point after touchdown, which would have given them a one-point margin and the victory. Hunthausen called a time out and devised a plan to block the kick. It worked. The Saints knocked down the kick, recovered the football, and the game was over.

Hunthausen recited from memory the concluding words of the sportswriter who raved about the game in the next day's *Rapid City Journal*. "The score," he wrote, "is no indication of how close the game was."

The priest coach was also a shrewd sports promoter. In the winter of 1954, Hunthausen noted that University of Montana in Missoula, the state's largest public institution and a sports powerhouse, had a very talented freshman basketball team. Known as the Grizzly Cubs, the freshmen were so good that they had twice defeated Montana's varsity team. Hunthausen cooked up a plan to pit the Grizzly Cubs against his Carroll varsity squad who were about to win their second straight MCC title. Both teams played electrifying fast-break basketball, sometimes topping 100 points and generally beating their opponents by more than 20.

Interest was so high that Hunthausen arranged two games, a Saturday night contest in Helena preceded by a Friday night face-off in Anaconda. On its sports page, the *Independent Record* threw down the gauntlet: "Who has the better team: the Fighting Saints of Carroll

College or the Fabulous Frosh of Montana University?" The Saints were undefeated in conference play while the Grizzly Cubs were un-defeated—period. The Cubs had a six-foot-seven former Helena high school star at center matched against the Saints' six-foot-three Walt Romansko.

Five thousand screaming fans crammed into Anaconda's Memorial Gym that February Friday night to see Romansko pour in 29 points and lead the Saints to a stunning, come-from-behind 90 to 83 victory. Carroll outshot the Cubs, 44 to 31 percent. Coach Hunthausen told the *Independent Record* it was the best game his team had ever played. The following night in Helena before another packed house the Saints led the Cubs through three quarters but fell apart in the final minutes, losing 76 to 70.

Nonetheless, Hunthausen received a congratulatory Valentine's Day telegram from the president of the Carroll College Alumni Association. "Your victory in Anaconda thrilled us all," wrote Charles R. White, "and will long be remembered when Carroll fans get together."

Hunthausen, who had maintained the sports programs along with all his teaching and religious duties, got a big helping hand when his brother Jack, now Father Jack Hunthausen, was assigned to Carroll in the fall of 1956. Jack Hunthausen, as athletic as his older brother, taught math, assisted with football, and became head basketball coach. For at least one football season, there were two men in black pacing the Carroll sidelines.

For Dutch Hunthausen, the relief was short lived. Freed of most of his coaching responsibilities, he had expected to teach full time while devoting more hours to counseling priesthood candidates. It was not to happen.

Within three months of Jack's arrival, "Doc" Neuman, head of the chemistry department and the college's vice president, died of a sudden heart attack. He was only fifty-one. His death left Hunthausen with full responsibility for the department.

Four months later, Monsignor Kavanagh, whom Bishop Gilmore had named college president in 1951, fell ill and slipped into unconsciousness during a business trip to Denver. Doctors discovered a brain tumor and operated. Kavanagh died in March 1957, after undergoing surgery. He was fifty-two.

Gilmore, who had journeyed to Denver to be at the bedside of the unconscious Kavanagh, celebrated the requiem High Mass for the late president at St. Helena Cathedral. Earlier he had offered the absolution at the funeral Mass for Doc Neuman.

Within days of Kavanagh's burial, Hunthausen went to talk with Gilmore about some ideas he had for furthering religious vocations. The two had a private conversation in Gilmore's office at the chancery and then Hunthausen returned to St. Charles Hall. Shortly afterward, the hallway phone rang. A student answered, found Hunthausen, and told him that Father Bob McCarthy, the chancellor and the bishop's right-hand man, was on the line.

Hunthausen picked up the phone and McCarthy told him, "Dutch, I think you ought to get your picture taken."

"Why?" Hunthausen asked. "There's pictures of me all around the place."

"You'll need a formal portrait photo," McCarthy replied. "You're going to be the new president of the college."

Hunthausen was dumbfounded. The line went silent. McCarthy, sensing the astonishment at the other end, said, "Didn't the bishop tell you when you were in here? . . . Oh dear, you better come back and see him again tomorrow."

The following day Hunthausen went back to the bishop's office. Gilmore asked him to kneel down and gave him his blessing.

"I am appointing you the president of the college," the bishop said. And, then after a long pause, he added, "You'll do okay."

Father Raymond Hunthausen was thirty-five years old when Bishop Gilmore announced his appointment as president of Carroll College on April 5, 1957. He was energetic, industrious, and devoted to the school. He was full of ideas about how Carroll could better accomplish its mission of educating students for life.

The 1957–58 school year officially opened in September with the Mass of the Holy Spirit at St. Helena Cathedral. Gilmore celebrated the Mass and Hunthausen, the new college president, delivered the homily. He told the students how fortunate they were to be attending a Catholic college. He described a world torn by war and rumors of war, by fear of nuclear annihilation, by false gods of materialism, secularism, and communism.

"So many live with no knowledge of why they are here or where they are going," he said. "In a world where there are so many who do not know Christ, you have a possession of inestimable worth, the gem of great price."

Hunthausen thought Carroll should display that gem by making its education exceptional and its campus beautiful. He was tired of hearing the grounds mocked as a prison yard without walls. He promised the Helena Rotary Club that with the landscaping and construction projects either under way or planned at Carroll the school would become the city's "beauty spot." In the first month of the 1957 school year, Bishop Gilmore dedicated a new science-library building designed by Doc Neuman and the new Borromeo Hall for priesthood candidates.

The new college president went to Gilmore with ideas for landscaping the front side of the campus, installing a statue of the Virgin Mary, building a new dining hall and—now that the school was going co-ed— a women's dormitory. Hunthausen wanted to set up an exclusive endowment for Carroll so the school could plan its own future without worrying whether the diocese would provide the money. He wanted the college to be free to raise its own funds and receive its own gifts. In a manner not untypical of bishops, Gilmore was not keen on the idea. But gradually he relented, allowing Hunthausen to separate Carroll's monies from diocesan funds and establish an independent college board of trustees empowered to make financial decisions. The bishop sat on the board but did not have veto power.

Hunthausen was obsessed with making Carroll a place of joy and beauty. Typically he'd be in his office in the morning, dealing with administrative matters, but if the afternoon was pleasant and sunny, he'd be inspired to go outdoors and get involved in yard work.

"I'd go over to Borromeo Hall and walk up and down the corridors, clap my hands, and say, 'All right, you guys, let's get to work,'" he recalled.

Hunthausen and his hastily assembled crew would seed lawns, plant trees, and put in concrete walkways. They had use of a dump truck donated by a local businessman and Carroll benefactor. They named it the "Green Hornet."

In the summer of 1959, Hunthausen enlisted the Borromeans and other student volunteers, borrowed dump trucks from local contractors, and persuaded the city of Helena to deliver discarded railroad tracks and other debris. They used the material to fill in an ugly depression called Lake Bluff, just west of St. Charles Hall, then covered it over in lawn and shrubs. The following year the school mounted an eight-foot Italian marble statue of the Blessed Virgin Mary on a pedestal at the foot of the broad staircase that ascended to St. Charles Hall.

Hunthausen much preferred working on the grounds to shuffling papers in his office. One day U.S. Senator Mansfield, the Montana Democrat who was then the powerful and influential Senate majority leader, showed up unannounced at his office. Ellen Ryan, Hunthausen's secretary, flustered and embarrassed that her boss was not there, went out looking for him. She discovered the college president on the back lawn, pushing a mower. His clothes were soiled with dirt, grime, and grass stains. She told him Senator Mansfield was waiting in the office. Hunthausen trotted back, but before he could throw a cassock over his work outfit, Mansfield spotted him. The senator let out a hearty laugh. "Good afternoon, Reverend President," he said.

With help from Mansfield, Hunthausen secured a forty-year federal loan of $1.04 million to build a women's residence hall and a new student center. He raised an additional million dollars for those projects and others by tapping successful alumni and the Helena business community. He established a public relations office, an alumni office, and a new department of elementary education.

Meanwhile, Hunthausen shored up the faculty by recruiting qualified lay staff that loved Carroll as much as he did. He hired Guido Bugni to take over his chemistry classes; Al Murray to teach math; and the Huber brothers, Hank and Bill, to instruct students in drama, speech, and debate. He negotiated with Bishop Gilmore to attract and retain the best priest professors.

As president, Hunthausen's style was consultative and inclusive. He would stop by a professor's office and ask: What do you think we ought to do here? Or how would you suggest we solve this problem? What's your input on this?

Al Murray, an Anaconda boy and math professor who spent his entire academic career at Carroll, said Hunthausen was impressed with good teaching, not degrees.

"He wanted our kids to do well and be able to go on to graduate school," said Murray, who with a wife and seven children took a pay cut to teach at Carroll.

Bugni was single and twenty-two years old when Hunthausen hired him to teach in 1959. He moved right back into St. Charles Hall. "I probably would have worked for nothing," he said. "I loved the place."

Hunthausen asked Bugni to wear a dress shirt and tie when he taught class. He told him, "If you look nice, you'll do a good job." The chemistry prof wore a shirt and tie on class days for the rest of his life.

Even as president, Hunthausen continued to live in Borromeo Hall with the young men considering priesthood. One day shortly before he was to preach at the first Mass of a newly ordained priest in Butte, he playfully got into a wrestling match with Jim "Killer" Stanaway, a squat, compact kid whose nickname was well deserved. The two fell to the floor, trying to pin each other. Stanaway wrenched Hunthausen's arm behind his back, breaking it so severely that the bone protruded through the skin.

Nonetheless Hunthausen persuaded the doctor to bind the arm without a sling so he could hide the injury and thus avoid awkward explanations about what had happened. He drove to Butte one-handed using a steering wheel knob. At Mass, no one was the wiser.

Hunthausen maintained the college discipline he had enforced as dean of men, delegating authority to others and exercising oversight. The 1960s counter-culture of the baby boomers had infected campus life even at a little Catholic college in Montana. But the biggest change came when Carroll went co-ed. Female nursing students had been around for more than a decade, but now the school welcomed women into all its classes. Girls had their own dormitory, but they shared the dining hall, the chapel, the classroom buildings, and the athletic facilities with the boys.

Hunthausen and Father Harrington, who succeeded him as dean of students, felt strongly that Carroll should continue to exercise its *in loco parentis* role. Girls were to wear skirts or dresses, no slacks or T-shirts. Their weekend curfew time was set fifteen minutes before the boys' midnight deadline. The school cracked down on drinking. The first two times students returned drunk to campus, they were grounded. The third time, they were hauled before a disciplinary board and either sent home for a while or expelled altogether.

Carroll was even tougher on sex. A student who spent the night with a member of the opposite sex—even off campus—was summoned to the disciplinary board and usually expelled. Parents of expelled students would sometimes plead their son's or daughter's case first with Harrington and then with Hunthausen.

"He wouldn't relent," Harrington said, approvingly. "He would hold to tough decisions."

Hunthausen was especially vigilant of the Borromeans, the seminary candidates whom he feared might fall in love with a girl if they spent too much time in female company. Tom Haffey, a Borromean who later became a diocesan priest, recalled asking Hunthausen for permission to join the Carrolleers, a co-ed singing group. Seminarians were prohibited from joining mixed groups.

"I asked him to make an exception but he said he had to hold onto the rule," said Haffey, also an Anacondan. "I remember him trying to explain, being embarrassed, and fighting himself about it."

Students were required to attend Sunday Mass and a 6:30 AM Mass on either Wednesday or Thursday. Seats were assigned and roll was taken. Those who failed to show up were grounded. Harrington suggested to Hunthausen that the weekday Mass requirement might be excessive. But the president insisted.

"This is a Catholic college," he said. "This is something their parents expect and something we should do."

Yet both priests knew that times were changing. Harrington, ten years younger than Hunthausen, laughingly recalled how his boss was totally unprepared for "the twist." The dance craze, popularized by

Chubby Checker's 1960 hit song, was a national sensation and soon spread from the Peppermint Lounge in New York City all the way to Helena.

One evening, Hunthausen happened to walk by the Carroll Commons, heard a lively recording of Checker's "Twistin' USA," and saw his students gyrating their hips and swinging their arms away. He immediately called Harrington and said, "Joe, this has got to stop. We can't have that on campus."

Flummoxed, Harrington didn't know what to do. "I mean, everybody's doing the twist, every kid in the school," he recalled.

So Harrington recruited another priest and the two of them, dressed in their black cassocks, walked over to the Commons and watched the students do the twist. How could they put a stop to what looked like such innocent fun? they asked each other. So they did nothing. Hunthausen never said another word about it.

The college president developed a close relationship with Bishop Gilmore, who remained the school's and Hunthausen's biggest supporter. The two Anaconda natives liked and appreciated each other. Gilmore valued Hunthausen's hands-on ability to make decisions and get things done.

The bishop, in office since 1936, gave much thought to the future of his far-flung diocese. Although his health was reasonably sound, his eyesight was failing and he no longer drove a car. An auxiliary bishop who could help with confirmations and other episcopal tasks would be a godsend.

One day in March 1962, Father Emmett Kelly, Gilmore's vice chancellor, watched the bishop pull Hunthausen's biography out of the personnel file in the chancery records. Because of his poor eyesight, Gilmore asked Kelly to type an envelope addressed to Archbishop Egidio Vagnozzi, the papal delegate to the United States. Gilmore then took the addressed envelope, returned to his office, shut the door, and presumably wrote a letter asking that Hunthausen be named his auxiliary bishop. Later that day, Kelly happened to see Gilmore, who rarely went anywhere on foot, walking to the post office, letter in hand.

On April 2, 1962, Gilmore was at a private dinner in San Francisco to celebrate the installation of that city's new archbishop when he collapsed during the meal's main course. A doctor rushed over to assist him and briefly detected a faint pulse. But within two minutes Gilmore expired. He was sixty-nine.

In Helena, Hunthausen and Father Joe Oblinger, the diocesan chancellor, were chatting in Hunthausen's room at Borromeo Hall when a student interrupted to tell the chancellor that he had an emergency call. Oblinger rushed down the hallway to the phone. When he returned, his face was ashen and drawn. "The bishop is dead," he said.

Three months later the diocesan clergy were in Butte to attend the funeral of a priest colleague. Just before Mass began, a priest from Carroll, acting on strict orders from Hunthausen's secretary, privately handed him a large envelope marked "CONFIDENTIAL." The return address read "Papal Nunciature, Washington, DC."

Hunthausen felt an immediate sense of foreboding. He'd never received a letter from the Vatican. He stuck the envelope in his pocket and waited. After the funeral, he drove to Anaconda to see his mother. Before he arrived at the family home, he stopped at St. Paul's Church, where Bishop Gilmore had ordained him sixteen years earlier, and stepped into the empty sanctuary. The church was so still that he could hear the flicker of the votive candle at the altar. He knelt and opened the envelope marked confidential. Inside was another sealed envelope. He opened that one and drew out an embossed letter on creamy white stationary. It was signed by Vagnozzi, the apostolic delegate.

"It is my duty to inform you that the Holy Father has in mind to appoint you Bishop of Helena," the letter read. "However, before doing this, His Holiness wishes to have an expression of your willingness to accept." The letter went on to say that Hunthausen had permission to "discuss this matter with your confessor, if you wish" and asked for a confidential reply as soon as possible. If Hunthausen agreed to accept the appointment, he should send Vagnozzi the following telegram: "COLLEGE REPORT TO BE FORWARDED."

Sworn to secrecy, Hunthausen drove to Spokane to talk and pray with Bishop Topel, his spiritual advisor. Once again, he heard Topel speak about being open to God's will, of saying "yes" to what life places before us. While his lifelong mentor didn't make the decision for him, Topel provided a spiritual framework for making the decision.

"If this is the way the Lord has chosen to speak to me," Hunthausen said of the Vatican's request, "I'll do what I can."

Still, he drove back to Helena unsettled, puzzling over what God was asking of him. A week went by. He got a phone call from a secretary of the Vatican Congregation for Bishops enquiring about the confidential letter. In veiled language, the secretary fished for an answer but Hunthausen naively thought he should stick to the script. He told the secretary he would respond soon. Two days letter he sent the coded telegram to Vagnozzi.

The Vatican announced Hunthausen's appointment as bishop of Helena on July 11, 1962. But the cat was already out of the bag. Someone had leaked the news to the *Independent Record,* which reported on its front page the appointment of "the genial president of

Carroll College" before the chancery had time to arrange a press brief-ing. Hunthausen, in fact, was in Billings chairing a conference of small college presidents. He had brought his mother with him so they could visit with his sister, Marie Walsh, and her family.

On an earlier visit with Marie's family in Billings, Hunthausen had also had to leave hastily for an evening appointment. The table had just been cleared and he was getting ready to go when one of Marie's young daughters approached him.

"We've got to say the family rosary now, Dutch," she informed him. "Are you a Catholic?"

This time he and his mother rushed back to Helena before the evening rosary. The chancery, the Carroll College staff, and the press were waiting for him.

He hastily prepared a formal statement in which he said that he regarded his appointment as bishop of Helena as a "clear indication of God's will for me." Then he continued, "As chief spiritual shep-herd, it will be my duty to be a docile instrument of the Good Shep-herd, Christ Himself."

Privately Hunthausen felt woefully unprepared. "I didn't have the foggiest idea what it meant to be a bishop," he confessed.

His family, friends, and colleagues at Carroll were delighted with the news. Hunthausen was popular, respected, and well regarded. Fa-ther Greytak, his colleague at Carroll, jokingly told the bishop-elect that he ought to note his improbable appointment by designing an episcopal coat of arms that included the Latin for "I believe"—"Fido."

Vagnozzi himself came to Helena to consecrate Hunthausen as bishop at St. Helena's Cathedral on August 30, 1962. The two men had never met. No doubt Vagnozzi, an effervescent, loquacious Ital-ian, was curious about the young priest whom Bishop Gilmore, whose scholarly reputation he respected, had recommended so highly. A Roman-born-and-educated career diplomat for the Vatican, Vagnozzi was skeptical of the U.S. church, which he regarded as im-mature, unsophisticated, and prone to doctrinal error. At Marquette University in Milwaukee the previous year, he had criticized U.S. bib-lical scholarship and disparaged the teaching ability of laypeople.

Because of Vagnozzi's presence, an unexpected number of U.S. bishops, most of whom Hunthausen did not know, came to Helena for the consecration ceremony. The evening before, the bishops gath-ered for a festive private dinner in the new dining hall at Carroll. The priests were relegated to a separate dinner in the old cafeteria of St. Charles Hall. After dinner, the bishops walked up the hill to join the priests for a reception.

On the way up, Vagnozzi chatted with Hunthausen. He was mystified by the bishop-elect and his background.

"How in the world did you ever study chemistry?" he demanded. "Why would you as a priest study chemistry and not theology?"

Hunthausen explained that, at the time, Carroll needed chemistry teachers more than it needed theologians, so he obliged. Vagnozzi seemed unsatisfied. He dropped the subject but Hunthausen understood the implied message: Here's a guy I'm making a bishop who may not know the right stuff or follow the right line.

At a solemn High Mass at the cathedral the next morning, Vagnozzi, assisted by Bishop Topel and Bishop William Condon, of Great Falls, consecrated Hunthausen as the bishop of Helena. A long, colorful entourage led by a feather-plumed honor guard of the Knights of Columbus processed into the vaulted Gothic cathedral with its beautiful stained glass windows. Some two hundred priests and more than twenty bishops and archbishops took their places as the pipe organ resounded, trumpets sounded, and a sixty-voice choir sang out *Ecce Sacerdos Magnus* ("Behold the great priest"). Hunthausen family members, friends, Carroll colleagues, and students filled the dark-stained pews and stood lining the walls.

Bishop-elect Hunthausen, wearing the robes of his new office, entered the crowded sanctuary, stood between Topel and Condon, and faced Vagnozzi, who was seated on a temporary throne at the altar. Reading from the ritual of consecration, the papal delegate asked Hunthausen to affirm his commitment to the Gospel, to Catholic tradition, and to the Holy Father.

"Will you be faithful and obedient to Blessed Peter the Apostle and his successors, the Roman Pontiffs?" he asked. Hunthausen assured him that he would.

Vagnozzi then consecrated Hunthausen, placing his hands on the head of the kneeling bishop-elect and praying, "Receive the Holy Spirit." Topel and Condon did the same. Vagnozzi anointed Hunthausen's head and hands with oil and gave him the symbols of his new authority to teach in Christ's name: a miter, a staff, and a gold episcopal ring. Hunthausen, now fully installed in office, walked from the altar into the main body of the cathedral to give his blessing to all who had come to honor him. He had taken for his episcopal motto the Latin phrase from the Lord's Prayer: *Fiat Voluntas Tua.* "Thy Will Be Done."

Ed Dolan, his childhood friend from Anaconda, watched as the new bishop, a white miter atop his head and a gold crosier in his left hand, processed down the aisle to bless the congregation. Seated in the front pew were his mother, his siblings, and their families. Dolan thought surely Hunthausen would bless his mother first. But instead he walked by way of the far aisle to the back of the church, blessing those standing against the sanctuary doors, and then those in the back pews. Finally he went forward to bless his mother and his family.

"I had to do it that way," the new Bishop Hunthausen told Dolan afterward. "I was too choked up."

Dolan, a sentimental Irishman to the core, felt his eyes well up with tears.

5

VATICAN II

Vatican II was a force that seized the mind of the Roman Catholic Church and carried it across centuries from the 13th to the 20th.
—Lance Morrow

Within weeks of his consecration in Helena, Bishop Raymond G. Hunthausen was in a balcony seat at St. Peter's Basilica in Rome to participate in the Second Vatican Council, the most significant event in the life of the Roman Catholic Church since the Protestant Reformation.

Hunthausen was the last U.S. bishop appointed before the Council began on October 11, 1962, and, at forty-one, the youngest of the American bishops. He was so far down the list of twenty-eight hundred bishops invited from around the globe that there was no seat for him in the main body of the basilica. Instead he and a few other recently named bishops had seats in the front row of the balcony on the left side of the nave. Unlike many bishops who had to peer down the long central aisle to see the speakers at the main altar, Hunthausen sat right above them.

"I had the best seat in the house," Hunthausen said. "Right over the cardinals."

For four autumns from 1962 through 1965, Hunthausen watched the Vatican Council fundamentally change the way the Catholic Church would preach the Gospel to the world. The core doctrines of God made man in the person of Jesus Christ and manifested in Christ's life, death, and resurrection would remain absolute. But how the church would conduct itself in worship, serve others, and engage the world would change irrevocably.

At Vatican II, the church asked itself for the first time in its two-thousand-year history: Who are we? What are we about? Where are we going? Unlike previous church councils, Vatican II was not called to address heresy or schism or some other threat to the church. Pope John XXIII, the unlikely pontiff who convened the Council, said its purpose was to reform the church and revive the spirit of the Gospel. Asked for a simple explanation, John went to the nearest window, flung it wide open, and let in the fresh air. The Council, he said, would be an *aggiornamento,* a bringing the church up to date.

The first council in nearly a century, Vatican II was unlike any of the twenty previous church councils. It issued no laws, no anathemas, and no condemnations. It abandoned the authoritarian power words and spoke in language that was inviting, inclusive, and even kind. It expressed itself in words such as dialogue, partnership, cooperation, friendship, dignity, freedom, holiness, conscience, liberty, and brothers and sisters. It turned the image of the church from a pyramid with the pope at the top, the bishops in the middle, and the faithful at the bottom into a circle it called the "People of God," wherein all believers, by virtue of their baptism, were equals in pursuing Christ's mission although they would pursue it in different ways.

The Council envisioned a new Catholicism, writes John O'Malley, a Jesuit scholar and Vatican II expert, that would move from commands to invitations, from laws to ideals, from definition to mystery, from threats to persuasion, from coercion to conscience, from monologue to dialogue, from hostility to friendship, from suspicion to trust, and from ruling to serving.

Vatican II, however, was much better envisioning than it was enacting. In large part, it trusted the pope and the curia, the powerful heads of the various Vatican offices, to carry out the reforms set forth by the Council. But successive popes and the curia, which was virulently opposed to the Council in the first place, ignored, watered-down, and reinterpreted the Council to suit their own ends. The church is still waiting to realize the full fruits of the Council.

Nonetheless, because of Vatican II, the Roman Catholic Church of the twenty-first century looks very different from the pre-conciliar institution that reared, schooled, and ordained Bishop Hunthausen. For most Catholics, especially Hunthausen, the most significant changes came in several key areas:

The role of the laity and shared responsibility. Prior to the Council, laymen and laywomen were expected to "pray, pay, and obey." The Council recognized that all believers have responsibilities as followers of Christ. Consequently, laypeople were empowered to serve as lectors, eucharistic ministers, catechists, parish administrators, and in other roles not specifically reserved for priests. The Council reinstated the office of permanent deacon, an ordained position open to married men.

While priests, nuns, and laypeople were to share responsibility at the parish level, Vatican II envisioned a similar shared responsibility between the bishops and the pope. The bishops at Vatican II, the so-called "Council Fathers," called it "collegiality." They expected dioceses to establish pastoral councils comprised of clergy, religious, and laity to govern the diocese in partnership with them. The Council struggled mightily, however, to define how the bishops, as successors to Christ's apostles, should direct the church in concert with the pope, the successor of St. Peter. How centralized should the church be? Where should decisions be made? What decisions were the pope's alone? Vatican II established national conferences of bishops to make many of those decisions and also set up a special advisory council, or synod, of bishops to advise the pontiff.

Scripture and liturgy. The Council emphasized that the church is subservient to the divinely revealed Word of God. Hence Catholic liturgy should focus on teaching and preaching from scripture. Mass should be celebrated in the local language rather than in Latin. Catholics were encouraged to read the Bible. Vatican II recognized what it called a "hierarchy of truths," subordinating some beliefs and practices to others. Belief in the death and resurrection of Christ was far more important than not eating meat on Friday.

Vatican II sought to restore the emphasis of the early church on community participation with Christ as the center of worship. As a result, the altar was turned around so the priest faced the people during the celebration of the Mass. The altar rail separating the priest from the congregation was removed. The faithful were urged to pray and sing together rather than retreat to a back pew to recite a silent rosary. Communicants received both the bread and the wine.

Ecumenism and religious freedom. Prior to the Council, Catholics were taught "outside the church, there is no salvation." To enter a Protestant church was to commit a sin. Encouraged by John XXIII, the Council Fathers recognized a common baptism with other Christians and affirmed the positive content of the world's other great religions including Judaism, Buddhism, and Islam. Vatican II expressed an openness to joint worship, scripture study, and dialogue with Protestants. It apologized to the Orthodox for the excommunications it had issued a millennium earlier. And it admitted that the Catholic Church was not perfect, that, on the contrary, Christ summoned it to be *semper reformanda*—"continually being reformed."

Perhaps most significantly, it acknowledged centuries of prejudice and persecution against the Jews by deploring its own anti-Semitism. Vatican II recognized the Judaism of Christ, the Jewish roots of Christianity, and the special relationship God has with the Jewish people.

Furthermore, the Council affirmed religious freedom for all people regardless of their belief or non-belief. In seeking and understanding the will of God, it declared, we must first follow our conscience. Even a misinformed conscience has to be respected.

The church in the modern world. No Council document resonated more with Hunthausen than *Gaudium et Spes*, which set forth how the Catholic Church should relate to the "the joys and hopes, the grief and anguish of the modern world." Much of the document, the Council's longest and the only one written in a modern language (French), is addressed to the whole world.

It challenges Christians to read "the signs of the times" and to extend Christ's love to a poor and suffering humanity. It affirms the dignity of the human person as made in the image of God, emphasizes the importance of the common good, and commits the church to work for a more humane world in which the human spirit can reach its full potential. The document redefines the purpose of marriage as a loving relationship open to the possibility of procreation. It reiterates Catholic social teaching, arguing that economic development must serve people over profits, that labor takes precedence over capital, and that workers have a right to organize for decent wages. Describing the nuclear arms race as a curse on mankind, it denounces the indiscriminate destruction of modern warfare as "a crime against God and humanity," the strongest condemnation of the entire Council.

In a startling reversal from tradition, *Gaudium et Spes* says the church needs and learns from the world.

On the partially overcast, opening day of the Council, Bishop Hunthausen, wearing the ill-fitting white damask cope that had belonged to his deceased predecessor, filed into St. Peter's Basilica with more than two thousand other bishops. It was a dazzling spectacle. Tens of thousands of people filled St. Peter's Square and lined the Via della Conciliazione to sing, chant, and welcome the Council Fathers to Rome. The bishops, in rows of eight, marched across the square and ascended the broad steps toward the great, open doors of St. Peter's. The scarlet-clad ranks of the cardinals followed them. And finally, there was Pope John XXIII, looking a bit overwhelmed, faintly smiling and waving at the crowd, carried aloft in a special papal chair until he dismounted at the entrance of the basilica and walked up the long nave to the high altar.

As Hunthausen made his way along the nave, he all but pinched himself. Am I really here? The small-college president and former

football coach who'd never been to Europe was now at the Vatican
Council rather than the late, Roman-educated Bishop Gilmore, who
had been a leading intellect among the U.S. bishops. After John XXIII
announced the Council in January 1959, Gilmore had prepared assid-
uously. He had pored over the preparatory documents he had received
from the Vatican, making notes, suggesting revisions, and offering
comments. A group of U.S. bishops, including the televangelist Bishop
Fulton J. Sheen, had asked Gilmore to conduct night classes in Rome
so they could improve their Latin, the official language of the Council.
Sheen, the handsome, charismatic host of the nationally televised program, "Life Is Worth Living," wrote his Helena colleague trying to
arrange class times.

Gilmore was confident about his Latin; he wanted to work on his
Italian. Eight months before the Council began, he phoned Hunthausen to inquire about Giuseppe Anceschi, an Italian-born professor
who taught math at Carroll College.

"I'd like to brush up on my Italian," the bishop told Hunthausen,
then the college president. "I wonder if you could arrange for the two
of us to go over to Giuseppe Anceschi's house for dinner."

Hunthausen called the Anceschis who were delighted to host a
dinner for the bishop and the president. The Italian couple served an
elaborate meal, replete with regional dishes and a vintage wine from
Modena, the professor's hometown. Following the bishop's lead, they
conversed in Italian throughout the dinner. But their six-year-old son
kept pestering the adults at the dinner table.

Finally, Hunthausen, who understood the conversation no better
than the little boy, said to the child, "Let's you and I go in there and
play some games." So the two of them went to another room, got out
some toys, and played for the rest of the evening.

Gilmore, elated by the night of Italian conversation with the Anceschis, continued to study the language until the April day he dropped
dead.

"The irony of it all," Hunthausen said, marveling at God's curious
ways. "Here's the bishop preparing for the Council with great anticipation, spending the whole evening practicing his Italian. And he never
went. I should have been practicing my Italian and he should have been
on the floor playing with the little boy. . . . Oh, how the Lord works!"

Hunthausen's Italian wasn't his only shortcoming as far as preparing for the Council. He had given very little thought to what a council
might do. And he had had very little time to review the reams of draft
discussion documents that ten Council preparatory commissions had
sent to Gilmore and were now sending to him. When the time came,
Hunthausen joined Bishop Topel, who was leading a pilgrimage of

Spokane Catholics to religious shrines in Europe before heading to
Rome. Topel, who had free passage as tour director, got the Helena
bishop a cut-rate air ticket, and Hunthausen arrived four days before
the Council began.

Pope John XXIII must have marveled at his presence at this place at
this point in history as much as Hunthausen did. The elderly pope was
no more of a theologian than the bishop of Helena. Born Angelo
Giuseppe Roncalli into a peasant family in northern Italy, he had a
humble, earthy simplicity that endeared him to others. Genial and
portly, he told jokes, laughed often, and openly expressed his affection
for others. After entering the priesthood, Roncalli taught church history at the diocesan seminary in Bergamo, and, when World War I
broke out, served as a chaplain in the Italian Army. His pastoral and
administrative skills attracted the attention of Rome, which named
him a bishop in 1925. He entered the Vatican diplomatic corps and
was the papal delegate to Bulgaria, Turkey, Greece, and, ultimately,
France, where he quietly eased out prelates who had supported the
Nazi-sympathizing Vichy regime. His diplomatic assignments required
him to work with the Eastern Orthodox, with Islam, and with de
Gaulle's Fourth Republic, tasks that deepened his respect for other
faiths and broadened his understanding of the world. In 1953, Pope
Pius XII made him a cardinal and assigned him to Venice. He was sev-
enty-two and assured Venetians that his life ambition to serve as a pastor was now fulfilled.

When Pius died six years later, however, the College of Cardinals
could not agree on a successor and belatedly elected Cardinal Roncalli, who took the name John XXIII. They expected John, who was
nearly eighty and in questionable health, to act as a caretaker. Yet
within three months of his election, he shocked the church, especially
the all-powerful curia, by deciding to call a council. The curia saw no
reason whatsoever for a council. In their minds, the last and only
other Vatican council in 1869–70 had settled questions of church
teaching once and for all. Vatican I stipulated that when the pope
speaks *ex cathedra*, or with the full authority of his office, he cannot
err on matters of faith or morals. Such pronouncements are infallible.
If new issues arose for the church, the pope, assisted by the curia,
would exercise his authority to decide them.

Unlike the experience of the early church, where authority was
shared, popes in the nineteenth and twentieth centuries concentrated
power in their hands and in the hands of the cardinals they named to
the curia. They bluntly exercised their authority in their various encycli-
cals, railing against the evils of the world. Gregory XVI denounced a

"conspiracy against clerical celibacy" and "the evil of freedom of conscience." Pius X rejected modernism as "the synthesis of all heresies."
And Pius XI condemned ecumenism and all forms of birth control.

Only Pius XII, John's predecessor, displayed some openness to re-
thinking and reforming the church. He endorsed historical and literary
analysis of the Bible, eased the rigid fasting and worship requirements
for Mass, and suggested that the church's hierarchical structure needed
to leave more room for the work of the Holy Spirit.

While Pius XII may have cracked the blinds, John XXIII was
about to thrust the window wide open. At the end of the solemn High
Mass inaugurating the Council, the plump, bald, old pontiff slowly
rose to speak. Hunthausen strained to understand the pope's Italian-
accented Latin. Pope John had written his own address, carefully
choosing the words that would convey his charge to the Council Fathers to reform the church and engage the world.

"*Gaudet Mater Ecclesia,*" he began, his resonant voice amplified
throughout the basilica. "Mother Church rejoices." After his joyful
opening, however, John went on to say that he was tired of listening
to "the prophets of doom" among his advisors. He did not believe
their contention that the modern world was slipping toward disaster
nor that it was "full of prevarication and ruin." Turning his back on
five hundred years of Catholic fortress mentality, the Holy Father
urged the Council to take a positive approach, to recognize the
progress of human genius, and to face the future without fear.

In a slap at the inquisitorial and condemnatory behavior of the
curia's Holy Office, the pope said the church prefers "to make use of
the medicine of mercy rather than that of severity." The church
should teach in the light of new biblical, theological, historical, and
scientific knowledge, he said. The church needs to bring itself up to
date so that the message of the Gospel can be heard and understood
by men and women throughout the world. The substance of the faith
is one thing, he said, the way in which it is expressed is another. The
challenge of the Council is to leave behind old methods that are no
longer relevant and lay out new ways of applying the Gospel to both
the church and the major concerns of the day.

In concluding his address, John XXIII boldly embraced Christian
unity and his desire for interfaith respect and understanding. The key
to the unity of all humankind, he said, is love. Hence, the Catholic
Church ought to be a be "the loving mother of all, benign, patient,
full of mercy and goodness toward the children separated from her."

After his opening address, Pope John did not attend the Council
again until the day the first session adjourned. He followed the proceedings with deep interest over closed-circuit television but rarely in-
truded on the bishops' work. Reforming the church was their job.

For the first session of the Council, Bishop Topel had made arrangements for himself, Hunthausen, Bishop Sylvester Treinen of Boise, and Bishop Hilary Hacker of Bismarck, North Dakota, to stay in a convent on the outskirts of Rome that accepted students and other itinerant guests. The convent, run by the Precious Blood Sisters of Canada, served simple meals in a common dining room. Most bishops attending the Council stayed in more centrally located hotels, monasteries, or other lodgings that could accommodate larger numbers. As a result, they had chartered bus service to and from St. Peter's Square. The four Northwest bishops had to arrange their own transportation.

A couple of days before the Council began, Hunthausen happened to meet an American priest who was selling a Volkswagen Beetle for $1,300. Hunthausen bought it. The other three bishops contributed toward the purchase on the condition that Hunthausen do all the driving in a city well known for its aggressive, unruly motorists.

So, every morning the four bishops, attired in their red cassocks and black birettas, squeezed into the VW bug and set off for St. Peter's with Hunthausen at the wheel. It was a tight fit. Topel and Hacker were well over six feet tall. Climbing into the back seat of a Beetle in full episcopal garb was a bit of a challenge.

One morning they were riding in the VW when they came to a busy intersection within viewing distance of the white marble colonnades of St. Peter's. A traffic policeman waved Hunthausen through the intersection. But when the light turned red, the Beetle's rear end was sticking out into oncoming traffic. So Hunthausen nudged the car forward, tapping the bumper of the car in front of him.

The driver's door on the car ahead burst open. The driver leapt out. He dashed back to inspect his automobile. Head wagging, arms waving, hands gesturing, he unleashed a torrent of Italian invective at Hunthausen. The bishops looked at Hacker, who spoke the best Italian, and said, "Say something! Say something!"

"Oh, no," Hacker replied. "I don't think so."

The Italian motorist then peered into the VW and stopped short. He couldn't believe his eyes—four princes of the church, dressed in their ecclesial finery, crammed into this little car. He went silent, shrugged, and with a final gesture of helplessness, got back into his car and drove off.

The Council Fathers took up the charge that Pope John XXIII had given them with great alacrity—so much so that the first business session of the Council was over within fifteen minutes. Much to the surprise of the curia, French Cardinal Achille Liénart, a respected scripture scholar, rose to ask that the bishops postpone voting on who should sit on the ten commissions that would draft the Council documents until the Council Fathers spent more time getting to know one other. Liénart's proposal was greeted with sustained applause.

Italian Archbishop Pericle Felici, the affable, urbane, and diplomatic secretary-general of the Council, reversed the decision to elect commission members immediately and delayed balloting for several days. With that, he abruptly adjourned the session. The bishops exited the basilica, swarming into St. Peter's Square and down the Via Conciliazione.

Watching from his window in the papal apartment, a bewildered Pope John turned in utter dismay to a visitor and exclaimed, *"Cosa c'e?"* ("What's happening?") Had the bishops given up already?

Liénart's move was of utmost significance. It meant that members of the curia and curial loyalists would not dominate the commissions. It also meant that the Council was not going to rubber stamp the draft documents prepared by the ten preparatory commissions that the curia had set up. The Council would do things its own way and not be subservient to Vatican bureaucrats who saw little need for church reform. The bishops, meeting in national conferences, drew up their own lists of recommended candidates for the various commissions. And, when voting occurred several days later, they elected a good number of them.

The successful intervention by the French cardinal put the Vatican Old Guard on notice. It especially drew the ire of Italian Cardinal Alfredo Ottaviani, who as head of the Congregation of the Holy Office was the most powerful member of the curia, chair of the Theological Commission, and the de facto leader of the traditionalists. Shrewd, intelligent, and witty, he chose for his coat of arms as cardinal the Latin motto *Semper Idem*—"always the same." Ottaviani, whose eyesight was failing, believed that the church was unchanging and unchangeable.

"I am an old soldier," he explained, "who serves the church blindly."

Ottaviani was ably supported by two other influential Italian cardinals, Giuseppe Siri and Ernesto Ruffini. Siri, a respected leader among the Italian bishops, had hoped to continue the authoritarian ways of Pius XII by succeeding him. Ruffini argued that the purpose of the Council was to put an end to any confusion in doctrine, morality, and biblical interpretation by laying down the law. He spoke more often than anyone else at Vatican II.

Perched in the balcony above them, Hunthausen watched as Ottaviani and the other cardinals dominated the Council proceedings. The cardinals, by virtue of their rank, were entitled to speak first. Only when they were finished were archbishops and bishops free to speak from any of the three dozen microphones placed throughout the basilica. All speakers were limited to ten minutes each.

Ottaviani commanded Latin so well that he could ignore his text and hold forth extemporaneously, gesticulating, pacing about, and throwing his hands up in the air. He got especially worked up about changes proposed for modernizing the Mass, fearing that the faithful would be scandalized.

"Are the Council Fathers planning a revolution?" he taunted the reformers.

Fulminating away on one occasion, Ottaviani ignored repeated signals that he had run well beyond the time limit. Suddenly, power was cut to his microphone and he was silenced. The basilica broke out in sustained applause. Insulted and humiliated, the mighty head of the Holy Office boycotted the Council for the next two weeks.

Surprised first by Liénart's intervention and then by Ottaviani's silencing, Hunthausen saw plainly that the curia was losing ground, that the Council Fathers were determined to take the church in a radically new direction. He was amazed how the speakers, especially the northern European cardinals who were the major advocates of reform, were willing to overturn centuries of church tradition. Contrary to the usual, well mannered show of episcopal unity and conformity, here were prelates speaking their minds, voicing sharp disagreement with each other, and vigorously attacking each other's ideas.

"Most of the American bishops, certainly most of my close friends and I, stood with our mouths open, waiting to see what would happen next," Hunthausen recalled. "I was simply overwhelmed; I had no understanding of the church beyond Helena and Great Falls. And now the Council put me in contact with the church around the world. I got an awareness that I would never have acquired in a lifetime without the Council."

The bishops threw out virtually all of the documents drafted by the Council preparatory commissions. Instead of discussing them as drafted, the Council Fathers either rejected them altogether or sent them back to the now-reconstituted commissions for rewriting and consolidating. As a result, the first session of the Council accomplished very little beyond reorganizing itself. Not a single document won final approval. Only the draft document on liturgy—after heavy and extensive revision—got a friendly reception.

Cardinal Liénart, Cardinal Leo Suenens of Belgium, Cardinals Josef Frings, Franz Konig, and Augustine Bea of Germany, and other reformers clearly routed the curia traditionalists at the first session. All bishops were permitted to bring a theological consultant, or *peritus*, with them to the Council, although most did not. The exceptions were the northern European prelates who were assisted by the ablest theologians of the day, including Karl Rahner, Yves Congar, and Henri de Lubac, scholars who had been silenced and condemned during the long reign of Pius XII. Cardinal Frings brought with him the then-reformist theologian Joseph Ratzinger who would ultimately head the former Holy Office under Pope John Paul II and then be elected his successor as Pope Benedict XVI.

Council sessions began with Mass each day at 9 AM. A bishop from the Latin rite or any of the twenty Eastern rites in communion with Rome (Maronite, Melkite, Byzantine, etc.) led the service. The eucharistic sharing of the body and blood of Christ in the form of bread and wine was central to every Mass. But the music, the prayers, and the overall liturgical display varied enormously. The Eastern rite services included choirs that chanted and sang polyphonic harmonies quite alien to the Western ear. After the Eucharist, a richly adorned Lectionary was placed on the altar and incensed as a reminder that the church stands under the revealed Word of God.

Hunthausen was astonished by how diverse the Masses were. Sometimes he recognized nothing other than the central act of eucharistic consecration. The Ethiopian rite Mass, celebrated by the archbishop of Addis Ababa, included spirited chanting, bell ringing, tambourine shaking, and African drums. It caused such a sensation that a headline in the *New York Post* shouted "Bongo drums beat at the Vatican."

Following Mass, the Council moved into the business of the day, opening the discussion with the words: *Adsumus, Domine Sancte Spiritus, adsumus* ("We are here, Holy Spirit, we are here.") For many of the bishops—at least until they received the written translations later—the content of the business day was elusive. Despite their classical seminary education, few bishops had a real comprehension of spoken Latin. Even when they did, a heavily inflected native tongue, whether German, Spanish, African or something else, often confounded communication. Moreover, some Latin presentations were little more than doggerel pasted together from a dictionary.

As for the argument that Latin was the church's universal language, one bishop wryly commented: It's true. No matter where you are in the world, it is equally unintelligible. Nonetheless, virtually all speakers adhered to the official Council language. One big exception was the Melkite patriarch, His Beatitude Maximos IV Saigh, an outspoken advocate of national bishops' conferences and use of the vernacular. He consistently addressed the Council in French.

Cardinal Richard Cushing of Boston offered to pay for a simultaneous translation system, but the Council leadership decided against it for fear the "secret" deliberations—particularly the more controversial and tempestuous ones—would leak out. Never mind that they leaked out anyway. With no live translations, the U.S. bishops got by with English summaries of the speeches put out at the end of the day.

John XXIII realized that most of the Council Fathers, particularly those who were old, frail, or not fluent in Latin, would find it excruciating to sit through hours of ten-minute monologues. Consequently, he ordered the installation of coffee bars on the main and upper levels of the basilica. The bars offered a variety of refreshments and afforded bishops a place to meet, talk, and smoke. At times, more bishops seemed to be gathered at the bars than listening from their seats, especially when speakers tended to repeat things that had already been said. Council Secretary-General Felici frequently asked the bishops to remain in their places rather than wander off to the "thermopolium."

When the daily Council session adjourned around one o'clock in the afternoon, Hunthausen and his American bishop housemates returned to their lodgings to eat the main meal of the day and perhaps take a nap, much as the Italians did. After the first year of the Council, the four Northwest bishops moved to the Instituto Madri Pie, a four-story, brown stucco rooming house operated by women religious two blocks from St. Peter's. An unpretentious place, it offered small private rooms with shared baths. Eight dollars a day covered room, board, and laundry. In the mornings it could be noisy, since the sisters also ran a day school for kindergarten kids. About three dozen bishops, most of them Latin Americans, booked rooms there for the Council.

Madri Pie's location put the heart of the Eternal City at the bishops' doorstep. In the afternoons, which were free, Hunthausen, Treinen, Hacker, and George Speltz, the new auxiliary bishop of Winona, Minnesota, explored Rome on foot. They strolled down the city's cobblestone streets to the Coliseum or the Piazza Navone or any of the medieval churches throughout the city. In the afternoons and evenings, there were numerous activities to occupy them and the other bishops. During the first session, the U.S. prelates met every Monday at the North American College to review the events of the day, prepare for upcoming discussions, and, when possible, present a united front on issues, such as religious liberty, that were of special concern to the American Church.

The *periti*, the consultant experts on theology, liturgy, scripture, church law, and other subjects, were readily available to the bishops. A bishop might accost a *peritus* for an informal conversation over a cappuccino or attend a more formal presentation by a *peritus* theologian on ecumenism, collegiality, or seminary formation. Hunthausen and the American contingent at Madri Pie often walked over to the

English-language press briefing at the USO to hear the *periti* and representative bishops comment on the Council debates. Hunthausen found himself getting the theological education that he had missed as a chemistry major.

Sometimes the experts came to Madri Pie to chat with Hunthausen and the others about whatever excited them. One expert was Father Godfrey Diekmann, the Benedictine priest who was an international authority on liturgical reform. He didn't have to travel far for these chats. Diekmann occupied the room across the hall from Hunthausen at Madri Pie.

Hunthausen's continuing education and exploration went beyond the Council and Rome. The bishop of Helena visited Florence, Naples, and Venice and traveled beyond Italy to pray at the Marian shrines in Lourdes and Fatima. He took advantage of a four-day recess over the All Saints Day weekend to visit a Helena priest studying in Zurich and the motherhouse in Speyer, Germany, of the Dominican sisters who served at Carroll College. During a break in the last session of the Council, he joined fifty other bishops on an eight-day pilgrimage to the Holy Land. The group celebrated Mass in Bethlehem, visited various Christian sites, and spent time in both the Israeli and Jordanian-held sectors of Jerusalem.

During each Council session, the U.S. ambassador and his wife hosted a garden reception at their private Roman villa for the American bishops. At Thanksgiving time, the rector of the North American College engaged a Roman chef to serve a traditional turkey dinner with all the fixings. Although briefed on the intricacies of candied yams and mincemeat pies, the caterer produced a turkey carcass stuffed with salami and festooned with artichokes. Dessert was Neapolitan ice cream studded with dried fruit and nuts.

Between the first and second sessions of the Council, Hunthausen spent a month at the Mayo Clinic in Rochester, Minnesota, recovering from back surgery. Toward the end of his stay, he was mobile enough to attend the consecration ceremony for Speltz, who had just been appointed bishop and would be attending the Council for the first time. Timid, soft-spoken, and theologically cautious, Speltz soon embraced the Council as enthusiastically as Hunthausen and the two became fast friends.

In September 1963, Speltz checked into Madri Pie with Hunthausen and the others for the second session. Pope John XXIII had died three months earlier, so this was the first time that the newly elected Pope Paul VI would preside. There was great anticipation about what Paul VI would say in his opening address to the Council Fathers. Would he endorse what John XXIII had begun? In what direction would he steer the Council? How active was he likely to be in shaping the agenda?

Speltz, who had just purchased a portable tape player, was determined to record the pope's address. He worried about getting it past the Swiss Guards. But Hunthausen and the others suggested he hide the recorder in his briefcase and just stride in. So that's what he did.

Because seats for the second session were not yet assigned, Speltz and the American bishops from Madri Pie proceeded to sit halfway up the main seating section in the middle of the basilica. They were in formal dress, wearing white miters, gold pectoral crosses, and ornate embroidered copes. When the time came for Paul VI to speak, Speltz reached inside his briefcase and pulled out the tape recorder. He had not tested it. In fact, he had no idea that to record he had to simultaneously press the "play" and the "record" buttons. He simply pushed "play." And all of a sudden, a demonstration tape in the recorder burst out at full volume. As the pope assembled his speaking papers, a John Philip Sousa march rang through the basilica.

Forty years later at a Seattle University symposium commemorating the Council, Hunthausen told that story.

"The bishops—it seemed to me for miles and miles—all turned around," he said, chuckling. "Bishop Treinen and I looked the other way as though we didn't know the fellow next to us. Oh, poor George, he didn't touch a tape recorder for two years."

Sometimes the trio of Hunthausen, Treinen, and Speltz ended their walks around Rome by returning to St. Peter's Square and sitting on the basilica's grand steps. There they talked about the matters the Council was discussing: divine revelation, the liturgy, church governance, and the global issues of poverty, war and peace, human rights, and religious liberty.

Speltz, who held a PhD in economics, was excited about what he saw happening at the Council. "I had a sense that there would be a new church, a more open church with a more prominent place for laypeople," he said.

Hunthausen and Treinen felt the same way.

Schooled in the genteel notion that bishops always agreed with each other, Treinen was initially shocked at how some of the cardinals went at each other's throats. A bald, whimsical man with large protruding ears and a keen wit, the bishop of Boise had never witnessed such behavior among his brother bishops.

"I was scared after the first session by the open confrontation on the Council floor," he admitted. But gradually he and the other junior bishops from Madri Pie came to enjoy the sharp verbal jousting and the pointed repartee.

"By the second session, it was altogether different because we knew each other," Treinen said. "We were like schoolboys coming back from summer vacation. The Council was getting good reviews at home and it felt good."

Hunthausen was particularly excited about the changes that the Council intended for the church. "It all made good sense to me," he said. "By golly, you know, my own thoughts and feelings about what the church ought to be were being validated."

He, Treinen, and Speltz, like most of the Council Fathers, consistently voted for the documents proposed by the reformers, all of which passed by overwhelming majorities of 90 percent or more. None of the three Northwest bishops ever spoke from the Council floor although they signed joint statements that were then read or entered into the record by one of the American cardinals. As junior bishops, they were expected to make their sentiments known through more senior prelates.

In fact, the only prelate from the Northwest who did speak from the Council floor was Seattle Archbishop Thomas A. Connolly, whom Hunthausen would succeed a decade later. In the fourth and final session, Connolly was moved to speak on the document about the ministry and life of priests. A top-down administrator who ran the archdiocese with military aplomb, he complained that the Council was creating "a crisis of obedience . . . owing to a false notion of freedom and independence" among some priests. "In these days of ferment," Connolly warned, "priests are more apt to have their own opinions on many important matters."

Despite Connolly's concerns about disobedient priests, the Council majority had clearly moved to reformist positions on virtually all of the sixteen documents approved at Vatican II. Over the course of Council's four years, the bishops went from concerns about firming up doctrine to concerns about how Catholic belief could best be lived out in the modern world. It was a remarkable transformation. Most of the bishops were products of a closed seminary environment that stressed apologetics as the way to defend the faith against a hostile secular culture. They started with an answer and then developed the arguments to prove that the answer was the only correct one. Most of them came to Council convinced that there was no salvation outside the Catholic Church, that the pope's authority was absolute and extended to the various bodies of the Holy See, and that the church reforms of the Protestant Reformation were illegitimate, heretical, and to be roundly condemned.

Their transformation was evidenced, for example, by the change of leadership and direction within the caucus of the two-hundred-some U.S. bishops. At the beginning of the first session, the American heavyweights were Cardinals Francis J. Spellman, of New York, and James F. McIntyre, of Los Angeles, who assumed the role of speaking for the other U.S. bishops. Spellman, who had been a close friend of Pius XII, saw little need to call the Council in the first place. He and McIntyre wanted to retain the Latin Mass, reiterate Catholic doctrine, and keep the laity in its appropriate place.

"Active participation by the faithful in the Mass is nothing but a distraction," said McIntyre, admonishing the reformers. He and Spellman, strong advocates of papal primacy, opposed national conferences of bishops as a threat to the monarchical structure of the church.

As the Council unfolded, however, most U.S. bishops shifted toward more open, collegial, and inclusive positions on a variety of issues. Cardinals Joseph E. Ritter of St. Louis and Albert Meyer of Chicago, emerged as the leaders of this new majority. They spoke out for Mass in the vernacular, for appropriate sharing of responsibility with the pope and the laity, and for committing the church to respecting liberty of conscience. They envisioned bishops as "servant leaders" rather than autocratic lords. Ritter boldly called for an end to the Counter-Reformation by seeking unity with other Christians and respectful understanding of other faiths. True unity in Jesus Christ requires it, he declared. By the end of the Council, Ritter and Meyer were clearly speaking not only for their own constituency but also for most of the Council Fathers.

The U.S. prelates were unanimous in their support of the declaration on religious liberty, the most bitterly contested document of the Council. The declaration was contentious because it forced the church to reverse itself, to admit that it had been wrong. For most of its history, the church had condemned religious liberty, a position taken as a way of protecting itself and preserving its privileged relationship with the state. The argument went like this: The Catholic Church possesses the truth, therefore it alone has the right to practice and proclaim the faith. "Error," it famously decreed, "has no rights."

Because the U.S. Constitution separated church and state, the American bishops recognized that the church had to embrace the diversity of the modern world and promote freedom of belief. Spellman recruited Father John Courtney Murray, a Jesuit expert on church-state relations, as a *peritus* to help resolve the issue. Murray, whom the Vatican had silenced in the 1950s, convinced the Council that neither "error" nor "truth" has rights because they are abstract concepts. Only human beings have rights. And one of those rights is the right to religious liberty.

Hunthausen was very pleased with the Council declarations on religious liberty, Christian unity, shared responsibility, the liturgy, the laity, and especially, the role of the church in the modern world.

"I thought the church is the people," he said, "and it's high time that we invite people to take responsibility for their own lives. We can't keep talking down to them."

Even in his early years as a priest, Hunthausen had been troubled by the church's claim that it was the only path to salvation. He recalled a Protestant woman who visited him one time to talk about converting to Catholicism. She asked him: What happens to all these other people out there, all these people who aren't Catholic?

"I remember telling her," Hunthausen recalled, "that I think we're all going to be surprised when we get to heaven and see who else got there."

Gaudium et Spes, the Council document on the Church in the Modern World, brought together topics not specifically addressed elsewhere: human dignity, marriage and family, culture, economic and social life, and war and peace. Hunthausen was particularly cheered by the Council's all-out condemnation of war in the wake of John XXIII's 1963 encyclical, *Pacem in Terris,* with its powerful call for an end to the nuclear arms race. Even Cardinal Ottaviani bluntly told the bishops, "War must be completely outlawed." For which he was warmly applauded.

Even so, *Gaudium et Spes* recognized the right of nations to defend themselves and was ambiguous on the morality of stockpiling nuclear weapons. In the very last week of the Council, New Orleans Archbishop Philip Hannan, with the backing of Cardinal Spellman, engineered a campaign to further water down the document. Hannan argued that the possession of nuclear weapons had preserved freedom for much of the world. Moreover, he contended, a limited use of atomic weapons was possible without inviting global destruction. The Council Fathers rebuffed him. Eighteen years later, during the U.S. bishops' climactic debate over the legitimacy of nuclear weapons, Hannan would face off with Hunthausen.

At the Council, Hunthausen shared his thoughts on the moral evil of nuclear weapons in conversations with Treinen, Speltz, and other bishops.

"I struggled mightily with some of the inconsistencies and the absolute contradictions I could see between the arms race and what I thought Jesus was about," he recalled. "In that document, 'The Church in the Modern World,' it was all there. Now I had to hear how the Spirit was speaking to me."

John Courtney Murray's winning argument for religious liberty was emblematic of a larger struggle that characterized the debates at the Council, a debate that continues in the Catholic Church today: Is the church of the world? Or is it apart from the world? Is its mission to build the kingdom of God in this world? Or is it to help the faithful achieve salvation in the next world?

These questions and their answers illustrate two fundamentally different theological traditions evident in the church even from its earliest days: the Augustinian and the Thomist.

The Augustinian tradition is named for Augustine, the fourth-century Father of the Church, theologian, and bishop, whose writings were extremely influential in shaping Christian thought and Western philosophy. In the *City of God,* his twenty-two-volume opus, Augustine asserted the superiority of the church to human society, arguing that only the church holds the true wisdom found in Christ. While the church must be in the world, he wrote, it is not of it. Rather, it holds itself apart, protecting itself from heresy, corruption, contamination, and the evils of the times. Augustine saw the church as a holy mystery in opposition to the world. He emphasized the theology of the cross—the crucified Christ—as the heart of Christianity.

The Thomist tradition is named for Thomas Aquinas, a thirteenth-century Father of the Church, Dominican priest, and theologian whom the church considers its greatest theologian and philosopher. In *Summa Theologica* and other works, Aquinas placed a strong emphasis on reasoning as he employed the Greek classics and Christian theology to develop his ideas on morality, natural law, and political theory. He stressed the convergence of reason and faith as the underlying foundation of Catholic teaching. Aquinas engaged the world, drawing a distinction between the natural and the supernatural and reconciling the Christian faith with human culture. An optimist, he was inclined to see goodness rather than sin, joy rather than sorrow, and God's grace rather than God's judgment. He believed that the church could learn from the world and should adapt accordingly. While Augustine emphasized the cross, Aquinas emphasized the incarnation, God made man in Christ.

Nowhere did these two traditions find themselves in more tension than in the writing of *Gaudium et Spes.* At the time, the neo-Thomists triumphed, managing to secure overwhelming passage of an optimistic, forward-looking document that reversed the condemnations of modernity that Pius IX had issued a century earlier. *Gaudium et Spes* put the church on record as committing itself to addressing the world's problems in partnership with other people of good will—regardless of faith—for the common good of all mankind.

Ultimately, however, the Augustinians would prevail. Almost immediately, they attacked the document as overly optimistic and naïve. It minimized the power of sin and obscured the distinctive nature of Christianity, they contended. The church should put the emphasis on proclaiming Christ to the world, not on dialoguing with it. Among these critics were Polish Archbishop Karol Wojtyla, the future Pope John Paul II, and Joseph Ratzinger, the *peritus* theologian and future Pope Benedict XVI, and virtually all the members of the Roman curia, the group charged with implementing the reforms of Vatican II. The Council could say what it liked, but the Vatican hierarchy would decide what the church would do. The future was in its hands.

The cause of church reform lost its most influential champion with the passing of Pope John XXIII. Two weeks after his death on June 3, 1963, the College of Cardinals elected Giovanni Battista Montini, the cardinal archbishop of Milan, as Pope Paul VI.

Paul, who had spent much of his career in the curia, generally supported the reformist aims of the Council, but was indecisive, anxious, and frustratingly vague about what he hoped to see accomplished. In the subsequent Council sessions of 1963–65, he intervened often, exercising his influence with the Council's leadership at private meetings in the papal apartment. He pored over Council documents with a red pen, making recommendations, and marking sections he wanted to see revised. At several points, he threw his weight behind the traditionalist minority to delay or stop discussion, and, at one point, he ordered the burning of a secret advisory ballot meant to gauge the Council Fathers' opinions on collegiality, the diaconate, and celibacy.

Paul removed three issues from the Council agenda altogether. The Council Fathers would not discuss priestly celibacy, church teaching on birth control, or reform of the curia. These matters, Paul decreed, he would reserve to himself.

In 1967, as thousands of priests were leaving the priesthood to marry, Paul issued an encyclical insisting on celibacy for Latin-rite priests. In 1968, he rejected the majority recommendation of the papal birth control commission that he had established and sided instead with its minority members—including the future Pope John Paul II—in continuing the church's ban on artificial contraception. The encyclical *Humanae Vitae* justified that prohibition, disappointing and angering Catholics, particularly in the United States, where most of them rejected the pope's rationale for the "rhythm method" and kept using contraceptives.

Paul refused to reform the curia despite the urgings of the Council majority. He flatly told Cardinal Suenens, one of the Council moderators, that no major reorganization was needed and he intended to retain all the heads of the Vatican congregations. In a concession to the reformers, he did issue a document ostensibly reforming the Holy Office, the curial department headed by Ottaviani that drew much of the Council's wrath. Paul renamed the office the Congregation for the Doctrine of the Faith (CDF), hoping to emphasize promotion of good doctrine rather than punishment of error.

He accorded the CDF precedence over all other congregations because it "deals with the questions of greatest importance." His decree sought to make the CDF's work transparent, establish legal representation and a right of appeal, ensure consultation with national bishops' conferences and theological experts, and abolish the Index of Forbidden Books. But with the exception of ending the Index, little happened. Two decades later, when Hunthausen was investigated, punished, and humiliated by the CDF, he had no official legal representation, no right of appeal, and no due process. In fact, the Vatican refused to show him its report of the allegations against him.

Paul VI did establish a synod of bishops, which the Council Fathers had envisioned as an elected consultative body that would govern the church, carrying out the reforms of Vatican II in collaboration with the pope. The synod, they hoped, would balance the influence of the curia by operating collegially with the pope and the national conferences of bishops. Paul had a somewhat different idea. The synod, he said, would be subject "immediately and directly to the power" of the pope. His successor, Pope John Paul II, made that abundantly clear at subsequent synods in which he determined the agenda, chose most of the bishops who attended, and then asked the bishops to rubber-stamp statements and recommendations drafted by the curia.

On the cool, sunny morning of December 8, 1965, Pope Paul VI concluded the Council by celebrating Mass at an elevated, outdoor altar in St. Peter's Square. Hunthausen and the other Council Fathers, attired in their episcopal robes, stood as the pope delivered a brief homily in Italian. Each of them had received a gold ring and an apostolic blessing as an expression of the pope's appreciation.

Archbishop Felici, the Council secretary-general, read the pope's official letter declaring the Council over and enjoining "everything the Council decreed be religiously and devoutly observed by all the faithful." Then the pontiff rose, raised his hand to bless the bishops and a crowd of more than three hundred thousand people, and dismissed them. "Go in peace," he said.

Hunthausen flew home to Montana, tired and exhilarated. The Council had transformed him. He had a new concept of the church as the "People of God" sharing responsibility in building the kingdom of God on earth. He had a new idea of his role as bishop, as a "servant leader" who convenes, collaborates, and inspires rather than dictates, reprimands, and proscribes. And he had a new vision of his Catholic faith in which Christ liberates and loves all—regardless of their beliefs or their sins—especially the poor, the suffering, the abandoned, and the victims of war and injustice.

"For me to have attempted to be a bishop without the Council would have been a disaster," Hunthausen said. "My goodness, the spirit and theology of the Council turned my head around."

BISHOP OF HELENA

Reason is in fact the path to faith,
and faith takes over when reason can say no more.
—Thomas Merton

Bishop Raymond G. Hunthausen returned from Vatican II with a new vision and a new mandate for his ministry in western Montana. The headline in the *Montana Catholic Register*, the diocesan newspaper, proclaimed: "With Closing of Vatican Council Begins the Church of the Future."

"God's will for us, then, my dear people," the young bishop and Council Father wrote in an accompanying letter, "is the successful implementation of all that the Council has and will decree."

The church of the future envisioned by Hunthausen began by implementing the liturgical reforms of Vatican II: the Mass celebrated in English rather than Latin, the priest at the altar facing the people, communion distributed in the form of bread and wine to standing rather than kneeling recipients, the shared "kiss of peace" among Mass-goers as a recognition of their community in the Body of Christ, and laypeople participating in Mass as readers, eucharistic ministers, and homilists.

Hunthausen brought Father Godfrey Diekmann, the internationally renowned liturgist and his fellow lodger at Madri Pie, to western Montana. Diekmann spoke throughout the diocese, attracting hundreds of laypeople curious and excited about how Catholic worship was changing. The young bishop reinforced the liturgist's message.

"You must desire to become not mere silent spectators at the Mass," he told the Montana Knights of Columbus at their annual convention banquet in Lewiston in May 1964, "but active participants." Often he expanded his remarks to address the larger themes of the Council. At the Knights convention in Anaconda the following year, Hunthausen said the Catholic laity was on the threshold of reclaiming a church that was rightfully theirs.

"The Catholic laity is in the phase of another 'sleeping giant,'" he said. "Once it is truly awakened to its full potential there will be inaugurated a kind of Catholic Great Awakening that will renew and inspire the world."

At the dedication of the new St. Mary's Church in Helena in August 1966, Hunthausen explained that great awakening. "The laity are full-fledged, co-responsible members of the church," he told the large crowd gathered for the dedication ceremony. "They are expected to be dynamic promoters of the cause of Christ and not merely passive recipients of the services of the ordained."

He struck a similar note at the diocesan Council of Catholic Women convention in Anaconda in August 1967. He urged the women to embrace the Council's reforms and wholly participate in the modern church. He described the Vatican II documents as containing a "living message from God addressed to you." The Council presents the church with "a new Pentecost, a new opportunity that cannot be grasped in the old ways," he said.

Embracing the Council's call for shared responsibility, Hunthausen initiated the creation of a Priest Senate, a diocesan pastoral council, a finance council, parish councils, and special commissions charged with implementing various church reforms. None of these bodies had existed before.

In October 1966, Hunthausen assembled the priests of the diocese at a retreat center at St. Joseph's Hospital in Deer Lodge. He invited them to elect twelve of their number as a "priest senate" to advise him on matters pertaining to the welfare of the local church. The priests did so and the new body conducted its first bi-monthly meeting in January 1967. Hunthausen sat in on the meetings but he did not chair them nor did he set the agenda.

The Priest Senate, whose members were elected by deaneries, became Hunthausen's most important sounding board. It subsequently established a priest personnel board and set up a mediation and arbitration process for priests involved in disputes with the bishop or their parishioners. It issued public statements on concerns such as the MX missile and the nuclear arms race, the religious right to conscientious objection, the immorality of the Vietnam War, and the need for priests and laity to be involved in the selection of their bishops.

After establishing the Priest Senate, Hunthausen set up the diocesan pastoral council, the purpose of which was to collaborate with him and other diocesan leaders in furthering the ministry of the church in western Montana. Pastoral council members were selected after wide consultation with pastors and parish leaders. The twenty-three-member council met for the first time in the library reading room at Carroll College in March 1969. It consisted of thirteen laypeople, six priests, three sisters, and a Christian Brother. They were young, old, ranchers, businesspeople, pastors, teachers, and homemakers. The bishop was the presiding officer.

"We put together a process that I think was way ahead of its time," said Hunthausen, recalling the first meetings of the group. "We spent a lot of time reviewing materials that came to us from Rome, discussing them, making our comments, and then sending them off."

The Pastoral Council embraced its task with enthusiasm and determination. Members started their discussions on Saturday morning, ate meals at the college, prayed and celebrated Mass together, and then closed their deliberations on Sunday afternoon.

"It was their church as much as it was mine," Hunthausen said. "We acknowledged that the Spirit works through all of us and we have to provide the vehicle for the Spirit to speak."

He found the Pastoral Council absolutely essential for developing lay leadership, educating the faithful, and building the church of the future. Not once did he reject or overrule its recommendations.

"I made sure that the discussions were prayerful and thorough and I would voice my opinion," he said. "But I was not about to countermand."

One of the first pieces of advice he received from the Pastoral Council was to help parish councils understand their role and responsibilities. Some parishes had set up councils while others, often headed by pastors reluctant to share authority, had not. So Hunthausen announced a "Congress of Parish Councils" that convened at Carroll on July 26–28, 1970.

"There was a lot of scurrying around, let me assure you," Hunthausen recalled. "But as it turned out, every parish was represented and, from that point on, all the parishes took it seriously and it was off and running."

More than 250 people representing all fifty-six Catholic parishes in western Montana showed up for two and a half days of presentations, workshops, prayer, and worship. In addition to the three official representatives from each parish council (the pastor and two laypeople), other Catholics, some Protestants, and Bishop Eldon Schuster from Great Falls came as observers. A theologian from Catholic University gave a keynote address on "The Layman and the Mission of the Church." Participants discussed religious education, liturgy, finances, and social issues such as poverty, abortion, and racism.

Hunthausen wandered among the tables, listening to those in small groups ask each other: What should a parish council deal with? Is it just for practical matters, or does it explore spiritual issues? Does the pastor have the final word, or do we try to reach a consensus?

Some of the questions had to do with understanding the cultural changes unleashed by Vatican II: Why have some priests stopped wearing their collars in public? Why are nuns discarding their habits? Why has Father moved out of the rectory and into his own apartment?

The attitudes and beliefs behind these questions had prompted the Priest Senate to push for an extensive research study, which the diocese began in 1969. With help from social scientists at the University of Montana, the diocese conducted scores of interviews and sent questionnaires to nearly three thousand homes to measure the religious values, attitudes, and commitment of Catholics in western Montana. The Priest Senate and the Pastoral Council reasoned that they could not plan for the future of the local church unless they knew what Catholics felt, thought, and desired. The research findings led to establishing diocesan committees on spirituality, liturgy, social concerns, the family, and ecumenism.

The findings also showed that the overwhelming majority of diocesan clergy and laypeople supported the bishop and the reforms of Vatican II. They liked the changes in the church and felt the diocese was headed in the right direction at the right speed. Jon Driessen, the sociologist who led the survey team, told Hunthausen that he couldn't say for certain what the diocese was doing right.

"All I can tell you is that whatever you're doing, keep doing it," Driessen said.

Establishing grassroots deliberative bodies to guide and govern the church was radically new. To be sure, Vatican II had not made the church a democracy. The bishop—and ultimately the pope—still ruled. But he was expected to rule in such a manner that his decisions reflected the knowledge and wisdom of the faithful. The purpose of the consultative bodies was to uncover that knowledge and find ways of using that wisdom.

In the post–Vatican II years of the Helena diocese, no one did that better than Father James Provost, the bright, creative canon lawyer whom Hunthausen made his chancellor in 1967. A Carroll College graduate from Missoula, Provost studied church law at the Catholic University of Louvain, Belgium, and received a doctorate from the Lateran University in Rome. An usher at the Council while he was studying in Rome, he returned to Montana eager to initiate its reforms as Hunthausen's right-hand man. He later served as president of the Canon Law Society of America and was a professor of church law at Catholic University in Washington, DC.

Drawing from the documents of Vatican II, Provost argued that the universal church is not a monarchy headed by the pope but rather a communion of diverse churches that adapt church law to suit their local cultures and circumstances. Rome doesn't provide a cookbook with set recipes, he said. "[Canon law] is a general set of guidelines in which you've got to work out the recipe for your diocese."

Provost said that Vatican II, with its recognition of the common dignity and equality of all believers, put the focus on the parish community rather than on the priest. "We used to say: What are we going to do with Father Harry, the pastor?" he explained. "Now we say: What are we going to do with St. Harry's, the parish?"

Provost envisioned a Catholic Church in which laypeople led many parishes while priests provided the sacraments. In Helena, he assembled the learning material, designed the process and structure, and created the modus operandi for church reform.

"Jim Provost is one of the brightest guys I've ever known in my life," Hunthausen recalled years later. "He had great common sense. He could analyze and synthesize and bring us to a conclusion."

Slender, with distinctive black eyebrows, penetrating dark eyes, and a long, boyish face, Provost was very organized and spoke convincingly. His presentations flowed logically toward next steps and conclusions that welcomed engagement and involvement. Unaffected and approachable, Provost eschewed clerical garb in favor of a sport coats and turtleneck sweaters.

Father Sarsfield O'Sullivan, an erudite, aristocratic, blue-eyed Irish pastor from Butte, credited Provost with helping Hunthausen understand what he had experienced at the Council and apply it to the local church.

"Bishop Hunthausen's transformation took place after the Council was over," O'Sullivan claimed. "What did it? The charismatic and fine mind and influence of Father Jim Provost."

Provost's brilliance lay in developing a decision-making process for the Priest Senate, the diocesan pastoral council, and other collaborative bodies that was designed around prayer and consensus building. The various groups discarded Robert's Rules of Order in favor of consensus-type statements that gauged the strength of feelings about various concerns and possible solutions. Participants indicated what they thought and how strongly they felt it.

"It seemed to me a great way to hold people together instead of letting an issue tear them apart," Hunthausen said. "It allowed for win-win situations once we knew something was ready for a decision. ...Once we let the process unfold, we were going to come to a conclusion. Thank the Lord."

The process that Provost and Hunthausen pioneered in Helena became a model for a national Parish Leadership Development Program that spread across the country. As a result, Provost was in constant demand as a speaker and consultant.

For his part, Hunthausen was elected in April 1971 at the U.S. bishops' meeting in Detroit as the first chair of the conference's Region 12, which included Alaska, Idaho, Montana, Oregon, and Washington. He was the youngest of all the bishops in the region's eleven dioceses. The regional bishops' group, like the Priest Senate and the parish and diocesan councils, was also a response to the Vatican II call for collegiality and shared responsibility.

Hunthausen took the chairmanship seriously. With Provost's help, he organized annual meetings of the regional bishops with priest, women religious, and lay representatives from their respective dioceses. The Vatican had called for a synod of representative bishops from national bishops' conferences to meet in Rome in the fall of 1971 to discuss two topics: priesthood and justice in the world. Hunthausen wanted to give the Catholics of Region 12 an opportunity to discuss the issues and inform the four U.S. prelates attending the synod. He invited the four synod representatives, the Northwest bishops, and six delegates from each diocese for prayer and discussion at St. Thomas Seminary near Seattle on August 31–September 1, 1971. Altogether three archbishops, ten bishops, sixty priests, twenty nuns, and sixty laypeople attended. It was a historic occasion. Never before had a U.S. body of bishops met openly with clergy, women religious, and lay representatives to talk about important church matters.

"We were somewhat unique," Hunthausen conceded. "The Northwest was seen as moving with the spirit of the Council, trying to discover and understand what shared responsibility meant in all its ramifications."

Only one of the four prelates going to the synod came to this first-ever regional meeting of Northwest Catholics. Coadjutor Archbishop Leo Byrne, of St. Paul, Minnesota, cautioned the participants that while the synod was part of an ongoing process of church renewal, it would not work instant changes. The meeting participants didn't expect instant change, but they did expect action. They urged Byrne and the other three U.S. bishop representatives to argue for married priests, term limits on bishops, better church accountability, and greater decision-making at the local level. They also called for more church attention to vocations, poverty, racism, and environmental degradation.

Some attendees, including more than one bishop, were reluctant meeting participants and were not calling for anything. At one point, Archbishop John J. Ryan of Anchorage rose to object to some matter in the proceedings. Hunthausen, as the meeting chair, suggested to Ryan that the matter be referred to the archdiocesan Pastoral Council in Anchorage. A loud guffaw followed; there was no such council in Anchorage.

The two-day regional meeting concluded with Hunthausen thanking the participants for engaging in open and honest dialogue. Their sessions, he observed, illustrated the readiness and capability of the church in the Northwest to work collegially. The next step, he said, was to find effective ways of sharing that responsibility at all levels of church life.

The Vatican synod on the priesthood and justice proved to be a huge disappointment. A cautious and anxious Pope Paul VI, still reeling from the rejection of his 1968 encyclical on birth control, let the curia set up a process designed to thwart reform and frustrate decision-making. It was the converse of the Provost method: set speeches, repetitive presentations, no dialogue from the floor, little discussion time for serious subjects, poor use of experts and background material, and no way of assigning any weight to what was said.

Nonetheless, the Catholics of Region 12 soldiered on. At their second regional meeting at the University of Portland on March 3–5, 1972, Hunthausen urged the diocesan delegations to be more intentional in including youth and minorities. He led a Helena diocesan group of sixteen who shared in workshop discussions on topics such as farm labor, human life, war, poverty and the agenda at the upcoming national meeting of the U.S. bishops. In April 1973, Hunthausen chaired the Region 12 meeting in Spokane where eighty participants discussed issues related to youth, marriage and family, conscience formation, and communications. The following year, he convened the region's annual meeting at the Providence Sisters novitiate east of Seattle where participants put together a plan that established Catholic Communications Northwest, a public affairs and communications office for sharing the message and witness of the church through radio, television, press and film.

Vatican II's exhortation to involve the church in the joys and sorrows of the modern world was heeded in western Montana. The diocesan Pastoral Council created a Commission on Social Action and Human Development charged with implementing the social justice teaching of the church. The Montana Catholic Conference, representing the state's two bishops, helped convince state lawmakers to reject a 1971 bill that would have legalized abortion. In a joint public statement, Hunthausen and Bishop Schuster challenged Montanans to provide counseling and practical care for women with unwanted pregnancies. The abortion bill was soundly defeated. Two years later, however, the U.S. Supreme Court's *Roe v. Wade* decision recognized a woman's constitutional right to an abortion, thus overturning Montana's prohibition.

In October 1971, the diocese and Carroll College committed themselves to Project Equality, which called for strong affirmative action efforts to employ minorities and protect them from discrimination. In Montana, this meant paying special attention to Native Americans, many of whom are Catholic. In April 1973, Hunthausen and Bishop Topel, along with key priests and other diocesan leaders, attended a special two-day gathering in Spokane where the Indians spoke and the clergy listened. The Indians shared their hopes for self-determination, jobs, schooling, respect, and incorporating Native American ritual within Catholic worship.

"This was a first for Indian people," said Father Joe Obersinner, the Jesuit pastor of St. Ignatius Mission in Montana.

In response to Vatican II's call for Christian unity, Hunthausen reached out to Protestant denominations in western Montana. The pre–Vatican II Church had treated Protestants as lost and "separated brethren" who would find salvation only by coming back to Rome. Consequently, there was some bridge building to do. Slowly trust grew. By Holy Week 1968 the diocese was able to invite Protestants and Catholics to a joint ecumenical service at St. Ann Church in Butte. More than fourteen hundred attended. Hunthausen, who preached the sermon, told them, "It behooves us to realize how great is our agreement and how insignificant are our differences."

Later that year, Hunthausen invited the presiding bishop of the U.S. Episcopal Church to use the spacious St. Helena Cathedral for the installation ceremony of the new Episcopal bishop of Montana. Hunthausen, Bishop Schuster, and a thousand others watched as the Rev. Jackson Gilliam, a married father of three, was consecrated an Episcopal bishop in a Catholic church.

In 1969, the all-Protestant Montana Council of Churches invited Father Provost and John Frankino, the layman who was the diocesan lobbyist, to attend its annual October assembly as "official observers." The door was opening. Three years later Hunthausen and Schuster accepted an invitation from the Protestant denominational executives to join them in a pilgrimage to churches around the state to listen to the common concerns of Montanans. And finally, on October 1, 1973, the Protestant churches dissolved their council and joined with the Catholics in forming a new Montana Association of Churches committed to Christian unity in preaching the Gospel.

Vatican II challenged the Diocese of Helena to speak out on the implications of the nuclear arms race unfolding in its own backyard. Hunthausen endorsed 1969 and 1970 statements by the Priest Senate objecting to the installation of MX anti–ballistic missiles in Montana. The first statement argued that the top priority of the federal government ought to be human needs, not weapons of mass destruction.

"We cannot remain silent when our government is about to embark on a new round in the suicidal arms race," the statement read. The 1970 statement said that squandering money on arms destroys the nation's ability to eradicate the causes of war—hunger, disease, illiteracy, and violation of human rights.

The FBI office in Helena clipped the statements from the newspaper and placed them in a confidential file that agents started keeping on Hunthausen. The case file would later figure in the Reagan administration's effort to portray him as a threat to national security.

Hunthausen's enthusiasm for social justice, ecumenism, and church reform was not shared by some of his flock, including a fair number of diocesan priests, most of them older and established in their ways. They simply felt that too much was changing too fast and they weren't buying it.

Msgr. Michael English, the Irish-born pastor of St. Patrick's in Butte and one of the most influential priests in the diocese, absolutely refused to make the worship changes specified by the Council. Opinionated, cantankerous, and obstinate, English regarded St. Patrick's as his personal fiefdom. He insisted on keeping Masses on standard time even after Montana embraced daylight savings time.

"No bishop will take me out of here over my dead body," he told Hunthausen.

Despite the Council mandate, English persisted in saying Mass at the altar with his back to the congregation.

"I've been standing with my ass to the people all these years and I'm not going to turn around now," he told his Irish priest pals.

Hunthausen bided his time. When English died in October 1967, he presided at the funeral Mass in Butte. English's corpse lay before him in a coffin at the foot of the altar. Hunthausen celebrated the Mass facing the coffin and the congregation, the first time it had ever happened at St. Patrick's.

At the cathedral in Helena, Msgr. Edward Gilmore played a cat-and-mouse game with Hunthausen on liturgical form. A genial, hardworking, well-regarded pastor, the monsignor was in his seventies and stuck in his ways. He agreeably said yes but did as he pleased. At

Hunthausen's request, Gilmore hired an architect who designed and built an altar facing the congregation. But it was constructed as a temporary altar, easily dismantled and reassembled as needed.

"Gilmore put it out whenever the bishop was coming," recalled Father Joe Oblinger, Hunthausen's chancellor at the time. "Then it would disappear afterward."

When Msgr. English died, Hunthausen sent Gilmore to St. Patrick's in Butte, where the altar now faced the people, and installed Oblinger, his trusted lieutenant, at the cathedral.

Oblinger himself initially had issues with Hunthausen. "There was a lot of tension between us because he was changing a lot of things," said Oblinger, who had also been chancellor under Bishop Gilmore. "He moved out of the bishop's house and turned it over to the nuns. He just made his mind up and did it. And then some of the early appointments I didn't like."

Nonetheless, Oblinger appreciated Hunthausen's openness and his willingness to listen and take action. "You could fight with him and argue with him and it didn't make any difference in terms of our relationship," he said.

Hunthausen seemed to have the capacity to listen forever.

Father Emmett O'Neill, who went into parish work after teaching political science at Carroll College, said Hunthausen's listening skills won people over, even those hard set against him.

"He sat down one to one with somebody, listened very openly to what was going on in their life, and then said what he needed to say," O'Neill said. "Even the conservatives would feel pretty good after having talked to him."

Hunthausen preferred face-to-face conversation to phone calls and letters, especially when dealing with priests. He would get in his car and drive two hundred miles to talk to a troubled priest in a small parish in some forlorn Montana town. He passed the time enroute listening to audiocassette tapes on spiritualty, personal psychology, and theology. He might not get home till one in the morning even though he had to say the 6 AM Mass.

The bishop was equally willing to meet with laypeople concerned about the changes in the church. Typically, he'd respond to a letter of complaint with an invitation to meet and talk at the parish office. In April 1970, for example, he wrote Mrs. A. B. Chenovick of Helena inviting her to call him to arrange a visit to discuss the liturgical changes that "are upsetting and disturbing to you."

Such meetings were not always pleasant. Father O'Sullivan recalled seeing Hunthausen assailed in the lobby of an Anaconda hotel where the Diocesan Council of Catholic Women was holding its convention.

"An exceedingly neurotic and rather vicious lady was standing there and insulting the bishop, not giving him a chance to talk at all," O'Sullivan said. "He looks at her, not getting angry, not looking hurt, nothing at all. It was remarkable."

The Helena diocese, with its Irish priests and Montana's cowboy culture, had a reputation for hard drinking. A story went around that Archbishop Vagnozzi, the papal delegate to the United States, had warned Hunthausen to keep priests away from the booze. Hunthausen, who enjoyed an occasional drink himself, wanted priests to get together for mutual support. If that occurred around after-dinner drinks, so be it. Nonetheless, he was generally quick to address excessive drinking and alcoholism. Sometimes a priest disappeared from the diocese so suddenly that the others would ask, "Was the problem punch or Judy?"

Hunthausen sent several priests away for treatment, typically to the Guest House in Lake Orion, Michigan, which specialized in treating alcoholic clerics. Priests in recovery joked that the house had a room with the bishop's portrait on the wall because someone from western Montana was always there. Father Tom Haffey, one of those recovering alcoholics, credited Hunthausen with helping him achieve sobriety.

The bishop's response to clerical sex abuse was less sure. He and Oblinger, the chancellor, shared the limited understanding of pedophilia characteristic of the time. They thought of child molestation as a grave moral weakness that could be resolved with confession and treatment. Often they figured the root of an abuser's problem was alcohol. Dry them out, they reasoned, and they won't act out sexually. They later realized how wrong they were. So did the diocese, which in January 2014 filed for bankruptcy protection as part of a $15 million settlement of lawsuits involving priests who had sexually abused an alleged 362 children over five decades.

The most preoccupying issue for Hunthausen during his thirteen years as bishop of Helena was not clergy sexual abuse, nor even creating a post–Vatican II church. It was closing Catholic schools. The closures, which shuttered most of the parochial schools in western Montana, were especially disconcerting because they were so unexpected and happened so fast.

"That whole dream [of Catholic education] got crushed and had to be reversed," recalled Father Jack Hunthausen, the bishop's brother and principal of the new—and soon doomed—Helena Central Catholic High School. "I know Dutch went through all kinds of agonizing times over that."

Father William Greytak, the Carroll College history professor and Hunthausen confidante, served on the special panel that ultimately recommended closure of most of the schools. "If anything caused Dutch problems with priests and people," Greytak said, "it was the closing of the schools. People never ever forgave him for that."

When Hunthausen succeeded Bishop Gilmore, he figured that the diocese would continue to serve a booming Catholic population by building yet more churches and schools. In 1964, the diocese reported a record enrollment of 9,325 students in twenty-four parish elementary schools and eight Catholic high schools. One out of every seven of the sixty-eight thousand Catholics registered in the diocese were enrolled in a Catholic school, a very high participation rate.

The schools offered a Catholic education at very little cost, making them accessible to virtually all Catholic families. The religious order women who taught in the schools worked for little pay and, as long as there were plenty of them, tuition was modest. In 1958, women religious comprised 80 percent of the Catholic schoolteachers in the Helena diocese. Ten years later, they occupied less than half the teaching posts and their numbers continued to fall.

The loss of teaching sisters was a national phenomenon. For decades Dominican, Mercy, Benedictine, Ursuline, Franciscan, and other orders of sisters had filled most of the teaching positions in parochial schools. Vatican II, however, with its talk of "shared responsibility" and "outreach to the world" opened up the possibility of nuns taking on many other tasks. They did. They left the classroom in droves to become nurses, doctors, missionaries, social workers, and parish staff members. And, in the social tumult of the 1960s, many simply left religious life altogether.

The departure of the sisters drove up tuition costs, priced out most Catholic families, and left empty desks in newly built classrooms. The schools could no longer pay for themselves. The handwriting was on the wall even as Father John J. McCoy, the diocesan school superintendent in Helena, announced the record enrollment of 1964.

"Within ten years, the cost of education will double," he warned readers of the *Register*.

He was wrong. Within ten years, education costs were so prohibitive that most Catholic schools in western Montana were closed.

Virtually everyone, including Hunthausen, was amazed at how quickly the schools became unsustainable. They were compelled to hire more lay educators to replace the nuns and somehow find the revenue to pay them fair wages. A lay teacher, at a cost of about $10,000 a year, was nearly seven times more expensive than a nun. Meanwhile, the new schools were carrying heavy construction debt.

"At first, we thought we could amortize the debt in eight years, then it was fifteen, and then it was thirty," Hunthausen recalled. "And then we weren't even able to pay the interest on the debt. The obvious was staring us in the face. What had seemed so wonderful five or six years earlier had all fallen apart. We couldn't support ourselves. We had to do something."

The diocese's biggest battles over Catholic education occurred in its most Catholic towns: Helena, Butte, and Anaconda. In all three, making the decision to consolidate or close schools was a contentious and agonizing process. But, in the end, it wasn't Hunthausen's decision to close the schools; it was the Catholic community's.

In February 1967, a mere year after the grand opening of Helena Central Catholic, Hunthausen met with school leadership, those pastors with parish schools, and the Priest Senate. He told them that with the rapidly rising costs, he did not see a future for most of the Catholic schools in the diocese. To pay costs, school tuitions would have to be set so high that only the wealthy could afford a Catholic education. We must find other ways to instill the Catholic faith and preach the Gospel, he said.

Over the coming months and years, parish councils in towns that had Catholic schools agonized over Catholic education. Could they afford to keep their school? Was maintaining a school hurting other parish programs and services? Without a school, how could they best teach their children the Catholic faith? What was the Gospel calling them to do?

At a meeting at Carroll College on October 2, 1968, Bishop Hunthausen called for development of a five-year education plan for the diocese. Father McCoy pleaded for a professional study that would look at the possibility of central financing for all Catholic schools in the diocese. Others said the study would only find what they already knew: the schools were unaffordable. Msgr. Gilmore, dean of the clergy in Butte, complained that the city's nine parishes were impoverishing themselves trying to pay for their respective grade schools while covering a growing deficit at the city's two Catholic high schools.

Two months later, a group of influential Catholics formed the Montana Association of Private Schools with the sole purpose of seeking state funding for private education. They pointed out that 12 percent of Montana's school-age children were in private schools (virtually all of them Catholic schools). If these schools were forced to close and their students thrust into the public system, the group argued, it would cost the state three times as much as assisting the existing private schools. The following month, Hunthausen and Bishop

Schuster created the Montana Catholic Conference whose purpose was "to serve the common good of the people of Montana" by coordinating the public efforts of the state's two Catholic dioceses. The first big task was to persuade the state legislature to support private education.

The effort failed. In February 1969, the Montana House defeated a bill to provide aid to private schools by a vote of 60 to 43. In the wake of the vote, Hunthausen told an assembly of diocesan priests that Catholic parents—not the clergy—would decide the school issue.

"The people will make the final decision," he said, "but the people must get the facts."

Hunthausen laid out the facts. The modest $80 a year per student that parishes and high schools typically charged for tuition didn't come close to covering actual costs. Moreover, the sisters continued to depart.

The diocese had tried to rescue Catholic schools through fundraising efforts. In 1965, Hunthausen established a "sacrificial giving plan" in which Catholics were encouraged to tithe 10 percent of their income (5 percent for the parish and diocese; 5 percent for charities). The plan replaced a number of special diocesan collections and assessments and was meant to simplify giving to the church. It fell significantly short, however, collecting in its first year less than half the income that the diocese had realized under the old system. Consequently, there was even less money for schools.

In the 1968 campaign, laypeople spoke at Sunday Masses explaining the financial plight of the schools and urging a renewed commitment to sacrificial giving. Every parishioner received a mailing outlining likely school cutbacks if funds were not forthcoming.

"Every year we made an appeal to people to support the parishes because the parishes have to support the schools," said Father Oblinger, Hunthausen's first chancellor. "But we got no response, no response. So we told them: We cannot keep this system going."

Unable to raise sufficient funds at home, Hunthausen pursued connections with wealthy people outside the diocese in hopes of raising money for the schools as well as for Carroll College. He managed to get an introduction to Benjamin H. Swig, a Jewish philanthropist whose multi-million dollar real estate holdings included the Fairmont Hotel in San Francisco and multiple properties in Boston and New York. Swig, who lived in a penthouse suite at the Fairmont, supported Catholic causes and institutions and was twice knighted by the Vatican for his humanitarian work.

Swig took a particular interest in Carroll and offered to match whatever the school could raise in contributions from its alumni. One autumn day, Hunthausen got a phone call from the development officer at the Archdiocese of San Francisco who urged him to fly to California for a fundraising opportunity with Swig and other philanthropists. Reluctantly, Hunthausen agreed to go. He had little stomach for soliciting the rich.

He flew to Los Angeles where Swig and California Governor Edmund "Pat" Brown, a Catholic, met him at the airport. The threesome then drove to the Los Angeles Coliseum to watch the Notre Dame–USC football game. USC, led by O. J. Simpson, was undefeated; Notre Dame, its archrival, was 7-2. The Fighting Irish had a two-touchdown lead at halftime, but Swig and Hunthausen had to leave in order to arrive in Palm Springs for a fundraising dinner that evening. After they left, USC roared back, Notre Dame missed two field goals, and the 1968 matchup ended in a 21-21 tie.

Gov. Brown playfully wrote Hunthausen afterward, "If you had stayed, I am sure the faithful would have won, but you felt it necessary to leave in order to gather the coin of the realm."

There was not much coin to gather however. Swig sat next to Hunthausen at dinner in Palm Springs and surveyed the moneyed crowd at the tables around them. He was not impressed. Leaning toward the bishop, he whispered, "They're all a bunch of deadbeats. Let's get out of here; they won't give you a dime."

Swig wrote Hunthausen the first of several generous checks for Carroll College and diocesan schools. He visited Helena in 1970 to lunch with Catholic benefactors at the Montana Club. But he was disappointed that they were unwilling or unable to match his contributions.

"If they're not interested," he wrote Hunthausen afterward, "how can they expect a person of another faith from miles away to be interested?"

By early 1969, the Catholic schools in Butte, Helena, and Anaconda were all in dire financial straits, running large deficits that could not be covered by the parishes. When Hunthausen told an auditorium full of parents at Boys Central in Butte that the diocese was abandoning plans to build a new high school on land purchased just four years earlier, he was shouted down.

But over the course of many hours of deliberation, diocesan school officials, school board members, parish council leaders, and pastors grudgingly decided to close most of Butte's Catholic schools and consolidate the students into four buildings. The boys' and girls' high schools were combined in their two existing buildings. Two parish schools were kept open for seventh and eight graders. But primary school education in Butte—from first through sixth grade—ended altogether.

At one point, when the various parishes were caucusing, it looked as if the Butte consolidation plan might unravel because St. Patrick's, the most affluent parish, was determined to keep its grade school open. Hunthausen told the parish leadership that they were free to make that choice but it would undermine the whole consolidation plan.

"We can't do it unless we do it together," he told them. The St. Patrick's group re-caucused, returned, and said they'd go along with the master plan.

"It was marvelous," Hunthausen said, "as painful as it was."

In Helena, deliberations proceeded at parish and community levels much as they had in Butte. In March 1969, an ad hoc committee representing parish councils, pastors, and school board members recommended closing all the city's Catholic schools, including the new high school the diocese had opened just three years earlier. Catholic schooling in Helena—the seat of the diocese and the capital of the state—would end with the 1969 school year. The recommendation surprised the two Hunthausen brothers and it shocked Oblinger, now vicar general, all of whom thought the committee would want to keep the high school open. "Instead we dumped a thousand students on the public schools," Oblinger said.

Hunthausen commended "the hard work and frank courage" of the committee's recommendation. "I concur in their decision," he told the diocesan paper, "as genuinely providing for what, in the long run, will be best for all citizens of Helena." Two months later, the diocese concluded the sale of Helena Central Catholic High School to the public school district for $1.5 million. The district reopened it as Capitol High.

The hardest-fought battle to save Catholic schooling occurred in Anaconda, Hunthausen's hometown. After the state legislature rejected public aid to private schools, Anaconda voters passed a levy that allowed the public school district to hire eight full-time teachers who would be assigned to teach secular subjects at the city's Catholic high school. The county assistant district attorney described the measure as "aid to the student, not to the church." But opponents obtained a restraining order and filed suit with the Montana State Supreme Court, which ultimately ruled against the plan.

By January 1972, Anaconda's Catholic high school and three parochial schools were drowning in debt. Hunthausen, McCoy, and the diocesan business manager met with pastors and parish council leaders to discuss consolidation and closure proposals. A group of high school students formed an SOS (Save Our Schools) Club and partnered with the Knights of Columbus to ask five hundred people to pledge $200 each toward a school survival fund. The drive collected pledges of $43,000, well short of its $100,000 goal.

Finally, in February 1973, the three Anaconda parish councils conducted a secret vote on whether to close the city's entire Catholic school system. The first ballot resulted in a tie. On a second ballot, the vote for closing prevailed, 32 to 26.

So, on May 23, 1973, under the ornate domed ceiling of the Washoe Theatre in downtown Anaconda, the city's Central Catholic High School conducted its final commencement exercises. The principal, Father Bill Stanaway, gave the graduation address. He compared the people of Anaconda to Christ's apostles gathered in the upper room after Jesus has ascended into heaven. The bewildered apostles didn't know what to do.

"They were afraid," Stanaway said. "They were afraid until the Spirit came and moved them to go out and share themselves to help build the dream Jesus had."

The Catholic schools are gone, the principal said, but the people and their faith will carry on. The diocese sold Central Catholic High School to the public school district. And the three Anaconda parishes closed their grade schools forever, including St. Paul's, where Bishop Hunthausen had begun his formal Catholic education forty-six years earlier.

Pope John XXIII had challenged the churches of rich nations to share 10 percent of their resources, including personnel, with the churches of poor nations. Hunthausen responded by inviting priests and laypeople from his diocese to do mission work in the Diocese of Solola, Guatemala. Over the years, the Helena diocese sent priest volunteers along with women religious and laypeople with nursing, teaching, and other skills.

Hunthausen, who previously had never been to a developing country, faithfully visited his mission team every spring. He celebrated Mass in thatched huts, his English translated first into Spanish and then into K'iche, the indigenous tongue, in remote villages reached by red dirt roads winding into the green mountains around Lake Atitlan or descending abruptly into the steamy subtropical forest toward the Pacific Coast. Under the cloak of Catholicism, native beliefs thrived.

Mostly, Hunthausen experienced culture shock. He felt he had stepped back three centuries in time to witness utter poverty. Yet he was touched by the kindness and generosity of the native people, stoic descendants of the Mayans.

"I would come into a little village and they would give me a gift. Often it would be a bottle of pop, a Coke, or strawberry soda," he recalled, noting that the cost of the imported pop was equivalent to almost a day's wages. "I'd find myself incapable of drinking it. I'd take a sip or two, say thanks, and then I'd give it to the kids."

The natives, poor, semi-literate, and divided by dialect and subculture, were especially vulnerable to exploitation. Hunthausen admired the courage of the mission volunteers who put themselves at risk by confronting unscrupulous plantation owners or advocating for indigenous rights in local courts. They helped their parishioners build water projects, establish land claims, and receive fair prices for coffee and bananas. It was dangerous work. One diocesan priest found his name on a murder-for-hire "hit list."

Following his 1974 visit, Hunthausen sent a letter to Sheila McShane, a nurse and diocesan volunteer who had put her life in peril by caring for wounded rebels. "It is not in me to do what you people are doing," he wrote. "I console myself with the thought that it's because God has not called me to such work. [But] in my more honest moments, I admit my inability to give as completely as you have."

Six years later when Hunthausen was archbishop of Seattle, Father Pete Byrne, a Maryknoll missioner and childhood friend, invited him and his sister, Edna, to experience mission work in Peru. With Byrne as their tour guide, the Hunthausens saw hungry children rummaging through burning trash piles in the slums of Lima and women in skirts and bowler hats trying to coax potatoes from the frozen ground of the Peruvian altiplano. In the Andes, Hunthausen was so overcome with the nausea, chills, and migraine pain of altitude sickness that he thought he was going to die.

At a retreat house near Lima, they talked with Peruvian church intellectuals including Gustavo Gutiérrez, the father of liberation theology. Hunthausen joined Byrne for several days at his parish in Ciudad de Dios, a sprawling slum whose newest residents lived in thatch and cardboard huts on barren hillsides. They visited parishioners' homes and concelebrated the 7 AM Mass. After church one morning, a little boy latched on to Hunthausen's leg and wouldn't let go. So he walked about with the boy attached.

Upon his return from mission trips, Hunthausen gave talks and showed slides, trying to convey the overpowering reality of what he had seen and experienced.

"But words and pictures don't do it," he said. "You have to walk among them. You've got to become one of them. That's what Jesus did."

Hunthausen took particular interest in his brother priests—so much so that the U.S. bishops' conference named him in 1974 to chair a sub-committee on priesthood. The committee's purpose was to reaffirm priesthood at a time when priests were experiencing significant change, doubt, and loneliness, and many were leaving. The reforming spirit of Vatican II challenged many of the traditional premises of priesthood: Why was it limited to men? Why were priests required to be celibate? Why were priests expected to make a lifelong commitment? Why? Why? Why?

Hunthausen ordained 54 men to priesthood during his years as bishop of Helena. But losses to death, marriage, and disillusion kept the total number of priests in the diocese flat at about 155. The departure of many good priests, usually because they wanted to marry, pained the bishop.

"I've never seen such suffering as goes on in the lives of those who find themselves in this struggle," Hunthausen said. "It hurt them. It hurt the whole presbyterate. And it hurt me. Still does."

Hunthausen made sure the diocese helped departing priests by providing a severance payment, insurance coverage, and pension rights. And, if they were willing, he saw them through the Vatican's process of "laicization," a lengthy, cumbersome procedure in which priests are returned to a lay state.

"Many of these guys remained friends, some of my best friends," he said.

In a case that would cost Hunthausen dearly, one of the diocese's more talented priests wanted to marry yet continue to be a priest. Father Michael Miles was co-pastor at Resurrection Parish in Bozeman where he also served as chaplain of the Newman Center at Montana State University. There he met and fell in love with Joan Doyle, an MSU psychology professor.

Miles was convinced that Vatican II reform and the loss of so many priests to marriage would cause Rome to abandon its requirement of priestly celibacy. After all, Eastern-rite Catholic priests could marry and the church recognized married Anglican priests who converted to Catholicism. Clearly, Miles argued, the ministerial life of a priest could include a spouse and children as it did for other Christian faiths.

Persuasive and assertive, Miles visited Hunthausen's small apartment above the chancery one evening to tell the bishop about his two loves—Joan Doyle and the priesthood. He wanted to keep both. He said loving Joan was making him a better priest. Taken aback, Hunthausen conceded that celibate life was difficult but reminded Miles of the promise he had made at ordination several years earlier.

Hunthausen thought highly of Miles and knew him well. They had skied, hiked, and ridden horseback through the Rockies together. More importantly, he was an effective, well-regarded pastor, especially popular among students and parishioners in Bozeman.

"It would delight me if you could stay, Mike," Hunthausen told him. "But there's no way. You know the law of the church as well as I do. The Holy Father is especially adamant on this point."

Miles told Hunthausen about a married Catholic priest he'd recently met in Holland who had managed to exercise much of his priestly ministry by taking advantage of loopholes in church law. Hunthausen looked dubious. He told Miles that he would have Father Provost research it. Provost did. The canon lawyer didn't like the idea but he told Hunthausen that church law on priests dispensed from their vows appeared vague enough, especially in exceptional circumstances, to allow the bishop some latitude.

Typically, a priest who left ministry to get married left town and quietly disappeared in disgrace and disapprobation. Out of sight, out of mind. Hunthausen believed this was cruel to the priest, to the partner he wed, and to the parish he left behind. As bishop, one of his obligations was to avoid creating scandal in the church. Surely, he reasoned, forcing a defrocked priest to abandon family, friends, and community was more scandalous than allowing him to play some continuing role in the parish. Vatican II entitled a layperson to take on several ministerial roles including speaking from the pulpit, distributing communion, pastoral counseling, and, in emergencies, even performing the sacraments of baptism and the last rites. Why shouldn't a former priest have all the rights of a layman?

Hunthausen mulled over Miles's request. He knew that Miles was a vociferous advocate of married priesthood. Once he married Joan, his presence at the altar could give the impression that the church accepted married priests. Father Con Kelly, the co-pastor at Resurrection Parish, further complicated the matter because of his own enthusiastic support for Miles and a married priesthood. Hunthausen asked himself: What will parishioners think? How will the priests of the diocese react? What will Rome say? And what, in good conscience, is the right thing to do?

Hunthausen took the matter to the priest personnel board, which unanimously recommended that Miles be allowed to stay on the parish staff. Admittedly, two board members had deep reservations but were willing to acquiesce to the bishop's judgment.

Hunthausen insisted that Miles complete the laicization process before he would consider what pastoral duties he might be permitted to do at Resurrection. Miles agreed and was eventually returned to a lay state. He married Joan Doyle in a wedding ceremony before two hundred people at the Newman Center in Bozeman and continued on the parish staff at Resurrection.

But he went beyond the role of an active layman. He preached; he wore the priestly alb and stole; he participated in the consecration of the Eucharist. Parishioners continued to call him "Father" and treat him as the co-pastor. He claimed that Hunthausen had given him de facto permission to function as a married priest. Several years later, he told his story in a paperback potboiler titled *Love Is Always*. The book cover, which depicts a handsome man in a Roman collar about to kiss an attractive woman, describes the tale inside as "a true story of a man and woman's challenge to Catholicism's forbidden world of the married priesthood."

By the time the book was published in 1986, Hunthausen's successor had removed Miles from all ministry—priestly or lay—in the Diocese of Helena.

Hunthausen remained friends with Miles and continued to talk with him over the years. He believed his decision to allow the married Miles to remain on the parish staff was correct as long as Miles functioned as a layman and not a priest. Whether Miles did or not was a matter of some debate.

Father O'Sullivan, a keen observer of diocesan politics, considered Miles duplicitous. "He caused a great deal of grief for Dutch," he said.

Father Oblinger cited the Miles case as an example of Hunthausen's willingness to give people the freedom to discover God's will for them.

"I saw Bishop Hunthausen as having that classic masculine virtue of being venturesome, of being willing to take a risk," Oblinger said. "He would let people try things out. If they crashed around him, he would help them out. But he was willing to risk it. Ultimately, that virtue would cost him. He would have to pay for taking that risk."

Hunthausen was particularly venturesome in the great outdoors. He loved skiing, fishing, and camping in Montana's mountain wilderness. In the winter, he and a group of priests went skiing on Thursdays at Bridger Bowl north of Bozeman where the runs dropped twenty-seven hundred feet through chutes and gullies and over moguls. They'd discuss business while riding the chair lifts.

"We called it a holy day of obligation," joked Father Emmett Kelly, one of the ski crowd. "Sometimes there'd be a many as a dozen of us."

Other times they'd drive up to Whitefish and ski at Big Mountain. One time there was a half dozen of them flying down the slope when a young priest named Charlie teetered sideways and crashed hard. A hip, independent fellow, Charlie had grown a full, lush mustache, a facial adornment that didn't impress the bishop. He fell with such force that he lost his poles, skis, glasses, mittens, stocking cap, and pride.

Describing his spectacular fall afterward, Hunthausen said, "Charlie lost everything but his mustache."

In the warmer months, Hunthausen scheduled appointments with John Frankino, the state Catholic conference director, and diocesan department heads at the pro shop or the ninth green at the Meadows Golf Course in Helena. They'd deal with diocesan matters while teeing off.

Soon after being named bishop, Hunthausen instituted an annual pilgrimage to St. Mary's Peak, named by Father Pierre Jean DeSmet, the pioneer Jesuit missionary who brought Christianity to Montana. On an August Sunday, scores of Catholics, ranging in age from seven months to seventy years, would set out on the 4.5-mile hiking trail to the top of the 9,335-foot mountain. Along the way, they recited the rosary. At the summit, with its stunning view of the entire Bitterroot Valley, Hunthausen celebrated Mass, using a large stone boulder as the altar. Afterward, the Missoula Knights of Columbus hosted a picnic at the Bass Creek campground on the valley floor.

The wilderness—that virtually untouched splendor of God's creation —gave Hunthausen time for contemplation, reflection, and unhurried conversation with family and friends. Many of those friends were priests and bishops, who carried the burden of their office along with the loneliness of celibate life.

For several summers, Hunthausen organized weeklong horse packing trips into northern Montana's Bob Marshall Wilderness, a roadless area that was home to moose, mountain goats, wolves, elk, and the largest grizzly bear population outside of Alaska. Riding horses up steep mountain trails was not for lightweights. While planning a July 1969 trip, Hunthausen wrote the three bishops going with him that "I will need your rugged individualism to keep us going." He made arrangements through a wrangler from Whitefish named Pat Timmons, a crotchety old mountain man who provided the pack train of horses, the food, and a cook, usually his son. The bishops brought their own sleeping bags, outdoor gear, and fishing poles as well as chalices, wine, and altar bread to celebrate morning Mass together.

Once on the trail, they had to ride their mounts up some dicey inclines and ford some heavy streams, many of them running high and full with snowmelt. Chuckling, Hunthausen recalled Timmons's advice,

"If you slip off the horse in the middle of the river, grab onto its tail. Horses know how to swim."

For one of their trips, the old wrangler assembled a group of horses that were not all his and, consequently, not acquainted with each other. The steeds reared, bucked, and kicked at each other whenever the pack team halted. The group reached a large meadow alongside a river where they planned to fish and camp for a few days. Timmons tethered his horses in a small grove of trees near the campsite and cut loose the borrowed ones to roam and graze. Then, after a time, he tied up the borrowed horses and let his steeds run free. For a while, it worked. But then one of the loose group got into the tethered horses and got kicked so hard that the blow shattered its hind leg.

With no means to mend the leg or transport the injured horse, Timmons told the astounded bishops that he would have to kill the animal and then burn it. It was too big to bury in the rocky ground. If they didn't dispose of the injured horse, they could expect grizzlies in their camp.

"None of us had the heart for helping him," Hunthausen recalled. "We went off in the woods where we could hear the shots. It was so sad. That horse was the most beautiful one of the lot."

While the bishops were off in the forest, Timmons and the other wrangler built a gigantic bonfire. They dismembered the horse with an axe and flung its head, limbs, and trunk into the flames. They stoked the fire with dry wood, making it as hot as possible. Eventually it incinerated the remains of the horse, leaving only brittle white bones and a lingering smell of burnt leather.

In early 1975, Hunthausen received an official letter from Rome that Pope Paul VI wished to appoint him archbishop of Seattle. The Vatican's apostolic delegate to the United States, Archbishop Jean Jadot, asked Hunthausen to give the invitation prayerful reflection and reply as soon as he felt confident in his answer. As he had done when named bishop of Helena thirteen years earlier, Hunthausen drove to Spokane to consult with Bishop Topel, his mentor.

"In this instance," Hunthausen explained, "I felt the obligation to re-discern, re-examine, and wonder what is it that is making this all happen."

One thing that was making it happen was Jadot, the Belgian-born apostolic delegate, who had a Vatican II vision of the church very different from that of earlier delegates from Rome. Jadot had served as a pastor in Belgium and then as a chaplain to Belgian troops in the Congo. He later directed the Belgian office of Propagation of the Faith, which took him to missionary lands around the globe. In that role, he caught the attention of Cardinal Joseph Suenens, the influential Council reformer and confidante of Paul VI. On the advice of Suenens, Paul named Jadot apostolic delegate to the United States in 1973.

Paul told Jadot that too many American bishops were business types, political wheeler-dealers rather than pastors. He wanted bishops who were healers and bridge-builders, modest, unassuming men who modeled Christian virtues. He expected Jadot to find those men.

Jadot did not disappoint. During his seven years as the Vatican's delegate to the United States, the bald, stooped, chain-smoking Belgian transformed the American episcopacy through his nomination of 103 new bishops and assignment of fifteen archbishops. He chose and promoted men—the so-called "Jadot boys"—committed to the vision of Vatican II. Speaking at the U.S. bishops' national meeting in 1976, he criticized the American church for its failure to embrace diversity, its lack of creativity in developing new models of parish life, and its seeming inability to address the priest shortage and the role of women in the church. Some of the prelates, including cardinals with strong connections to the curia, were furious at Jadot's remarks. Rome received so many letters of complaint that Jadot offered to resign. But Paul VI insisted he continue.

After Paul died in 1978, several U.S. cardinals began undermining Jadot with the new pope, John Paul II. In 1980, John Paul recalled Jadot to Rome, relegating him to an unimportant office in the Vatican Secretariat of Non-Christians where Jadot languished until his retirement four years later. Unlike his predecessors and successors, Jadot was never named a cardinal. He returned to Belgium, where he died in 2009 at the age of ninety-nine.

In selecting nominees, Jadot sent a questionnaire to bishops, priests, women religious, lay leaders, and others regarding prospective candidates. The questionnaire inquired about the candidate's health, character, temperament, judgment, Christian virtues, behavior, knowledge, cultural sensitivity, orthodoxy, fidelity to church teaching, pastoral fitness, leadership qualities, administrative skills, and public esteem. (This wide consultation process ended with John Paul II.)

In 1974, as Seattle Archbishop Thomas A. Connolly approached the mandatory retirement age of seventy-five, the priests of the Seattle Archdiocese submitted a profile of the sort of archbishop they would like next. They asked for a man of deep spirituality, sensitive to social concerns, committed to decentralized, democratic management, and able to enliven the church community with a fresh spirit of love and caring.

Jadot, who visited Seattle and met with the priests, took this information along with what he had gleaned from questionnaires and personal conversations and submitted three nominees for the pope's consideration. He also indicated whom he preferred—Hunthausen. Paul VI accepted Jadot's recommendation and asked Hunthausen to be archbishop for the church in western Washington.

Even after the prayer time with Bishop Topel, Hunthausen remained hesitant and unsure. He had little experience of big cities and diverse communities and was reluctant to leave his family and friends in Montana.

"Lord, it doesn't make sense to me," he decided. "But if this is where I am being led by the Spirit, I will go and do my best. That is all I can do."

Hunthausen told Jadot that he would honor the pope's request. But he needed to tell his mother before the news was made public. On the February 1975 day of the announcement, Hunthausen phoned her in Helena at five in the morning.

After apologizing for calling so early, he told her, "Ma, I'm fine. Don't worry. But somebody is likely to tell you and I want you to hear it from me first. I'm being sent to Seattle."

There was a long pause on the phone line. Then Edna Hunthausen told her first-born child, "Oh, dear, I don't want that."

"Ma," Hunthausen replied. "I don't either."

There was another long pause. "Well, okay," she said. "We'll pray about it."

That brief conversation with his mother haunted Hunthausen the rest of his life. She was eighty-one years old and lived happily in an apartment down the hall from her oldest son, the bishop. Now that would end. She accepted her fate, and when her son moved to Seattle she returned to Anaconda, living her final years in a senior citizen home where her children and grandchildren visited regularly. She died in 1983.

After the heart-wrenching phone conversation with his mother, Hunthausen returned to St. Paul's Church in Anaconda where he was leading a mission retreat. He celebrated the morning Mass. The congregation had just received communion and was kneeling in the pews in silent prayer when a huge banner, posted on the sanctuary wall to promote the mission, suddenly came undone and fluttered down before them. The banner read: "The Gospel of Our Lord Jesus Christ Invites You. RSVP."

Startled, Hunthausen watched as the banner gently fell from the wall.

"I wasn't asking for a sign," he said. "But if I had been, there it was."

ARCHBISHOP OF SEATTLE

People will forget what you said, people will forget what you did,
but people will never forget how you made them feel.
—Maya Angelou

A keen observer attending the installation ceremony for the newly appointed Catholic archbishop of Seattle on the chilly Thursday evening
of May 22, 1975, quickly sensed a break with the past. The venue,
the attendees, the symbols, and the words were different. Clearly
Raymond G. Hunthausen was a new kind of church leader with a vision of a new kind of church.

Rather than a limited, by invitation-only ceremony at St. James
Cathedral, the usual locale for such an event, this was a "people's celebration" at the Seattle Center Arena, a sports pavilion. Anybody
who walked in the arena door was welcome. To be sure, there was
the honor roll of church and public dignitaries. On the church side
were Archbishop Jean Jadot, the Vatican's apostolic delegate, Cardinal Timothy Manning of Los Angeles, ten other Catholic archbishops
and bishops, four hundred priests, and three abbots. And on the civic
side were the county executive, the mayor of Seattle, the lieutenant
governor, state legislators, and city council members. There were also
Protestant and Jewish leaders. And there were more than five thousand everyday people, including Hunthausen's mother, his siblings,
their spouses and their children.

An especially keen observer noticed the difference in ecclesial
symbols. Hunthausen wore a simple white alb and a white cloth miter
without adornment. His episcopal ring, which Catholics traditionally
kiss out of respect for the office, was a plain gold band lacking the
bejeweled amethyst stone typical of bishops. His crosier, the shep-
herd's staff symbolizing his position and authority, was a smooth mahogany stick curved at the top, void of decoration. His predecessor's
crosier, richly ornamented in intricate gold and silver, was gently
placed aside.

Finally there were the words. Calm, smiling, and surprised by the spontaneous outpouring of applause, Hunthausen began his address with a long litany of acknowledgments to the church leaders and public officials seated before him. When he got through all the names and titles, he paused, grinned, and quietly said, "Good evening." The crowd responded with laughter and more applause. He added, "I've been wanting to say that for some time."

In his brief speech, Hunthausen emphasized what he saw as his primary role as archbishop: to share responsibility with the "People of God" in building the kingdom of God. He confessed his apprehensions and his feelings of inadequacy.

At times, he said, "I feel not so much like a burning bush but like a cold radiator. I know God is there, but my efforts seem to be wasted."

He asked the faithful of western Washington to join with him in the journey ahead. Quoting Augustine, he said, "What I am for you terrifies me; what I am with you consoles me."

At receptions before and after the ceremony, Hunthausen drifted through the crowd, shaking hands and patting backs. There was no ring kissing. His smiles and laughter hid the low-level anxiety that gnawed at him. He felt woefully unprepared for the big city, the bright lights, and the high expectations ahead.

"In my innocence, you know, it was the beginning of something that I didn't have the foggiest idea of what it would be," he recalled years afterward.

Western Washington was very unlike western Montana in so many ways—the weather, the geography, the industry, the people, the culture, and the church. In fact, it was mostly unchurched. Only 40 percent of state residents, four-fifths of whom lived in Hunthausen's new territory, said they belonged to a church. A quarter of the state's residents reported no religious belief whatsoever, the highest rate of unbelief in the nation. Washington's peculiar history of immigrants, radicals, and restless entrepreneurs fleeing more traditional, churched communities back East was said to account for it.

Hunthausen was the sixth bishop, and second archbishop, to govern the Catholic Church in western Washington. Catholicism first came to the Pacific Northwest in the form of French-Canadian missionary priests who arrived in 1838 with the Hudson's Bay Company and catechized the native peoples. Father Augustin-Magliore Blanchet, one of those missionaries, was named the first bishop of the region in 1846 and set up his see at Fort Vancouver on the Columbia River. But the Native Americans, soon decimated by disease, all but disappeared, replaced by American and European settlers. Blanchet borrowed recklessly to build churches, schools, orphanages, and hospitals and then recruited religious order priests and nuns to staff them.

When he retired in 1879, the diocese was so stretched for cash that his successor, German-born Bishop Aegidius Junger, stinted on personnel costs by playing his violin at Mass. Bishop Edward John O'Dea succeeded Junger in 1896 and presided over the diocese for the next thirty-six years. Like Blanchet, he established parishes, opened hospitals and religious institutions, and built churches, including St. James Cathedral in Seattle, which in 1907 became both the official see and the name of the diocese.

The Boston-born son of Irish immigrants, O'Dea was piously devout, administratively astute, and politically adept. During the labor strife of the Depression, he defended new immigrants and championed the rights of workers. In 1924, working behind the scenes, he mobilized Catholic businessmen, Protestant clergymen, and civic leaders to work together to defeat an initiative that would have outlawed parochial schools. O'Dea, who died on Christmas night 1932, left his library and his gold snuffbox to St. Edward Seminary, which he had opened the year before.

Bishop Gerald Shaughnessy, a former classics teacher who once coached Hunthausen's mother on the girls' high school basketball team in Anaconda, succeeded him. Shaughnessy had earned a doctorate in theology and worked in the apostolic delegate's office in Washington, DC, before his appointment to Seattle. A stickler for detail and decorum, he put the deeply indebted diocese back on a strong financial footing by consolidating loans and starting a revolving capital fund. He was rigid, haughty, obsessive, and feared.

"He always had a right way," recalled Father William Gallagher, who, as a newly ordained priest, served as Shaughnessy's personal secretary. "The first time he told me to answer the phone, which was sitting right next to him, I picked it up, answered it, and then put it down. He went into a fit. I had put the phone down wrong. It had to be put down so the cord didn't go across the phone."

Shaughnessy lived isolated and often sick in the majestic brick mansion that O'Dea had purchased as the bishop's residence. He kept toys and teddy bears that he intended to give to kids, but he rarely encountered children. He suffered a cerebral hemorrhage in 1946 and died in 1950.

Because of Shaughnessy's illness and limited capacity, Pope Pius XII appointed Thomas A. Connolly in 1948 as coadjutor bishop of Seattle with right of succession. At the time, Connolly was an auxiliary bishop in San Francisco. He was raised in that city, studied at St. Patrick's Seminary in nearby Menlo Park, and was ordained to the priesthood in 1926. For nine years he was pastor at Mission Dolores Church in San Francisco where he personally handed out report cards to the eleven hundred students in the parish school.

Hard working and decisive, Connolly was an impressive figure, tall and regal, his wavy black hair combed straight back. He immediately set to work addressing issues that had languished because of Shaughnessy's illness. He convinced the Vatican to reduce the diocese to just western Washington because he didn't like traveling over the mountains to the eastern side of the state. The Vatican complied, carving out new dioceses in Yakima and Spokane, and elevating Seattle to an archdiocese and hence Connolly to an archbishop.

Connolly was a take-charge guy, confident and tough, with an indomitable will and an overpowering desire to succeed. He did not back away from confrontation.

"He could be as friendly and playful as a kitten," recalled the Most Rev. Cornelius Power, who served as Connolly's chancellor before being appointed bishop of Yakima. "But when the need arose, he had the jaws of a pit bull."

Connolly, archbishop of Seattle for twenty-five years, was a builder and promoter in the boom times of American Catholicism. On his watch, forty-three parishes were founded and more than 350 churches, schools, rectories, convents, parish halls, and religious education centers were constructed. Vocations to the priesthood and religious life were abundant. Thanks to the baby boom, Sunday Masses were well attended and Catholic schools were full. Connolly made a practice of personally baptizing the twelfth child of any Catholic family in the archdiocese. *The Progress* regularly published photos of the smiling archbishop posed next to the mother, the newly christened infant in her arms, surrounded by her husband and a passel of kids.

St. Edward Seminary, designed for 111 students, was crammed with 256 students by 1956. Consequently, Connolly built an adjacent major seminary named for St. Thomas the Apostle. He dedicated it in 1959. With his blessing, five orders of religious women created a sisters' formation program and built Providence Heights College on a ridge east of Seattle. Some 256 sisters from thirty-six different communities enrolled at the convent school when classes began in 1961.

On social justice issues, Connolly was a progressive. He opposed right-to-work ballot initiatives and required all church construction projects to include a clause forbidding discrimination in hiring workers. He successfully lobbied for a Seattle open housing law that ended the practice of "redlining," which real estate agents used to keep minorities from buying homes in certain neighborhoods. He expanded the role of Catholic Charities beyond orphans and disadvantaged youth to include assistance for the poor, the elderly, and refugees from Southeast Asia.

After the first session of the Council, Connolly pronounced himself a "Vatican II bishop," celebrated the Mass in English, and turned the altar around. As Hunthausen did in Helena, he established a Priest Senate and a priest personnel board and encouraged the formation of parish councils. He urged laypeople to get involved in parish life by teaching faith formation, serving as youth ministers and discussion leaders, and assuming other responsibilities previously taken on by priests and nuns.

Thanks to the Council, Connolly warmed up to ecumenism. He accepted a standing invitation for Catholic participation in a KOMO-TV program in which a rabbi, a Protestant minister, and a priest would discuss theological and social issues. He appointed Father William Treacy, a thoughtful, soft-spoken priest committed to interfaith dialogue, to represent him. The "Challenge" program drew a substantial audience and lasted fourteen years.

Connolly found some Vatican II reforms difficult. He stumbled over collegiality, shared responsibility, and consensus decision-making. Although he started the Priest Senate, he never went to the meetings. Instead, the senate leadership forwarded its recommendations and he either accepted or rejected them. He attended the regular breakfast meetings of the region's Protestant denominational executives, but none of them ever felt comfortable enough to address him by his first name.

In fact, when Hunthausen first took Connolly's place at the ecumenical breakfasts, one of the Protestant bishops asked, "What are we supposed to call you? We called your predecessor 'Archbishop.'"

"So did I," Hunthausen replied. "But you can call me 'Ray.'"

Connolly was equally intimidating to his priests and staff. He referred to the archdiocese as "mine," not "ours." One young priest, in a Vatican II spirit of collegiality, decided that he would henceforward address Connolly as "Archbishop" rather than use the formal title of "Your Excellency." Connolly was in a reception line after a church dedication ceremony when the priest decided to try the new greeting.

"Good morning, Archbishop," the young priest said cheerfully.

Scowling, Connolly retorted, "Good morning, priest."

An accomplished speaker who relished grandiose language and figures of speech, Connolly demanded and received attention. Sometimes his candor and bluntness caused reactions he hadn't anticipated. As commencement speaker at the 1969 graduation ceremonies for Seattle University, Connolly justified the escalation of the Vietnam War including the bombing raids that President Nixon had ordered on Viet Cong bases in Cambodia. Two dozen SU graduates, dressed in caps and gowns, immediately stood up and walked out without receiving their diplomas.

If Connolly was bothered by their abrupt exit, he never said so. He was not one to agonize or temporize. He enjoyed life, especially the celebrations and the banquets he hosted for visiting bishops and dignitaries. A sportsman, he had a favorite salmon fishing hole in Puget Sound off Point No Point. When he caught fish or things were going particularly well, he'd throw back his head, laugh, and proclaim: "God is good."

With might and right on his side, the autocratic Connolly felt free to intervene in the lives of people ranging from chauffeurs to governors. When Mike McKay, who occasionally drove for him, told the archbishop that he planned to get married, Connolly demanded to meet the girl in his office. He grilled her, then McKay, and after they both passed muster, he insisted on performing the wedding ceremony himself at the cathedral.

Connolly's intervention in the life of Albert D. Rosellini, the Democratic governor of Washington State from 1957 to 1965, was equally direct. Connolly heard that Rosellini, a married man and a Catholic, was having an affair with his secretary. He phoned the governor and threatened to denounce him from every church pulpit in the archdiocese if Rosellini continued the illicit romance. The governor ended the affair. In fact, he later thanked Connolly for helping him through a difficult time.

At age seventy-five, Connolly was still healthy, vigorous, and not eager to relinquish the archdiocese to Hunthausen at the Seattle Center Arena that May evening in 1975. He had mixed feelings about the bishop from Helena and would have preferred someone else to succeed him, someone more like him. He did not want to hand over his First Hill mansion to Hunthausen, a moot issue since the new archbishop had no intention of living there. In fact, Connolly continued to live in the archbishop's regal residence until his death in 1991.

"His name is Hunthausen," Connolly growled at the time. "Let him hunt his own house."

Hunthausen was so different from Connolly that staff and clergy were bowled over.

"Dutch was just plain folks," said John Pinette, who was a seminarian at St. Edward's when he first met Hunthausen, "unassuming, shuffling through the cafeteria line to get his peas and beef stew with everybody else."

Father David Jaeger, whom Connolly had ordered to direct the Catholic Youth Organization, made an appointment with Hunthausen within a week of the archbishop's installation.

"I went in and I was just disarmed," Jaeger recalled. "You had to go in wearing battle array with Connolly. Hunthausen listened. He didn't solve my problem in the slightest. He listened and wished me the best. CYO was clearly on my shoulders. He was a supportive boss but he wasn't going to interfere or take over. He treated me like an adult."

Under Connolly, there had been no formal organizational structure at the chancery. All decisions came to him. Hunthausen began a monthly meeting of the fifty-some chancery staff and created a cabinet of a half dozen department heads who consulted with him regularly. Often they met with him over breakfast at the seminary, where he had taken up residence after moving from Helena.

Father Don Espen, a canon lawyer who later left the priesthood and became a technical writer, was one of the cabinet members. Espen found Hunthausen's approach of setting forth a vision without giving specific directions both liberating and exasperating. The archbishop treated staff as colleagues, gave them autonomy, and let them work out their own way of getting things done. It was a management style that was anathema to legalistic minds that demanded rules and black-and-white clarity.

"It's like having cyanide around the edge of your plate and just being careful not to eat any of it, " Espen said. "That was his philosophy. Great for us; an occupational hazard for him."

Hunthausen's management philosophy wasn't designed or calculated. It was simply him, the expression of a reflective, soft-spoken introvert who was humble, guileless, and blessed with personal integrity. A few years into his administration, the archbishop joined the priests of the archdiocese at a workshop on the Enneagram presented by Father Richard Rohr, a Franciscan priest and internationally known spiritual director. The Enneagram, whose purpose is better understanding of self, others, and God, posits nine interconnected personality types. Hunthausen identified himself as a "Nine." Nines tend to be passive, status-quo people dependent on the energy of others to move them along. They don't like change, but if change comes, they deal with it. Nines avoid conflict, are sensitive to others, and make good peacemakers. And they are loyal even when the persons and institutions they trust disappoint or cross them.

Maury Sheridan, the Montana native who served as Hunthausen's first communications director in Seattle, worried about his new boss's naiveté, especially with the media. Sheridan gently told Hunthausen that he wasn't in Montana anymore and needed to be more guarded about what he said and did. Hunthausen listened, but he didn't change.

"His style," Sheridan concluded, "was one of his greatest assets and one of his greatest liabilities."

Why a liability?

"Because Archbishop Hunthausen spoke what was on his mind and in his heart," Sheridan said. "That's what made people around him crazy and political. How do you shut this guy up? How do you control what he's going to say?"

Looking back years later, Sheridan added, "The clergy as much as the laity wanted to control that man for what he said. But trying to manage the archbishop was like trying to hold onto a fish."

Within two weeks of taking office, Hunthausen set out to visit the then 126 Catholic parishes in western Washington. Nearly every weekend he got into his blue Volkswagen Beetle and drove off to celebrate Mass, preach the sermon, and mingle with the pastor and parishioners at the coffee hour afterward. He called on churches from the Canadian border to the Columbia River, from the Pacific Ocean to the crest of the Cascade Mountains.

"I didn't know this archdiocese," Hunthausen said. "And that helped me greatly."

The new archbishop was so low key that sometimes people forgot he was there. In Sedro Woolley, an old railroad town in the Cascade foothills, the parishioners at Immaculate Heart of Mary Church invited him to a potluck dinner in the park across the alley from the church. After they had laid out their salads, casseroles, baked beans, fried chicken, and desserts, folks dug in. Hunthausen grabbed a paper plate, served himself, and then looked for a place to sit. All the picnic tables were occupied. So he found himself a spot on the lawn next to a youngster wolfing down the meal. The boy, who had no idea who Hunthausen was, rattled on about his school, his friends, and his new bike. When he paused to eat some more, the archbishop asked him, "Where'd you get that tin plate? Everybody else has a paper one."

The boy motioned at a house across the street. "At home," he replied. "I saw there was a picnic going on so I got my tin plate and came on over."

For years afterward, in sermons and on retreats, Hunthausen told that story to illustrate God's message: We are called to share with anyone who comes along. Bishop or boy.

In his homilies, Hunthausen often explained how Vatican II was changing the experience of church.

"There has been too great a reliance in the church on law and institutions," he said. "The urgent message of Vatican II was that we return to the primacy of love in the life of the church. I don't mean to eliminate law, but to say that the primary law is love."

Hunthausen continued the Bicentennial Project initiated by Connolly. In the spirit of the Council and in conjunction with the two-hundredth anniversary of the nation, the U.S. bishops had launched a church renewal project that culminated in a national gathering of bishops, priests, nuns, and lay leaders in Detroit in October 1976. The purpose of the three-day gathering, which met under the banner of "A Call to Action," was to draft a five-year social action program for the bishops' approval the following spring.

The Bicentennial Project marked an unprecedented effort by the nation's bishops to create a dialogue on the issues that concerned church members. By inviting representatives of the "People of God" to join with them in discussing the issues, the bishops staged the broadest grassroots consultation of Catholics in U.S. history. It was a true test of the Council's concept of shared responsibility.

Cardinal John Dearden, who, like Hunthausen, had his idea of church transformed by the Council, welcomed 1,340 delegates from 152 dioceses plus 1,000 observers (Protestants, Jews, media, etc.) to Detroit's Cobo Hall. A tall, sensible, and sensitive prelate, Dearden had served as the first president of the newly formed U.S. Conference of Catholic Bishops and was regarded as a leading church reformer and social justice advocate.

Meeting in small groups, the delegates discussed global issues such as nuclear arms, human dignity, racism, poverty, labor, and war. But they also talked about the contentious church issues: birth control, the ordination of women and married men, the exclusion of divorced and remarried Catholics, homosexuality, and the role of conscience in moral decision-making. The Call to Action conference produced 182 recommendations, ranging from the majestic to the mundane, for the bishops to consider at their semiannual meeting the following spring. Most of the recommendations had been passed by overwhelming majorities and called for significant reforms in church policies, practices, and, in some cases, doctrine.

Philadelphia Cardinal John Krol, the acerbic, cold-eyed Polish-American prelate who would soon rejoice at the election of a Polish pope, complained that the delegates were not representative of the U.S. church. He described them as "naïve, old ladies who wanted to help people but don't know anything about canon law." *The Wanderer,* the independent Catholic weekly and self-appointed champion of ultra-orthodoxy, sniffed that the conference was more socialism than social justice.

The twelve-member delegation from the Archdiocese of Seattle, headed by Hunthausen and Father James Dunning, the archdiocesan Bicentennial Project director, arrived in Detroit able to speak for more western Washington Catholics than just themselves. They brought with them data collected from more than eighty-six thousand parishioners who completed questionnaires on church issues. They also had feedback from the fifteen thousand Catholics who had participated in "discussion-action" groups in the parishes.

The Bicentennial survey found that Catholics in western Washington were at odds with a number of church teachings and practices. Two-thirds said divorced Catholics should be able to receive communion. Seventy percent said the church should reevaluate its position on birth control. And 59 percent said they would accept a married priest as their pastor. Half of those surveyed did not object to engaged couples having sex before marriage. The questionnaire also explored Catholic attitudes toward abortion (53 percent always opposed), capital punishment (67 percent in favor), and worshiping with Protestants (70 percent in favor). And it asked for feedback on subjects such as parish collections, the liturgy, religious education, and Mass attendance.

For the most part, the data from the Seattle archdiocese mirrored the findings of similar surveys from other dioceses and countrywide polling done by the National Opinion Research Center. The research demonstrated that the bishops were presiding over a church in which many Catholics disagreed with church teaching and wanted change.

Hunthausen hoped that the Call to Action Conference would mark a turning point in the course of the U.S. church. He participated with great enthusiasm, sharing in the general sessions and joining the small group meetings, including a workshop on the arms race in which discussions with several military chaplains got quite heated.

"The spirit was one of excitement, one of hope, one of expectation," Hunthausen recalled. "This was a new beginning. There was talk of a national pastoral council."

In an open letter published in *The Progress*, the Seattle archbishop wrote, "The pains and joys shared in Detroit touched our hearts." He conceded that he, like many bishops, was uncomfortable with some of the proposals. But so what? The point of the conference was to share the needs, hopes, and dreams for the church—openly and lovingly.

"We have raised our hopes," Hunthausen concluded. "Failure to act, on all levels, would simply cause greater frustration."

The Call to Action delegates submitted their recommendations to the bishops who took them up at their semiannual spring meeting in Chicago in May 1977. The bishops established an ad hoc committee to study the proposals and formulate a five-year action plan. But it was obvious that most of them were not prepared to share responsibility with the laity nor ready to discuss church teaching on contraception, a celibate priesthood, or homosexuality. In a nod to the Detroit meeting, they did remove the penalty of automatic excommunication for Catholics who divorced and remarried outside the church, and they simplified procedures for obtaining an annulment.

Cardinal Krol and the other traditionalists carried the day, however, dismissing the Call to Action delegates as "liberal extremists" and pawns of activist peace and women's groups. Ignored was the fact that the delegates, often elected members of parish or diocesan councils, had been appointed or approved by their respective bishops. The ad hoc bishops' committee for implementing the Detroit recommendations slipped into obscurity and disappeared altogether with the election of Pope John Paul II in 1978.

"We all expected the committee to take some dramatic steps in the directions indicated by the [Call to Action] experience," Hunthausen said. "After all, most of the experience of the Call to Action was occasioned by the documents of the Council and this [format] seemed to offer the church a way of conducting itself.... But nothing much happened. That was the surprise. This was the end of it."

While the U.S. bishops' conference abandoned a five-year social action plan, the archdiocese of Seattle launched one. Hunthausen and diocesan leadership took the Bicentennial survey data and information gleaned from parish and diocesan gatherings and drafted "Ministries 1976–81." The planning document set goals and assigned responsibilities for renewing and reforming the church in western Washington. Based on the feedback from parishioners, the archdiocese hired a youth faith formation director, assigned a priest-ethicist to address life issues, appointed a state legislative advocacy director, named a liturgy director, initiated a social justice office, and enlarged the capacity of the marriage tribunal to handle annulments. It also created a finance council, a parish leadership development program, and a commission for ecumenical and interreligious affairs.

Hunthausen expanded the role of the consultative groups established by Connolly and, unlike his predecessor, met with them. He empowered the Priest Senate, which began making significant and far-reaching decisions such as establishing new parishes. He affirmed the priest personnel board, expected parishes to have councils, and, as in Helena, formed an archdiocesan pastoral council of representative laypeople, women religious, and priests to collaborate with him in governing the archdiocese.

"I wanted us to share and learn together," Hunthausen said. "That was my idea and still is."

The archdiocese engaged Management Design, Inc., a Cincinnati-based church consulting firm headed by Father George Wilson, SJ, to help set up the Pastoral Council, improve the work of existing deliberative bodies, and school pastors on adjusting to change. One of the consulting firm's tasks was training pastors to govern by consensus rather than dictate by fiat. Hunthausen hoped that pastors would see how the post–Vatican II model of church enhanced their ministry while encouraging parishioners to grow in the practice of the faith.

Hunthausen convened ten regional "Faith and Sharing Retreats" where nearly seven hundred parish representatives had discussions similar to what he and the Seattle delegation had experienced at the Call to Action in Detroit. And he came to virtually every meeting of the archdiocesan Pastoral Council and the other high-level consultative groups.

"He didn't say very much in many of those meetings," recalled Father Mike McDermott, who, at various times, directed research, business and finance, administration, and ministerial services for the archdiocese. "But he gave a fine sense of direction to things."

McDermott, also one of Hunthausen's skiing companions, compared his boss's oversight to that of a good athletic coach. The archbishop had an overall game plan—largely set by Vatican II—and, while offering his guidance and support, he trusted others to play it. McDermott likened Hunthausen's coaching to that of Lenny Wilkens, a former player for the Seattle Supersonics basketball team and an all-time NBA winning coach.

"Lenny Wilkens was a great coach for a mature team but a lousy coach for an immature team," McDermott said. "Dutch was a great archbishop for a mature church but not for a church that needs a lot of parenting."

Sometimes the players didn't want to follow the plan. Early in his administration, Hunthausen sought to hire a fundraising director and initiate an annual Catholic appeal much as he had done in Helena. He took the proposal to the Priest Senate and they overwhelmingly voted it down. The priests argued that the archdiocesan tax on their parishes was already too high. They doubted that their parishioners were willing to give more. But mostly, they didn't trust the chancery.

Hunthausen invited the Senate to place some of its members on the archdiocesan budget and funding committee, which would study the financial picture and report back. The Senate agreed. A year later, it decided to give the appeal a shot. The first effort in 1978 more than exceeded the goal, and the appeal became an annual event thereafter.

The whirlwind of activities and initiatives with which Hunthausen began his ministry in Seattle did not compensate for the initial loneliness he felt in his personal life. He missed his friends, his mother, and his brothers and sisters and their families back in Montana. He especially missed the counsel of Father Provost, his top advisor and brainy organizer in Helena.

Father Larry Reilly, an ethicist and moral theologian teaching at St. Thomas Seminary, encountered Hunthausen one evening in the priest-dining hall. The room had been empty except for Reilly who had been having his nightly beer when a non-descript gray-haired man entered and helped himself to some cereal and milk. Reilly thought the man might be a Sulpician priest whom he had not yet met. So he introduced himself, explaining that he was new to the seminary faculty.

"Welcome," the man said. "I heard you were coming; it's really nice to meet you."

"And who are you?" Reilly inquired.

"Well," the man replied, a bit ill at ease, "I'm the bishop."

Reilly and Hunthausen had many more conversations after that first one over beer and cereal. They grew close. Reilly quickly recognized that the archbishop had very different views than Connolly, yet remained surrounded by Connolly's appointments.

"I realized the poor man was very isolated," said Reilly, a cerebral man with a large forehead and thin lips who speaks slowly and chooses his words carefully. An adept spiritual director, Reilly heard the confessions of seminarians and priests.

Hunthausen asked Reilly to advise and represent him on theological and moral issues, especially on hot topics such as abortion, homosexuality, or women's ordination. Reilly reluctantly agreed. During those first months as Hunthausen slowly developed other trusted friends and advisors, Reilly frequently served as his representative. At least once a week, Hunthausen knocked on Reilly's seminary door, gave him a fistful of pink phone slips, and asked him to return calls from a newspaper reporter, or a television editor, or someone organizing a conference or a panel discussion. Reilly hated the job, but he understood that Hunthausen needed both his expertise and his emotional support.

"He'd come home and these bad things had happened, so we'd go for a walk around the property," Reilly recalled. "Our conversations were always about subjects he wished to discuss."

One time the archbishop came back to the seminary very troubled after a tense personnel discussion with a priest. He related the story to Reilly, who listened closely and then told Hunthausen, "I fully agree with the priest. He is right and you are wrong."

Hunthausen slammed his fists on the table in anger.

"Your job is to give me support and right now I need support," he said.

Reilly responded, "If I'm going to minister to you, I'm going to tell you the truth whether you like it or not."

A few months later, Father Peter Chirico, a Sulpician priest and moral theologian, returned to the seminary to resume his teaching post. Reilly sent Hunthausen a handwritten note saying that Chirico was better suited for the role of his key theological advisor, spokesperson, and confidante.

"Trust and confide in Peter and get to know him," Reilly said. "He'll serve you very, very well."

Hunthausen took Reilly's advice. Chirico served as his top theological advisor for most of his administration, including the tempestuous years of the showdown with Rome.

Another advisor Hunthausen recruited during his early days in Seattle was Father Michael G. Ryan, the savvy, persuasive young priest who would become his chancellor and vicar general. Roman-educated and wise in the ways of the church and the world, Ryan had a pleasing pastoral touch, making his points with a broad smile, a jovial laugh, and a gentle squeeze of his listener's arm. He was neat and tidy and had a perfectionist's love of classical music.

Ryan first met Hunthausen at a semiannual meeting of the Region 12 bishops a couple of years before he was appointed to Seattle. Among other things, the bishops discussed St. Edward and St. Thomas Seminaries, which trained priesthood candidates for the entire five-state region. At the time, Hunthausen was chair of the seminary board and Ryan was vocations director for the Seattle archdiocese. Hunthausen thought the traditional seminary model of educating young men isolated from secular culture and then thrusting them into the world as ordained priests a dozen years later did not work. Too often these sheltered priests knew too little about themselves and too little about the people they were to serve. Hunthausen didn't have a sure alternative but he was convinced there was a better way to prepare priests for ministry.

At the regional bishops' meeting at the seminary in April 1975, Archbishop-elect Hunthausen asked Ryan if they could have a chat after dinner. The two adjourned to Ryan's seminary apartment where Hunthausen questioned him about the vocations situation and the vi-ability of the two seminaries. Both were hurting for students, particularly St. Edward's, which housed the high school program.

"I told him the place was in serious trouble and recommended that a study group assess it," recalled Ryan, whom Connolly had appointed vocations director over the young priest's objections. "I felt for the first time that I was dealing with someone who treated me as a colleague."

Once in office Hunthausen followed Ryan's advice, asking him to chair a six-member seminary study group that included Bishop Elden Curtiss, his successor in Helena, three priests, and a nun. Six months later, the committee recommended that St. Thomas Seminary, which offered undergraduate and graduate-level theology courses in preparation for priesthood, be shut down. St. Edward Seminary had already closed, quietly shifting its forty-four students to Kennedy High School in Seattle. Hunthausen took the recommendation, which he supported, privately advised retired Archbishop Connolly, who gave him no reply, and then went to the Region 12 bishops' meeting in the spring of 1977.

It was a painful meeting in which the bishops grudgingly reached a consensus that St. Thomas Seminary was finished. As they neared a final decision on the matter, Connolly, who no longer had a vote but was entitled to attend the bishops' meetings, arrived in the room and took over.

He pointed at Portland Archbishop Cornelius Power, his former chancellor, and demanded, "Do you agree with closing the seminary?"

"Yes," Power responded.

Connelly pointed to another bishop and asked the same question.

"Yes," the bishop replied. So did the next bishop. And the next.

Shaken and defeated, Connolly moaned. "You're destroying my creation," he said. "I'm not going to sit here for the closing of my seminary."

With that, he turned and bolted from the room. He never again attended a bishops' meeting. He regarded St. Thomas Seminary, which he had opened with such pride and fanfare less than a decade earlier, as his greatest accomplishment. Now it was history, a white elephant that would soon become home to a school for naturopathic medicine.

Embittered, Connolly later told *The Progress*, "I have been tossed out on the garbage dump."

Closing the seminary did not go down any better with many others who blamed Hunthausen for its demise. When the archbishop made the announcement at a priests' meeting, more than a few rose to attack him. Father Donald Conger, his face flushed with anger, launched into a diatribe in which he accused his old seminary class-mate of lying and concluded by disparaging the signature closing of Hunthausen's letters: "May God be with you in all his peace, love, and joy."

"Peace, love, and joy," Conger mocked. "I'm sick of it."

Hunthausen, unruffled, made no response. He understood the anger and hurt of those grieved by the closure of an institution that they loved so much. But he remained unaffected by it.

In closing the seminary, Hunthausen announced that an ad hoc commission headed by Bishop Nicolas E. Walsh, his recently named auxiliary, would design a new program of priestly formation. The commission included Ryan, Father Melvin Farrell, SS, the former semi-nary rector, and Bishop William Skylstad of Yakima. While Walsh was the titular head, Farrell did most of the work. The commission asked itself: What does the church need in priests today? Who are today's seminarians? How do we recruit them?

Ultimately, the commission came up with a plan to mainstream priesthood candidates at Kennedy High School and an enhanced School of Theology at Seattle University. The seminarians would re-ceive concentrated spiritual direction characteristic of a traditional seminary while learning alongside other students.

It sent its plan to Bishop John Marshall, chair of the U.S. Bishops' Committee on Priestly Formation, the papal nuncio, the regional bishops, and others with a vested interest in training priests. They asked Marshall, of Burlington, Vermont, and other bishop committee members to visit. When they finally did visit, in 1981, they gave the fledgling priestly formation program good marks. Their observations, however, were not treated as kindly in Rome. The Vatican, it later emerged, was bothered by the involvement of lay people and psychia-trists in the screening of seminary applicants. Nor did it like the ex-tended discernment process or some of the test questions used to weed out unsuitable candidates.

"It became lodged in the minds of the powers that be that there was a litmus test for becoming a seminarian in Seattle," Ryan later surmised. "You had to be for optional celibacy, in favor of the ordi-nation of women, and be liberal."

The Archdiocese of Seattle, which numbered 350,000 registered Catholics in 1975, had had an auxiliary bishop since Connolly's time. There were simply too many confirmations, dedications, and other events requiring the presence of a bishop for one man to do it all. But with the death of Bishop Thomas E. Gill, Connolly's auxiliary, in No-vember 1973, the archdiocese had but one bishop—the archbishop.

Jadot, the apostolic delegate, had promised Connolly, and then Hunthausen, that Seattle would soon have one or more auxiliaries. In May 1976, Jadot asked Hunthausen for a favor: Would he consider taking Bishop Walsh as his auxiliary? Walsh, appointed bishop of Yakima two years earlier, was struggling. He suffered from asthma and high blood pressure and was indecisive, unfocused, and unable to complete projects. Thin-skinned, he often felt ignored or slighted by others, which compounded his difficulties. Jadot was candid about Walsh's limitations and let Hunthausen know that if he accepted Walsh, he would also get a second auxiliary.

Hunthausen agreed. He dared not assign Walsh to lead a chancery department but found him to be a great help with confirmations, parish and school visits, and short-term assignments, such as the commission on priestly formation. Walsh became fiercely loyal to Hunthausen. Later, in the midst of the Vatican's investigation of the archbishop, Walsh flew to Rome on his own initiative to meet with Pope John Paul II and members of the curia and vouch for Hunthausen.

The archbishop never got a second auxiliary bishop. And, after Walsh retired in 1983, Hunthausen waited three years for another auxiliary. This time, the auxiliary was Bishop Donald Wuerl, imposed by Rome to keep watch on him.

It would be hard to say why George Kotolaris had a special affection for Archbishop Hunthausen, because George claimed to be crazy. He certainly acted like he was. He showed up uninvited at various church events—confirmations, weddings, anniversary Masses, and especially funerals. He wedged his way forward, took a seat in the front pew, and snapped pictures with a pocket camera, often of the deceased displayed in an open casket. He dressed in loud sport coats, white bucks, and a polka dot navy cap under which he secured his long gray hair with bobby pins. He had a rosy-cheeked complexion like a porcelain doll.

George frequently showed up at church services where the archbishop was presiding and sheepishly asked Hunthausen for a ride home afterward. So the archbishop would drive George back to his First Hill apartment. After one such service, George sidled up to the archbishop and asked for a ride to Yakima, a three-hour drive over the mountains, where he knew that Hunthausen was consecrating a new bishop. The archbishop agreed on the condition that George be ready outside the cathedral rectory at six in the morning. He was. Riding there and back, George offered Hunthausen an unabridged critique of the abilities of various priests. At least one of them was so awful, George insisted, that Hunthausen ought to assign him to Camas, a dismal mill town in the far reaches of the archdiocese.

On other occasions, George would awkwardly hit up the arch-bishop for a five-dollar bill. After Mass at the cathedral one morning, he caught Hunthausen in the vestibule and nodded toward a tall, aloof fellow he identified as his friend Bill.

"Bill needs $5," he told the archbishop.

Hunthausen produced a five-dollar bill and handed it to George who ambled over to give it to Bill. A few moments later, George returned and cornered the archbishop again.

"I need $5 too," he said.

George's presence at religious services could be discomfiting at times. He showed up one morning at a Mass that was part of a cursillo at St. Patrick's. Two men walked in after the Mass had started. George, sitting in the front pew, peered down the aisle and said in a voice loud enough for the entire congregation to hear: "Didn't I see you two at the homosexual Mass last night?"

At one point, Hunthausen heard that George was about to be evicted from his subsidized apartment because it had become a health hazard. Plastic sacks of garbage lined the walls. Spoiled food filled the refrigerator and kitchen shelves. Papers, magazines, photos, brochures, and books were stacked four feet high across the living room floor. Flies, mice, and cockroaches gorged themselves on the rotting decay.

Early one Saturday morning, Hunthausen, dressed in khaki work pants and accompanied by several folks he had recruited, arrived at George's apartment door. They spent the whole day hauling out garbage, washing down the walls, cleaning the toilet and bath, and scrubbing the kitchen floor. When they were done, George asked the archbishop to bless his new home.

When George died of a sudden heart attack in 1990, Hunthausen and nine other priests concelebrated the funeral Mass at St. James Cathedral. It was done in a style that George would have appreciated. Yellow daffodils decorated the altar. The choir sang "Amazing Grace." The ushers distributed memorial cards with a photo of George in his trademark pink tie.

More than five hundred people came to bid him goodbye. Father Treacy, who like the other celebrants knew George well, delivered the homily. "I pray you have a heavenly banquet, George," he said, "and may I suggest you take some pictures."

In the summers, Hunthausen left Seattle for vacation back home in Montana. One August he rendezvoused with his sister Edna and two of her fellow Sisters of Charity for a drive up into Canada. The four-some crossed the border and overnighted near Lake Louise, the spectacular alpine lake in the heart of the Canadian Rockies. During the drive, Sister Helen McDevitt told the others about a recent retreat in which she had learned about dream interpretation and the significance of dreams for our conscious lives.

That night Hunthausen dreamed that he was in a private meeting in his chancery office when Marilyn Maddeford, his personal secretary, interrupted to say there was a monsignor from Rome waiting to see him. The archbishop was not expecting a visitor. He said he would come out as soon as possible. He emerged a few minutes later to find the monsignor, dressed in a full black cassock with raised buttons and purple piping, livid with anger.

In a loud, foreign accent, the monsignor berated the archbishop. "Don't you realize that I've come all the way from Rome," the stranger shouted, "that I represent the Holy Father and the sacred curia?" On and on, he raged, ranting about the importance and the power of the Vatican congregations.

Hunthausen remained calm. Softly and evenly, he said, "Monsignor, I thought the curia were the servants of the bishops and not the bishops the servants of the curia."

And then, all of a sudden, he woke up. He had no idea how to interpret the dream but he immediately wrote it down. In time, it would prove to be prophetic.

The following day the foursome drove along the rim of the Rockies from Banff to Jaspar, enjoying exhilarating views of evergreen forests, rushing rivers, craggy peaks, luminous glaciers, sparkling snowfields, and meadows carpeted in wildflowers. In the car, Hunthausen played some instrumental music that he had recorded from a Christian radio station. For miles and miles no one said a word in the car. The music, with its soaring harmonies, suggested God's creation in all its breathtaking beauty and grandeur. It had rained earlier in the day and there, amidst the sun and remaining clouds, was the arc of a perfect rainbow.

"We couldn't speak," Sister Edna recalled. "I looked back and Helen McDevitt was crying. We were overwhelmed. We felt lifted into some divine connectedness with all this beauty."

Hunthausen called it a "wow" experience, a God moment, and spoke about it at retreats for years afterward. He made each of the sisters a cassette copy of the recorded music and mailed it to them. He labeled it "Music to Watch Glaciers."

The post-conciliar Vatican, which many expected to focus on inclusion, shared responsibility, and social justice, instead became increasingly preoccupied with enforcing church teaching, especially on moral and sexual issues. Unnerved by the negative reaction to his encyclical forbidding artificial birth control, Pope Paul VI retreated into a cautious reactionary mode, fearful of pushing many of the reforms envisioned by the Council. When John Paul II assumed the papacy, he set out to make very clear the doctrinal absolutes on which Catholic teaching is grounded now and forever. There would be no ambiguity, no gray areas for making prudential decisions that might be inconsistent with church law or practice.

John Paul zeroed-in on three doctrinal issues of particular concern: (1) abortion; (2) excluding women from priesthood; and (3) homosexuality. Hunthausen soon found himself immersed in all three.

No issue has defined Catholic identity more in the United States than the issue of abortion. *Roe v. Wade*, the 1973 U.S. Supreme Court decision legalizing abortion, hardened the Catholic position that life begins at the moment a sperm fertilizes an egg. The Catholic Church argued that a fetus had a right to protection within the womb regardless of how it was conceived, what deformities or defects it might carry, or what the wishes of the mother or father might be about giving birth.

With legalized abortion now the law of the land, earlier Catholic speculation about when human personhood began and how much protection should be afforded to the fetus faded away. Aquinas, the church's greatest philosopher, had taught that a fetus acquired a soul when it became identifiably human, perhaps two to three months into pregnancy. Catholic ethicists had applied the principle of "proportionality" to abortion, arguing that there were times when ending fetal life could be justified to achieve a greater good, such as saving the life of the mother. They asked: Why should the ban on abortion be absolute? Why does the fetus have a priority claim over the mother? What about a fetus with severe abnormalities? Or one conceived by rape or incest? How can a church that bans contraception ask a teenager to carry an unwanted fetus to full term?

Before *Roe v. Wade* and the papacy of John Paul II, Catholics openly discussed and debated these questions. Now the discussion, if it occurred at all, went underground. There was to be no ambivalence on the question of abortion. It was a black-and-white issue. Pro-choice Catholics were ostracized; pro-choice priests and nuns were reprimanded and punished; pro-choice Catholic politicians were denied communion and forbidden from speaking at Catholic institutions. Abortion—not the sacraments or social justice or care for the poor and suffering—became THE litmus test of Catholic identity.

Abortion trumped everything else. It became the lens through which virtually every other issue was viewed. In 1980, Hunthausen, seeking to temper the abortion obsession, persuaded the state's Catholic bishops to publish a statement titled "The Morality of Being a Single Issue Person." Drafted by Father Chirico, the statement argued that elevating a single issue above all others "is to erect an idol," replacing God with a cause. Voting for politicians solely on the basis of their stance on abortion is contrary to the richness of Catholic tradition, the statement said. "A Catholic Church which thinks in terms of only one issue has given up its birthright."

To be sure, Hunthausen had no scruples with church doctrine on abortion. He believed that life began at the moment of conception and demonstrated that belief through his words and actions. He spoke at the annual Right to Life rally on the state Capitol steps in Olympia on the anniversary of the *Roe v. Wade* decision. He prayed with protesters standing in the wind and rain outside an abortion clinic in Everett. And he parted company with the Protestant church executives with whom he breakfasted weekly by advocating for a state ballot initiative that would cut off public funding for abortion.

The initiative was one of several measures on the 1984 general election ballot headed by the presidential race between the incumbent, Ronald Reagan, and his Democratic challenger, Walter Mondale. Mondale's running mate was U.S. Congresswoman Geraldine Ferraro, the first-ever woman on the presidential ticket of a major party and a Catholic. Ferraro was also for abortion rights, which resulted in a scolding by New York Cardinal John O'Connor. In response, eighty Catholic theologians and religious leaders signed a full-page ad printed in the *New York Times* on October 7, 1984, that said Catholics held a diversity of opinions on the abortion issue. The U.S. bishops' conference roundly condemned the ad; the Vatican demanded that the signers recant; and, in the minds of many Americans, the official Catholic Church all but endorsed Reagan, the pro-life Republican.

I went to interview Hunthausen two weeks before the November 6 election. As the religion reporter at the *Seattle Post-Intelligencer,* I wanted to ask how much the abortion issue should weigh on the Catholic conscience in the voting booth. Does it indeed trump other issues?

Hunthausen and Chirico, his voluble theologian, sat with me at the dining room table in the rectory of St. Patrick Church. Hunthausen looked tired and unanimated. We started with abortion. Chirico argued that as long as there is scientific doubt about the precise point when life begins, the fetus should be recognized as human. Hunthausen said that aborting any fetus, even one that shows signs of severe defects, cheapens life. He noted that he was close to a number of families who were raising children born severely handicapped.

"I can't answer why they happen but they have been the salvation of those families," he said.

Nonetheless, voting for or against a politician solely on the abortion issue bothered Hunthausen. There are other issues of equal moral significance, he said, such as human rights, war and peace, social and economic justice. Ultimately, how a Catholic voted and whether a woman had an abortion was a matter of personal conscience.

"I would never deny that the woman has the right to choose," Hunthausen said. "No one can take that away from her. It's the consequences of that choice that we are really talking about."

The church certainly has an obligation to speak out for the life of the fetus, he said. But once you do that, you make it almost impossible to relate to a woman considering an abortion. In fact, Hunthausen conceded, he had never counseled a woman who had had an abortion or was contemplating one.

"You see the dilemma," he continued. It's hard to give much solace to someone whom you believe is taking a human life. "It's so complex and I'm so hesitant to make a judgment about an individual because it's really between them and God. That's where the decision should be made."

The emphasis on an informed conscience was a constant theme in the archbishop's ministry. But elevating conscience over church law did not sit well in Rome. Hunthausen would suffer for it.

In his first full year in Seattle, pro-life groups pressured the archdiocese to withdraw its support from United Way because the agency helped fund Planned Parenthood, which offered abortion referrals. (United Way also provided funding to Catholic social programs.) The archbishop decided to address the matter in "a pastoral letter on moral decision-making" addressed to the Catholics of western Washington. It was classic Hunthausen, emphasizing the primacy of conscience and the need to determine the greater good.

"In our times, the church rarely tells us what to do and what not to do," he wrote. "Rather, she encourages us to act responsibly, to act as men and women who believe in God, as men and women whose belief affects our life."

Acknowledging that "it is often very difficult to make practical and concrete applications of moral principles," Hunthausen sought "to offer some guidelines for responsible Catholic decision-making." He noted the norm that human life is sacred, and the principle that human life must always be respected.

Yet, he wrote, we face "conflict of value" questions when we seek to apply that norm and that principle to war, capital punishment, abortion, euthanasia, suicide, self-defense, and other issues. The sacred value of one person's life can come into conflict with other values in life. When that happens, Hunthausen continued, we might have no choice but to choose one value over another. In the case of United Way, he was choosing the value of an organization that did much good over the wrong that one of its member organizations did.

That thinking, however, did not endure. In 1988, Planned Parenthood announced that it would begin performing abortions at its clinics. As a result, the archdiocese, now under close Vatican supervision, pressured the United Way Board to drop the organization as a member and a funding recipient, which it did. It was a Pyrrhic victory for Hunthausen and the archdiocese, however. They looked like bullies; other faith leaders denounced them; and Planned Parenthood soon raised record funds on its own. Hunthausen tried to assuage the situation by urging Catholic support for United Way but the abortion funding issue left the community deeply polarized.

Several years earlier, a chancery staff member had arranged a meeting between Hunthausen and Lee Minto, the grandmotherly family counselor who headed the Seattle office of Planned Parenthood. Hunthausen asked Father Reilly to come with him.

The theologian refused because he was convinced that Minto was trying to manipulate the archbishop. He showed Hunthausen a copy of Planned Parenthood's public relations strategy, which advised its executives to make friends with bishops who would then be less likely to attack them. Reilly told Hunthausen that he doubted that Minto desired a sincere dialogue.

"I like to think that Jesus, if he were here, would say that what I am doing is what he would do," Hunthausen responded.

Reilly shrugged. "I don't know Jesus as well as you but I do talk to him a lot," he said. "If that's his opinion, he can tell me."

So Hunthausen took Father Chirico with him. Minto, a Unitarian who opened the first place in the state where low-income women could get contraceptives, established a comfortable rapport with the archbishop. They talked candidly about their differences over birth control, a woman's right to privacy, and abortion. Later their dialogue was expanded to include people from other churches, the YWCA, and civic groups wrestling with the abortion issue. Chirico regularly represented Hunthausen in these talks. The dialogue eventually foundered, however, when the discussion got to the status of the fetus.

"I think that was unfortunate," said Chirico, noting that Seattle was probably the only place in the nation where the Catholic Church actually talked to Planned Parenthood.

Vatican II did not fling church doors wide open for women. They were still barred from ordination to priesthood and the diaconate and could not serve as pastors, bishops, or popes. The Roman Catholic Church remained a patriarchy.

In Seattle and elsewhere, Catholic leadership asked itself how best to include women in the full life of the church. Hunthausen participated in a priests' retreat in which the retreat master extoled the mystery and magnificence of priesthood and how grateful priests should be that God had called them to this wonderful ministry.

"All of a sudden it crossed my mind," the archbishop recalled. "I cannot believe in a God who has instituted a priesthood that is this magnificent and then denied it to half the human race. I can't believe that."

Encouraged by several women religious, Hunthausen proposed that the Washington State Catholic Conference (WSCC), the legislative advocacy arm of the state's three dioceses, issue a pastoral letter on women. The letter would address issues of inequality and discrimination against women in both the church and the larger society.

It was not an auspicious time to be raising the women's issue, especially the very contentious issue of women's ordination. In 1976, Pope Paul VI had cited various theological and historical reasons justifying the church's position that women cannot be admitted to priesthood. Two years later, John Paul II had declared the subject of women's ordination decided and closed to discussion. During his first papal visit to the United States in 1979, he pointedly looked away when Sister Theresa Kane, the president of the Leadership Conference of Women Religious (LCWR), the nation's largest association of nuns, asked that women be permitted to serve in all ministries of the church.

Nonetheless, Hunthausen and other Vatican II bishops continued to dialogue with lay and religious women about their full participation in the life of the church. Two dozen U.S. bishops, including Hunthausen, publicly endorsed the Equal Rights Amendment to the U.S. Constitution. *U.S. Catholic* magazine gave Hunthausen an award for furthering the cause of women in the church. But as John Paul II began packing the U.S. bishops' conferences with like-minded men, Vatican II bishops were cold-shouldered and marginalized.

The two other bishops on the WSCC at the time, Lawrence Welsh, of Spokane, and Skylstad, of Yakima, were not enthusiastic about Hunthausen's proposal for a pastoral letter on women. *The Wanderer* had published a vitriolic attack on Hunthausen for not preventing a regional gathering of the Women's Ordination Conference at a parish hall in Federal Way, south of Seattle. Hunthausen sought to calm his colleagues' anxiety by arguing that the letter ought to rec-

ognize the enormous contribution of women to the church and invite
them to assume a larger role. He agreed that the women's ordination
issue could create a backlash and defeat the broader intent of the letter. Hence, leave it out.

Skylstad was reasonably comfortable with this approach. But
Welsh refused to sign any such letter. The three bishops had a standing agreement that if they could not reach consensus on an issue, they
took no action. The WSCC protocol, however, did allow a bishop to
speak in his own name in his own diocese. So Hunthausen decided to
write his own letter on women, one that would ultimately result in a
scolding from Cardinal Joseph Ratzinger, the Vatican's doctrinal
watchdog and pope-to-be.

The archbishop sought drafting help from women religious, including Sisters Sharon Park and Margaret Casey, who served on the
WSCC staff, and Sister Diana Bader, a moral theologian and president of the archdiocesan Sisters' Council. The three women went
through several revisions of the letter with Hunthausen.

"It was not intended to be confrontational but it was certainly intended to be future oriented," Bader explained. "The big issue was
justice."

Hunthausen had strong feelings about church discrimination
against women and pushed the justice issue as far as he could without
openly defying the pope. A loyal son of the church, he certainly had
no intention of rushing out to ordain women. But he wanted the
church to discuss the issue. He saw no convincing historical, scriptural, or theological argument for an all-male, celibate priesthood.

The Pastoral Letter on Women, addressed to the "People of God"
and published under Hunthausen's name and signature, appeared in
the October 2, 1980 edition of *The Progress*. The letter began by noting the six hundredth anniversary of the death of St. Catherine of
Siena, a laywoman and doctor of the church who obeyed church authority yet challenged popes to face the issues of the day. The archbishop could have been describing himself.

"Jesus gave a prominent place to women; all are called to equal
roles as disciples," Hunthausen wrote.

Yet women continue to suffer injustice, he pointed out. Citing
Gaudium et Spes, the Vatican II document on the Church in the Modern World, the archbishop wrote that discrimination, whether based
on culture, race, or sex, is to be overcome and eradicated as contrary
to God's will.

"We cannot expect women to accept a role that limits their
growth, opportunity, freedom, dignity, and particularly their rights,"
Hunthausen wrote. "Women are working to effect change and, in

justice, to become equal partners in the human community.... Change is mandated for the church of western Washington."

In mandating that change, the archbishop called for affirmative action in all parishes and archdiocesan offices; equal access to theological and pastoral education; the elimination of sexist language and imagery from church rites, documents and communications; equal employment opportunities and compensation for qualified women and men in church positions; and active recruitment of women as lectors, eucharistic ministers, and parish and diocesan team members. Finally, Hunthausen recommended creation of a Commission on Women to work with him and the archdiocesan Pastoral Council to guide and monitor the policies he had proposed.

The commission, comprised of eight women selected from more than two hundred women and men who applied, held its first meeting five months later.

The local response to Hunthausen's bold step in writing a pastoral letter on women was strongly positive. In letters to *The Progress*, the provincial superiors of the Providence Sisters and the Sisters of St. Joseph of Peace said their respective orders unanimously affirmed the pastoral. The co-chairs of the Seattle Church Council's Task Force on Women and Religious applauded the archbishop for calling on the Catholic Church to "stand as a liberator of women rather than an oppressor." The head of the state church association suggested that Hunthausen's proposals for eliminating sexual discrimination in the church were instructive to all Christian denominations.

At least one diocesan priest was not supportive. Father Paul Auer, pastor of St. Paul Parish in Westport, a fishing town on the Pacific coast, wrote *The Progress* that the letter was untimely, insubordinate, and theologically wrong. "Priestly ordination is reserved by divine institution to men alone," Auer asserted.

Women aren't the only ones excluded from full ministry in the church. Married men are shut out as well. In the Latin rite, only celibate men can be ordained priests, although John Paul II and Benedict XVI welcomed married priests who converted to Catholicism from other denominations.

"What kind of mind admits married Episcopal priests but turns away those who have been ordained in our own tradition and chosen to marry?" asked Sister Bader, the moral theologian. "What kind of mind is that?"

Hunthausen wondered as well. Why should celibacy be an absolute prerequisite for the ordination of men or women? Too often he found himself in painful conversations with priests who had fallen in love with a woman—or a man—and felt compelled to forsake a vocation they loved. Hunthausen spent hours listening to them.

The case of Father Andrew Prouty was particularly painful. Prouty and Hunthausen were good friends from their days together at St. Edward Seminary. In fact, Prouty, like Michael Miles, the would-be married priest in Montana, had been on horse packing trips in the Rocky Mountains with Hunthausen. While Prouty was extroverted and impetuous—the opposite of the archbishop—the two got along well.

Prouty, who had served as pastor in several parishes, fell in love with a social worker named Marnie Beattie, a mother of eight, and needed to tell Hunthausen about it. So he invited the archbishop for dinner at the parish rectory. He had the housekeeper prepare strawberry cream pie, Hunthausen's favorite dessert. But he couldn't summon the nerve to tell him that, after more than three decades of priesthood, he planned to leave so that he could get married. He invited the archbishop to a second dinner at the rectory. After another strawberry pie, a puzzled Hunthausen asked, "Andy, what is it? What are you trying to tell me? Do you want out?"

Prouty mumbled, "Yes."

Hunthausen made no objection. He had come to listen, not to oppose or persuade.

As with Miles, he asked Prouty to complete the Vatican-required process of laicization so that the church would be able to bless his marriage to Beattie. He offered to assist with the paperwork and gave Prouty the name of a psychiatrist who had been helpful to other clergy separating from the church. It proved to be a long wait. John Paul II had made laicizations much more onerous and difficult. Many priests gave up, got married outside the church, and were thus barred from receiving the very sacraments they used to dispense. But in deference to Hunthausen, Prouty waited.

Finally, Rome released him from priesthood. He and Beattie married three months later.

Shortly before Prouty died in 1990, he and his bride attended the national CORPUS Convention in San Jose, California. Founded as a support and advocacy group for married priests, CORPUS evolved into a church reform movement promoting an inclusive priesthood of men and women, married and single. It held its June 1990 convention in San Jose because the U.S. bishops were holding their annual spring meeting in nearby Santa Clara.

On Saturday morning, the CORPUS group staged a rally on the lawn in front of the hall where the bishops were meeting. Marnie Beattie, now Marnie Prouty, recalled the occasion.

"As the two hundred or more bishops and archbishops processed by in their white robes and miters, they all pointedly ignored our group standing there, except for four of them," she wrote.

One of the four was Hunthausen who called out Andy Prouty's name and walked over to say hello. The next morning the CORPUS group of married priests celebrated Sunday Mass together in the Student Union Building at San Jose State.

"Happy tears blinded Andrew's eyes at Mass," Marnie Prouty wrote, "[because] he suddenly realized it was okay for him to be both ordained and married ... [He] felt free to celebrate the Eucharist again."

Suggesting that the church should ordain women and married men was a sure way for a bishop to incur the wrath of Rome. But an even surer way was to suggest that the church should bless same-sex marriages or welcome sexually active homosexuals into full church participation.

The traditional Catholic view on human sexuality is based on the teachings of Aquinas who contended that the primary purpose of sex is procreation, which properly belongs within a heterosexual marriage. Aquinas condemned sodomy, masturbation, adultery, and extramarital sex as contrary to God's purpose in uniting a man and woman for the purpose of conceiving and nurturing children. For him, homosexuals were simply wayward heterosexuals committing immoral acts.

A modern scientific understanding of human sexuality and the sexual revolution of the 1960s put the church's traditional teaching under question and attack. With the approval of Pope Paul VI, the Congregation for the Doctrine of the Faith (CDF) issued *Persona Humana*, a "Declaration on Certain Questions Concerning Sexual Ethics," in 1975, Hunthausen's first year in Seattle. The document sought to address what the Vatican called a corruption of morals, especially "the unbridled exaltation of sex" that is "infecting the general mentality." It repeated long-standing church teaching that sex belonged within a heterosexual marriage.

What was new was the CDF's treatment of homosexuality. The document defined two types of homosexuals: (1) treatable heterosexuals who engage in homosexual acts; and (2) incurable homosexuals who have "some kind of innate instinct or pathological constitution." The second category should be treated with understanding, the document said, and "their culpability judged with prudence."

Persona Humana raised a huge pastoral challenge for bishops charged with teaching Catholic doctrine as well as with priests, women religious, and laypeople counseling Catholic homosexuals. How do you tell a gay man or woman that God made them homosexual but with no morally licit way to express their homosexuality?

Hunthausen had virtually no experience in dealing with the gay issue before coming to Seattle. In Montana, homosexuality had been a taboo topic. During his time at Carroll College, Father Topel had advised the future bishop that some of the young men he was directing toward priesthood might tell him that they were attracted to men.

"But I never had any of the young men speak to me about it or admit it," Hunthausen said. "I never thought about it, never read about it, never made a critical judgment. Is this a choice or a fact of life? That issue never crossed my mind."

In Seattle, the archbishop got a quick and thorough education. More than one priest, often those who had entered the seminary as naïve fourteen-year-old boys, came to him to confess their homosexuality.

"I came to have a very compassionate view," he said. "I knew these men and I knew them well and I knew they were good people. I heard their stories and experienced their anguish as they came to an awareness of who they really were."

Hunthausen wanted to keep them as priests as long as they—like heterosexual priests—were committed to celibacy. But his overriding goal was to affirm them for who they were. Regardless of their sexual orientation, he said, God loved them.

"I don't believe that any of us can minister in a loving way unless we've somehow come to terms with our own selves," he said. "It's terribly important for an individual to rejoice in who he or she is as a gift from God."

It hurt Hunthausen to see gay priests depart. Many of them were talented pastors, caring, dynamic leaders genuinely committed to the Gospel. But the archbishop understood their decision.

"When they see the way society treats homosexuals and the things their own church says about them, how can they really believe that God loves them?" Hunthausen asked.

The archbishop became convinced that homosexuality was simply God's gift to some people. He didn't know why. And he had to deal with the arguments of others, including his cousin, a respected Anaconda internist, who sent him reams of literature supporting the position that homosexuality was a treatable disorder.

As he met and counseled more gays, he was sure that they had to be who they were: homosexual. Yet if God made them gay, would God also require that they be celibate? He noted that St. Paul extolled the celibate life but also recognized that celibacy was not for everyone. Should we presume that all homosexuals receive the gift of celibacy? The church teaches that sexuality is a natural expression of our human nature, Hunthausen observed. But it also teaches that homosexuals have to abstain from sex. There was a contradiction there that perplexed the archbishop.

"I haven't sorted it all out nor do I suppose I ever will," Hunthausen said. "I'm simply telling you the dilemma that has gone through my mind as I have come to know homosexual people."

In 1972, a group of gay Seattle Catholics quietly affiliated with Dignity, a national Catholic organization started three years earlier whose purpose was to provide an opportunity for gay men and women to share their faith together. They met in each other's homes, sometimes inviting priests and religious educators to dialogue with them. In 1977, they asked to meet on church property where they hoped to have Mass together. The pastor at Sacred Heart Church adjacent to the Seattle Center agreed.

"It's not my church," Father Lyle Konen explained. "It's the people's church. I'm just the custodian—in the spiritual sense."

A while later the Dignity Mass moved to St. Joseph Church, the Jesuit parish on Capitol Hill, the heart of Seattle's gay community. Dignity members hung banners, distributed gay-friendly religious literature, and organized church socials afterward. The celebration of the Sunday evening Mass was no different than any other Mass.

"The only difference was that there were all kinds of gay people there worshiping together," said Pat Roche, a bank communications director and later national president of Dignity. "I immediately felt at home."

Meanwhile, Hunthausen, citing a 1976 statement by the U.S. bishops on the human rights of homosexuals, urged Catholics to oppose public measures that discriminated against gays in employment, housing, licensing, or civic participation. His letter, published in *The Progress*, argued that sexual orientation is not grounds for discrimination.

"To discriminate against this group of men and women is not only contrary to sound religious principles," he wrote, "but in conflict with protection of basic rights in our American civic life."

In 1977, Hunthausen endorsed Seattle Mayor Wes Uhlman's first-ever proclamation of a Gay Pride Week. Avoiding the words "gay pride," the archbishop described the week as an opportunity to focus on injustices committed against homosexuals. Hunthausen later called for a "no" vote on a 1978 Seattle ballot initiative that would have repealed the city ordinances protecting employment and housing rights for gays and lesbians.

His defense of gay civil rights through application of new Catholic thinking about the inherent nature of homosexuality did not sit well with some of the faithful. "Homosexual conduct is contrary to God's laws," a Snohomish reader wrote *The Progress*. "Shall we also bring into [the Christian community] murderers, rapists, extortionists, abortionists, and all their buddies?" A Seattle reader worried that anti-discrimination laws would force Catholic schools to employ homosexuals.

Others wrote *The Progress* praising the archbishop for his support of sexual minorities. "I am a human being, a Catholic, and a gay," wrote a Seattle man. "I know I had NO CHOICE in the matter of my sexual identity."

Norman DeNeal, president of Dignity's Seattle chapter, thanked Hunthausen for opening the door to gays who had felt rejected by the church.

In an effort to calm emotions and instill understanding, *The Progress* published a three-week series in March 1978 on "the Homosexual and the Church." The series began with an article about Dignity, quoting Father Kirby Brown, a chaplain to the Seattle gay group, who said requiring gays to be celibate is unrealistic and unsound. He suggested that a faithful, loving, and committed gay relationship could be considered equivalent to heterosexual marriage. In the second part of the series, *The Progress* interviewed DeNeal and another Seattle Dignity member about how and when they realized they were gay. Both said that Dignity gave them a place where they could be accepted as gay and Catholic. And both rejected the church's argument that homosexual acts are inherently sinful.

In the final installment, Father Brown, the Dignity chaplain, and Father Reilly, the moral theologian, discussed how the church should minister to homosexuals. Reilly reiterated church teaching (homosexuals, good; homosexual acts, bad) but he could not offer absolute answers in dealing with pastoral questions involving gays (Should gays receive communion? Should they teach in our schools? Should gay unions be tolerated?). "Good moral decisions of a practical nature require wisdom and prudence," he wrote.

Father Brown countered that the church needed to dialogue with gays to better understand their sense of alienation and isolation. "I'm asking that those who want the church's teaching to be changed be heard and be given a chance to [talk about it]," Brown wrote.

By 1983, the deadly AIDS virus had begun to take its toll in the gay community, raising the question of homosexuality and homosexual relationships to new intensity within the church. In June, during the gay pride celebrations in Seattle, the state's three bishops, led by Hunthausen, issued a teaching document under the name of the WSCC titled "The Prejudice against Homosexuals and the Ministry of the Church." The document, originally drafted by Chirico, again explained church teaching but then went out of its way to affirm and praise homosexuals. It attributed to gays a special sensitivity for human warmth and attention to the needs of others. "Church teaching is positive with regard to homosexual persons in the totality of their beings," it read.

Taking up more than two pages of dense type in the June 16, 1983, edition of *The Progress,* the document argued that "the prejudice against homosexuals is a greater infringement of the norm of Christian morality than is homosexual orientation or activity." Why? Because prejudice hampers personal growth for both gays and "straights," offends human dignity, and is contrary to God's law. The document went on to say that "the manner in which church teaching has been concretely conveyed has contributed to the prejudice against gays and lesbians."

Suggesting that prejudice was a greater evil than homosexual sex soon rang alarm bells at the Vatican.

That same month, Hunthausen accepted an invitation to speak to the Dorian Society, a gay businessmen's group, at a downtown hotel. While invited to talk about peace and disarmament, the archbishop paused during his speech to acknowledge the significance of the occasion. Never before had an American Catholic bishop met and spoken publicly with a gay activist organization.

"I hope it's not the last time," he told them.

Hunthausen also met with the organizers of Dignity's biennial national convention planned for Labor Day week 1983 at the downtown Sheraton Hotel. The convention theme was "Building the City of God." The organizers sought the archbishop's permission to celebrate their closing Mass at St. James Cathedral, a short walk uphill from the hotel.

Hunthausen knew that a gay Mass at the cathedral could ignite a firestorm. He also knew that his absence from the diocese—he and the other Northwest bishops were scheduled to be in Rome—would further complicate things. He thought the cathedral request was reasonable, however, one he certainly would have granted for a convention of disabled, charismatic, divorced, or virtually any other Catholic group. Nonetheless, he decided it would be best to consult with others, including Father Ryan, the chancellor; Father William Gallagher, the cathedral pastor; and the priest personnel board. No one raised any major objections, although Gallagher made it clear that he would have nothing to do with the Mass. He'd be hunkered down in the rectory.

Because Hunthausen would be away, the Dignity organizers asked Ryan, as chancellor, to deliver the welcoming remarks at the cathedral. The politically astute Ryan thought otherwise.

"I became pretty alarmed and nervous about it," he recalled. "In those days, frankly, I was not prepared to compromise my future and, I thought, this will surely do it."

Ryan, who wanted to keep both himself and his boss out of trouble, came up with the idea of a videotaped welcome from Hunthausen with an explanatory Q&A with the archbishop printed in *The Progress*. So he and Maury Sheridan, the communications director, concocted the interview, ran it by Hunthausen, and then scripted and filmed the video.

In *The Progress* interview, Hunthausen acknowledged that the gay issue was sensitive, volatile, and likely to excite heated emotions of fear and hostility. "Those are painful risks we take if we are to grow in our faith," he said.

He carefully noted that he did not embrace some of the positions held by some members of Dignity. Yet, he pointed out, these are "our people," members of the Body of Christ with the same rights to the sacraments and use of the church as any other Catholics. Remarking that church treatment of gays had driven many of them away, he said, "As chief pastor of this church I want to do all I can to halt this exodus."

In the videotaped message shown in the cathedral, Hunthausen told the Dignity delegates, "While I am not able to be with you in person, I am surely with you in spirit and in prayer. . . . I pray that your presence here among us will be a blessing."

The archbishop went on to note that some find it difficult to understand why the church has a special ministry to gays. For them, he said, your presence in the cathedral is a source of wonderment and confusion, even anger and resentment.

"Perhaps your first duty in love will be toward those very people who find it so difficult to understand you and why you have come here," he concluded.

More than twelve hundred people, including eight hundred Dignity members, participated in the Saturday evening Mass. Forty-five clerics concelebrated the service with Father Pete Peterson, an archdiocesan priest. Sheridan, who attended on Hunthausen's behalf, described the Mass as a fine religious experience conducted with sensitivity and seriousness.

Despite Ryan and Sheridan's damage control and Hunthausen's mollifying words, Catholics hostile to Dignity fought back with a vengeance. On the day of the cathedral Mass, a full-page ad purchased by a group calling itself the "National Parents League," appeared in the *Seattle Times*. Under the bold headline "DON'T BE MISLED," the ad denounced Hunthausen for welcoming Dignity and for allowing the group to use the cathedral. It excerpted quotations from scripture, church documents, Pope John Paul II, and Dignity speakers and publications to demonstrate its point that a "clear contrast" existed between Dignity's position and "God's law as continuously taught by the Catholic Church." The Dignity convention with its the cathedral Mass, the ad concluded, is an occasion of confusion and scandal.

That evening, some 150 people, including members of Catholics United for the Faith (CUF) and two priests from Portland, marched outside the cathedral while the Dignity delegates attended the Mass. As the marchers paced back and forth on the sidewalk, they recited the rosary and sang hymns. One of the Portland priests decried Dignity's use of the cathedral as "a profanation" and "sacrilege." Some of the marchers carried signs. They read: "Remember Sodom and Gomorrah." "God is not GAY." "Pray for Gays."

Meanwhile, Archbishop Hunthausen had begun a long, roundabout journey to Rome where an infuriated Cardinal Ratzinger awaited him.

"Dutch" Hunthausen dressed for first communion at St. Paul's Church in Anaconda, Montana, 1927.
(Courtesy Hunthausen family)

Hunthausen graduated from Carroll College in 1943.
(Courtesy Hunthausen family)

Hunthausen, far left, attended St. Edward Seminary, 1943-46.
(Courtesy Hunthausen family)

At Carroll College, Hunthausen taught chemistry and math and served as head football coach and dean of men.
(Archives, Catholic Archdiocese of Seattle)

As bishop of Helena, Montana, Hunthausen, left foreground, participates in the Second Vatican Council in St. Peter's Basilica in Rome from 1962-65.
(Catholic Northwest Progress)

Assigned to Western Washington in 1975, Archbishop Hunthausen chats with a youngster at a church picnic in Sedro Woolley.
(Catholic Northwest Progress)

Hunthausen waits to speak at a peace rally on Puget Sound in 1982. Thousands came to oppose the Trident submarine, the world's most lethal weapons system.
(Catholic Northwest Progress)

At a peace demonstration at the Trident base at Bangor, Hunthausen quietly watches from the crowd.
(Catholic Northwest Progress)

Hunthausen, center, and other Pacific Northwest religious leaders scan the horizon from the bow of the Heather Queen as they await arrival of the first Trident submarine in August 1982.
(Catholic Northwest Progress)

Hunthausen wrote a pastoral letter that called for full inclusion of women in the life of the church. The Vatican reprimanded him for it.
(Catholic Northwest Progress)

At the Vatican in January 1986, Hunthausen introduces the delegation from Seattle to Pope John Paul II.
(*Catholic Northwest Progress*)

Hunthausen and Auxiliary Bishop Donald Wuerl face questions about Wuerl's authority as they prepare to celebrate Mass at Kennedy High School in Burien on September 7, 1986.
(*Seattle Post-Intelligencer* Collection, Museum of History & Industry, Seattle)

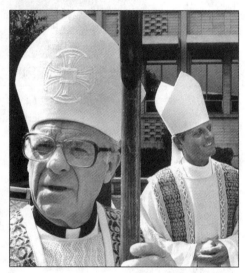

Archbishop Pio Laghi, the papal nuncio, lectures Hunthausen at the U.S. bishops' conference in Washington, D.C., in November 1986.
(*Sooner Catholic*)

Editorial cartoon by Brian Basset in the Seattle Times, *November 13, 1986.*
(Used with permission, *Seattle Times*)

Hunthausen greets supporters at SeaTac Airport after
defending himself against Vatican accusations at the
November 1986 U.S. bishops' conference.
(*Catholic Northwest Progress*)

*The Vatican appoints Bishop Thomas J. Murphy, left,
as coadjutor archbishop of Seattle and restores
Hunthausen's full authority on May 26, 1987.*
(Catholic Northwest Progress)

*The Vatican named Archbishop John Quinn, center, Cardinal Joseph
Bernardin, right, and Cardinal John O'Connor, not pictured, to an ad hoc
commission to resolve the "Hunthausen affair."*
(Catholic Northwest Progress)

Hunthausen, center left, and the Rev. William Cate, head of the Church Council of Greater Seattle, center right, lead a 1987 Seattle march in memory of assassinated Archbishop Oscar Romero to promote the cause of Central American refugees seeking sanctuary.
(Catholic Northwest Progress)

Hunthausen links arms with U.S. Congressmen Jim McDermott and Mike Lowry, left, and state religious leaders in protest of the 1991 Gulf War.
(Catholic Northwest Progress)

THE VISITATION

You blind guides, straining out a gnat and swallowing a camel!
—Matthew 23:24

Archbishop Hunthausen's long 1983 journey to Rome began with the disturbing coffee-break conversation he had had with Archbishop Pio Laghi, the papal delegate, at the U.S. bishops' meeting in Chicago in May. Laghi had told him in a rather enigmatic manner that the Archdiocese of Seattle was to receive an "apostolic visitation." But he offered few details, then disappeared.

Weeks later Laghi phoned Hunthausen to inform him that Archbishop James A. Hickey, of Washington, DC, would be named as the "apostolic visitator" to Seattle. In Luke's Gospel story of "the visitation," Mary, soon to be the mother of God, goes to the home of her pregnant cousin, Elizabeth, to assist her with the birth of John the Baptist. The story demonstrates the virtue of love of neighbor in the hour of need. Hickey, like Mary, would offer counsel and support to a brother bishop whom Rome judged to need serious help.

A formal, austere man who held graduate degrees in canon law and theology, Hickey was an obvious choice. Educated in Rome, he had been rector at the Pontifical North American College and had served as bishop in Saginaw, Michigan, and archbishop in Cleveland. He was an influential, behind-the-scenes player in the church and with U.S. political leaders. More important, he was a trusted colleague and carbon copy of Pope John Paul II—strong on social justice yet unstintingly orthodox on doctrine and discipline.

"The most serious of my charges," Hickey said, "is maintaining the purity of church doctrine."

In his Washington, DC archdiocese, Hickey had ended church funding for a nonprofit pregnancy crisis center when it declined to stop dispensing contraceptives. As chancellor of Catholic University, he had removed moral theologian Father Charles Curran because of his dissent from Catholic teaching on artificial contraception. And he had all but shut down the ministry of a local nun and priest, Sister Jeannine Gramick and Father Robert Nugent, for what he regarded as their ambiguous position on church teaching regarding homosexuality.

Hickey was a stickler for by-the-rulebook celebration of the Mass and the sacraments, clamping down on substitutions or changes that he felt deviated from the norm. As the U.S. church's point man in the nation's capital, he cultivated a close and sometimes conflictive relationship with the Reagan administration. At the height of the civil war in El Salvador, he testified before Congress in opposition to U.S. military aid to its right-wing government. Like Hunthausen and other bishops, he advocated for nuclear disarmament in the face of the administration's massive arms buildup. And he also lobbied the Reagan government for formal diplomatic ties with the Vatican and appointment of a full U.S. ambassador to the Holy See.

Hunthausen was baffled by the planned appointment of Hickey to investigate Rome's concerns. He had been unable to get specifics from Laghi and had little idea what Hickey would come to Seattle to do. In frustration, he phoned Archbishop John Roach, of St. Paul, Minnesota, the incoming president of the bishops' conference.

"Jack, what do you think of this thing?" Hunthausen asked. "I think this is something that has come out of the curia, out of Cardinal Ratzinger's office. I just feel that the Holy Father would dismiss this thing if he could know the whole story."

There was a pause on Roach's end of the phone line. "No, I don't think so," Roach said. "I don't think things like this happen without the Holy Father's knowledge and decision."

Roach suggested that Hunthausen get a bill of particulars from the Vatican. Find out what's disturbing them, he told the Seattle archbishop.

Hunthausen took Roach's advice. He asked Father Ryan, his Roman-wise chancellor, to help him draft a letter to Laghi. In the letter he said that the coffee-break conversation in Chicago had given him no indication of the nature of the Vatican's concerns, only that there were some. What were they? he asked. Then he questioned the wisdom of sending in Hickey as a secret investigator.

"Assuming that the proposed visit is an extraordinary way of proceeding, would it not be a cause for serious confusion for our priests and our people?" Hunthausen wondered. "To be very frank, I hope that I will be able to consider carefully with you whatever concerns there may be before a decision is made [about sending an apostolic visitor]."

A month went by before Laghi responded. The papal delegate revealed that he had received instructions from Cardinal Ratzinger that "the Holy Father himself" was initiating the apostolic visitation in Seattle because of "serious reservations of a pastoral and doctrinal nature." The only reason he hadn't told Hunthausen more about this in Chicago, he wrote, was because the Vatican had not yet identified the visitator. Now Ratzinger was naming Archbishop Hickey to do the job.

Hickey would bring with him two experts in theology and canon law and also receive assistance from Bishop William Levada of Los Angeles, Laghi noted. Levada was on the Vatican's fast track. He had worked under Ratzinger at the Congregation for the Doctrine of the Faith and would later serve as archbishop in Portland and San Francisco before succeeding Ratzinger as CDF prefect when the latter became Pope Benedict XVI.

Laghi's letter did not respond to Hunthausen's question about Rome's concerns other than to say that they had started before his time as papal delegate. "I can only urge you to respond in a most gracious and cooperative way," he wrote Hunthausen.

Unsatisfied, Hunthausen phoned Laghi, asking again to know the reasons for the investigation. Laghi demurred, suggesting that Hunthausen talk to the visitator.

When Hunthausen called Hickey, he discovered that the Washington archbishop was suffering from a very serious case of pneumonia and was unavailable. Hunthausen became increasingly uneasy as the summer weeks slipped by. Finally, Hickey called Hunthausen from the hospital.

"His voice was very weak, so weak that I could hardly understand him," Hunthausen recalled. "He was very apologetic about the delay and suggested that we meet in Chicago in September."

In September, Hunthausen had planned to be in Rome for the *ad limina* visit of the Pacific Northwest bishops with the pope and attend a month-long theological colloquium. To accommodate Hickey, he agreed to forgo most of the colloquium and meet him in Chicago on his way to Rome.

Meanwhile, he felt he should tell a few others what was happening to him. He unburdened himself to Yakima Bishop William Skylstad, a close colleague and trusted friend.

"It was a heavy conversation," Skylstad recalled. "He was trying to understand: why him?"

He then drove to Helena, where he picked up his brother, Father Jack Hunthausen. The two brothers drove north to Browning, the forlorn, windswept town on the Blackfeet Reservation, where they

met their sister, Edna, in her trailer home. The archbishop felt compelled to share the news of the visitation with the two siblings who
had also committed their lives to the church.

As the wind rattled the aluminum walls of Edna's trailer,
Hunthausen said, "I've got to share this with you. I don't know
where it's going." Then he explained what had transpired.

Edna recalled how humiliated and wounded her older brother
felt. He had thought things were going well in the archdiocese, that
Rome was pleased with his leadership. And now this.

The siblings talked for several hours before the archbishop and
Jack drove back to Helena. The conversation in Edna's trailer had
cheered him up. But deep in his heart he remained troubled and hurting. How could an institution he loved so much be so distrusting of
his loyalty and love?

On September 15 and 16, 1983, Archbishops Hunthausen and Hickey
met in a Chicago hotel room. It was just the two of them. After some
initial pleasantries, Hickey opened the first of several file folders filled
with letters, notes, and newspaper clippings. Despite the fraternal talk
about "brother bishops," Hickey and Hunthausen scarcely knew one
other. They shared a strong commitment to nuclear disarmament and
social justice although Hickey would never have entertained a tax
protest. A cautious intellectual with a cultivated air of amicable reserve,
Hickey went about his job with meticulous and dispassionate attention
to detail. Hunthausen, though ill at ease, was his usual self, friendly,
guileless, and transparent. Unlike Hickey, he had come to the meeting
without notes or documents. And hence he was utterly unprepared.

"I was absolutely appalled when he dragged out all of the newspaper clippings and the letters that had been received in Rome," Hunthausen said.

The letters were full of accusations of alleged liturgical abuses, of
failures to heed church law, of the archbishop's unwillingness or inability to instruct and enforce Catholic teaching. In Hunthausen's
mind, virtually all of the accusations were misrepresentations, had
logical explanations, or were totally inconsequential.

"I can't believe this, Jim," Hunthausen told Hickey. "I just can't
believe this. Jim, this is petty. I could develop a file like this on you or
any other bishop."

Unmoved, Hickey continued to pull letters and clippings from his
files, displaying them one at a time, going from one to the next. He
didn't have a list of questions and he didn't ask many. It was obvious
that Hunthausen was on the spot to offer explanations.

One letter objected that two archdiocesan priests had participated in an ecumenical Thanksgiving Day service at St. Mark's Episcopal Cathedral during which they distributed communion. Surely, the letter complained, a Catholic priest giving out communion at a Protestant event is an egregious violation of church law. Hunthausen told Hickey that, yes, this was "probably clumsy ecumenism," and he had asked the offending priests not to do it again. And they hadn't. Case closed.

Hickey produced a July 1980 newspaper column by Ray Ruppert, the religion editor of the *Seattle Times*. Ruppert had interviewed Hunthausen on a number of issues including the nuclear-armed Trident submarines, the archdiocesan goals for the next five years, and a spat covered in *The Wanderer* about alleged misuse of altar breads. Some Catholics, disturbed by parish liturgy committees baking their own bread, had objected to using anything other than traditional unleavened communion wafers. Rome, without consultation, eventually decided in their favor. In the interim, a great deal of tattling had gone on about baked bread at communion.

Once Rome had ruled, Hunthausen instructed his priests to please use unleavened bread in celebrating the Eucharist. For someone horrified by the possibility of nuclear holocaust, the altar breads issue seemed incredibly trivial. The archbishop told Ruppert that fussing about altar breads was "being like the fellow on the Titanic who just moves his chair around to get a better view of the disaster."

Hickey, stone-faced, did not appreciate Hunthausen's analogy. Later, when he re-interviewed the archbishop as part of the formal visitation process in Seattle, he gave an example of how he had handled a situation of questionable altar bread. He was in the middle of celebrating Mass when he discovered the communion bread had been made with yeast. He stopped the Mass, he told Hunthausen, called the dismayed pastor to his side, and told him that he could not continue until he had appropriate bread. The pastor had no unleavened bread in the sacristy. So, leaving Hickey at the altar, he ran to his car, drove to a neighboring parish, borrowed some communion wafers, and came back. Hickey then resumed the Mass.

"That's how strongly I feel about this," he said.

Stunned, Hunthausen spoke his mind. "I really feel that was destructive of good liturgy, Jim. It was destructive of Christian community. I would never do that. I would just never do that."

Undeterred, Hickey produced more letters and articles. There were complaints about former priests still administering the sacraments. About annulments granted to divorced Catholics who offered lame explanations for their supposedly invalid first marriages. About psychological tests that allegedly weeded out the seminary candidates most committed to the Holy Father. And, finally, there were letters accusing Hunthausen of being soft on abortion, approving of homosexual behavior, being beholden to Marxist liberation theology, and failing to teach and uphold the unchanging, eternal Catholic truth as decreed by the pope and the magisterium.

Hunthausen was dumbfounded. He knew that some of his critics had written to the papal delegate, to Ratzinger, and to the pope. But he couldn't believe that the Vatican took most of these complaints seriously. He knew about some of them because he'd received copies of the letters.

"My feeling when I heard from these people was, by golly, Rome will see through this in two seconds," Hunthausen said. "They know what kind of people they're dealing with."

Indeed, Rome did know.

Foremost was *The Wanderer*, the ultraorthodox Catholic weekly published since 1867 in St. Paul, Minnesota, and distributed to all the key offices at the Vatican. Edited by its sole owner, A. J. Matt Jr., the newspaper is independent of ecclesial oversight and purports to maintain a fiercely vigilant adherence to Catholic doctrine. It lives uncomfortably with Vatican II, arguing that the Council was about renewing the church, not reforming it. It helped organize Catholics United for the Faith (CUF), a national lay organization founded in 1968 "to support, defend, and advance the efforts of the teaching Church."

Criticism of Archbishop Hunthausen began to appear in *The Wanderer*'s news and opinion pages long before the papal delegate approached the archbishop about an apostolic visitation. Catholics unsettled by the reforms of Vatican II and riled by Hunthausen's opposition to Trident wrote *The Wanderer*, *The Progress*, the local dailies, and the Vatican. For the most part, criticism of the archbishop's protests against nuclear arms landed on deaf ears in Rome. But around 1982, after Hunthausen initiated his tax protest and became the U.S. bishops' point person on unilateral disarmament, things shifted. Letters that had typically gone unanswered now received responses that the matter was under review. Hunthausen critics discovered that the letters most likely to get a response documented a liturgical abuse or alleged a teaching or practice that was contrary to church doctrine or law.

A few loudmouth critics who claimed to represent the true church bedeviled the archbishop. Their intemperate remarks made sensational copy for the press but shed little light on what was really happening.

Perhaps the most vociferous critic was Erven Park, a heavy-equipment salesman in the Columbia River town of Kelso, a father of eight and a former grand knight in the Knights of Columbus. Park published and circulated a newsletter called *Catholic Truth* in which he regularly detailed the "unauthorized and forbidden" practices and teachings in the Archdiocese of Seattle. He sent the newsletter free of charge to every priest in western Washington. Among his allegations were mishandling of communion, altering the prayers of the Mass, preaching liberation theology, encouraging women to seek ordination, and disputing the biblical account of Adam and Eve.

Another strident critic was Danny Barrett, a parishioner at St. Philomena's Church in the Seattle suburb of Des Moines and the spokesman of an ad hoc group called Catholics Against Marxist Theology. Barrett, a naturalized Irishman and retired Boeing employee, attacked Hunthausen as a pacifist who would rather "be Red than dead." He and his cronies charged that the archbishop had perverted the intent of Vatican II by turning the Mass into "a communist-influenced social event."

Catholics United for the Faith, buttressed by *The Wanderer*, was much more effective in its criticism of Hunthausen than Barrett or Park. In western Washington, CUF had chapters in Seattle, Tacoma, and Everett, and claimed a mailing list of twelve thousand. And it had priest supporters in the archdiocese who believed that Hunthausen had indeed led the local church astray.

As the religion writer at the *Seattle Post-Intelligencer*, I went to interview one of these priests, Father William Ogden. A frail former seminary professor and chaplain, Ogden lived in a downtown Seattle retirement home where he said a private Latin Mass in his room. Like other traditionalist Catholics, he complained that Hunthausen and other Vatican II bishops were contravening church law in multiple ways. For example: by allowing youngsters to receive first communion before their first confession, by permitting liturgical innovations (e.g., guitar playing and interpretative dance) that "blasphemed" the Mass, or by suggesting that a Catholic can dissent from the official teachings of the church and still remain in good standing.

"With all the heresy that is going around," Ogden told me, "there is going to come a time when it will be difficult to determine what is church teaching."

Ogden insisted that Catholic teaching is unerring and forever unchanging. Thumping a large black book of canon law, he said, "It is not possible that any of these certain truths can be changed."

The Wanderer filled its pages with like-minded thinking. It denounced what it viewed as the heretical beliefs and practices imposed on the Catholic faithful by bishops like Hunthausen. Its most cogent and articulate writer was Frank Morriss, a contributing editor whose columns also ran in *The Progress* along with those of George Weigel, Jim Douglass, and, occasionally, Archbishop Hunthausen.

Morriss was in Seattle at the invitation of the local CUF chapter the month before Hickey grilled Hunthausen in Chicago. He titled his presentation "Indignation" because, he said, like most traditional Catholics, he was indignant.

"Don't get the idea that Christ was always dripping with sweetness and honey and saying your sins are forgiven," Morriss told a small, sympathetic audience at Seattle University. "He was utterly excoriating with corrupt religion and indifference to truth."

Morriss attacked pacifism, the substitution of good intentions for morality (e.g., allowing gay Masses), and the elevation of conscience over church authority.

"If the church says contraception is wrong, you don't follow your conscience," he said. "You get it fixed. Nothing's right for you that isn't right for everybody."

Morriss urged local Catholics to resist what was happening in the Seattle archdiocese by taking action. Speak out, he said. Stage public protests. Subscribe to *The Wanderer*. Object to the homosexual Mass and demand that the cathedral be reconsecrated. Write Hunthausen and copy the papal delegate, the heads of Vatican congregations, and the pope.

CUF, *The Wanderer*, Morriss, and other Hunthausen critics kept Father Chirico, the archdiocesan theologian, very busy. Smart, clever, and good-humored, Chirico often served as the archbishop's advocate and spokesman, repeatedly explaining what many Catholics seemed to have missed. Because of Vatican II, the church of the 1980s was not the church of the 1950s, he pointed out time and again. Things had changed.

Chirico's apologetics went like this: The core beliefs of Catholicism are eternally true: Christ is God made man. He suffered, was crucified, died, and was buried to redeem mankind from sin. And he rose again that all humanity might share in eternal life. Around that fundamental core, however, is a great body of theological teaching that is subject to change and even reversal. The church, albeit quietly, has demonstrated that. It has changed its teachings on slavery, usury, Judaism, religious freedom, evolution, biblical literalism, and the sun-centered universe. It has altered its practices on matters such as fasting, marriage annulments, reception of the sacraments, and lay participation in the Mass. Vatican II clearly acknowledged the "development of doctrine" in response to "the signs of the times."

"Theology has never remained static," Chirico explained over and over again. "Theology, like science, moves on."

He noted that some Catholics were unable to accept the fact that the Gospels are not official biographies of Christ but rather divinely inspired spiritual accounts of what it means to be a Christian. A Gospel parable can contain truth even if the particular events never happened, he said.

As for church teaching, Chirico said decrees from Rome are official but rarely infallible. In fact, the pope has declared church teaching infallible only two times: the dogma of the Immaculate Conception of Mary (1854) and her Assumption into heaven (1950). Consequently, Chirico pointed out, an informed Catholic, under certain circumstances, *can* dissent from official teaching.

Those who complained to Rome, he said, "see heresy behind every tree. They can't see how something new can be as good as what they had before. Unfortunately for them, we have an archbishop who challenges people to think."

Hunthausen's critics detested Chirico whom they saw as a devil-tongued obfuscator. Some trailed the theologian around the archdiocese with tape players hoping to record a "Chirico-ism" they could use to get him in hot water with Rome.

At some point in that Chicago hotel room that warm September afternoon, Hunthausen had seen enough. "I'm going to Rome," he told Hickey, who finally put away his notebook and files.

Hunthausen insisted that conducting a visitation in Seattle would do damage to everyone—to him, to Hickey, and to the Holy Father. Hickey replied that he was simply doing what he had been asked to do—conduct a visitation. He suggested that Hunthausen call on four prelates when he was in Rome: Ratzinger; Cardinal Agostino Casaroli, the Vatican secretary of state; Cardinal Sebastiano Baggio, head of the Congregation for Bishops; and Bishop Levada, the Los Angeles auxiliary who had formerly worked at the CDF. With the exception of Levada, Hunthausen realized that Hickey was suggesting he talk to the men at the very top of the Catholic Church.

Obviously, he concluded, the concerns about his ministry in Seattle were being dealt with at a very high level. Ratzinger, Casaroli, and Baggio met every Friday morning with Pope John Paul II.

In Rome a few days later, Hunthausen managed to arrange appointments with three of the four prelates. Casaroli was out of town. Hunthausen also decided to see Archbishop Jadot, the former papal delegate now consigned to an obscure Vatican office.

He started with Levada, an icy, ambitious, by-the-book bureaucrat and future CDF prefect. Levada was in Rome to give a talk at the North American College where he, Hunthausen, and Nicolas Walsh, Seattle's auxiliary bishop, were all lodging. Hunthausen arranged to meet him privately at the seminary. Levada, through his earlier experience at the CDF, presumably knew Ratzinger's concerns. After all, Hickey had suggested the two of them talk.

Levada, however, was not going to do any talking.

"He said nothing," Hunthausen recalled. "Literally nothing. Yet he must have known what was going on."

Shut out by Levada, Hunthausen then called on Jadot, who received him warmly. Jadot said he knew nothing about the visitation but assured Hunthausen that the Holy Father would receive a favorable report about the Archdiocese of Seattle once Hickey's visit was concluded. He was also confident that Seattle would receive one or more auxiliary bishops since Walsh would be resigning soon for health reasons.

Comforted by Jadot, Hunthausen next called on Baggio, who received him after hours in his apartment just off St. Peter's Square. A squat, affable Italian nicknamed "Viaggio Baggio" for his many travels, the powerful cardinal was responsible for recommending episcopal appointments and overseeing the work of bishops around the world. Named to head the Congregation for Bishops by Pope Paul VI, he was retained in office by John Paul II despite his previous preference for recommending conciliar-minded appointments like Jadot's. Baggio quickly pleased his new boss, however, seeking out bishop candidates in the mold of the pontiff.

Baggio served Hunthausen tea and listened to the archbishop's accounts of his conversations with Laghi and Hickey about the visitation. Assuming that he would quickly put the visitation behind him, Hunthausen then went on to appeal to Baggio for the appointment of two auxiliary bishops to Seattle.

Gesturing expansively, the cardinal shrugged. "One for sure," he said, "but two, maybe."

In Italian-accented English, Baggio returned to the subject of the visitation. "You know," he said slyly, "I don't know much about [the reasons] for this visitation."

And then, shrugging again, he implied that Hunthausen's lack of auxiliaries, his peace activism, and the pending visitation were all related.

"He kind of equated the fact of the visitation with my involvement in the arms race issue," Hunthausen recalled. "He gave me to believe there was some connection. That's the only place [at the Vatican] that I ever, ever got that sense."

The implication was so oblique that Hunthausen didn't pursue it. After all, his primary agenda with Baggio was getting auxiliary bishops. He appreciated Baggio's graciousness but upon leaving the apartment he realized that he knew little more than when he had arrived.

Cardinal Ratzinger was next. Hunthausen had never met him. He went alone in the early afternoon, traversing St. Peter's Square to enter the courtyard of an imposing, medieval building that housed the former Holy Office, now the CDF. He walked up the steps to the second floor where the cardinal and his secretary, Father Thomas J. Herron, the young priest who had succeeded Levada, received him in a high-ceilinged conference room. Ratzinger and Hunthausen sat in armchairs, facing each other across a low mahogany table.

The tall, white-haired cardinal, though unsmiling and reserved, was courteous and prepared to listen. Herron, an American from Philadelphia, did some initial translation but it was soon evident that Ratzinger and Hunthausen could communicate fine in English. The archbishop reviewed his conversations with Laghi and Hickey and suggested, as he had to Hickey, that a secret apostolic visitation initiated by the Vatican would harm the Holy Father and the church. If there are concerns about my ministry, he told Ratzinger, let me take the initiative and publicly invite Archbishop Hickey to Seattle to review our work on behalf of the Vatican.

"Your Eminence, we've got nothing to hide," Hunthausen insisted. "You're free to explore and examine anything you want in the archdiocese."

Hunthausen was adamant that it would be impossible for Hickey to come to Seattle for a week of interviews and keep the whole matter quiet. Moreover, he added, the Catholics of western Washington had a right to know what was happening in their church.

Ratzinger mulled it over. "It makes some sense," he conceded. "But we've already begun in the other direction and I cannot tell you yes or no until I consult with the others who are involved."

He promised to get back to Hunthausen as soon as possible. He then opened up discussion of the issues that Hickey had quizzed him about in Chicago: first communion before first confession, the use of laicized priests in teaching roles, intercommunion with Protestants, the granting of annulments to divorced Catholics, and so on.

"My response in each instance," Hunthausen said, "was that we're no different than any other diocese. Some of these things are very common practices."

As he had with Hickey, the archbishop insisted that he and his staff had dealt responsibly with most of these issues. Some of the information that Rome had was clearly false, he maintained. And, in his opinion, some of it was just not "terribly serious."

Ratzinger complained about Hunthausen's 1980 pastoral letter on the role of women in the church not for what it said but for what it didn't say. The letter didn't mention the subject of women's ordination, Ratzinger objected. That's true, Hunthausen replied. Well, it should have, the cardinal griped, because it missed an opportunity to explain why women can't be priests.

At one point in the conversation, Hunthausen raised the issue of the church's treatment of men who had left the priesthood. He suggested that the Vatican allow former priests to perform some ministerial roles. Ratzinger wouldn't hear of it. Light treatment of ex-priests and reconciliation with the church would give a bad example to seminarians, he said.

Ratzinger had no documentation on the table in front of him. He was simply repeating what he'd read or been told. He kept his heavy artillery until last. Why, he demanded to know, was the archdiocese supporting Dignity and why had the archbishop welcomed the homosexual group into his cathedral? The question poisoned the already heavy air.

Meeting Ratzinger's cool gaze, Hunthausen blanched. A Gospel story popped into his mind. In John 8:11 the Pharisees bring to Jesus a woman caught in adultery. They want Jesus to invoke the law of Moses and order the woman to be stoned. "Let the one among you who is without sin be the first to throw a stone at her," Jesus tells them. The Pharisees disappear one by one, beginning with the elders, until Jesus alone is left with the woman. He asks her, "Has no one condemned you?" "No," the woman replies. Then Jesus says, "Neither do I condemn you."

Hunthausen was recounting the Gospel story when Ratzinger, his voice full of wrath, interrupted him. "Are you presuming to lecture me?" he demanded.

The archbishop paused, caught his breath, and quietly continued. In regards to Dignity, he explained, "I tried to do what I thought Jesus would do. Jesus didn't wait until people changed before he talked to them. He began a dialogue and I think that's what the church ought to do with the gay community."

Infuriated, Ratzinger silenced him again. "Don't preach to me," he said.

Their discussion ended on this unhappy note. Ratzinger excused himself and abruptly left the room. Father Herron, his secretary, remained to continue the conversation. For the next forty-five minutes, Herron tried to convince Hunthausen that the archbishop's approach to gay ministry was misguided, that letting homosexuals into the cathedral was scandalous, and that Dignity was committed to infiltrating and subverting the church.

By the time Hunthausen left the room, he was as angry as Ratzinger.

That evening, the Seattle archbishop attended a reception at the North American College where he spoke with Archbishop Francis T.

Hurley of Anchorage and Archbishop Rembert Weakland of Milwaukee. He respected both men and valued their opinions. Hurley would become his episcopal advisor in the Vatican ordeal that lay ahead. Hunthausen told the two archbishops what had transpired in his meeting with Ratzinger.

A look of alarm crossed Weakland's face. "I'm next," he said. "They're using you to tell everyone else [the U.S. bishops] to pay attention."

Hunthausen's final meeting at the Vatican was with Pope John Paul II himself. But in this case it was a group meeting along with the other Northwest bishops in Rome for the *ad limina* visit. Every five years diocesan bishops are required to make a pilgrimage to the Vatican to present a written account of the state of their dioceses to the pope and the curia. Typically, the pope addresses them as a group with no more than a few minutes allotted for private one-on-one conversation.

In his group address, John Paul insisted that the bishops proclaim "without fear or ambiguity" the teaching of the church against divorce, contraception, homosexual acts, and premarital sex. Furthermore, he said, bishops must not support any individual or group that promotes the ordination of women to priesthood.

Following his address, the Holy Father sat down with the dozen Northwest bishops for a group discussion. Generally, such conversations are light and convivial, steering clear of painful topics. However, Bishop Michael Kenny, of Juneau, Alaska, proposed to Hunthausen beforehand that the two of them each raise a serious subject. Hunthausen agreed. Kenny would talk about the church's treatment of women. Hunthausen would talk about its treatment of former priests.

Kenny, his high-pitched voice pinched with anxiety, went first. He gently suggested to John Paul that women could do so much more for the church if only the Holy Father would open the door to their participation in ordained ministry. If the church remained determined to bar women from priesthood, he said, it would need better arguments. The pope batted down Kenny's suggestion like an annoying fly. Women, he countered, are complementary—not equivalent—to men and the principal role for which God made them is to serve in the home as wives and mothers.

Hunthausen spoke next. He was sitting directly across from John Paul and looked him squarely in the eye as he spoke. He asked the pope to write a letter to all former priests thanking them for their years of dedicated service to the church. Many good men, in good conscience, leave their priestly ministry for good reasons, he said. Yet, after they complete the Vatican process of laicization, they typically receive orders from Rome barring them from teaching in Catholic institutions or from serving in parish positions open to laypeople. This is not fair or just, Hunthausen said.

Scowling, John Paul defended the process and the outcome. "Letting priests out of their lifetime commitment so easily would be scandalous to married people who also make lifetime commitments," he told the archbishop.

Hunthausen persisted. "Your Holiness," he continued, "these good men feel that they have been rejected by the church."

"The church hasn't rejected them," the pontiff snapped back, "they've rejected the church."

Stunned by the pope's rebuff of Hunthausen and his dismissal of former priests, several bishops rallied to the Seattle archbishop's defense. "Oh, no, no, Holy Father," they insisted, "it isn't that way at all."

But John Paul remained intransigent.

In their brief private conversation, Hunthausen told the Holy Father that he wanted to share something that lay very heavy on his heart. He noted that he had visited earlier with Cardinal Ratzinger about the looming visitation.

"Holy Father," he said, "I have done my level best to be a bishop of the church and a disciple of the Lord. If I am an embarrassment or if I am a problem for you or the church, I am more than willing to step down."

John Paul, taken aback, minimized the seriousness of the visitation, assuring Hunthausen that he should not regard it as unusual or troubling.

Hunthausen then made the same suggestion that he had made to Ratzinger: Let me invite the Vatican to publicly review our ministry rather than have Rome initiate a secret investigation. The outcome will be better for all, he suggested.

"No, no, no," the pope responded. "If you'll just go along with what we're going to do, it will all work out."

The archbishop explained that his efforts to implement Vatican II reforms had caused Catholics resistant to change to flood Rome with complaints. Many were unfounded, he insisted, and where there were legitimate issues, he was addressing and resolving them.

John Paul nodded. Smiling slightly, he said something in Polish, which he then translated for Hunthausen's benefit. "Some people are more papal than the pope," he said, adding that he also suffered false accusations.

Hunthausen was both relieved and puzzled by John Paul's sympathetic reaction. At first he asked himself: Does the Holy Father really know what's going on? And then he realized, of course he does. The realization made him feel all the worse.

A few days later Hunthausen was at a deanery meeting of priests on the Olympic Peninsula in the far western region of the archdiocese when he was summoned to the phone to take a long distance call from Washington, DC. It was Hickey who told him that, after talking it over with Ratzinger and Laghi, the visitation was going forward. Please keep it secret.

Within the week, Hunthausen received another sudden call from Hickey. The word was out. Hickey's own diocesan newspaper had asked why he was going to Seattle. So Hickey and Hunthausen simultaneously released public statements saying that, at the request of the Holy See, Hickey would carry out an apostolic visitation in the Archdiocese of Seattle from November 2 to 8, 1983. Hickey was coming as a brother bishop to observe the situation firsthand and offer appropriate assistance in response to criticism of Hunthausen's ministry, the statements said.

On the advice of Father Ryan, Hunthausen added some additional words to his statement. He noted that much of the criticism of his ministry and that of other U.S. bishops "has come from reactionary elements within the church which seem bent on undoing the renewal begun in our church by the Second Vatican Council. Because my faith tells me that this renewal in the church is the work of the Holy Spirit and because I am convinced that our efforts here in this archdiocese are in keeping with the spirit and intent of the Council, I do welcome Archbishop Hickey's visit."

Archbishop Hickey stepped off a plane at Sea-Tac International Airport on the wet, gray afternoon of November 2, 1983, to find a scrum of news reporters, Hunthausen supporters, and Ryan, the chancellor, awaiting him. I was one of the reporters. Hickey, dressed in black clericals and a black fedora, looked determined to get through a distasteful assignment as speedily as possible.

Hunthausen supporters waved signs reading: "We Love Our Archbishop." Earlier, 252 of the 280 priests in the archdiocese, the members of the archdiocesan Pastoral Council, and the regional leaders of six orders of women religious had signed statements in support of the archbishop. The priests announced their support with a full-page ad in *The Progress.*

At the airport gate, Hickey halted in the glare of the television lights to take a few questions from the media. I asked him if his visit had anything to do with the archbishop's tax protest in opposition to nuclear arms or his call for unilateral disarmament. (An article had just appeared in *The Progress* quoting an unnamed Vatican official who explained that bishops who take strong public stands on political issues often cause complaints to Rome.)

"That is not part of my charge," Hickey insisted, adding that he had come at the request of the Holy See to evaluate "various problems" related to church doctrine and practice.

"What are the problems?" I asked.

"To be more open about those criticisms would not serve the welfare of the people and the church," Hickey responded. "Sometimes, you do things in a quiet way."

While Hickey declined to talk specifics, he acknowledged that the Seattle situation appeared to reflect a church-wide conflict between those adhering to the old traditions and those embracing the reforms of Vatican II. The doctrinal and liturgical matters dividing Catholics in Seattle, he conceded, are also national issues.

"So why focus on Hunthausen?" I wanted to know.

Hickey pursed his lips and dodged the question. "Not everything in the church is up for grabs, up for debate," he cautioned. "We have to be clear about that."

The television lights went off. Ryan grasped Hickey by the arm and guided him toward the baggage claim. Hunthausen was quietly waiting in the car to drive them to the cathedral rectory. The visitation had begun. Hickey's expert advisors, Father T. William Coyle, a Redemptorist priest from Fargo, North Dakota, whom Hickey knew from his work on priestly formation, and Father Lorenzo Albacete, a Puerto Rican theologian, writer, and physicist who advised the U.S. bishops' conference, also arrived. Coyle, the note taker for the coming week of interviews, was a kind and discreet elderly man. Albacete, in contrast, was an effusive, argumentative, Roman-educated dandy who boasted of his close friendship with John Paul II.

Hickey and Albacete, assisted by Coyle, conducted a total of sixty-five interviews with priests, women religious, and laypeople of the archdiocese over the next six days. Nearly half of the interviewees were priests. Hickey had asked Hunthausen for a list of leadership people he should interview. Hunthausen sent him the archdiocesan directory with names, job titles, and job descriptions. It was Hickey's investigation, not his.

The three visitors lodged in private rooms in the rectory, sharing the parlor, dining room, and other common areas with Hunthausen, Chirico, and Father Gallagher, the pastor. They conducted their interviews in the rectory and in the chancery building across the street. It was an awkward situation. Hickey and Albacete questioned people in closed-door rooms as the everyday business of the archdiocese swirled around them.

Hickey interviewed Hunthausen for nearly five hours in the rectory's "VIP Room," the nicely appointed apartment in which Hickey was lodged. He went over many of the same liturgical and doctrinal matters the two of them had discussed in Chicago, but this time the conversation was recorded. Hickey assumed a friendly, professional tone, asking a prepared set of questions as objectively as possible. He was efficient and thorough despite his discomfort with his investigative role.

In regard to some matters, for example, the matter of altar breads, Hickey told the archbishop that he would have done things differently. Yet, he conceded, things really weren't much different in Seattle than they were in his own archdiocese of Washington, DC. In fact, Dignity also hosted Masses there.

In the rectory interview, Hickey questioned church employment of former priests. Specifically, he asked, what about Kevin Hanley, a teacher and ex-priest trained in Rome who had once worked at the chancery?

Hunthausen told Hickey that nothing saddened him more than a good priest forced to leave the ministry because he had fallen in love and wanted to marry. He assured Hickey that Hanley, in accord with Rome's laicization demands, had severed his relationship with the archdiocese and was neither ministering nor teaching at church.

"What about his wife?" Hickey inquired.

"And what about his wife?" Hunthausen responded.

"She's the principal of a Catholic grade school," Hickey said.

"Oh, my golly, my golly, Jim," Hunthausen replied. "Don't tell me you want to get rid of her!"

He couldn't believe it. He regarded Hanley and his wife, Geri, as "marvelous people" who were the bulwark of Assumption Parish in Bellingham. He credited her with saving the parish school from possible closure.

"Jim," Hunthausen pleaded with Hickey. "How can we do this to ourselves? How can we deprive the church of their ministry?"

Working himself into a steely anger, Hunthausen told his inquisitor that the way the church treated former priests was heartless, scandalous, and cruel. Testily, he went after Hickey: "So many of these men were loved by their parishes and had so much to give. And when they're gone, there's a deep gaping hole in the lives of their people. Most of our laity would have no difficulty at all having these men come back and serve as married priests. Why can't they at least have all the rights and privileges to serve as laymen?"

"If you look around other dioceses," he stormed on, "you know there's a good number of laicized priests working in various [ministerial] positions. You see the contributions they're making. Where's the scandal? What's the scandal?"

Hickey listened impassively. He had known Hanley when the former priest was a seminary student at the North American College. He knew he was bright and talented. But that was not the issue.

Hickey dropped the subject of Hanley and laicized priests. But Cardinal Ratzinger would pick it up again.

Moving on, Hickey revisited more of the subjects that he and Hunthausen had discussed in Chicago. The Seattle archbishop's anger subsided. Now he was tired and frustrated, unnerved by Rome's preoccupation with what he regarded as so many minor matters in which bishops were traditionally free to make their own prudent decisions. Throughout the interview, he wondered where it was going and when and how it was going to end. This visitation was a big mistake to begin with, but now that it was under way someone at the top was unwilling to back down. Hunthausen felt undermined, his authority diminished, and his credibility ebbing away.

The critics who saw Hickey worked hard to discredit the archbishop and his ministry. Hickey heard from Park, publisher of the *Catholic Truth*; Barrett, of Catholics Against Marxist Theology; David Mitchell, past president of CUF's Seattle chapter; and William Gaffney, a retired attorney and CUF member who regularly wrote the archbishop citing alleged aberrations in liturgy or doctrine by local priests and nuns. (When Gaffney was on his deathbed a few years later, Hunthausen quietly visited him in the hospital.)

Hickey shunted some critics off to Albacete who met with Betty Sifferman, vice president of CUF's Seattle chapter and a mother of six. She complained that women were functioning in church roles prohibited to them. "They're pushing this feminist business on us," she charged.

For the most part, the critics restated to Hickey the complaints they had already taken to the archbishop, the papal delegate, or to Rome. Many of their concerns cut little mustard with Hickey who was the likely source of Laghi's later comment that Hunthausen had been subjected to "exaggerated and mean-spirited criticism."

Park, for example, presented Hickey with a four-page list of Hunthausen's alleged heresies and abuses. Although Hickey swore all interviewees to an oath of confidentiality, Park was quite happy to report their conversation immediately afterward.

With more credible interviewees, Hickey explored the issues that had raised hackles with Ratzinger and the pope. He focused on the operations of the archdiocesan marriage tribunal in separate interviews with Father Ed Holen, the tribunal director, and Father Matthew Naumes, the tribunal's judicial vicar.

Hickey confronted Holen with a copy of a tribunal letter that said that under certain circumstances a pastor could allow a divorced and remarried Catholic to receive the sacraments without a church annulment of the earlier marriage. Remarried Catholics in these circumstances might exercise the so-called "internal forum," an act of good conscience in which they honestly decide that annulment is impossible, imprudent, or harmful to the other party. The Vatican was convinced that marriage tribunals in the United States grossly abused the prerogative of conscience in adjudicating annulments.

Hickey's interview with Holen did not go well, even after the tribunal director pointed out that the offending letter was no longer used. In fact, the apostolic visitator ordered Holen to write an essay on the proper use of the internal forum and return it to him before he left town. Holen complied but left the tribunal and the priesthood shortly thereafter.

When Hickey interviewed Naumes two days later, the atmosphere in the archbishop's conference room was tense and confrontational. Albacete, who did a good deal of the questioning, and Coyle were also there. Naumes sat directly across from Hickey who presented the same letter he had shown to Holen and demanded an explanation.

He and Albacete spent most of the interview time harping on the letter: Who told you that you could do that? Don't you know better?

Naumes was surprised by the obsessive focus on the letter. They asked no questions about Hunthausen or parish life or "whether I used fruitcake when I said Mass," he said. Obviously, they had an agenda and a clear idea of what they wanted.

"They were looking for confirmation, a second or third source for some incident or some policy which, from their point of view, was off the mark," Naumes concluded.

Fuming about what he regarded as a setup, Naumes decided to play "the hog on ice" when the interview was finally over. Danny Barrett and his anti-Marxist gang were in the corridor waiting to present Hickey with a three-hundred-page document listing Hunthausen's "political shenanigans." Barrett was the next interviewee. Naumes, citing the required oath of secrecy, told Hickey that he was not about to blow his cover and leave through that crowd. So Hickey and Naumes slipped from the conference room into the adjacent office of the archbishop, leaving the door ajar just a crack. Albacete then ushered the Barrett gang from the corridor into the conference room.

While Albacete got them seated, Hickey idly picked up an engraved glass plaque from Hunthausen's desk. In the darkened office, he struggled to read the words etched on the glass. So Naumes explained that U.S. Catholic magazine had given the archbishop the award in recognition of his contribution to the role of women in the church.

"It was almost as if someone had put a live grenade in his hands," Naumes said, giggling.

The apostolic visitator put down the plaque and re-entered the conference room while Naumes exited into the now-empty corridor and out of the building.

Hickey also quizzed Sister Diana Bader, the moral theologian and member of the archbishop's medical moral advisory committee, on the "internal forum" issue. His questions implied that there was no room for conscience in moral decision-making, Bader said. "If you were divorced and remarried [without a proper annulment], you were living in mortal sin, and you're out."

Bader, the primary drafter of Hunthausen's pastoral letter on women, found the interview situation reminiscent of the Inquisition. Hickey had his dossier of materials. He asked leading questions. She tried to offer a defense. And he documented whatever she said.

"I really found it unbelievable that in this day and age a cleric would call me in to investigate one of his own brother bishops," Bader said. "It's unimaginable and inexcusable."

Father David Jaeger, the vocations director and an anti-Trident activist, was equally disgusted by the secret procedure and lack of due process. After Hickey grilled Jaeger about the seminary program, the Dignity Mass, and the marriage tribunal, he asked if the priest had anything else to say.

"Yes," Jaeger responded, glaring at Hickey. "I think it is an injustice for this to be taking place."

"Thank you, Father, for your cooperation," Hickey replied and dismissed him.

Hickey's interview with Father Chirico was more cordial. After all, he was a guest in the cathedral rectory, Chirico's home, and they shared meals together. They conducted the formal, recorded interview in the rectory's front sitting room.

Hickey asked how many people were really upset, how the archbishop was received, and what Chirico thought the theological concerns were. He also inquired about Chirico's book on papal infallibility, which had been maligned by some of Hunthausen's critics as full of "heretical Chirico-isms."

The conversation was friendly and courteous. In Chirico's mind, Hickey hadn't uncovered anything that was clearly contrary to church doctrine or practice. So what was the big deal?

The theologian became convinced that the motivation behind the Vatican investigation—despite Rome's protestations to the contrary—

was Hunthausen's stand on unilateral disarmament and his tax resistance. In the minds of many American Catholics, withholding taxes to protest nuclear weapons was unpatriotic and tantamount to treason, a crime far worse than heresy.

"The archbishop was stirring people up," Chirico concluded, "so the Vatican decided to do something."

Sometimes Hickey had narrow, specific concerns with the interviewees. For example, he asked Father Michael McDermott, past research director for the archdiocese, about a 1979 questionnaire that included queries such as: Do you believe Jesus is true God and true man? The question came from a national Catholic survey designed by Father Andrew Greeley, the sociologist and author. Yet Hickey, reflecting one of the Vatican's fears, expressed concern that Catholics in western Washington were voting on what they believed.

"I tried to assure him that was not the case," McDermott said.

Hickey questioned Michael Reichert, the president of Catholic Community Services of Western Washington, about the agency's policies and practices around hiring gays and placing infants and foster children with gay parents.

His interview with Father Ryan, the chancellor, was broader and more far ranging. Ryan thought it went on forever. By telling stories and citing examples, he emphasized to Hickey that Hunthausen was first and foremost a pastor. The archbishop welcomes, he includes, he listens, Ryan said. He lets people make their own decisions guided as best they can be by the Gospel and the church.

He is not theologically precise because he is not a theologian, Ryan told Hickey. "But don't confuse that with his deep, deep loyalty to the church and to the Holy Father."

At the end of the interview, Hickey thanked Ryan as if he had had a sudden revelation. "This is extremely helpful," he said. "I wish we had heard all this at the beginning."

Another revelation occurred during Hickey's interview with Father Larry Reilly, the seminary theology professor who preceded Chirico as the archbishop's theological advisor. Hickey interviewed Reilly in the rectory on Sunday afternoon just hours before he flew back to Washington. Albacete, who had played bad cop to Hickey's good cop, had departed earlier in the day with a plaster statue of the Virgin Mary, a gift from Father Ryan who had heard the Puerto Rican gushing over the kitschy representation of the Madonna.

With Albacete gone, the atmosphere in the rectory parlor was convivial and relaxed. Hickey, knowing the job was nearly done, let his guard down. He knew Reilly from their interaction in the mid-1970s when Reilly was the spiritual director at the American College seminary in Louvain, Belgium, while Hickey was rector at the rival North American College in Rome. The two had enjoyed talking together while walking around their respective campuses. Hickey addressed Reilly as "Larry."

After turning on the tape recorder, he asked Reilly for his impressions of the archbishop. Reilly responded by comparing Hunthausen to Cardinal Suenens, the influential reform leader at the Second Vatican Council.

"I consider Archbishop Hunthausen one of the greatest men I have ever known," Reilly told Hickey. "He's a man of the Gospel, an authentic Christian man, and I have the greatest respect for him."

Surprised, Hickey recovered and said, "Yes, it's true. He's a very wonderful man."

Then Hickey opened his file folder and drew out Hunthausen's pastoral letter on "proportionality," with its argument that it was sometimes necessary to risk the possibility of evil to achieve a greater good. Or, in the case of the archbishop's letter, that a conscientious Catholic could support the good done by United Way, even if the agency provided funding that facilitated contraception and abortion referrals at Planned Parenthood. Reilly had written the letter's first draft.

Hickey produced a sheaf of letters from doctors and nuns who claimed that Reilly's faulty theology about freedom of conscience was being used to justify sterilization, abet contraception, and undermine the teaching authority of the church. Shuffling through the letters, he demanded: Is this accurate? Is this true? Did you say this?

Reilly replied that most of the allegations were false. But, in fact, some of them, for example, sterilization under certain circumstances at Catholic hospitals, were indeed true. There are some situations, he told Hickey, where sterilization is the lesser evil and therefore a moral responsibility.

A look of horror crossed Hickey's face. "It is inconceivable to me how you, as a Roman Catholic priest, could hold a position that is the opposite of our Holy Father's," he said to Reilly.

"It's simple," Reilly shot back. "I'm like a whole lot of other people. Our convictions are different from the Holy Father's."

He went on to argue that many of Hickey's brother bishops also held positions different from the pope's. The color rose in Hickey's face. The friendly warmth seeped from the room.

Frostily, Hickey replied, "We're not here to sit in judgment of my brother bishops."

Reilly realized that no matter what he said, Hunthausen was doomed. Either Reilly was a bad theologian whose incompetent bishop acted on bad advice, or he was a good theologian whose incompetent bishop failed to follow good advice. Either way, no matter how the interview went, Reilly thought, the archbishop would lose.

Overcome by the impossibility of the situation, Reilly's crossed leg began to twitch uncontrollably. He put his foot to the floor to keep the leg from trembling.

Finally, Hickey had exhausted his paper files and completed his questions. He turned off the tape recorder and closed his books. The room was sociable again.

"Well, Larry," he said. "I guess we both know why I'm really here, don't we?"

"Yes, Archbishop," Reilly replied. "You're here because of Ronald Reagan and the archbishop's position on nuclear disarmament."

"That's right," Hickey said. "That's right, Larry."

Nothing more was said. Both men stood and shook hands. Reilly left the room, ending what he called "one of the worst experiences of my life." The two clerics never spoke to each other again.

After the final interview was over, Hunthausen and Ryan took Hickey and Coyle to dinner at McCormick's, a fish restaurant on Fourth Avenue. The dinner conversation was awkward, consisting of small talk and ignoring the substance of the past week. And then it was time to go to the airport.

On the way out of town Hickey told the press that he would be "very, very surprised" if the Vatican made any changes in Seattle as a result of the confidential report he would file with the papal delegate. The disagreements and misunderstandings he had found in the archdiocese could all be resolved through mutual understanding and goodwill, he said.

Privately, Hickey told Hunthausen that the job was done, and he didn't know what would happen next. Like Pontius Pilate, he was washing his hands of the whole affair.

A month later, Cardinal Ratzinger wrote Hunthausen to tell him that Hickey's task was indeed concluded. His letter, which he ordered the archbishop to publish, was decidedly less rosy than the comments the apostolic visitor had made when leaving Seattle. Ratzinger noted that Hickey had gone to Seattle to investigate "a number of issues which have been of concern to the Holy See for some time." Because Rome "did not want to give uncritical acceptance to extremist viewpoints," "this demanding work was undertaken," he wrote. He praised Hickey's work and thanked Hunthausen for his cooperation and devotion to the Holy See.

Ratzinger told the archbishop that he would study Hickey's report so as "to overcome the specific problems which have been encountered." He closed by wishing Hunthausen a peaceful Christmas.

On January 26, 1984, Ratzinger wrote Hunthausen again. He reiterated some of the concerns that he and Hickey had highlighted in their previous conversations with the archbishop: sterilization at Catholic hospitals, general absolution of sins (rather than individual confession), intercommunion with Protestants, first communion before first confession, the Kevin Hanley case, and Hunthausen's granting of an "imprimatur" for the book *Sexual Morality*.

Hunthausen decided to take up these matters by scheduling a private meeting with Ratzinger when the cardinal was in Dallas for the biennial U.S. bishops' workshop hosted by the National Catholic Bioethics Center. The workshop provided ongoing education for bishops on bioethical issues such as abortion, contraception, cloning, and euthanasia. Ratzinger was the keynote speaker at the February 1984 workshop. In his address, titled "On Conscience," he warned about overreliance on subjective reflection and the dangers of relativism.

Hunthausen and Ratzinger met in the cardinal's hotel room. Just the two of them. Ratzinger, collected and reserved, took the Seattle archbishop through the concerns he'd noted in his January 26 letter. In each case, Hunthausen explained what actions he had taken or planned to take at the Vatican's request. He was asking Catholic hospitals to end sterilizations for contraceptive purposes. He had already instructed archdiocesan priests that general absolution and intercommunion were not permitted under the revised code of canon law. He was requiring youngsters to confess their sins before receiving first communion. As for the Hanley case, he argued that firing Hanley's wife would cause scandal and harm the church. Ratzinger nodded in faint agreement but urged Hunthausen to look for an opportune time to rectify the situation.

The archbishop also assured Ratzinger that, at the CDF's request, he would withdraw his imprimatur from *Sexual Morality*, a 1977 book written by Father Philip S. Keane, a Sulpician priest and seminary professor and a personal friend. The imprimatur is a bishop's official declaration that a book is free of doctrinal error. Keane, whose book became a Catholic bestseller thanks to the CDF's action, set forth church teaching on topics such as premarital sex, homosexuality, and masturbation, then explored them in the light of recent anthropological, psychological, and theological thinking. Keane and Hunthausen accepted the Vatican's order to remove the imprimatur although both noted that the rules had changed. Prior to the papacy of John Paul II, imprimaturs were granted to responsible theological books, even though they might express disagreement with the "non-defined" teaching of the church. How else do you encourage free and open theological inquiry?

At the end of his forty-minute conversation with Ratzinger, Hunthausen thought he had answered the cardinal's questions satisfactorily. He knew what the Vatican expected of him. And he believed that he could now put the whole investigation behind him. Emboldened, he asked Ratzinger to support his request for two auxiliary bishops in Seattle. Though non-committal, the cardinal made no objections.

"When I came back from Dallas, I did the things I was asked to do," Hunthausen recalled. "So I thought it was over."

Over the spring and summer of 1984, Hunthausen repeatedly asked Laghi for an official Vatican declaration that the investigation was complete and that he had passed muster. He wanted exoneration, papal approval of his ministry, and two auxiliary bishops to help him. Laghi, whose diplomatic status had been elevated from delegate to nuncio, was encouraging but, like Hickey, gave the impression that these matters were decided upstairs. Nothing was forthcoming from Rome.

In August, Hunthausen left for Montana on his annual vacation, much of it spent with family and friends in Helena and Anaconda and at the cabin on Moose Lake. Bishop Walsh, now retired, met him at breakfast one morning in the dining hall at Carroll College. The two retreated to a far table where they could talk in private. Hunthausen told Walsh that he felt defeated by the Vatican's silence. Without the backing of the Holy Father and church leadership he felt "a certain loneliness" that no amount of support from his family or the faithful could make up for. He missed talking with Bishop Topel, his spiritual mentor, now in a Spokane nursing home where his mind had drifted off into dementia.

Walsh noted how dispirited the archbishop seemed, how his job had become a burden. "There is not much light in his eyes or buoyancy in his voice," Walsh wrote in his journal.

On October 1, 1984, Laghi wrote Hunthausen offering him a deal. The Vatican would close the investigation on the condition that Hunthausen accept a coadjutor bishop with special faculties to oversee certain areas of archdiocesan ministry. Laghi put the best spin possible on the proposed deal. After all, he noted, Hunthausen had wanted an auxiliary bishop. And, while the coadjutor would have final authority in certain areas, the archbishop would still be the archbishop. Plus, he added, Rome invites you to suggest candidates to be the coadjutor.

"As you give prayerful reflection to this decision of the Holy Father," Laghi wrote in closing, "I pledge my own abiding, fraternal support."

Hunthausen was stunned by the proposal: the pope wanted to assign him a minder. The Vatican had so little confidence in him that it wanted someone else to make the decisions in the areas in which he was deemed deficient. He couldn't believe it.

Father Ryan helped Hunthausen write a response to Laghi's letter. Outraged by Rome's treatment of his boss, Ryan drafted a lengthy letter in which he summoned every argument imaginable for rejecting the Vatican deal. Hunthausen read the draft and signed it. The letter informed Laghi that for "the good of the church"—a phrase the nuncio had also used—Hunthausen could not accept the Holy See's offer. For the good of the church, he contended, Rome should close the investigation and affirm his ministry. He noted that he had corrected or was correcting the shortcomings that Ratzinger had cited.

"I welcome constructive criticism and evaluation," Hunthausen wrote. "But I am convinced that there are few if any areas of difficulty —disciplinary or otherwise—which are not common to most of the other dioceses and archdioceses of this country."

As for the Holy Father's offer of a coadjutor bishop with special faculties, Hunthausen was certain that such an appointment would make it virtually impossible for him "to continue in any meaningful way" as archbishop of Seattle. It would cause further division and polarization in the church, he predicted. "In a word, the good of the church would suffer immeasurably."

Over the next year, Hunthausen and Laghi went back and forth via correspondence and personal conversation about how to affirm the archbishop's leadership while resolving the Vatican's concerns. The archbishop insisted he had addressed Rome's issues and would continue to do so. Rome felt he could not be trusted on his own. The Vatican knew, however, that demanding Hunthausen's resignation would create a public furor and likely do great harm to the church.

Hunthausen spoke with Laghi in person at the November 1984 meeting of the U.S. bishops in Washington. Again, he asked for an official end to the investigation, a blessing of his ministry, and appointment of an auxiliary bishop from the Northwest. Again, there was no response from Rome.

Four days before Christmas, Hunthausen was admitted to the coronary-care unit at Providence Hospital in Seattle after experiencing chest pain and numbness in his arms and hands. He thought perhaps he had overexerted himself skiing backcountry ridges with priest friends in the Cascades.

Doctors ordered an EKG and confirmed that the archbishop had suffered a mild heart attack. Consequently, he spent Christmas in the hospital. A couple of days later, he was back in his room at the cathedral rectory, where Marianne Coté, the matronly staff cook, nursed him back to health on a regimen of fish, skinless chicken, and short walks.

With the New Year, it was obvious that Hunthausen's negotiations with Laghi were going nowhere. Like Hickey, the nuncio was simply following orders. Cardinal Ratzinger and the pope were issuing the commands.

At the February 1985 Workshop for Bishops in Dallas, Laghi admitted to one of the Northwest bishops that the Hunthausen affair was out of his hands. The regional bishops got wind of the Vatican's proposal of a coadjutor bishop with special faculties for Seattle. And they were furious.

"This has to be one of the grave injustices of my forty-three years as a priest and bishop," retired Bishop Walsh wrote in his diary after learning how Rome planned to discipline Hunthausen. "No matter how it turns out, Dutch will carry the wounds to his grave . . . and the religious and laity will never view the Church in the same light."

Laghi and Hunthausen remained at an impasse. Rome insisted on appointing an auxiliary bishop with special powers; Hunthausen refused. On April 19, 1985, Laghi wrote the archbishop to tell him that he was going to Rome where he would request two auxiliaries for Seattle. He told him that one of the three men that he would suggest for an auxiliary would be Father Ryan. Then he added that another would be Father Donald Wuerl, of Pittsburgh.

"I genuinely pray that one will be chosen from your own clergy," he wrote.

On July 4 weekend 1985, Ryan was in New York for the U.S. convention of Serra International, a Catholic lay organization that fosters vocations to religious life. Laghi was also a guest. After the closing banquet, Ryan introduced himself to the nuncio, who pulled him aside, eyed him closely, and said, "Whatever happens in Seattle, you will be very key to the solution."

Ryan didn't know how to interpret Laghi's comment. Was he being induced to pressure Hunthausen? Enticed with the prospect of being named a bishop? He didn't know.

The following evening Ryan had dinner with a seminary classmate from his days in Rome who was now working in New York. The classmate brought along one of his own friends from the seminary— Donald Wuerl. The threesome dined at an expensive Manhattan restaurant where Wuerl picked up the tab. He said nothing about Rome's plans for him.

A couple of days later, Hunthausen phoned Ryan from Montana to say that the Vatican had decided he would get just one auxiliary bishop. That auxiliary would be Donald Wuerl, a priest of the

Diocese of Pittsburgh, a Roman-educated theologian and a former secretary in the curia.

Laghi had called Hunthausen earlier that day to tell him of Wuerl's pending appointment. The nuncio abandoned his suave persuasiveness and played hardball. Accept Wuerl as your auxiliary, he told the archbishop, or resign. Moreover, he continued, Wuerl would come with "special faculties" that would give him final authority in the ministry areas where Rome had judged Hunthausen to be lacking. Laghi followed up the call with a letter, putting on paper what he had said on the phone, and enclosing Wuerl's curriculum vitae.

By this time, Hunthausen, with Laghi's consent, had enlisted Archbishop Hurley to help him in dealing with the Vatican. A rugged, witty, blunt-spoken bear of man, Hurley had embraced his adopted state of Alaska. He had learned to be a bush pilot so he could visit the people in the hinterlands of his domain. Laghi and Hunthausen both viewed Hurley as astute, fair-minded, and reasonable, likely to steer things in a positive direction.

Hurley had been associate general secretary for the U.S. bishops' conference and knew how the Vatican worked. He suspected that Hunthausen's simple, honest, and transparent answers to questions from Hickey, Ratzinger, and others were what had gotten him in trouble with Rome.

"They were dealing with you in a legalistic fashion," Hurley told his Seattle colleague. "You never should have answered a lot of those questions until you had an attorney present."

Hunthausen shrugged. "I don't have anything to hide," he said.

Upon learning of Wuerl's imminent appointment, Hunthausen, Hurley, and Ryan hastily agreed to meet on July 12 in Spokane, a convenient rendezvous point. They booked rooms for Friday and Saturday nights in the Sheraton Hotel on Riverfront Park and strategized. By Sunday morning, they had a letter of response for Laghi.

Hunthausen informed the nuncio that he would accept Wuerl as his auxiliary bishop. However, he continued, giving Wuerl special faculties would "take from me some of the most essential administrative and deliberative powers" of an archbishop. Granting an auxiliary such sweeping authority, he wrote, "clearly appears to be punitive."

Hunthausen followed up his letter by flying to Washington to talk to the nuncio in person. Laghi thought he would use the occasion to introduce the archbishop to Wuerl, who was vacationing with his sister's family on the Jersey Shore. He quickly summoned Wuerl to the nunciature where he planned to spring him on Hunthausen.

"He's right here in the building waiting to meet you, " Laghi told the archbishop.

"I don't want to meet him," Hunthausen stubbornly said. "That wouldn't be fair to him or to me. I haven't accepted this [deal] and I don't wish to meet him."

So the stalemate continued.

In early September 1985, Hunthausen, Laghi, and numerous other prelates were in Los Angeles for the installation of Roger Mahony as that city's new archbishop. Hunthausen found a suitable moment to reopen the discussion with the nuncio and asked Laghi if he could see a copy of the Hickey report. With the investigation still open and unresolved, Hunthausen wanted to know the exact charges against him, what conclusions Hickey had drawn, and what recommendations he had made to Rome. Wasn't that only fair? Didn't church law ensure due process for the accused?

Laghi agreed and made arrangements for Hunthausen and Hurley to visit with him at the nunciature in Washington on October 9 and 10. In anticipation of their visit, the two Northwest archbishops met first with Father James A. Coriden, a canon lawyer who taught church law at Catholic University and was an expert on the rights of Catholics in the church. Hurley had suggested to Hunthausen that they prepare for the discussion with Laghi by consulting with Coriden, a short, self-effacing scholar popular with his theological colleagues. Hunthausen agreed.

The meeting with Coriden was an eye opener for the Seattle archbishop.

"We sat with him for several hours and I told my story up to that point as clearly as I could," Hunthausen said. "He asked questions and tried to put it all in perspective. And his response at the end was: You know, if this debacle ever became public in all its ramifications, it would cry to heaven for vengeance."

Coriden could offer little advice, since the Vatican seemed to be making up the rules as it went along. Hunthausen, who had come to Washington in hopes of resolving the whole matter, felt disheartened and hopeless.

The next morning he and Hurley arrived at the Vatican's Apostolic Nunciature to the United States, a stolid, three-story, beige-colored building on Embassy Row. They were ushered into a small conference room where the papal nuncio and Archbishop Hickey awaited them. The four archbishops sat across from each other, two to a side.

On the table between them was a huge bound tome that was obviously the Hickey report. During the course of their conversation, however, Laghi told Hunthausen, "I can't let you see it." He argued that because Hickey had sworn interviewees to an oath of secrecy, he could not in good conscience share what they had said with Hunthausen. The Seattle archbishop got the impression that Hickey had persuaded Laghi to withhold the "secret" testimony from him. Never mind that the apostolic visitator, his investigative team, Laghi, Ratzinger, other members of the curia, and perhaps even the pope had already read it.

Hunthausen, the ire rising within him, looked at Hickey and said, "Jim, this whole thing was wrong from the very start. You know that."

Startled by Hunthausen's sudden anger, Laghi launched into a long explanation, defending himself and the Vatican's actions. At no point did he concede that Rome might have operated differently or might have resolved matters without mounting a full-scale investigation. He justified the Vatican's lack of due process, noting that church law is different from American jurisprudence. He refused to acknowledge that the alleged liturgical and doctrinal aberrations lodged against Hunthausen could be found in dioceses across the United States.

Laghi's unwillingness to concede a single point infuriated Hunthausen, who after months of privately nursing his hurt and anger, launched into a harangue of his own. He spoke for a long time, arguing that the visitation should have been conducted as an open dialogue with him and his accusers. He charged that the investigation had maligned him, dispirited the people of the archdiocese, given credibility to extremist critics, and, most important, hurt the good name of the Holy Father and the universal church.

Glaring at Laghi, he seethed, "I really feel I've been betrayed. I think this whole procedure has been unnecessary and unjust. Never, never do this again. Just never do it again."

The nuncio winced. The Hickey report remained unopened on the table as the meeting adjourned. Hunthausen and Hurley made their way upstairs to their rooms to prepare for lunch.

Hurley, shaking his head in disbelief, was astonished at what had just transpired and what Hunthausen had said.

"I've never seen you like that before," he told his Seattle colleague. "You were eloquent."

Eloquent or not, Hunthausen was crushed.

"Every time I thought I was moving out of the woods, I found myself more deeply entrapped," he recalled. "It had become a nightmare."

On their second day at the nunciature, Laghi ended the discussion with the two Northwest archbishops by handing Hunthausen two official letters from the Vatican.

The first was signed by him and dated October 7, 1985. It said that he been asked by his superiors to detail for Hunthausen the special areas of concern to be given to Wuerl. The auxiliary bishop, the letter read, would exercise primary responsibility for five areas: liturgy, the marriage tribunal, clergy and seminarians, ex-priests, and moral issues related to health care and homosexuals. The letter, however, did not say who had final authority to make decisions, an omission that would cause grave misunderstanding and turmoil later on.

The second letter was signed by Cardinal Ratzinger and dated September 30, 1985. Soon known as "THE Ratzinger letter," it laid out the concerns of the Holy See regarding the administration of the Archdiocese of Seattle and demanded corrective action. Laghi gave it to Hunthausen with the understanding that it was not to be made public.

In his letter, Ratzinger told the Seattle archbishop that after a thorough review of the testimony in the Hickey report and related documents, statements, and letters, the apostolic visitation process was officially over. He praised Hunthausen for implementing the renewal envisioned by Vatican II, including lay participation, the creation of consultative bodies, and applying the Gospel to world concerns.

"You have been repeatedly described as a man of Gospel values, sensitive to the needs of the suffering and the aggrieved," Ratzinger wrote. "Your concern for justice and peace is well known. Time and time again you have given clear evidence of your loyalty to the church and your devotion and obedience to the Holy Father."

Nonetheless, wrote the Vatican's doctrinal watchdog, there are problems that require correction. Ratzinger then listed a dozen areas in which the archdiocese was failing to follow church practice or doctrine. The list included the concerns that Ratzinger and Hickey had addressed in discussion with Hunthausen, but some seemed to come out of the blue.

There were the familiar allegations of laxness in the operations of the marriage tribunal, of permitting contraceptive sterilization, of allowing first communion before first confession, of replacing individual confession with general absolution, of accepting illicit intercommunion, of letting former priests serve in parishes or teach in Catholic schools, and of confusing survey questionnaires with voting on Catholic doctrine. Ratzinger also reiterated the charges that Hunthausen had failed to clearly communicate that women cannot be priests and that homosexual activity by its very nature is an "intrinsic evil."

The cardinal gave special emphasis to the gay issue. He insisted that the archdiocese withdraw support from any homosexual group that does not unequivocally support church teaching and scolded the archbishop for his "ill-advised welcome of a pro-homosexual group to your cathedral."

New was the Ratzinger letter's identification of "a number of basic doctrinal problems" that affect "the day-to-day life of the church in Seattle." The cardinal then listed concerns so broad in scope that any bishop, Hunthausen included, would be hard pressed to resolve them. He charged that many priests, women religious, and lay leaders in the Seattle archdiocese misunderstood the nature and mission of the church and had faulty understandings of Christ and the sacraments, especially the sacrament of holy orders (ordination to priesthood). These Catholics are unduly influenced by an understanding of man based on "the tentative conclusions of the human sciences," he wrote. As a result, they are "reluctant to accept the magisterium as capable of giving definitive direction in matters of faith and morals."

Ratzinger made his most forceful point last. A Catholic conscience, he stressed, makes decisions based on the authoritative teaching of the church.

The underlying message of the Ratzinger letter was clear: There is no room for exceptions or extenuating circumstances in moral decision-making, no room for proportionality or prudent pastoral judgment, no room for an informed conscience to make up its own mind. You will follow the letter of the law of the church.

The two letters, one taking away much of his episcopal responsibility, and the other enumerating his many failures as a Catholic archbishop, devastated Hunthausen.

"When I got the [Ratzinger] letter after all of this, I felt deceived and betrayed," he said. "Where in the world is this coming from? I thought things had been resolved and now the letter contained so much more."

He tormented himself, pondering over and over how he had failed. He thought: "I'm not direct enough. I'm not strict enough. I don't issue edicts."

With the letters in hand, a disconsolate Hunthausen flew back to the Pacific Northwest with Hurley. On the flight to Seattle, they talked about what he should do. Should he resign? Should he retire? Should he turn over final authority to Wuerl? Or was there another way?

After two weeks of "intense soul searching," Hunthausen wrote Laghi to assure him that he would take measures to correct or prevent the problems set forth in Ratzinger's letter. Second, he would accept the appointment of Wuerl as auxiliary bishop and assign him oversight for the areas of Vatican concern. He would not, however, give Wuerl special faculties as Laghi had requested. Final authority would stay with the archbishop.

"I have made it very clear that accepting them [special faculties] would involve a serious compromise of my integrity both as a person and as a bishop," he informed the nuncio. "I am not the sort of person who pretends to be what I am not."

Laghi next saw Hunthausen at the U.S. bishops' annual meeting in Washington, DC, in mid-November 1985. He arranged an afternoon meeting at the nunciature for Hunthausen and his soon-to-be named auxiliary. The two had a cordial, hour-long conversation in which Hunthausen told Wuerl that he thought the visitation had been unnecessary and things were going quite well in the archdiocese.

Then Laghi finally gave Hunthausen what he had sought for nearly two years—official notice that the apostolic visitation was concluded and closed. Hunthausen asked for something in writing that he could publish for the people of the archdiocese, since it was their local church that Rome had investigated. The nuncio, who preferred to keep things secret, reluctantly agreed. His official letter, dated November 14, 1985, was an abridged version of the still undisclosed Ratzinger letter, at times using identical language. It too praised the archbishop as a good man, dismissed the mean-spirited critics, and then laid out a more condensed version of the Vatican's concerns.

Hunthausen released his own letter along with Laghi's. In it, he expressed gratitude for an end to the investigation and told the people of the archdiocese that he was committed to dealing with the Vatican's concerns. He asked both his supporters and his critics "to join together to build up this church."

With the investigation behind him and Wuerl in the wings, Hunthausen pressed the nuncio on the terms of the new auxiliary's assignment. He had rejected the Holy See's wish to grant Wuerl special faculties under Canon 403.2 of church law. In a December 2 letter to Laghi, however, he agreed to a compromise: he would give Wuerl responsibility for the Vatican's areas of concern but he, not Rome, would grant the special faculties as he deemed fit. On the advice of Archbishop Hurley, Hunthausen's letter made it very clear that he would remain in charge. This arrangement, the letter stated, "will not impinge upon my ultimate authority as ordinary [the leader] of the archdiocese." Later that clarity disappeared.

Meanwhile, Father Ryan, at the archbishop's suggestion, made a quiet trip to Pittsburgh to congratulate Wuerl and brief him about the archdiocese and the investigation. The former seminary classmates spent three days together in the snowbound city discussing substantive issues, including the Ratzinger letter and the Hickey report. Ryan concluded that Wuerl, given the amount of detail he knew, had to have read the report that Hunthausen had not been permitted to read.

In Pittsburgh, Ryan tried to disabuse Wuerl of information about the archdiocese that he thought was simply untrue or unfair. He was unsuccessful.

"Don Wuerl's got a picture that's been given to him by Rome and by Hickey," he told Hunthausen and Father McDermott, the chancery administrator, upon his return to Seattle. "We're going to be starting in the hole."

On December 3, 1985, the day after reaching the compromise agreement on special faculties, the Vatican announced the appointment of Father Donald Wuerl as auxiliary bishop of Seattle. In his letter of appointment, Pope John Paul II wrote that he was granting Hunthausen's request for an auxiliary and called upon the bishopelect "to be at one with the archbishop" for the good of the church.

Wuerl, forty-five at the time, was certainly at one with the pope and the Vatican. He had spent much of his career in Rome. He was seminary-trained at the North American College and the Gregorian University and later served as personal secretary to Cardinal John Wright, the prefect of the Congregation for the Clergy. After Wright's death in 1979, Wuerl returned to Pittsburgh as rector and professor of theology and philosophy at St. Paul Seminary. In 1982, he was appointed executive secretary to Bishop John Marshall for the Vatican-ordered study of U.S. seminaries. A writer and co-author of the adult catechism, *The Teaching of Christ*, Wuerl had established a reputation as a religious educator, a reputation he would enhance in the years ahead.

Hunthausen's critics were delighted with Wuerl's appointment. Some noted that he was strong on church teaching and doctrine, an area where they claimed the archbishop was weak. For his part, Hunthausen told the media that he and Wuerl would get along just fine, working out any disagreements in dialogue and "total openness."

Retired Bishop Walsh, whom Wuerl was replacing, was not so positive. He had encountered the bishop-elect in Rome and did not receive any "warm vibes." He regarded Wuerl as a climber, an obsequious underling biding his time to be named to higher office. (In 2010, Pope Benedict XVI, the former Ratzinger, named Wuerl a cardinal.)

"It is a pity that there has been a tradition which warrants these aspirations," Walsh wrote in his journal, predicting "another period of pain now that this appointment has been made."

On January 6, 1986, the feast of the Epiphany, in St. Peter's Basilica in Rome, Pope John Paul II placed his hands on the head of Father Donald Wuerl as he knelt at the high altar beneath Bernini's sculpted canopy and ordained him a bishop of the Roman Catholic Church. Some twenty cardinals and thirty bishops, including Hunthausen, took part in the ceremony while Wuerl's family and friends from Pittsburgh and Rome, a delegation of western Washington Catholics, and hundreds of other observers and well-wishers looked on. John Paul, flanked by Cardinal Casaroli, the Vatican secretary of state, and Cardinal Bernard Gantin, the new head of the Congregation for Bishops, anointed Wuerl's forehead with holy oil, then placed a white miter on his head and a silver crosier in his hand. Wuerl, now a bishop, bowed to the pope and embraced him.

After the ordination ceremony, the Pittsburgh and Seattle delegations along with other invitees adjourned to the four-star Hotel Massimo d'Azeglio for a reception and banquet. Among the guests was Archbishop Hickey.

"Don Wuerl invited every American working for the curia," said John Pinette, the Seattle seminarian charged with organizing the dinner. Pinette, who was studying in Rome, said the diners presented "*la bella figura*" with flattering toasts delivered from all quarters.

Wuerl's Vatican connections afforded a private audience with the pope. The morning after the banquet, John Paul received the Pittsburgh and Seattle delegations in an ornate hall adorned with Renaissance paintings. Hunthausen introduced the Seattle delegation; Bishop Anthony Bevilacqua, of Pittsburgh, introduced those from the Steel City; and Wuerl introduced his family and friends. Photos were taken of the various groups with the Holy Father.

In heavily accented English, John Paul read from a prepared text: "Christ calls you, Bishop Wuerl, to this special service and the church sends you forth to a specific and beloved part of God's holy people to collaborate with the archbishop for the benefit of the flock." In the pope's unscripted remarks, Pinette and Ryan thought they heard a veiled reference to Wuerl's "special faculties."

The day after the papal audience, Hunthausen, Ryan, and Pinette lunched together at one of the pope's favorite restaurants, L'Eau Vive, run by Belgian nuns. The food was excellent; the conversation depressing.

"This was a low day for Raymond Hunthausen," Pinette recalled. "He was realizing the worst. The allusion in the pope's remarks. The no confidence stuff. The way Don was obviously wired into the curial world."

While Pinette and Ryan talked about the events of the previous two days, Hunthausen sat in gloomy silence, barely touching his food. He had just returned from an appointment with Cardinal Gantin, the West African prelate who had replaced Baggio at the Congregation for Bishops. Gantin, rumored to be pope material, was a fierce defender of John Paul and the curia. A native of Benin, he had spent most of his career in Rome where he had held several curial positions. He was close to Ratzinger and regarded as inflexible as Baggio was flexible.

Gantin met Hunthausen at his office in the semicircular marble building on St. Peter's Square where several curial congregations are housed. His office furnishings, substantial and bulky, suggested business rather than comfort. At first Gantin, who spoke fine English, met with Hunthausen alone. He seemed uncomfortable and not particularly well informed on the Seattle situation. He adopted an impatient, admonishing tone that Hunthausen described as "smothered anger." He was blunt and to the point, his attitude conveying as much as his words: Hunthausen was in the wrong; he had raised concerns in Rome; and he had better do what he was told.

Referring to Wuerl, Gantin told the Seattle archbishop, "You will certainly respect this man in his role as auxiliary and see to it that he has responsibility for the areas assigned to him."

"Of course, I will share my ministry with Bishop Wuerl," Hunthausen replied, meaning that he would give his new auxiliary responsibility for the five areas of Vatican concern. He heard no mention of "special faculties" under Canon 403.2 or of Wuerl having ultimate decision-making power.

Toward the end of the meeting, Gantin summoned the sub-secretary of the congregation, a Latin American archbishop. The sub-secretary had been meeting separately with Wuerl elsewhere in the building. The cardinal and his top aide discussed whether all four prelates should come together to talk but decided it wasn't necessary.

"So I never did meet with Bishop Wuerl in the presence of Gantin or his sub-secretary," Hunthausen said. "What was said among them, I haven't the foggiest idea. But within a few weeks of our return the whole thing all of a sudden came to a head."

Hunthausen was never comfortable with the Vatican's insistence on secrecy in its inquiries and communications. He believed the faithful of western Washington, particularly archdiocesan leaders and parish priests, had a right to know what was going on. He had insisted that Laghi's November 14 letter ending the investigation and listing the Vatican's concerns be made public. The nuncio had grudgingly complied.

But the Ratzinger letter went further than Laghi's summary. Hunthausen began to feel that, in good conscience, he could not withhold it despite Rome's request that it not be published.

"It was the only way I knew of conveying what had happened," Hunthausen said. "How do you tiptoe around something like that?"

So he decided to read the letter aloud. He first read it aloud at a meeting of the Priest Senate shortly before going to Rome for Wuerl's ordination. He read it a second time before a gathering of archdiocesan clergy and staff three days before Wuerl was to land in Seattle. The letter was not well received. While Ratzinger's allegations had crushed and humiliated Hunthausen, they offended and enraged many of his priests and staff.

Auxiliary Bishop Donald Wuerl arrived in the Pacific Northwest for the first time in his life on January 26, 1986. Four days later, he celebrated Mass with Hunthausen and greeted the priests of the archdiocese at the St. Thomas Center, the former seminary. He was gracious in his remarks, asking the priests to be patient with him as got to know the archdiocese. He noted that he had accepted the advice of a Seattle Jesuit who had suggested that he reconsider his decision to live in a pricey condo downtown. Living at the posh Watermark Towers would compromise his credibility and commitment to the poor, the Jesuit suggested. Wuerl took the advice. He broke the lease on the condo, abandoned the custom-made furniture, and moved into the rectory of Holy Rosary Church in West Seattle.

I met Bishop Wuerl at a press conference at the chancery, the day after the Mass with priests and staff. My print and broadcast colleagues were not kind. We peppered Wuerl with questions such as: You've been described as "rock-hard orthodox." Are you? Will you be tailing the archbishop and tattling to Rome? Are you a spy?

Wuerl, nattily attired in a neatly pressed cassock with a gold pectoral cross, handled the antagonistic queries with poise and occasional humor. He was deferential to the archbishop and cautious in his replies. Tall and gaunt, his brown hair neatly parted, he had soft brown eyes, a cleft chin and a toothy grin. Even then, long before he became a powerful and influential cardinal, Wuerl projected an air of confidence and knowledge. He spoke well in a mellifluous baritone and seemed without doubt. He looked good on camera and knew it.

At the press conference, Wuerl dodged or deflected questions about whether he would withhold taxes to protest nuclear arms or if his views were the same as those of the "existing hierarchy."

"Well," he replied to the latter question, "the 'existing hierarchy' and myself were out for a long drive the other day and found ourselves in complete agreement in many areas."

He commended Hunthausen for his recent pastoral letter advocating compassion and help for people with AIDS. He admitted, however, that he and the archbishop had yet to explore all the issues facing the church and the archdiocese.

Hunthausen quietly gave Wuerl responsibility for overseeing the ministerial areas that Rome had stipulated. The archbishop, Wuerl, Ryan, and McDermott decided they would delay an announcement of Wuerl's designated responsibilities so that the new bishop could first establish himself. Wuerl and the two chancery administrators went through the Ratzinger letter and planned how the archdiocese would continue to address the Vatican's concerns.

"We worked hard to make things work with Wuerl," said Mc-Dermott.

Hunthausen also worked to accommodate his new auxiliary despite their considerable differences in age, background, and vision of the church. He felt sorry for Wuerl, thrust by Rome into a contentious situation and asked to do a very difficult job. He tried to be open and candid.

"I felt proud of what we were doing and how we were doing it," Hunthausen said. "I had the feeling that he would come to see that and agree with it."

But Wuerl's Roman approach and unfamiliarity with the local church worked against his own best interests. At the chancery, for example, he decided to partition off his office from a larger open room. "The wall," as it became known, soon symbolized his isolation and alienation from other chancery staff.

Three months into the job Wuerl suddenly discovered that his operating instructions from Rome were different from Hunthausen's. A disagreement between the two of them emerged during a continuing discussion over what the archdiocesan position should be on political efforts to reverse recent city, county, and state measures outlawing discrimination based on sexual orientation. In 1978, with Hunthausen's support, Seattle was one of the first U.S. cities to affirm protection of employment and housing for gays and lesbians. In 1985, Washington Governor Booth Gardner issued an executive order forbidding state agencies from discriminating against homosexuals. And that same year in King County, home to Seattle and a third of the state's population, the County Council narrowly passed a fair-employment ordinance to protect gays from job discrimination. By 1986, however, a number of forces, including many churches, were campaigning to rescind these legal protections for homosexuals. The campaign was vicious and vitriolic. The petition circulated to collect signatures for Referendum 7 read: "Repeal special rights for homosexuals, transvestites, child molesters, sadomasochists, rapists and other persons with deviant sexual orientations."

Archdiocesan leaders were in a quandary. Church teaching upheld the rights of homosexuals but condemned homosexual acts. Separating the two wasn't easy. Some Catholics were saying, yes, respect their rights but don't let them near our children, schools, and churches unless they're sworn to chastity.

In early 1986, there were two meetings at the chancery to discuss how the church could speak faithfully to the issue of gay rights in this intense political environment. The meetings included Hunthausen, Wuerl, Ryan, McDermott, Seattle University President Father William Sullivan SJ, and the heads of public affairs, Catholic Charities, and the peace and justice office. The discussions were long and argumentative.

In the second meeting, Bishop Wuerl and Father Sullivan got into tendentious argument over the philosophical issues behind homosexuality and gay rights. In defense of their positions, they cited Augustine, Aquinas, and several medieval philosophers. Wuerl then advanced some of the thinking that Ratzinger would employ later in his infamous pastoral letter on homosexuality, which he described as an "objective disorder" and an "intrinsic moral evil."

Tony Lee, the archdiocesan lobbyist on poverty issues and an attorney, interrupted. He asked Wuerl if the bishop thought homosexuality was more objectively disordered than murder.

"Yes," Wuerl replied.

Ryan, silently steaming, scrawled in bold letters across his notepad the word STUPID.

Hunthausen, who had said nothing, took advantage of a momentary halt in the discussion to interject some personal remarks. He mentioned several people whose personal livelihoods would be endangered by the repeal of gay rights protection. One of them, he said, was a teacher with three children.

The general meeting ended with Hunthausen, Wuerl, Ryan, and McDermott remaining behind. The archbishop told the other three that he welcomed the information and advice he had received in the meetings. He then said he would oppose efforts to repeal anti-discrimination laws.

Wuerl, a surprised look on his face, said, "Archbishop, if you do that, I would have to countermand it."

Hunthausen, equally surprised, asked, "What do you mean by that?"

"I have special faculties," Wuerl replied, "and this is one of the areas in which I'm in charge."

"Yes," Hunthausen said, "this is an area in which you have oversight and responsibility but I have the ultimate say."

"No, Archbishop," Wuerl responded. "I do."

Ryan quickly left the room to locate Laghi's December 2 letter agreeing to leave the assignment of special faculties up to Hunthausen. He found it and handed it to Wuerl, who quickly read it.

"This is utterly at odds with the orders I have from Rome," he told the others. "There is no point in talking about this any further until we have clarification from Rome."

Wuerl stood and left the room. It was Holy Thursday, the day on which the church commemorates Jesus and the apostles at the Last Supper.

9

THE EXPLANATION

Blessed are those who are persecuted for righteousness' sake,
for theirs is the kingdom of heaven.
—Matthew 5:10

Msgr. George A. Kelly, a formidable critic of "misguided" church re-form, opened a chapter of his book, *Battle for the American Church Revisited,* with a story about how the Vatican makes its point. In Kelly's telling, an aide to a powerful curial congregation walks into the cardinal's office with folders of complaints against four American bishops.

The young priest places the material on his boss's desk and says, "Your Eminence, the pope has to fire these four bishops."

The older man replies, "As usual, you have it all wrong. The pope doesn't have to fire four bishops. He only has to fire one and tell the world why he fired him."

In the early 1980s, with Pope John Paul II consolidating ecclesial authority in Rome and U.S. President Ronald Reagan attempting to achieve global supremacy in nuclear arms, Archbishop Raymond Hunthausen was on the firing line. His nuclear pacifism, heightened by the civil disobedience of his tax protest, was imperiling the pope's anti-communist alliance with Reagan. Moreover, the Seattle archbishop's emphasis on the inclusive, collegial, and compassionate application of Vatican II was undermining the efforts of John Paul and Cardinal Joseph Ratzinger to impose their will on the American Catholic Church.

For the Polish pope and for Ratzinger, his doctrinal watchdog, Hunthausen was a double problem. The archbishop's call for unilateral disarmament was jeopardizing the Vatican's relationship with Washington. And his emphasis on the priority of conscience was compromising Rome's demands for unequivocal adherence to church teaching.

To understand why Hunthausen was zeroed in on by John Paul and Ratzinger, we need to understand them, the two men who dominated the Roman Catholic Church for thirty-five years, from John Paul's election in 1978 until Ratzinger's resignation as Pope Benedict XVI in 2013. These two prelates had a profound effect on the church, reversing the course of the future envisioned at the Second Vatican Council. They were determined to recentralize power in Rome while halting the thrust of most of the reforms initiated by the Council. Ratzinger bluntly described their task as stopping an "avalanche of ecclesial decadence."

Pope John Paul II, self-made and self-contained, was a charismatic leader of immense talent. Handsome, vigorous, and dynamic, he was a poet, a philosopher, an actor, an athlete, an outdoorsman, and an author. He could converse in a dozen languages and traveled to more than a hundred nations where he addressed millions of people, often at huge outdoor Masses. Known and recognized in the most remote corners of the globe, his many admirers hailed him as John Paul the Great and, in 2014, Pope Francis elevated him to sainthood.

On economic and social justice issues, John Paul championed the human rights and dignity of workers, immigrants, refugees, children, the disabled, and the suffering. He built bridges with other Christian churches, particularly the Orthodox, and he reached out to other faiths, notably the Jews. He apologized for the church's historic anti-Semitism and its silence and indifference during the Holocaust. On internal issues, however, he had his shortcomings. He was all but blind to clerical sex abuse.

Suspicious of pluralistic societies and enamored of clear lines of power and authority, John Paul brought his Polish experience of German fascism and Soviet communism to the world church. Although he had participated in Vatican II, he redefined its meaning afterward. Its purpose, he maintained, had been to restore and reaffirm traditional Catholic doctrine. His encyclical *The Splendor of Truth* argued that God's truth is revealed by Christ and preserved by the Catholic Church. This truth is absolute. It is knowable, attainable, and unchangeable.

Comfortable with the hierarchical church, John Paul was suspicious of many of the reforms of Vatican II. He balked at the collegial model of the "People of God" in which bishops governed in partnership with the pope and the laity. Collegiality for John Paul meant "the shared unanimous position," as he put it in his first encyclical, in which the bishops bowed before the supreme pontiff. Or, as Cardinal Bernardin described it, "acted like altar boys."

John Paul was convinced that secularism, moral relativism, ecumenical fuzziness, and theological speculation had eroded Catholic truth, compromising church teaching. He was determined to protect and preach what he saw as the inalterable doctrine the church had maintained for two thousand years. Among other things, he had no doubt that Christ intended priests to be male and celibate, that marriage was heterosexual and permanent, and that the Catholic Church was the only sure and true path to eternal life.

He was not interested in hearing arguments to the contrary. Notorious for windy preaching from a prepared text, he had little curiosity and a singular inability to listen. On his first papal trip to the United States in 1979, he arrived with a set of speeches written in Rome without consultation with the American bishops. When he met with the bishops, he didn't ask a single question about the local church, its challenges or aspirations, nothing. His duty was to instruct.

Cardinal Josef Ratzinger, John Paul's able lieutenant, shared his boss's core conviction that the church must be clear and consistent in its unchanging doctrine. His experience under Nazism in his native Germany taught him that a church that wavers in its teaching succumbs to the political and cultural consensus of the moment. Ratzinger was ordained a priest, completed a doctorate in theology, and participated as a *peritus* at Vatican II. Serving as the chief advisor to Cardinal Joseph Frings of Cologne, one of the Council's foremost reformers, he helped shape some of its most important documents.

After the Council, Ratzinger secured a position at Germany's leading university for academic theology, Tübingen. It was there that the chaotic, violent protests of 1968 deeply unsettled him. Students took over classrooms and barged into faculty meetings, demanding to be heard. They grabbed the lectern and distributed flyers blaspheming Jesus and ridiculing scripture. A rattled Ratzinger stalked out. He was never the same again. The open and communicative scholar vanished, replaced by a dogmatic and gloomy authoritarian who feared the world was falling apart.

The experience at Tübingen of "ideologies that were tyrannical, brutal, and cruel made it clear to me that the abuse of the faith had to be resisted," he later wrote. "Anyone who wanted to remain a progressive in this context had to give up his integrity."

In 1977, Pope Paul VI appointed Ratzinger archbishop of Munich and elevated him to cardinal. When Paul died the following year, Ratzinger and the future Pope John Paul II got acquainted at the Vatican conclave that would elect the next pope. Each was impressed by the other's intellect, orthodoxy, and communications skills. They both believed there was a need to restore order in the church after what they regarded as the ambiguity and excesses unleashed by the Council.

When the College of Cardinals elected John Paul, the new pope invited Ratzinger to Rome to head a curial congregation. The cardinal declined for the time being—he'd been archbishop of Munich for only a year—but in 1981 he accepted John Paul's request to head the Congregation for the Doctrine of the Faith, the former Holy Office.

United in a common cause, John Paul and Cardinal Ratzinger set out to restore the doctrine and discipline that they believed church reformers had severely damaged to the detriment of God's eternal truth.

"The Christian fabric must be remade," John Paul wrote in his first encyclical.

The two prelates remade that fabric by exercising their authority through an unprecedented campaign of condemnations, interventions, banishments, silencings, and excommunications that some commentators compared to the Inquisition. They went after theologians with a vengeance, particularly Latin American theologians who spoke of a "preferential option for the poor" and a "theology of liberation" that John Paul deemed influenced by Marxism. Ratzinger investigated Father Gustavo Gutiérrez, the Peruvian scholar regarded as the father of liberation theology, silenced Father Leonardo Boff, the respected Brazilian theologian who called for justice within the church, and wrote a CDF "instruction" denouncing the popular "base communities" of the poor.

He also punished those who questioned church teaching on contraception, abortion, sexual morality, women's ordination, papal infallibility and authority, and a host of other issues big and small. Ratzinger stripped Father Hans Küng of his right to teach or call himself a Catholic theologian and he barred Father Charles Curran from teaching moral theology at Catholic University in Washington, DC.

John Paul, at Ratzinger's instigation, authorized doctrinal investigations of seminaries, Catholic universities, and religious orders. He appointed his own man to run the Jesuits; he ordered priests and nuns to leave public office and refrain from partisan politics; and he put an end to the Dutch church's implementation of shared responsibility by forcing its bishops to sign a set of forty-six propositions dictated by Rome.

To the delight of traditionalists, John Paul reauthorized use of the Latin Mass, required priests and nuns to wear religious garb, and canonized or beatified nearly fourteen hundred saints, more than all his predecessors combined. He and Ratzinger were adamant that Vatican II did not envision any change in the church's traditional teaching on the indissolubility of marriage, priestly ordination (celibate men only), birth control, or the established prerogatives of priests, bishops, and the pope. In 1983, they published a revised code of church law, making their interpretation of the Council's intent a done deal. The canon law revision was followed by a universal *Catechism of the Catholic Church* that nullified all national catechisms and imposed Rome's interpretation of the faith on all.

All the while, John Paul appointed inflexible, legalistic, and often-mediocre bishops who could be counted on to toe the Roman line. Archbishop Jean Jadot, whom John Paul removed as apostolic delegate to the United States, described them as authoritarian loners who don't seek advice, can't relate to people, and don't like to hear confessions or preach. Within a decade, John Paul had radically changed the face of the episcopacy worldwide.

John Paul and Ratzinger shared a love-hate relationship with the United States. They admired the country's respect for human rights but they deplored what they saw as American culture's idolatry of money and superficial celebrities, its dog-eat-dog Wall Street capitalism, and its abandonment of traditional moral values. Ratzinger viewed U.S. culture as hostile to faith.

"Looking at North America, we see a world where wealth is the measure of everything," he said in 1984. "It becomes difficult if not impossible to present the authentic Catholic ethic as reasonable, since it is too far distant from what is considered normal and obvious."

The CDF prefect and the pope viewed the American bishops of the Jadot years as ineffectual, compromised, and constitutionally unable to lay down the law. Yet when the U.S. bishops' conference demonstrated some muscle by drafting a peace pastoral at odds with the Reagan administration, Ratzinger and John Paul found themselves in an awkward situation. They welcomed the bishops' vociferous opposition to nuclear weapons, but they wanted to ensure that the peace pastoral would not threaten the pope's international diplomacy, especially the warm relationship John Paul was developing with the Reagan White House. The pope wanted American help in toppling communism, particularly in his native Poland.

On November 22, 1983, two weeks after his "visit" to Seattle, Archbishop James Hickey celebrated Mass at Holy Trinity Church in Georgetown to commemorate the twentieth anniversary of the assassination of John F. Kennedy. President Reagan, Cardinal Agostino Casaroli, the Vatican secretary of state, and Archbishop Pio Laghi, the Vatican's apostolic delegate to the United States, were among the participants and spoke together informally afterward. The following day they met again for formal talks at the White House. Reagan and Casaroli signed papers establishing full diplomatic relations between the United States and the Vatican. The world's most powerful country and its most powerful church would exchange ambassadors at the highest level, enhance communications, and give each other greater access to information. The deal cemented the "holy alliance" that had begun a year and a half earlier when Reagan and John Paul had first met in the Vatican Library.

The prime mover behind the alliance was William A. Wilson, a wealthy California real estate developer who was a long-time personal friend of the president and a major contributor to the Republican Party. A convert to Catholicism, Wilson was also a member of the Knights of Malta, a secretive military order known for its works of charity and its dim view of church reform. In fact, he viewed Vatican II as an unmitigated disaster. Tall, assertive, and loose-lipped, Wilson helped parcel out jobs as a member of Reagan's "kitchen cabinet" after the 1980 presidential election. He gave himself the post of presidential envoy to the Vatican and immediately began lobbying to upgrade the assignment.

Wilson worked with Congress to reverse an 1867 law, passed at the height of anti-Catholic prejudice in America, that prohibited funding an embassy at the Vatican. In the summer of 1983, he arranged for House and Senate delegations to visit Rome to talk with members of the curia and have an audience with the pope. U.S. Representative Clement J. Zablocki, the Democratic chair of the House Foreign Relations Committee and a Polish-American Catholic whom Casaroli presented with the Order of St. Gregory the Great, introduced a House bill paving the way for full diplomatic recognition. U.S. Senator Richard Lugar, Republican from Indiana, brought a similar bill before the Senate. Congressional leadership then tacked a diplomatic relations amendment onto a larger State Department funding bill. The omnibus bill with its Vatican recognition clause passed without a public hearing. Reagan quietly signed it into law the day of his White House meeting with Casaroli. And ten days later, he named Wilson as the first U.S. ambassador to the Vatican.

Wilson's bigger role furthered what Richard Allen, Reagan's national security advisor, grandly called "the greatest secret alliance in history." While Washington and the Vatican did not conduct joint plans to bring down communism, they did share much information. CIA Director William Casey flew secretly to Rome in a windowless black C-141 jet and went undercover to the Vatican on more than one occasion.

Casey; William P. Clark, Allen's successor as national security advisor; General Alexander Haig, the U.S. secretary of state; Vernon Walters, Reagan's ambassador at large; Edward Rowny, the U.S. nuclear arms talks negotiator; and Wilson met multiple times with the pope and his advisors. (Rowny also tried to call on Hunthausen.) All six men were key players in the administration and practicing Catholics. Their faith in the moral leadership of the pope melded naturally with their mutual desire to defeat communism.

"There was a real coincidence of interests between the U.S. and the Vatican," said Casaroli.

Reagan's men provided U.S. intelligence information to the Vatican, including undercover CIA reports and analysis from Poland as well as satellite photos of Soviet deployments of troops and weapons in Eastern Europe. Allen was convinced that the satellite evidence of the Soviet threat prevented John Paul from criticizing the counter deployment of U.S. weapons, including nuclear missiles, in western Europe.

John Paul was caught in a Faustian bargain. To liberate his Polish homeland and other nations from communism, he had to countenance America's bellicose nuclear weapons policy. In May 1982, Reagan signed a secret national security directive (NSDD 32) committing the U.S. government to destabilizing the Soviet Union and its communist allies by whatever means necessary. And in January 1983, as the Vatican red-penciled the U.S. bishops' peace pastoral, Reagan approved a secret directive (NSDD 75) that called for a massive U.S. arms buildup to enable deployment of even more nuclear warheads against the USSR.

Meanwhile the Vatican gave Reagan's men, principally Walters, a former CIA deputy director, its own intelligence from Poland and messages from the pope to the president. Walters met with John Paul personally as many as a dozen times. The church, in close communication with the Solidarity movement and bishops and priests in Poland, had excellent information as that country headed toward a popular, labor-led uprising.

Laghi, the papal delegate, cultivated the U.S.–Vatican relationship in Washington. At critical times, Casey, the CIA director, and Clark, the national security advisor, dropped by the nunciature to have cappuccino with the archbishop. In turn, Laghi met with Clark at the White House, entering through the southwest gate to avoid reporters. Clark gave classified government information to Laghi. For example, in a private letter dated February 9, 1983, the papal delegate thanked the national security advisor for "the confidential report" that "I have made available to my superiors" under "the notation of secrecy."

"My role was primarily to facilitate meetings between Walters and the Holy Father," Laghi told *Time* magazine. "It was a very complex situation—how to insist on human rights, on religious freedom, and keep Solidarity alive without provoking the communist authorities further."

At one point, Laghi traveled to Santa Barbara to ask Reagan to lift some of the U.S. economic sanctions against Poland because they were hurting everyday people more than the communist government. The administration complied.

The Reagan administration's friendly relationship with the pope did not translate into a warm relationship with the U.S. bishops as they worked on their pastoral letter on war and peace. One archbishop claimed that Ambassador Wilson had given Rome a list of twenty or thirty troublesome bishops, although Wilson subsequently denied it.

In the midst of the administration's huge arms buildup, the bishops were on the verge of condemning possession of nuclear weapons as a grave and impermissible moral evil. Not only might they reject the doctrine of nuclear deterrence, they might also advocate nuclear pacifism or call for unilateral disarmament. Such positions, Reagan's dismayed advisors feared, would fuel the nuclear freeze campaign, jeopardize spending on nuclear weapons programs before Congress, embolden the Soviets to take advantage of American disunity, and perhaps even cost Reagan the 1984 presidential election. With the publication of the second draft of their letter, the bishops had emerged as the major moral critic of U.S. and Soviet nuclear policy.

Clark; Caspar Weinberger, the defense secretary; Eugene Rostow, the director of the arms control and disarmament agency; and Lawrence Eagleburger, the under-secretary of state, were dispatched to disabuse the bishops of their "fundamental misunderstanding" of U.S. nuclear deterrence. The Reagan officials testified before the bishops' five-member drafting committee, headed by then Archbishop Bernardin, and followed up with letters they made public.

Clark admonished the bishops for ignoring the administration's serious arms control efforts, for minimizing the Soviet threat, and for failing to recognize the right to fire nuclear weapons first, if necessary. Weinberger decried the draft letter's pacifist tone with its suggestion of unilateral disarmament.

"I find most troubling the draft letter's implication that the policy of deterrence itself should be forsaken if complete nuclear disarmament is not imminent," wrote the defense secretary, taking a direct shot at Hunthausen and the other peace bishops.

Weinberger followed up with a personal call on Archbishop Hickey to explain the administration's position.

The U.S. bishops might have resisted the supplications of the Reagan administration but they were not going to say "no" to the pope. As noted earlier, the Vatican ordered Bernardin and three other conference executives to Rome in January 1983 for a secret consultation. The Americans met with Casaroli, Ratzinger, and the bishop leaders of six western European nations. The German bishops, in particular, accused the U.S. bishops of selling out to the Soviets and provoking a schism in the church on the morality of nuclear weapons. Casaroli and Ratzinger, invoking the pope's name, backed them up. They told Bernardin that the letter could not condemn nuclear deterrence nor should it give credence to unilateral disarmament or nuclear pacifism.

The powerful U.S. prelates who dealt frequently with the pope welcomed the Vatican intervention. Cardinals Krol of Philadelphia, Law of Boston, Mahony of Los Angeles, and Bishop O'Connor, whom John Paul would soon name the cardinal-archbishop of New York, regarded Hunthausen and other peace bishops as making trouble for both Washington and Rome. The Seattle archbishop's well-publicized tax protest against nuclear arms was dividing rank-and-file Catholics and complicating the pope's relationship with the Reagan administration. After the secret meeting in Rome, O'Connor met independently with Casaroli and the pope and came back to the States with forty amendments intended to water down the pastoral. Bernardin, whom John Paul had just named a cardinal, was livid. But, ever the master of conciliation, he found a middle way to accommodate Rome and the peace bishops.

Per the Vatican's request, the bold second draft of the peace pastoral morphed into a third and final draft that gave conditional support for nuclear deterrence, softened its stance on a nuclear freeze, affirmed the just-war theory, and dismissed the idea of unilateral disarmament. The Reagan administration reacted as if it had dodged a bullet. The headline of the front-page story in the *New York Times* read: "Administration Hails New Draft of Arms Letter—Says Bishops 'Improved' the Nuclear Statement." Rowny, the head arms negotiator, claimed the administration's defense policies were "in harmony" with the views of the pope.

The Vatican's intervention on the peace pastoral mollified the Reagan administration, keeping Rome-Washington relations harmonious and fruitful. And it put the U.S. bishops on notice that the Vatican had veto power over any decisions by the conference. Yes, the bishops were free to suggest and advise, but final authority rested with the pope and the curia.

In the 1984 interview that became *The Ratzinger Report*, the CDF prefect bluntly dismissed the authority of national bishops' conferences. "No episcopal conference, as such, has a teaching mission," he said. "Its documents have no weight of their own save that of the consent given to them by individual bishops."

So much for the U.S. bishops' labors on the peace pastoral.

John Paul and Ratzinger had other concerns with the U.S. bishops besides the peace pastoral. They were preoccupied with the state of Catholicism in the United States where they saw "divisions and confusions" caused by a misguided spirit of Vatican II. Many dioceses were emphasizing shared responsibility over clerical authority, listening over instructing, inclusivity over exclusion, compassion over law, prudential judgment over moral absolutes, and an informed conscience above everything else. They were allowing, even encouraging, pastoral approaches to annulling marriages, providing general absolution, permitting sterilizations, giving children first communion before first confession, sharing the Eucharist with Protestants, letting former priests serve in lay roles, and welcoming and ministering to homosexuals, even when they disputed church teaching.

The pope and his doctrinal chief contended that many bishops were failing American Catholics through their inability or unwillingness to teach the definitive doctrine and practice of the church, even down to the most mundane issues—like the recipe for unleavened altar breads.

In Ratzinger's mind the most outrageous example of episcopal malfeasance was the U.S. church's ambiguity on homosexuality. "Indeed," he fumed in *The Ratzinger Report*, "it has come to pass that bishops have placed churches at the disposal of 'gays' for their gatherings."

An aloof, asexual loner, Ratzinger was obsessive about gays. He said and wrote more about homosexuality than any other Vatican official and singlehandedly toughened the church's position on gay sex. He began by revising the 1975 statement on sexual ethics in which the CDF concluded that some homosexuals were simply born that way and thus cannot be labeled sinners per se. The statement had led to interpretations in which homosexuality was regarded as neutral or even good and God-given. In 1986, Ratzinger responded with official guidelines, approved by John Paul and addressed to the world's bishops, but obviously written with the U.S. church in mind. He reaffirmed the church's condemnation of homosexual acts, and then took an additional step. Homosexuality, Ratzinger wrote, "is a more or less strong tendency ordered toward an intrinsic moral evil, and thus the inclination itself must be seen as an objective disorder."

The CDF prefect warned bishops about dissenters who undermine church teaching on homosexuality and spread the "deceitful propaganda" of gay activists. He advised bishops to be on guard against pastoral programs for homosexuals that either overtly or covertly pressure the church to change its teaching. His references were obvious: Dignity and New Ways Ministry, the Catholic organization founded by Father Robert Nugent and Sister Jeannine Gramick. He ordered bishops to withdraw support from any group that does not fully subscribe to church teaching.

Ratzinger's harsh, unforgiving language outraged homosexuals and offended many clergy and laypeople. But Ratzinger was not done yet. He would later incorporate his description of homosexuality as an "intrinsic moral evil" into the church's universal catechism. And when he became Pope Benedict, the first major publication of his pontificate was a document banning gays from the priesthood even if they were celibate. Homosexuality, Benedict said, was incompatible with the priestly vocation.

Ratzinger's hard line on homosexuality had enthusiastic supporters in the Reagan administration. These supporters included Ambassador Wilson. Through his connections with Paul Weyrich, Joseph Coors, and other wealthy Reagan backers, Wilson was introduced to Father Enrique Rueda, a Cuban-American priest who received funding through Weyrich's right-wing foundations. Rueda led a propaganda assault on bishops who questioned the nation's nuclear deterrence policy or sympathized with gay rights or liberation theology. Working from *The Wanderer*'s mailing list, he organized "truth squads" in Seattle and elsewhere to create "significant negative publicity for the bishops" and make them "squeal and squirm in anguish."

In September 1982, Wilson met Rueda at the State Department in Washington and helped him arrange airfare and Vatican connections in Rome. Once there, Rueda likely stopped by the CDF office and delivered a copy of his newly published book, *The Homosexual Network*, to Ratzinger. The 680-page tome is an encyclopedic expose of alleged gay infiltration in the church that, among other things, identifies twenty "prohomosexual" U.S. bishops, singling out seven of the group, including Hunthausen, as the worst offenders. Rueda defined "prohomosexual" as "promoting conditions favorable to the practice of homosexuality."

Ratzinger used the word "pro-homosexual"—a rather odd term—in his infamous September 30, 1985, letter to Hunthausen. In the fourteenth and final point listing the archbishop's failures, he reprimanded Hunthausen for "the ill-advised welcome of a pro-homosexual group to your cathedral." One wonders how closely Ratzinger had read Rueda.

In Rome, Wilson met regularly with Casaroli, the secretary of state, and other officials in the Vatican diplomatic corps. But he also had at least one private meeting with Ratzinger. What business did Reagan's political point man have with the pope's man in charge of doctrine? There is no public record of their discussion, which occurred at a private meeting in late March 1983. That was a month before Bernardin told the U.S. bishops' conference about the Vatican edit of the peace pastoral, and Laghi tapped Hunthausen on the shoulder at the coffee break.

In early 1983, as an unblinking world seemed to lurch toward nuclear genocide, John Paul and Ratzinger decided to send the U.S. bishops a very strong message. The message had two parts: (1) there will be no peace pastoral that upsets our relationship with the Reagan administration; and (2) we—not you—will decide and enforce Catholic teaching and practice in the American church.

The pope and the future pope figured that making an example of one U.S. bishop, as Msgr. Kelly's anecdote suggested, would bring the others in line. Investigate, embarrass, and punish one bishop, and the others will mend their ways. Look for a Jadot bishop, a pastoral type known for sharing responsibility, delegating authority, and exercising prudential judgment. Such bishops are the enablers of cafeteria Catholics. Find a bishop who is not too obscure—the point must be made—but also not too well connected, lest there be a hue and cry. Better to choose an outlier far from the Catholic heartland of the East Coast and the upper Midwest. If he's an archbishop, all the better. Bishops desirous of advancement will pay attention.

Rome had an ideal whipping boy: Hunthausen. A Jadot boy, an archbishop, a westerner from the most unchurched corner of the nation. Apolitical and ingenuous, a nonentity in the bishops' conference, a backbencher who never spoke at general sessions. By all accounts, he was also a faithful loyalist respectful of church teaching and the Holy Father. Once confronted, he would surely acknowledge his sins and quickly correct his ways. The Vatican would accomplish its purpose: bring the U.S. bishops to heel without a great deal of fuss or consternation. Hunthausen was perfect. Or so Rome thought.

John Paul and Ratzinger must have reasoned that by offering up Hunthausen as the sacrificial lamb, they could accomplish two purposes with one blow. Strike down Hunthausen and they'd please the Reagan administration. Strike down Hunthausen and the U.S. bishops would get the point that on all matters Rome rules—not them.

Hunthausen wasn't the only U.S. prelate to receive an apostolic visit as the U.S. bishops completed the peace pastoral in 1983. There was another, Bishop Walter Sullivan, of Richmond, Virginia. A cheerful, self-effacing man whose prominent front teeth and large-frame bifocals gave him an "aw shucks" look, Sullivan was a Vatican II bishop like Hunthausen, active in the world beyond church walls. Despite the large military presence in his diocese, Sullivan was an outspoken critic of nuclear weapons and the Reagan arms buildup. He suggested the bishops' peace pastoral be stated in one sentence: "We as leaders of the Catholic Church say 'no' to nukes, 'no' to their use, 'no' to their manufacture, 'no' to their deployment, and 'no' to their existence."

On church issues, Sullivan was also much like Hunthausen. He was a strong ecumenist, creating a joint Anglican-Catholic parish that later got him in trouble with Rome. He reached out to women, naming them to leadership positions as parish coordinators. He allowed Dignity to meet on church property. And, like Hunthausen, he was also compelled to remove his approval from a book on sexual ethics. In his case, it was an anthology edited by Father Nugent titled *Challenge to Love: Gay and Lesbian Catholics in the Church*.

In June 1983, the Vatican dispatched St. Louis Archbishop John May as "visitor" to Richmond. May interviewed more than a dozen people, including Sullivan, some priests, and members of an ultra-orthodox watchdog group. Afterward, he told Sullivan "you have the same crazies in your diocese that I have in mine." May sent a confidential written report to Rome, which Sullivan, like Hunthausen, was not permitted to see.

Shortly thereafter, Sullivan, again like Hunthausen, had a private meeting with Ratzinger in Rome. The CDF prefect ordered him to put an end to general absolution, intercommunion, liturgical innovation, and other things that Rome now found unacceptable. The tone of meeting and the Vatican's open file on his ministry intimidated Sullivan. He felt he was being watched, that people were after him, and that he'd better curry favor with Rome if he wanted to remain a bishop.

Unlike Hunthausen, Sullivan did not make the Vatican investigation public or talk about it with others, even his closest priest friends and advisors. In *The Tidings*, his diocesan newspaper, he portrayed the inquiry as Rome's way of determining the need for an auxiliary bishop, a hollow explanation that May publicly supported.

In retrospect, Sullivan regretted going along with the Vatican's demand for secrecy. It left him isolated, adrift, and unsure of himself. And, as time passed without closure or a clean bill of health, Sullivan felt like a permanent defendant in a Kafkaesque trial. After the U.S. bishops' November 1984 meeting, he wrote Bishop James Malone, the conference president, asking the conference to please do something. "There are some aspects of the apostolic visitation which I find both unjust and, if publicly known, quite scandalous," he declared.

Sullivan also wrote Hunthausen, whose fate had been well publicized, to complain that no one from the bishops' conference had contacted him. "The whole process is shrouded in secrecy," he objected. "A year ago I was in Rome and completed all I was asked to do. I am beginning to find the experience a different kind of 'mushroom cloud.'"

Malone forced Laghi to act. The Vatican ambassador finally told Sullivan that the Holy See was closing the investigation. Yet, as in Seattle, the ordeal continued. Laghi began a cat-and-mouse game with Sullivan about appointment of an auxiliary bishop of Rome's choosing empowered with special faculties. At one point, Sullivan wrote Laghi a blistering five-page letter absolutely rejecting an auxiliary bishop with final authority in areas where he had been judged deficient. But in April 1986 he capitulated. He accepted the appointment of Msgr. David E. Foley, a grade-school friend from Maryland, as auxiliary bishop with special faculties. Foley was known as a pious priest who recited the rosary outside abortion clinics but steered clear of peace protests. Sullivan knew and trusted him. He sent a letter to diocesan priests telling them that Foley had special faculties in matters of doctrine, liturgy, and sexual morality. The priests accepted it.

By the time I met and interviewed Sullivan in 1993, he and Foley had settled into a workable relationship despite the split authority between them. We talked in the hotel corridor outside a meeting of Catholic broadcasters in Virginia Beach. Sullivan, his gray hair unkempt, rubbed his chin and sucked on a ballpoint pen as he reviewed the Vatican investigation of his ministry.

He remained convinced that the Vatican had targeted him and Hunthausen for their peace activities, specifically for getting ahead of Rome and advocating unilateral disarmament. The Vatican was spurred on, he said, by conservative Catholics alarmed by their peace stand who then set out to nail them on alleged liturgical and doctrinal abuses.

"They go after where you're vulnerable," Sullivan said. "And we're most vulnerable on issues where the church is feeling the most pain, issues that push questions of conscience."

10

THE HUMILIATION

*One cause of corruption in religion is
the refusal to follow the course of doctrine as it moves on,
and an obstinacy in the notions of the past.*
—John Henry Cardinal Newman

Rome neither builds nor clarifies in a day. Months went by as Archbishop Hunthausen and Bishop Wuerl waited to receive a definitive ruling from the Vatican about who had final authority over the Archdiocese of Seattle. The Holy Thursday dispute that had erupted over gay rights legislation continued to hang in the air as the church of western Washington tried to move on. The looming question was: Who's in charge?

The two bishops initiated separate conversations with Archbishop Laghi, the papal nuncio, asking his help in clarifying the matter. Laghi, never quick and always cautious, asked them to wait until after he had had an opportunity to go to Rome to discuss the situation personally with his superiors. So spring became summer, and still the matter remain unresolved.

Meanwhile, the ad hoc committee of Wuerl, Father Michael Ryan, and Father Michael McDermott continued to work on addressing the five areas of Vatican concern raised by the visitation. In late April 1986, it submitted "an implementation review" to Hunthausen assigning responsibilities to various persons and archdiocesan offices. The "indicated concerns and deficiencies" included all the liturgical practices (general absolution, first confession/first communion, intercommunion, etc.), juridical matters (the marriage tribunal), pastoral issues (ministry to homosexuals, role of women, use of ex-priests, etc.), and doctrinal problems (mission of Christ and the church, the sacraments, role of conscience versus magisterium, etc.) enumerated in the Ratzinger letter.

But a fundamental culture clash hampered the ability to move forward. Wuerl's orientation was hierarchical, legalistic, and institutional; Hunthausen's was collegial, consultative, and pastoral. Wuerl's administrative style was top-down: explain your position and expect people to fall in line. Hunthausen's was bottom-up: create a dialogue, ponder the Gospel and church teaching, and apply your conscience.

On some issues, chancery staff believed Rome was overturning sound pastoral decisions with an insensitive and overly literal interpretation of church law. On other issues, it thought the Vatican had the facts wrong, exaggerated them, or, as the archbishop put it, went after mosquitoes with a sledgehammer.

McDermott, who did the lion's share of the nitty-gritty work on the committee, never understood why Rome was so wrought up.

Sister Diana Bader, the theologian and member of the archdiocesan moral advisory committee, read all the correspondence between the archbishop and the Vatican related to the visitation.

"There was not one area in which Hunthausen deviated from what was morally orthodox," Bader said. "He never taught or allowed to be taught a position that was in clear conflict with the teaching of the church." Like many other archdiocesan leaders, the Dominican sister believed the archbishop was being punished for exercising pastoral discretion in difficult situations, those gray, murky areas where the most prudent option was compassion—the sort of judgment, Bader argued, that Jesus exercised in scripture.

Don Espen, the canon lawyer on the chancery staff, was as perplexed about how to fix something that didn't seem to need fixing as Bader was. He spent hours gathering materials and assembling boxes of documentation in response to Ratzinger's list of errors. A paunchy, unflappable fellow who wore aviator-style glasses and spoke in a careful, modulated tone, Espen was often called into Wuerl's adjacent office.

"We spent a lot of time on these things: general absolution, altar girls, laicized priests, whether Father So-and-So had some ex-priest giving out communion," Espen recalled. "I'd tell him there was nothing wrong about this."

That was not what Wuerl wanted to hear. He ordered Espen to write a set of liturgical guidelines for pastors, guidelines that adhered scrupulously to canon law. Espen described the clash between the Wuerl church and the Hunthausen church in computer terms. Wuerl saw the world as digital; Hunthausen saw it as analogue. Wuerl saw folks as either inside or outside the box; Hunthausen didn't see the box.

"One of the great gifts that Archbishop Hunthausen gave me was seeing the world of shades and curves," said Espen, who later left the priesthood to marry.

At times, Wuerl must have felt like he had stumbled into the wrong church. Catholic culture in Seattle—informal, inclusive, collaborative

—was so different from the prescribed, closed, subservient Catholic culture he knew from Pittsburgh and Rome.

One day he called in Pat Sursely, who was responsible for archdiocesan finances and public affairs, for a briefing on the operations of his department. In anticipation of the meeting, Sursely had prepared a substantial report detailing the tasks and budgets of the various entities within his department. Wuerl brushed aside Sursely's report and plopped down a thick file folder containing articles and pages clipped from *The Progress*, for which Sursely had oversight.

"I want to talk about the paper," Wuerl said in a stern, peremptory tone.

"Okay, sure," replied Sursely, a gregarious, married layman who had once studied to be a Christian Brother.

Opening the folder, the bishop pulled out a newspaper clipping with a two-column photograph showing parishioners celebrating the hundredth anniversary of their church. For the occasion, some parishioners had dressed as nuns in full habits while one man was attired as a bishop wearing an embroidered white chasuble, a gold pectoral cross, and an ornate miter. He had a silver crosier in his hand.

"Look at this," Wuerl said, stabbing his finger at the picture.

Sursely peered closely and studied the photo. He was at a loss as to what perturbed the bishop.

"Look at it," Wuerl repeated. Sursely remained baffled.

Finally, Wuerl sighed and pointed out the fellow dressed as a bishop. "This isn't history," he scolded. "We dress like this today."

Things weren't much easier outside the office despite the efforts of Father James Mallahan, pastor at Holy Rosary Church in West Seattle, to create a comfortable home for the young bishop. A gregarious Irish raconteur, Mallahan happily shared the roomy, four-bedroom rectory with Wuerl and its other resident priest, Father Matthew Naumes. The pastor arranged regular evening meals preceded by what Naumes called "Mallahan's Manhattanland." Wuerl, who preferred Rossi aperitifs to the pastor's cocktails, was delighted when Mallahan gave him a fancy monsignor's cassock. He had it retailored and kept it on hand for Rome.

Despite the attempted camaraderie at the rectory, the unaffected Catholic culture of Seattle fit Wuerl as poorly as Mallahan's untailored cassock. On Pentecost Sunday, for example, he and Hunthausen were to concelebrate a big Mass in the gymnasium at Kennedy High School. That morning, Wuerl called Naumes into his room and opened a large box to reveal a stunningly gorgeous miter embroidered with gold images of the saints. It must have cost $1,000.

"I'm going to wear this for the first time today," said Wuerl, beaming with pleasure.

Naumes replied, "What do you think the archbishop is going to wear?"

"But this is Pentecost," Wuerl persisted.

"I think you'd better wear the plain white one," Naumes advised. "You know that's what he'll be wearing."

On another occasion, Wuerl, Naumes, and Mallahan celebrated Naumes's birthday with an expensive seafood dinner at the downtown Metropolitan Grill and then decided to take the beach drive around Alki Point afterward. It was a warm, sunny Sunday evening with hundreds of teenagers in convertibles and pickup trucks, music blaring from their car stereos, cruising along Alki Boulevard at a snail's pace. Mallahan's Oldsmobile was soon stuck in the traffic. As he inched the car along, the girls in the back of a pickup truck in front of them cavorted, danced, and flashed their breasts.

At one point, a young man whom Naumes knew from Holy Rosary thrust his head through their open car window and exclaimed, "Father, what are you doing here?" The bishop sank deeper in the passenger seat.

What Wuerl lacked for support in Seattle, he found in Washington and Rome. He spoke regularly to Laghi, who complained to others about how Wuerl was being thwarted in Seattle. At Holy Rosary, he rose at 6:30 in the morning, placed calls through the overseas operator, and talked with well-placed friends in offices at the Vatican. Then he'd put on his athletic gear and jog five miles around the track at West Seattle High School or swim twenty laps at the YMCA pool.

No matter how hard Wuerl tried, he and Hunthausen were fated to be an odd couple. John Pinette, who succeeded Espen as the chancery's canon lawyer, believed that it was Hunthausen's style, his compassionate approach to church, that made it impossible for him to work with Wuerl. And with the papacy of John Paul II. He was judged too softhearted by a papal administration obsessed with enforcing doctrine and discipline.

"For Don Wuerl, the absolute first question was: What does this do to the institution?" Pinette said. "For Ray Hunthausen, it was: What does this do for the person? They saw the world in such fundamentally different ways."

Hunthausen's style sometimes worked against him. Because he was such a good listener, people would interpret his silence or lack of argument for agreement. As a result, his top aides developed the habit of quizzing him after important conversations to make sure there was a written record of any promises or proposed actions.

Some reform-minded Catholics, even at the chancery, misread Hunthausen's orthodoxy. Given his opposition to Trident, his ecumenism, and his receptivity to gays, women, and divorced Catholics, some doubted that he really believed what he said on abortion, euthanasia, or other issues that put the church at odds with secular culture. They suspected that, at heart, Hunthausen was a "cafeteria Catholic" like them. They were wrong.

As the wait went on for Rome's clarification, the nation's largest organization of Catholic priests honored Hunthausen with its President's Award for his commitment to peace, dialogue, collaboration, and renewal of priestly life and ministry. The National Federation of Priests' Councils, representing twenty-seven thousand American priests, also commended the archbishop as "an inspiration in facing the Roman investigation."

Addressing the NFPC at its annual meeting in Salt Lake City in April 1986, Hunthausen shared some of his own struggle. "It is difficult to proceed as churchmen," he said, "when we sincerely believe that a given policy or practice is contrary to the best interests of both the Gospel and the church itself. Yet we remain churchmen."

He argued that while the church is *semper reformanda*, continually in need of reform, it is also the Body of Christ, deserving of our faith and our love. The award did not go over well in Rome. The U.S. bishop advisor to the NFPC received a letter of reprimand from Cardinal Gantin for having failed to dissuade the organization from presenting Hunthausen with its highest honor. The advisor was Bishop Thomas J. Murphy, then bishop of Great Falls–Billings, Montana, and soon to be named coadjutor archbishop of Seattle.

In mid-June 1986, the U.S. bishops gathered at St. John's University in Collegeville, Minnesota, for their annual spring meeting. Laghi, operating on instructions from Rome, took Hunthausen aside and told him that indeed Wuerl did have special faculties. The Vatican had ruled that the auxiliary bishop had full and final authority over the five ministerial areas where Hunthausen was judged deficient. That meant that Wuerl would make the final decisions regarding liturgy, the marriage tribunal, clergy and seminarians, ex-priests, and moral issues related to health care and homosexuals. The nuncio told Hunthausen to expect a letter from Cardinal Gantin spelling it out in black and white.

Once again, the archbishop felt deceived and betrayed. Surely he had not misunderstood something as basic as who's the boss.

"It's impossible to have a church with two heads," he protested to Laghi. "This only makes matters worse not only for me but for Bishop Wuerl."

Determined to hold the line, the nuncio dug in. He told Hunthausen, "You know, of course, that you have no credibility in Rome."

"If I have no credibility in Rome," Hunthausen responded, "why in the world do you want me to continue? I have offered to resign."

"Well," said Laghi, carefully forming his reply, "it's for the good of the church."

If Laghi's news wasn't distressing enough, there was soon more bad news. While Hunthausen was with the bishops in Collegeville, the Michael Miles book was published. News stories moved across the wire services with Miles's claim that Hunthausen, as bishop of Helena, had permitted him to serve as a married parish priest. The archbishop got the word as he was walking to dinner across the leafy St. John's campus. Archbishop Hurley had spotted him and rushed over.

"It's all over now; you're done," exclaimed Hurley, telling him about the Miles book. Hunthausen explained to his colleague how he had allowed Miles, once he was laicized, to serve in lay roles but never again as a priest. If Miles had done so, it was without Hunthausen's permission or knowledge.

Hurley, convinced that Miles had indeed stretched the truth, urged Hunthausen to issue a press statement denying that he had ever fostered an experiment in married priesthood. Hunthausen did so, putting out a mild clarification. Bishop Elden Curtiss, his successor in Helena, sent out his own press release, denouncing Miles's book as full of "half-truths and distortions, and even totally erroneous statements."

Hunthausen and Wuerl returned to Seattle from the bishops' meeting on the same flight from Minneapolis. As the two of them sat together on the concourse awaiting the announcement of their flight, Hunthausen decided to make a personal appeal to his auxiliary.

"Don," he began, "you've been in Seattle long enough that I think you understand and appreciate that there are a lot of good things happening there. Don't you agree?"

"Yes," Wuerl replied.

"Then would you consider making a statement to the effect that you don't think special faculties are necessary for you?" Hunthausen suggested. "That, in fact, this [arrangement] is more disturbing and disruptive than it is healing?"

Wuerl waited for the public address system to go silent before he responded.

"I can't do that," he told the archbishop.

"Why?" Hunthausen asked.

"Because this is the Holy Father's decision," Wuerl said. "This is his appointment and I will do my best to try to carry it out."

Sighing, Hunthausen said he understood the young bishop's position. "I'm simply trying to get you to see mine," he explained. "I really feel that I'm suggesting this for the good of the church."

Wuerl was unmoved; the conversation was over.

In late July, Hunthausen received an official and very direct letter from Cardinal Gantin informing him that Bishop Wuerl had complete and final decision-making power in the five problem areas. Hunthausen replied to Gantin that he would accept the Vatican's ruling but felt obliged to share knowledge of Wuerl's special authority with his staff and the church of western Washington. He would do that, he said, when he and Wuerl were both back from vacation.

So on September 4, 1986, the archbishop and his auxiliary told priests, archdiocesan staff, western Washington Catholics, and the media how their authority was now divided. The press was particularly skeptical. Hunthausen and Wuerl were bombarded with puzzled questions: Why are we learning this now? Why are special powers being assigned to an auxiliary bishop? Isn't this a public slap in the face to the archbishop? Is this the way the archdiocese will get more in line with church teaching?

Hunthausen and Wuerl sat side by side at a conference table covered with tape recorders and microphones and put on the best face possible. The archbishop sighed, ran his hand down his jaw, nodded, and, at times, managed to grin. The bishop, unsmiling, was well prepared, albeit a bit tense.

Conceding that the arrangement was "somewhat unusual" and administratively challenging, Hunthausen said he and Wuerl were working together in a spirit of shared responsibility. He emphasized that, even though Wuerl had final decision-making power in the five areas, he would retain authority over the department heads and the overall administration of the archdiocese.

"Why do you have final authority on some matters?" a reporter demanded of the auxiliary bishop.

"I can't explain it," Wuerl responded. "That was a decision that was made before I came into this."

Asked if he had seen Archbishop Hickey's report, Wuerl responded carefully, noting that he hadn't had access "to everything that was part of the visitation." He said he presumed that many of the concerns that emerged from the visitation had already been addressed. Why look backward?

After the slap-in-the-face question, Hunthausen was asked if he considered resigning. "I suppose there were times...," he started to say, caught himself, smiled wanly, and then continued, "I'd just as soon not answer the question. I'm as human as anyone else is. I've gone through a whole gamut of emotions and I've tried to understand. I really have."

Wuerl's emotional state was harder to read. But his situation had to be as trying as Hunthausen's. Laboring under a cloud of suspicion and distrust, the young bishop surely felt misunderstood and abandoned.

"I'm not seen as me," he grumbled in a later interview with *The Progress*. "I'm somehow seen as the incarnation of the visitation."

The reaction to Hunthausen's announcement that Rome had forced him to surrender final authority over key areas was greeted with disbelief, tears, and anger. Sister Kathleen Pruitt, an executive member of the archdiocesan Sisters' Council, said removing Hunthausen's authority punished a man who modeled pastoral leadership. Father Ibar Lynch, a pastor and former director of clergy personnel, called Rome's action contrary to the spirit of Vatican II.

Father Theodore Hesburgh, the president of the University of Notre Dame, said he was "devastated" by the news. "You are my ideal of the best kind of archbishop, courageous, idealistic, dedicated, fearless, and, most of all, unambitious," he wrote the archbishop. "Having a deep belief in the Holy Spirit, I know that in the long run you will be vindicated and the small-minded people will be forgotten."

A letter signed by 150 local priests, nuns, and laypeople was delivered to Hunthausen and Wuerl denouncing the Vatican's action and demanding answers. Headlined "What Kind of Church Are We Becoming?" the letter asked: What is Bishop Wuerl's real role here? How can he, in good conscience, just obey Vatican orders? What are Catholics supposed to do when they feel their archbishop is being publicly humiliated? The signers pledged to fast and pray one day a week.

The letter, drafted by an ad hoc group called Concerned Catholics, soon grew into a public petition seeking the restoration of Hunthausen's full authority. The group had met twice monthly in various church basements ever since Archbishop Hickey's visitation. Among them were chancery insiders such as Father David Jaeger, the director of seminarians; Father Michael Raschko, an archdiocesan theologian; Jim Burns, the development director; and Sister Carol Ann McMullen, associate personnel director for clergy. The core group also included several nuns in leadership roles and some influential laypeople. They regarded the Vatican's treatment of Hunthausen as unfair, unjust, unchristian. And dishonest.

"We never believed the investigation had anything to do with Dutch's pastoral practices," McMullen said. "We figured it had much more to do with his involvement in the peace movement."

The group tried to work within church structures, urging the bishops of the region to support Hunthausen in his struggle with Rome. McMullen and Jaeger enlisted the help of Bishop Skylstad of Yakima and Bishop Welsh of Spokane in drafting a letter to all the U.S. bishops deploring the Vatican's treatment of Hunthausen and asking that his full powers be restored. At the group's invitation, Hunthausen attended a couple of Concerned Catholics' meetings but was discomfited by their activities. He appreciated the support but didn't want the attention, which he felt would further aggravate the situation.

Wuerl regarded the in-house support group for Hunthausen as impolitic and subversive. When he got wind of the "What Kind of Church Are We Becoming?" letter, he summoned McMullen to his office and told her, "Sister Carol Ann, if that statement ever reaches the press, I can tell you right now, the archbishop will be gone tomorrow."

Born, raised, and educated in Seattle, McMullen was a warm, cheerful woman who'd been a teacher, catechist, and leader in the community of Holy Names Sisters.

"Are you threatening me?" she responded.

"Yes, I am," Wuerl retorted.

"Bishop Wuerl," McMullen replied, her voice rising in anger, "as far as you're concerned and as far as the Vatican is concerned, the archbishop is already on his way out and we know that. If he goes tomorrow, no matter how he goes, that's beside the point. We're not standing up for him. We're standing up for what he stands for; we're standing up for the church we believe in."

Overcome with emotion, tears trickling down her cheeks, McMullen began to sob. Wuerl, helpless, teared up as well.

Slowly composing herself, McMullen looked the bishop in the eye and demanded to know: "Do you plan to be here for a while?"

"Why, yes," Wuerl answered. "Yes, I do."

"Then," McMullen replied, "my suggestion is that you get down on your knees and pray that Raymond Hunthausen doesn't leave because he's the only friend you have in this diocese."

Consternation over the Vatican's treatment of Hunthausen erupted at several meetings in parishes, in the chancery, and at the St. Thomas Center over the next several weeks. The most contentious were two large meetings of priests, chancery directors, and members of the archdiocesan Pastoral and Finance Councils hosted by Hunthausen and Wuerl at the former seminary. The September 12 meeting, attended by more than half of the four hundred priests in the archdiocese, was an emotional, five-hour affair in which the archbishop and his auxiliary attempted to explain their new arrangement, how there had been an honest misunderstanding over the "special faculties," and how the Vatican had now clarified Bishop Wuerl's authority. The purpose of the closed-door meeting was to clear the air, state the facts, and tell the unvarnished truth.

Hunthausen convened the meeting. Well aware of the anger, suspicion, and hostility directed at Wuerl, he insisted that his new colleague was simply doing what he had been asked to do. "He's my brother bishop and friend," said Hunthausen, putting everyone on notice that he expected civil and respectful behavior.

Nonetheless, Wuerl was sharply grilled: Had he come to Seattle with specific instructions from Rome? Did he believe the way the Vatican conducted its investigation of Hunthausen was fair and just? What did he think was so wrong with the local church that required outside intervention and big changes?

Put on the defensive immediately, Wuerl tried to respond to the priests' questions. No, he had no special instructions and no agenda other than responsibility for the five areas. As for the visitation, he refused to call it "unjust," reminding the priests that church law and American law are not the same. In regard to the local church, he was just getting to know it and saw many positive things.

In response to one question, Wuerl maintained that all he knew about Seattle beforehand was what he had read in *The New York Times*.

At that point, Father Ryan, his old seminary classmate, had heard enough. In full Irish temper, Ryan rose from his seat and all but called Wuerl a bold-faced liar.

"You remember our meeting in Pittsburgh which no one in this room knows about," Ryan said, referencing the secret trip he made to brief Wuerl before his appointment was announced. "I went back there to visit with you, to try to build a bridge, and to prepare you for a transition. It was obvious you'd seen the Hickey report. How can you say you knew nothing?"

Ryan soon reached full throttle. "We came here today to lance a boil that has been building up in this church for a long time," he thundered on. "And instead we're just adding to it by refusing to come forth and tell the truth. We've got to get past this. Only the truth is going to open this thing up and set us free."

In the face of Ryan's onslaught, Wuerl sat still, red-faced, embarrassed and compromised. When the priests applauded Ryan's remarks, he turned ashen.

"Perhaps I should resign," he said.

Several priests rose to assure the young bishop that he was welcome in Seattle. They just wanted full governance of the archdiocese returned to Hunthausen. They wanted their church back.

The next day Ryan phoned Wuerl at Holy Rosary, not to apologize, but to say that he very much regretted how the meeting had unfolded. Wuerl was angry and deeply hurt. He said he felt betrayed, his character besmirched, and his efforts to build a positive reputation with the priests of the archdiocese in ruins.

The once sociable relationship between the two former classmates became cold and distant. A year later, after the Vatican removed Wuerl from Seattle, he sent Ryan a handwritten note from Assisi. He wanted Ryan to know that there in the Italian hill town of St. Francis, he had experienced a sense of healing and peace from the trauma of Seattle.

In the aftermath of the combative September 12 meeting, the Priest Senate proposed that Hunthausen and Wuerl go to Rome to resolve the Seattle situation in face-to-face conversations with Cardinals Ratzinger and Gantin and, if necessary, with the pope. Wuerl wrote the priests of the archdiocese to tell them that he was willing to accompany the archbishop to Rome for a "forthright discussion" of the Vatican investigation and the local reaction. Noting many good and positive things under Hunthausen's ministry, he stressed that the issue was "certain practices and aspects of archdiocesan administration that the Holy See indicated need attention." He went on to say that once those matters were addressed, he presumed that full authority would revert to the archbishop.

Imploring the priests for "a fresh start—a new beginning," Wuerl suggested that they reject an "either/or" choice (Hunthausen or Rome) and embrace a "both/and" approach that affirmed the archbishop while dealing with the Vatican's concerns. "To continue to debate the visitation, its process and outcome here in Seattle seems futile and ultimately divisive," he wrote.

Meanwhile the petition circulated by Concerned Catholics asking for restoration of Hunthausen's full authority topped twelve thousand signatures from members of 90 of the 132 parishes in western Washington.

On September 22, Hunthausen, Wuerl, and the other Region 12 bishops participated in the installation ceremony for Bishop William Levada, Cardinal Ratzinger's former secretary, as archbishop of Portland, Oregon. While Levada was supposed to be the headliner, media pursued the fifty-five prelates in attendance, including Laghi and Hickey, demanding to know what the U.S. bishops were going to do about the Hunthausen affair.

Boston Cardinal Bernard Law, who would ultimately resign in disgrace after covering up priest pedophilia, characterized the Vatican's actions in Seattle as "legitimate involvement." He predicted that Hunthausen and Wuerl would work together to restore unity. Cardinal Roger Mahony, whose rule in Los Angeles would also be undone by sex abuse scandals, rejected the idea that Levada, his former auxiliary bishop, was sent to the Pacific Northwest to stiffen doctrinal orthodoxy.

"That's ridiculous," Mahony told the *Seattle Times*. "The appointment of an archbishop in Portland is not linked to a whole scenario of international intrigue."

The seventeen Pacific Northwest bishops, minus Levada, used the morning of the installation to discuss the Seattle situation, and then issued a bland statement supporting the efforts of Hunthausen and Wuerl to achieve unity within the church in Seattle. In a private letter to John Paul II, the region's bishops praised Hunthausen as a fine bishop true to the Gospel and loyal to the church. They asked that the Seattle archdiocese be returned to normalcy as soon as possible. When they received no reply, they sent a second letter. It too received no response.

The second general meeting at the St. Thomas Center on September 26 didn't go any better than the first. Retired Bishop Walsh departed early in disgust.

"I left at the 2:30 break," he scrawled on his paper copy of the agenda. "I couldn't take it anymore. We were getting NOWHERE. Wuerl's remarks in the AM almost started a riot."

Trying to appeal for unity, Wuerl had told the gathering that Rome had ruled and, for the good of the church, people needed to buckle under and fix what was wrong. He complained that some of the very people charged with leading the local church—archdiocesan priests and staff at the chancery—were causing the divisiveness. He accused "these renegades" of undermining his collaboration with the archbishop and demanded that the petition campaign to restore Hunthausen's authority be stopped.

His remarks infuriated many of those at the meeting. Sursely, the chief financial officer, stood up and asked Wuerl if, after seven months of observing the archdiocese first hand, he really believed that the local church leadership was incapable and incompetent. Why do we need your special faculties?

Wuerl danced around the question, prompting several shouts from the crowd demanding an answer. Incensed, the bishop replied that he resented either/or questions and would not answer them. Things went further downhill from there.

Finally, Father Michael McDermott, the meeting facilitator, halted the questioning and asked participants to write down their thoughts and questions on three-by-five-inch notecards. He and other staff collected the cards and reviewed them with the Priest Senate over the lunch break. It was obvious that people were on the verge of exploding. Along with the impromptu feedback on the cards, there were letters and statements that some participants had written earlier in anticipation of the discussion. These, along with the cards, were taped to the walls of the meeting room so participants could study them.

The comments were narrow in scope—the Vatican investigation, the secret process, Rome's concerns, Wuerl's special faculties—but broad in emotion. Some comments were angry, disappointed, frustrated, and righteous, while others were puzzled, resigned, hopeful, and loving.

Six Seattle Jesuits, in a letter copied to Laghi, Ratzinger, and Bishop James Malone, president of the U.S. bishops' conference, charged that Rome's actions had ignored biblical justice, disregarded church teaching, and undermined the character of the church. There could be no healing, they wrote, until the church examined its own conscience with respect to justice and human rights.

Father Joe Kramis, pastor of St. Theresa Church in Federal Way, argued that the central issue was the nature of the church. "The collaborative model of leadership in the spirit of Vatican II is threatened by the exaggerated importance of the magisterium and [its] creeping infallibility," he wrote.

Father Gary Zender, of All Saints Church in Puyallup, bemoaned the "disappointingly weak" statement from the Region 12 bishops whom, he suggested, should be as "hurt, confused, and scandalized" as he and his parishioners.

A few priests, however, submitted statements kinder to Rome and critical of the archdiocese. Father Hans Olson, of St. Luke Church in north Seattle, said he was ashamed by the priestly arrogance, the "almost violent tone," and the narrow-minded view that seemed to characterize the archdiocesan response to Rome. "There needs to be a frank assessment of our fidelity to the universal nature of the church," he wrote.

Father Joseph Mitchell, who served with Hunthausen and Ryan at St. James Cathedral, suggested that the archdiocese look closely at the issues raised in the Ratzinger letter.

"Do we claim to function with a vision different from that of the universal church?" asked Mitchell. "Do we claim a broader approach to church discipline? Do we assume a greater freedom in juxtaposing church teaching with theological opinion?"

McDermott, calm and reasonable, reconvened the meeting and summarized the posted material as objectively as he could. Then the floor was open for questions and comment.

Father Al Marshall's hand shot up. A feisty, pugnacious pastor known for badmouthing the chancery, Marshall went after Wuerl.

"Bishop Wuerl," he said, "you talk about unity but what you said was divisive. You tried to divide us from the chancery."

Wuerl rose to the attack, vehemently denying that he was taking sides. Soon the two clerics were yelling at each other at full volume. Hunthausen, sitting next to Wuerl, slumped in his chair, head bowed, apparently resorting to prayer. Abruptly Marshall shut up and sat down. The fight was over.

While others spoke after Marshall, the heated argument had disturbed and dispirited the room. Some, like Bishop Walsh, slipped away in dismay. The meeting petered out with no conclusions and little likelihood that Hunthausen and Wuerl would be going to Rome anytime soon for a forthright discussion with the pope.

The alarm, outrage, and hurt caused by the Vatican's disciplining of Hunthausen and its criticism of the archdiocese extended far beyond the two unruly and inconclusive meetings at the St. Thomas Center. Parishes staged discussion groups and prayer vigils and demonstrations.

The lay ministers of the archdiocese organized a Sunday convocation at Kennedy High School as "a faith response to the current painful experience" of the archdiocese. About 250 Catholics, most of them parish staff members, arrived in cars with "Hunthausen is my Archbishop" bumper stickers. Many wore apple-sized, red and white "I Love Hunthausen" buttons on their lapels.

Father Raschko, the archdiocesan theologian and one of several speakers, explained that Seattle was the focal point for the question that Vatican II never quite answered: What does it mean to find unity yet respect diversity in a "catholic" church? How does the Gospel take root in the local situation?

"Does the church foster strict conformity for the sake of unity?" he asked. "Or should we let ourselves bend and break a little for the sake of compassion?"

Thirty-five members in the core group of Concerned Catholics, most of them priests and nuns, wrote a ten-page letter to the U.S. bishops asking that Hunthausen's authority be restored, that the results of the "inquisitional" investigation be disclosed, and that the Vatican employ an "open, just, and collegial" process when it has issues with a bishop and a local church.

Other faith leaders, elected officials, and everyday people filled the letter and op-ed sections of the region's newspapers commenting on Hunthausen and his predicament. In an op-ed in the *Seattle Times*, the Reverend Dale Turner, the éminence grise of Seattle's Protestant establishment, described Hunthausen as one of America's strongest moral leaders.

"It is precisely because Hunthausen is willing to risk alienation and misunderstanding by his involvement in controversial issues that I admire him so highly," Turner wrote. "He has humility without timidity, competence without arrogance, and he exercises authority without being authoritarian."

The reaction to the Seattle situation was not confined to the Northwest. The national organization of canon lawyers took up a resolution calling for a review of the Vatican's investigative processes. The *National Catholic Reporter,* a Kansas City–based independent weekly with a circulation of fifty thousand, devoted the entire front page and two inside pages of its October 3 edition to letters protesting the Vatican's punishment of Hunthausen. And, in San Antonio, Texas, more than two hundred priests attending a national conference of vocation directors watched as Spokane Bishop Welsh, the keynote speaker, broke down as he tried to respond to a question about the Vatican's disciplining of Hunthausen. Tearful and choked up, Welsh eventually said, "The archbishop is a friend of mine. I want you to know I am struggling along with you."

In late September, the archbishop's six siblings and four of their spouses gathered at youngest brother Art's home in Helena to discuss what they could do to help their beleaguered older brother. The archbishop did not know they were meeting. Somewhere over dinner or after prayer they hit upon the idea of writing personal letters to the three hundred U.S. Catholic bishops likely to be at the annual meeting in mid-November. They would do it privately.

"We didn't want Dutch and the whole world to know," said Sister Edna Hunthausen, the middle sister. "We just wanted the bishops to know the kind of person he is and that he has not done anything out of line with the church. He just hasn't."

Edna got a list of the bishops' addresses from Bishop Sylvester Treinen, who advised her to use high-quality, letterhead stationery, greet them as "Your Excellencies," and make it short. Jeanne Stergar, the youngest Hunthausen sibling, addressed the envelopes, affixed the postage, and posted them with her return address in Anaconda.

The letter asked the bishops to address Hunthausen's situation when they met in Washington, DC. It acknowledged that doing so would "require personal risk" on their part but argued that his case "cannot be overlooked if the church is to continue to preach justice with any credibility."

"The letter did not make any judgments," said Father Jack Hunthausen, the other priest in the family. "All it did was say that Dutch be given the opportunity to speak."

Marie Walsh, the oldest sister, took an additional measure. She sent an audiotape of her brother's peace talk at Notre Dame to John Paul II. "I figured if the pope would listen to it," she said, "he would see the type of man Dutch was."

Hunthausen's siblings knew that if they had told him about the letter beforehand he would have discouraged them from sending it. He feared that all the advocacy on his behalf was damaging the institutional church that he had vowed to serve. He didn't want an "us against them" situation. He respected church teaching. He revered the Holy Father.

He could only wonder what his mother, who had died the summer before the visitation, might have thought. He recalled how Jack and Edna had kidded her about her oldest son's involvement in peace demonstrations and civil disobedience.

"You know," they teased her, "you ought to talk to Dutch. He may get himself into some real trouble and get tossed into jail one of these days. Just look at what the secretary of the navy is saying about him."

Their almost ninety-year-old mother was unperturbed. "I don't care if he gets thrown into jail. I don't care what the secretary of the navy says about him. All I worry about is: What does the pope think of him?"

Chuckling as he retold the story, Hunthausen concluded, "Good thing she died when she did."

In a church climate that had become increasingly partisan, Hunthausen strove for unity. He gave no encouragement to letter writing or signature campaigns on his behalf. He declined invitations to appear at church meetings and rallies organized in response to Rome's actions. And when lay ministers invited Bishop Thomas Gumbleton to headline the convocation at Kennedy High School, he persuaded his fellow peace bishop to stay away for fear of exacerbating church tensions.

But there was no avoiding the limelight. When retired Bishop Topel, his lifelong mentor, confidante, and spiritual advisor, died in late October 1986, Hunthausen concelebrated the funeral Mass at Our Lady of Lourdes Cathedral in Spokane. As he stepped to the pulpit to eulogize Topel, the congregation of priests, nuns, and laypeople rose to its feet in a sustained, standing ovation. He wished the applause had been for the late bishop, not him.

The fall 1986 meeting of the National Conference of Catholic Bishops was supposed to focus on final discussion and approval of the bishops' pastoral letter on the U.S. economy. Titled "Economic Justice for All," the pastoral applied Catholic social teaching to the American free enterprise system and, by implication, the Reagan administration. It found both wanting. Laissez faire market capitalism, it argued, neglects the poor, undermines the dignity of labor, threatens the environment, and glorifies greed. The letter, successfully shepherded through the bishops' conference by Archbishop Weakland, would sit alongside the bishops' peace pastoral as the most significant teaching and advocacy documents that the U.S. bishops would ever write.

The pastoral was eclipsed, however, by the volatile internal matter of what to do about Hunthausen. The bishops were distressed and divided. If they expressed too much support for their brother bishop, they could appear disloyal to Rome and destructive of church unity. On the other hand, if they abandoned the Seattle archbishop like Jacob's sons selling their brother Joseph into slavery, they would look like cowardly puppets at the beck and call of the Vatican. To do too much would invite retaliation and create further division. To do too little would give up on the collegial independence many of them sought to establish with Rome.

The Vatican had U.S. bishops who shared its views, especially the powerful cardinals whose elevated rank gave them easy access in Rome. They preferred to conduct business directly with the curia and the pope rather than deal through the cumbersome, consultative processes of the bishops' conference. Cardinals Law, O'Connor, Mahony, and others were not going to allow an independent-thinking bishops' conference to take the Hunthausen matter into its own hands. They could be counted on to back whatever Rome wanted to do with Hunthausen.

How the conference handled the Hunthausen case would have implications for bishops' conferences and local churches around the world. Ultimately, the bishops had to ask themselves who they were: Functionaries carrying out the dictates of the Holy See? Or local church leaders applying the Gospel in good conscience to guide their people?

Archbishop Laghi was tired of what he viewed as the bad and distorted press coverage the Vatican was receiving over the Hunthausen affair. In anticipation of the bishops' meeting, he called Bishop Malone, the conference president, and asked him to send all the U.S. bishops Rome's version of what had transpired in Seattle. Malone phoned Hunthausen to advise him of Laghi's request, and the archbishop called the papal nuncio.

"What purpose is this going to serve?" Hunthausen asked Laghi. "If you do this, I just know that in good conscience I'm going to have to respond."

Laghi, under pressure from Ratzinger and Gantin to tell Rome's side of the story, was undeterred. Malone, after two emergency meetings of the U.S. bishops' executive committee, sent out the Vatican's "Chronology of Recent Events in the Archdiocese of Seattle." The cover letter noted that the document was being distributed "at the request of the Vatican and authorization of the Holy See." Malone wanted to maintain a scrupulously neutral position.

The genial, savvy, and fair-minded bishop of Youngstown, Ohio, then invited Hunthausen to present his own chronology and argue his own case in a closed-door executive session at the bishops' meeting in Washington on November 11–13. Hunthausen was surprised by the invitation.

"My natural response would have been to say: 'Jim, I don't need to defend myself; let's just let it go,'" Hunthausen recalled. "But I said, "No, Jim, I think it's fine. I think this has to be dealt with.'"

Laghi's four-page chronology began by claiming that the visitation was mounted because of "the high volume of complaints" received in Rome, as early as 1978—the year John Paul II took office—from priests, nuns, and laypeople in the archdiocese. It reiterated that the Vatican's interest had nothing to do with Hunthausen's peace activities or his tax protest. "The concerns were strictly and solely of a doctrinal and pastoral nature," the chronology insisted. Mentioned were the familiar issues of the marriage tribunal, the liturgy, contraceptive sterilization, clergy formation, use of inactive priests, and ministry to homosexuals.

The chronology blamed Hunthausen for twisting the facts, creating unwanted publicity, reneging on a promise to give Wuerl special powers, and, most damaging of all, "lacking the firmness necessary to govern the archdiocese." In short, insufficient backbone to do the job.

It claimed that Rome's decision to take further action after concluding the visitation was "primarily provoked by the documented responses of the archbishop himself." Hunthausen had either failed to act on significant issues or minimized their importance, it charged.

Rome's original intent, the chronology stated, was to send Hickey quietly to Seattle in a spirit of fraternal support to help Hunthausen address problem areas. But the archbishop, to Rome's dismay, insisted on making the visitation public. The chronology noted that Laghi had shared the results of the visitation with Hunthausen at the apostolic nunciature in Washington, DC, in October 1985 and said the archbishop did not dispute the facts. It claimed that a deal was worked out in which Hunthausen would accept Bishop Wuerl as his auxiliary and give him responsibility for the areas of Vatican concern. Yet, the document complained, while Hunthausen gave Wuerl responsibility, he did not give him final authority as Rome had envisioned.

"For more than six months after the arrival of Bishop Wuerl, the agreed-to faculties were not given," carped the chronology, which blamed Hunthausen for "misunderstanding or misinterpretation."

Acknowledging that the archbishop finally gave Wuerl special authority, the Vatican document concluded on a malicious note. "Regretfully," it said, "the surprise announcement made by Archbishop Hunthausen after granting the faculties was interpreted as portraying the whole process as a one-sided affair."

Hunthausen reacted to Laghi's chronology with a brief public statement, questioning much of what it contained. Father Ryan, who kept detailed records on all interactions with Rome, began drafting the full response the archbishop would take to the bishops' conference. The language was more Ryan than Hunthausen, an exacting, line-by-line rebuttal that ran longer than Laghi's original chronology.

Among other things, Hunthausen contested Laghi's assertion of "substantial complaints" about him and the archdiocese going back to 1978. If so, the archbishop asked, why was I not told about this until after the visitation was announced? If my earlier responses were unsatisfactory and thus occasioned the visitation, he further asked, why was I not informed of this at the time? Why was I politely and routinely thanked for the information I provided only to hear nothing more until Archbishop Hickey had begun to investigate?

Hunthausen said he was surprised to learn things from Laghi's chronology that he had not heard before. For example, the chronology said the all-encompassing theological concerns raised in the Ratzinger letter were related only to the continuing education of priests. He found this baffling since priests of the Seattle archdiocese took the same courses from the same personnel as priests from dozens of other dioceses. What was particularly surprising, however, was the chronology's allegation that he "lacked the necessary firmness" to govern the local church. That was a new one.

Hunthausen rejected the chronology's claim that he had been obstinate and intransigent by not granting Wuerl special faculties as ordered. Per the compromise deal struck with Rome on December 2, 1985, he noted, the special faculties were up to him to assign. It was Rome that unilaterally changed the terms of the deal after he and Wuerl sought clarification.

The chronology's suggestion that he had "acted in bad faith" riled Hunthausen. "I did not," he said.

Once Rome had ruled, the archbishop said he had accepted Wuerl's special faculties rather than resign because several bishops and close advisors convinced him that it would better for the ultimate good of the church to do so.

While Hunthausen, Ryan, and Archbishop Hurley strategized over Hunthausen's defense at the bishops' meeting, retired Bishop Nicolas Walsh was on a one-man mission to Rome to advocate for his old friend and colleague. Walsh undertook the trip on the spur of the moment, traveling from his retirement home in Boise, Idaho, on the $2,500 he'd saved to replace his old Volkswagen. In Rome, he met with Cardinals Gantin, Sebastiano Baggio, and William Baum, the American who preceded Hickey in Washington and now headed the Congregation for Catholic Education. He also spoke with Archbishop Alberto Bovone, Ratzinger's secretary, and twice concelebrated Mass with Pope John Paul II in the pontiff's private chapel. At every opportunity, Walsh told curia members and their staffs that Hunthausen was a devout, dedicated, and loyal bishop whose orthodoxy was beyond reproach.

The retired auxiliary bishop gave the cardinal-prefects and the pope a solution for the Seattle crisis that he reckoned would restore the good name and reputation of Hunthausen, Wuerl, and the Holy Father: As soon as Rome's issues were resolved, have Wuerl recommend that Hunthausen's full authority be returned. That way, Walsh reasoned, Wuerl would appear magnanimous, Hunthausen would be made whole, and the pope would be seen as just and fair.

In a private letter to John Paul, Walsh warned that the divisive Seattle affair threatened the whole church. He wrote that the faithful, including the bishops, were still in the dark about the nature and results of the visitation. "Was something more serious discovered which was so bad that it cannot be revealed?" he asked the Holy Father.

Walsh told the pope that "wonderment, questions, frustrations, and anger are now blanketed by fear of Your Holiness," then hastened to add, "whom they nonetheless love and highly respect as Christ's vicar."

Father Ryan continued to work on Hunthausen's speech to the bishops, clarifying, explaining, and rebutting the allegations and conclusions of the Laghi chronology. He read it aloud as he and the archbishop drove from the chancery to a priest personnel board meeting in Tacoma.

"It took all the way down to read it to him," Ryan recalled. "He didn't say anything. It just churned him up inside to think that he would need to say all these things. I told him: I don't think you have any choice. The record has to be set straight."

Hunthausen took Ryan's draft, marked it up, softened some of the language, and then talked it over with some of the other Region 12 bishops. The discussion occurred in a large van that Bishop Skylstad had rented to transport them from a regional meeting in Portland to a ceremony rededicating the cathedral in Yakima. Skylstad, the Yakima bishop, was driving.

"I was trying to pay attention to the road," he said, recalling the winding drive up through the Columbia River Gorge and into the Yakima Valley. "There was a lot of discussion."

In Yakima, Hunthausen gave the revised draft to Hurley. The politically astute Alaskan read it and was hesitant.

"I don't know if I'd say all these things," he told his colleague, suggesting that Hunthausen downplay it a bit.

"Well, Frank, they're the facts," the archbishop replied. "If I'm going to respond at all, I'm going to have to say something that I'll be at peace with. I wish this whole thing would just go away but it's not going away."

In the days leading up to the U.S. bishops' big meeting at the Capitol Hilton in Washington, the Vatican turned up the flame with two announcements. On October 31, Cardinal Ratzinger released what gay activists would call the "Halloween letter," the CDF statement that defined homosexuality as an intrinsic moral evil that must be seen as an objective disorder. Five days later, Rome announced that Pope John Paul II would visit the United States in September 1987, stopping in eight cities including three on the West Coast. It would not do to have the Hunthausen case unresolved with the pope coming to town.

On Monday morning November 10, 1986, Bishop Malone opened the U.S. bishops' meeting and wrapped up his three-year term as conference president with an address assessing the state of the Catholic Church in the United States. He praised the growth of collegiality among the bishops, citing their work on the two pastoral letters, their positive evaluations of seminaries, and their willingness to criticize American culture for its economic inequalities, militarism, foreign interventions, and "massive slaughter of the unborn."

At the same time, Malone said candidly, the U.S. church has had a troubled relationship with the Holy See in trying to find the proper balance between local autonomy and allegiance to higher authority.

"Some people feel that the local church needs more freedom. Others believe that more control is in order," he said. "Some feel that appeals to authority are being exercised too readily. Others applaud what they perceive to be a return to needed central control."

How do we function as one unified Body of Christ? Malone asked. "We cannot exist alone. We are a *communio*. We are a church."

The conference president went on to say that the bishops would take up the Seattle situation in a closed-door executive session. He cautioned that "our conference has no competence to interject itself into the special relationship between the Holy Father and a local bishop." Nonetheless, he added, the bishops would offer their fraternal support to Hunthausen and Wuerl as an expression of collegiality with each other and the pope. Malone left it up to the bishops to decide what that "fraternal support" might be.

The opening morning also included the customary address by the papal nuncio. Laghi devoted virtually all of his speech to reading a seven-page letter from his boss, John Paul II. Making no mention of the Seattle situation, the pope reminded the bishops that, while they served as pastors of particular churches, "you must always be in full communion with the successor of Peter." John Paul noted his upcoming visit to the United States and concluded by reiterating his central theme of church unity under papal authority. Speaking on his own behalf, Laghi expressed satisfaction at seeing nearly one hundred of his recommended episcopal candidates now sitting before him as bishops.

Hunthausen, Hurley, and Ryan lunched Monday at the University Club, where Hurley had lodged the three of them for the duration of the bishops' meeting. Hurley, a member of the genteel, venerable old club a block from the Capitol Hilton, wanted a location close enough to walk to the meeting but far enough away to avoid the press and strategize in private. Retired Bishop William McManus of Fort Wayne–South Bend, Indiana, joined them for lunch.

What Hunthausen would actually say to the bishops had occasioned a heated debate between Ryan and Hurley. Ryan's draft of Hunthausen's proposed remarks was specific, critical, and passionate. The Anchorage archbishop's draft was generic, considerate of Rome, and almost apologetic. Hurley insisted that he knew the bishops, and Ryan's version would alienate many of them. Ryan contended that it was time to stand up and speak the truth. Hunthausen and McManus listened quietly as the two argued back and forth.

"We'll pray about it," Hunthausen finally said as he got up to walk back to the meeting.

After the two archbishops departed, Ryan and McManus lingered over lunch. Like Hunthausen, McManus was a Jadot bishop, a kind, thoughtful man who had served as superintendent of Catholic schools in Chicago. He was impressed by Hunthausen's courage and faith.

"Stay with this man and continue to back him," he told Ryan. "The American hierarchy has produced very few great men. He is one of them."

The argument between his key advisors unsettled Hunthausen who was already troubled by the note that Bishop George Speltz, his old horse-packing buddy and Vatican II colleague, had left on his desk. The note advised Hunthausen to be careful about what he said from the floor. At the coffee break, the two old friends found each other and talked.

Speltz suggested to Hunthausen that defending what he had done would simply prolong the controversy and hurt the church. "Why question the nuncio? Why risk a public exchange of accusations?" he said. "Don't do it."

Hunthausen explained that he felt he had to tell his story, not for himself, but for the good of the church. Speltz shook his head and wished him well. Hunthausen sank further into worry and indecisiveness. He wondered what was really driving him. Was it pride? Or conviction? Or a need to redeem himself? Could he trust that still voice that said "Thy will be done"?

While Hunthausen agonized, hundreds had mobilized outside the closed doors of Capitol Hilton ballroom to support him. Some distributed flyers with a scriptural warning that the bishops "not become as blind guides who strain gnats and swallow the camel." Others held candles and signs and walked in orderly lines along the sidewalk. Some wore the letter "H," cut from red cloth, on their coats, red being the color of martyrdom. Father McSorley, the Georgetown Jesuit whose essay on the immorality of possessing nuclear weapons had captivated Hunthausen, wore one on his black clerical suit.

Hunthausen's brother bishops, even those most sympathetic to him, were not so demonstrative. Bishop Kenneth Untener of Saginaw, Michigan, recalled how the only unoccupied chair in the room when the bishops' meeting opened was the one next to Hunthausen.

"I took it," Untener joked, "and wondered afterward if it cost me [appointment to] Philadelphia."

The mood in the Capitol Hilton's grand ballroom Tuesday afternoon November 11 was subdued and anxious. The room was closed to the press so the television lights were gone, making the place darker and more somber, like a courtroom. The bishops entered without the usual banter and immediately went to their desks where they found three documents for their consideration: (1) Bishop Malone's draft statement on what they should say about the Seattle situation; (2) Hunthausen's response to Laghi's Vatican chronology; and (3) the full text of the speech the Seattle archbishop would reference in defense of himself and his ministry.

Malone called the meeting to order and invited Hunthausen to come forward to address the bishops. Tense, nervous, his mouth grimly set, the Seattle archbishop walked to the podium as if he were headed to the executioner. He hated being the center of attention. He would rather be anywhere but here, at the heart of this church controversy. In his twenty-four years as a bishop, he had spoken to the full assembly of bishops only once—by invitation. And that was to speak out against nuclear weapons and advocate for unilateral disarmament. Now he had to speak to justify himself and his ministry. How humiliating.

Hunthausen began by telling his brother bishops how distressed he was by the anguish and turmoil that the Seattle affair had caused them and the church. "I wish it would all go away," he said. "How I wish that."

Touching on some of the main points in his longer written text, Hunthausen said the Vatican's actions in Seattle were not "some sort of battle of wits between a maverick archbishop and the Holy See." Rather, he contended, what has happened in his archdiocese has serious implications for individual bishops, conferences of bishops, the pope, and how the church is governed.

Hunthausen then reviewed his experience with Rome. The secrecy with which the Vatican conducted its investigation does not and cannot work, he said. "Open disclosure and candor are far more consistent with respect for persons in a mature church." He said Rome's obsession with secrecy prevented transparent dialogue, denied him access to the information being used against him, and deprived him of the opportunity to face his accusers.

"Given the kind of open church we have become since the Second Vatican Council," Hunthausen said, Rome's process "seriously wounds the community of faith and trust in the church."

As for the five areas of concern over which the Vatican gave Bishop Wuerl final authority, Hunthausen suggested to his fellow bishops that all of them involved matters of "pastoral judgment," of making prudent decisions locally rather than requesting orders from some central office in Rome. He noted that every pastor soon comes to recognize that applying church law is a rather imprecise science. "In such matters," he said, "we never really get beyond the possibility of making a mistake no matter how hard we try to faithfully discern the Spirit."

Hunthausen said he had used his best judgment in making pastoral decisions that he believed were consistent with church law, or, at least with church law as it was before John Paul II's major revision of 1983. He mentioned the Vatican's concerns—the marriage tribunal, use of laicized priests, intercommunion, general absolution, contraceptive sterilization, and so forth—and said he had dealt with them responsibly whenever they were brought to his attention. He acknowledged that perhaps his most controversial decision was to allow Dignity to celebrate Mass at the cathedral.

"I am willing to stand corrected," he said. "But my decision does not differ in kind from the decision made by many bishops to allow local Dignity groups to celebrate Mass in one or another church on a regular basis."

Hunthausen ended the defense of his ministry by comparing himself to his colleagues. He wasn't a rebel or a dissenter from church teaching. From the very start, he said, he had made it clear that he would sooner resign than bring dishonor to the church. He had the same goal as every other bishop—"to be a teacher, a pastor, and a servant of the Lord and of the church." He held up the example of Christ: "Never did he compromise the truth he had come to reveal, but neither did he fail to extend to all he encountered the warm and compassionate embrace of a loving God. That's the challenge I face day after day in my ministry to the church in Seattle, and I know it is the struggle of each of us in this room."

The archbishop challenged his brother bishops to embrace the shared responsibility envisioned by Vatican II by engaging in a dialogue with Rome that would result in a clearer balance between local and universal church authority. How does a diocesan bishop exercise his rightful judgment in union with the Holy Father? And what is the proper role of national bishops' conferences? Hunthausen argued that the visitation should have been carried out by the bishops' conference in collaboration with the Holy See. Instead, the U.S. bishops were left in the dark.

In a thinly veiled appeal asking the bishops to stand up to Rome, the Seattle archbishop reminded them that local churches, while in communion with Rome, have their own histories, traditions, lifestyles, characteristics, and problems. The American bishops have the responsibility and should assume the authority to apply church teaching in their own contexts. Moreover, he added, they ought to be as ready to practice justice within the church as they have been to preach peace and justice outside the church.

In closing, Hunthausen asked his colleagues for help. He called the removal of his authority and the assignment of special faculties to Bishop Wuerl "unworkable." For the good of the universal church, he said, "governance of the church of Seattle needs to be returned to normal as soon as humanly possible. I would even say at once."

"The good of the church is what is at stake here. Nothing less."

As Hunthausen left the podium and walked back to his seat, the ballroom erupted in a loud, vigorous, and prolonged standing ovation. From most quarters, it was a resounding sign of support for the archbishop and what he had said. But not all. Laghi, as he had done during Hunthausen's refutation, continued to hold his head in his hands. Cardinal Law, expressionless, refrained from clapping. And Archbishop Hickey, according to one bishop, looked as "white as a sheep."

Bishop Malone reassumed control of the meeting, directing the bishops to the statement of "fraternal support" drafted to address the Seattle affair. The statement, which Malone wrote after consultation with the bishops' fifty-member administrative board, sought a safe, pragmatic middle ground by expressing sympathy for Hunthausen while upholding Vatican authority. It affirmed the bishops' loyalty to the pope, declared the dispute between Seattle and Rome beyond their jurisdiction, and expressed confidence in the Vatican to resolve the matter.

At the same time, it acknowledged the dismay and confusion experienced by many Catholics. Malone compared "the suffering in the church in Seattle" to the pain "that can only be felt by members of a family." He noted that a family takes steps to ensure that a painful situation does not occur again. Implicit was the suggestion that the Vatican improve its investigative and disciplinary procedures when it has issues with a bishop's ministry. Nonetheless, the draft read: "It is clear that the process employed by the Holy See was in accord with the law of the church and was just and reasonable."

Malone read the statement, and then invited any bishop who wished to comment to speak from the floor for up to three minutes. Twenty-seven bishops rose to address the statement that would purport to speak for all of them on the Seattle situation. The very first, at Malone's invitation, was Hunthausen.

He apologized again for the pain that his situation had caused them and the church. But, in all honesty, he felt that the statement provided little help to resolve the matter. "It disclaims any authority or judgment yet it says that the process is reasonable and just," he said. "I am at odds with that."

Bishops Treinen and Skylstad, Hunthausen's friends and confidants from Region 12, were the next to speak. Treinen described the Seattle archbishop as a faithful and loyal churchman who spoke truth from the heart.

"I am loyal to Archbishop Hunthausen and to the Holy Father," the Boise bishop said. "And I grieve for both of them, for Bishop Wuerl, and for the church. Nobody should be subjected to this."

Skylstad seconded Treinen's remarks and objected to the draft statement's description of the Vatican's process as just and reasonable. "The perception is to the contrary," he said.

Archbishop Weakland also objected to calling the process just. Furthermore, he argued that the whole role of the bishops' conference was at stake in Seattle.

Archbishop John Roach, the previous conference president, declared that Hunthausen's address had made a mockery of the Malone statement, which needed a major revision.

Yet Cardinal Bernardin, who said he spoke for the other cardinals, endorsed the statement. The larger issue, he contended, was church unity with the bishops united with the Holy Father. "We acknowledge the tension, especially among our priests," he said. "We now have to move beyond the impasse."

Bishop Wuerl also praised the statement. He called it realistic, encouraging, and forward-looking. "It dissipates the image of division that plagues the local church," he said.

Archbishop Hickey rose to defend his conduct of the visitation as a confidential, fact-finding mission consistent with canon law. He noted all the hours he had spent gathering materials and interviewing Hunthausen and some seventy others. "This was a just and equitable procedure," he said.

The Washington archbishop was quickly taken on by Archbishop Hurley, who said he was "saddened and alarmed" by the intent of Hickey's remarks, which would take the bishops from a neutral course to one that would further divide the church.

Brooklyn Bishop Joseph Sullivan turned up the heat by reading a statement signed by nineteen bishops. It said Rome's disciplining of Hunthausen had failed to achieve the Vatican's goal, undermined the bishops' conference, and polarized the church. It called for development of an open and transparent dispute resolution and disciplinary process in collaboration with the bishops.

Cardinal O'Connor complained that declarations from all over the country, including by implication the one just read by Sullivan, had become vehicles for attacking the Vatican. "The climate has become such that anything that comes from the Holy See is looked at with suspicion," he objected, adding that the bishops could make suggestions to Rome but "had no right to interfere with its integrity."

Time ran out before all the bishops who wanted to speak on Malone's draft statement were able to do so. Malone adjourned the executive session for the day, promising that they could address the assembly when they reconvened in the morning.

Immediately afterward, the bishops gathered in conference rooms for regional business meetings. At the Region 12 meeting, a weary Hunthausen slumped down in a chair and shook his head. He looked thoroughly wrung out and depressed.

"Why did I come here?" he asked aloud. "Why did I come?" He seemed to have no realization how well his presentation had been received.

When Malone reconvened the meeting Wednesday morning, he presented a revised statement that attempted to address the criticism of the previous day. The new version limited itself to describing the Vatican's action as consistent with church law but no longer called it "reasonable and just." It still made the point that the bishops were not "authorized to judge the facts of the case" and acknowledged that Hunthausen and Wuerl "have been given a job to do by the Holy See." Yet the bishops offered "any assistance judged helpful and appropriate by the parties involved."

The new version was not received with much enthusiasm from the floor. Untener, Hunthausen's seatmate, and other bishops objected that the redraft ignored the fact that the present arrangement in Seattle wouldn't work.

Cincinnati Archbishop Daniel Pilarczyk countered that fixing Seattle was beyond the bishops' purview. "We cannot second guess the Holy See," he said.

Bernardin, playing the role of mediator, told Malone that the revised statement did a fine job of reconciling the concerns of the bishops with the concerns of Rome. He urged his fellow bishops to close ranks around the statement, cautioning them that any remarks they made to the press should be within its framework.

"We have to stick together," he said.

In ending the five-hour discussion and debate, Malone once again invited Hunthausen to comment. The archbishop stood up and graciously thanked his brother bishops for their efforts.

"I appreciate what you have done. You have agonized with Bishop Wuerl and me and come to this," he said. Sometimes, he suggested, truth and unity are in tension. He then went on to ask: How does one try to identify what really needs fixing in the church without giving the impression of setting oneself up against the Holy Father?

"The last thing I want is anything against the Holy Father. We are not drawing up sides."

Appreciating the bind his colleagues were in, the archbishop said he would support the revised statement. He drew their attention, however, to their promise to help resolve the unworkable arrangement in Seattle. And then he sat down.

At 10:15 AM, Malone reopened the ballroom doors to the media. Kenneth Briggs, the *New York Times* religion editor, entered to find "a thick layer of despondency" over the seated bishops. He wrote that he had never experienced "a heavier, more sullen mood among them."

Malone read aloud the revised statement, which was greeted by subdued applause. The conference president said he took the applause to mean the statement had the full support of the bishops.

At a press conference afterward, O'Connor praised the statement for showing the unity of the bishops, their loyalty to the Holy See, and their love for Hunthausen. However, Bishop Michael Kenny, a Hunthausen ally, said he and a number of other bishops did not support it. "It does not adequately address the widespread perception that both the process and the decision were unfair," Kenny said.

That evening Archbishop Laghi, in his role as papal ambassador, hosted a buffet dinner for the bishops at the nunciature. Malone, O'Connor, and several other conference leaders took Hunthausen aside and said they were committed to working with him in resolving the Seattle affair. They then met privately with Laghi in a conversation that Hunthausen suspected was the beginning of the next solution for Seattle.

The archbishop returned to Seattle the following evening to find himself mobbed at an airport reception more typical of that given to star athletes than bishops. Hundreds of people greeted him with flowers, handshakes, hugs, and shouts of "We love you." Stepping gingerly atop a baggage counter, Hunthausen received a tumultuous cheer and then addressed his fans.

"You're great, great people," he declared.

"And you're a great archbishop," someone shouted.

The next day Hunthausen was back at the chancery to face the media alone. Wuerl was in Pittsburgh to visit his family. The archbishop, looking rested and confident, repeated what he had told the bishops: Dual authority is unworkable. Seattle should be returned to normalcy as soon as possible.

Sighing, Hunthausen predicted that frustration and confusion would continue. "I've mentioned to Bishop Wuerl that the only way he and I could carry this off would be to be handcuffed to each other twenty-four hours a day."

The archbishop said he had no plans to resign and had not been asked to do so. He described the recently concluded bishops' meeting as "one of the most moving, profound experiences of my life." He called it significant that the U.S. bishops would spend hours hearing, discussing, and struggling over a local church that had tried hard to embrace the vision of Vatican II.

Hunthausen insisted he was not disappointed by the bishops' tepid statement on the Seattle situation. "I don't see the statement from Bishop Malone as coming down on one side or the other," he said. "Of course, we support the Holy Father. I see it as willing to provide help and assistance to the local church."

In response to reporters' questions, the archbishop said that while he and his staff would continue to address the issues raised by Rome, he didn't see any need to change his ministry.

Despite Wuerl's special faculties and full authority over major archdiocesan departments, little had changed. Thus far the auxiliary bishop had issued no rules or guidelines for any of the areas for which he had final responsibility. In some cases, he had not yet met with the department heads that ostensibly reported to him. Dignity, whose convention Mass at the cathedral had incurred Ratzinger's wrath, continued to celebrate its own Masses, just not at the cathedral. The ultra-orthodox Catholics who had complained to Rome about Hunthausen now began whining about Wuerl.

Yoked together in an impossible power-sharing relationship, the two bishops endeavored to govern the archdiocese together. Following the bishops' meeting, Hunthausen encouraged Wuerl to move ahead in the ministerial areas for which he had special faculties. The archdiocesan planning office took the work of the ad hoc committee of Wuerl, Ryan, and McDermott and designed a blueprint for addressing Rome's concerns. With Wuerl's approval, commissions were established to oversee liturgical issues and develop guidelines for catechetical formation.

Hunthausen inspired a deep loyalty among his staff, most of whom viewed him as a kind, compassionate, innocent man horribly victimized by Rome. As a result, Wuerl became the scapegoat for the animosity they felt toward the Vatican. With his elite Roman education and his meticulous Roman ways, the auxiliary bishop was an easy target.

When he arrived at the office in the morning, word went through the chancery: "Jackboots is in the building."

At the contentious meetings at the St. Thomas Center, more than one priest had filled out an anonymous notecard demanding to know if Wuerl was gay. Another priest mailed the bishop a series of wicked post cards. One read: "You out-Uriah Heeped Uriah Heep."

The malicious, divisive environment that seemed to envelop the archdiocese disgusted Father Larry Reilly, Hunthausen's former theological advisor.

"There was no gray, everything was black and white," Reilly said. "People either loved the archbishop and hated the pope or loved the pope and hated the archbishop. It was the antithesis of everything the archbishop stood for."

Hunthausen was hurt and saddened when he heard that some of his priests were harassing Wuerl. He redoubled his efforts to show that he and his auxiliary were working together in fraternal solidarity. But their radically different personal styles and their radically different visions of the post-Vatican II church made it very challenging. Sometimes Hunthausen's serenity cracked and the pain, frustration, and resentment seeped out.

Barbara Geraci, the missions' director, abhorred the fact that chancery staff who were friendly to Wuerl were somehow seen as traitors to Hunthausen. She decided to do something about it and came up with the idea of a chancery reconciliation service involving both bishops. She went to Marianne Coté, the kindly cook at the cathedral rectory, in hopes that Coté would use her good rapport to help make it happen. Coté and her daughter, Terrie, who worked as a rectory housekeeper, enjoyed a playful, teasing relationship with both bishops.

On evenings and weekends, the archbishop would come down from his third-floor room to make a snack, find Coté in the kitchen and chat. He told her stories about his parents, his siblings, his nieces and nephews. For a while, he was carving his own crosier from a five-and-a-half-foot cedar limb he'd found while hiking on Tiger Mountain. He sat on the back stairway leading out of the kitchen, whittling away, while Coté prepared food and talked about the religious education classes she taught at the cathedral. Sometimes Terrie brought in a playpen and her toddler, whom Hunthausen amused with magic tricks.

Coté was uncomfortable doing Geraci's bidding. She kept her distance from church politics and genuinely liked both Wuerl and Hunthausen. But in the kitchen one day, she decided to broach the subject of a reconciliation service. Hunthausen was leaning against the refrigerator when she made the proposal. He suddenly became quiet and steely-eyed. Looking squarely at the cook, he began backing out of the kitchen and up the stairway.

"You have to remember one thing, Marianne, they did it to me," he said. "I did not do it to them."

There would be no reconciliation service at the chancery.

Nonetheless, more than a dozen parishes took the initiative to hold their own prayer services "for healing and hope" for the church in western Washington. At St. Anthony Church in Renton, for example, parishioners wrote down their hopes for the church on cards that were then collected and placed on the altar. They prayed that God would heed their prayers.

Father Raschko, one of the speakers at St. Anthony's, cautioned that healing would not come quickly because the forces at play in the church were much larger than Hunthausen and the archdiocese.

"The real struggle today is not between people; it's not between different factions in the church," he said. "It's the struggle of new ideas awakening and reacting," of living the Gospel in the modern world. It's the church *semper reformanda.*

Ten days after returning from the bishops' meeting, Hunthausen was attending a conference on sexual abuse when he received a phone call from his doctor. Lab tests and then a biopsy following his annual physical revealed his prostate was cancerous and the cancer may have spread to his lymph nodes. The archbishop absorbed the bad news, and then went to Montana for Thanksgiving with his siblings and their families. He said nothing about the cancer.

Upon his return to Seattle, he had two surgeries. Dr. Jerry Minzell, a urologist at Providence Medical Center, first cut out traces of cancer from two lymph nodes and later removed the entire prostate gland. He consigned Hunthausen to a week of recovery in the hospital followed by bed rest at home. Minzell doubted that stress had played a part in aggravating the cancer and described the sixty-five-year-old archbishop as a "rather vigorous man."

Within hours of the second surgery, Hunthausen was sitting up in his hospital bed and chatting with his sister, Marie, and her husband, Pat Walsh. They had driven over from Montana. They told him that they had been strolling along the Seattle waterfront when a homeless fellow approached them and asked if they could spare a dime. On his soiled overcoat, the fellow wore an "I Love Hunthausen" button. Walsh pulled out his wallet and gave the man a dollar.

"Under the circumstances, how could I give him less?" he told the archbishop.

Chuckling, Hunthausen replied, "I would have asked: 'What's a Hunthausen?'"

A couple of days before Christmas, with Hunthausen still in the hospital, Father Ryan received a phone call from Western Union regarding a special telegram for the archbishop. The telegram was from Pope John Paul II. At first Ryan thought it was a hoax. The pope doesn't send telegrams. He phoned Laghi's office in Washington and asked it if was for real. No, they told him, that just doesn't happen. But a little later, he received a return call from the nunciature advising him that indeed the telegram was authentic.

John Paul had gone outside normal diplomatic channels to tell Hunthausen that he was praying for him.

THE COADJUTOR COMPROMISE

To lead people walk behind them.
—Lao Tze

The "fraternal support" the U.S. bishops promised Hunthausen at their November 1986 meeting bore fruit three months later. On February 9, 1987, Archbishop Laghi, the papal nuncio, issued a two-sentence statement that Pope John Paul II had appointed Cardinal Bernardin of Chicago, Cardinal O'Connor of New York, and Archbishop Quinn of San Francisco, "to assess the current situation in Seattle."

The nuncio complained to the *New York Times* that the Vatican had tried to handle the Hunthausen case discreetly. But given what he described as the Americans' "Watergate complex" about secrecy, Rome was making a public announcement about the three-member ad hoc commission.

The commission members, along with Laghi, Hunthausen, and Wuerl, were all in Dallas for the U.S. bishops' biennial bioethics workshop. They began work immediately. Bernardin, O'Connor, and Quinn spent the morning of February 10 with the nuncio and the two Seattle bishops and then held separate meetings in the afternoon and evening with Hunthausen and Wuerl. Hunthausen, still recovering from prostate surgery, was weak and shaky.

He presented the commission with documentation of the work that the archdiocese had done to address the Vatican's concerns. But again, there was a disturbing sense of déjà vu about their questioning. Haven't we been through all this before?

"I was just repeating myself over and over again," Hunthausen recalled. "I was saying: 'Here's what I'm doing. What else do you want me to do?'"

Cardinal O'Connor, in particular, seemed to have some strange notions of what had transpired in the Archdiocese of Seattle. Shortly after the commission was formed, O'Connor happened to be in transit at the airport in Memphis when Father Larry Reilly, Hunthausen's first theological advisor in Seattle, noticed him. O'Connor was traveling alone and waiting for a flight to LaGuardia. Reilly, who was also waiting for a flight, introduced himself. O'Connor was friendly and talkative so Reilly spoke candidly.

"I'd like to tell you," the priest theologian said, "I think you're making a mistake about Seattle."

"You know," O'Connor volunteered, "twice in the past month I've been with the Holy Father and twice he has said, 'I'm worried about a schism in Seattle.'"

"So what did you say to him?" Reilly inquired.

"I told him that it's certainly a concern," O'Connor responded.

Incredulous, Reilly said, "You're really not serving the Holy Father well. There's no more chance of a schism in Seattle than there is in New York."

Meanwhile, Father Ryan, the archdiocesan chancellor, had a brainstorm: To best understand Seattle, the commission should talk to Hunthausen's key advisors and department heads. These people knew the facts. They knew what the archbishop was doing or failing to do. He phoned Hunthausen, who liked the idea and suggested that the commission also consult with some of the Region 12 bishops. Bernardin agreed to the proposal and sold the idea to O'Connor and Quinn. They settled on interviewing eight regional bishops, seven priest consulters, and four department heads.

"This was a very credible group," said Ryan.

So on the weekend of March 6–7, 1987, the three commission members ensconced themselves in the bishop's residence on the forty-acre grounds of St. Patrick's Seminary in Menlo Park, California, to interview Hunthausen's closest colleagues. Neither Hunthausen, who remained in Seattle, nor Wuerl, who had just returned from a private meeting with the pope in Rome, were invited.

With Bernardin acting as chair and the loquacious O'Connor asking most of the questions, the commission talked with the eight regional bishops on Friday, calling them in one by one for half-hour interviews. Among them were Hunthausen's confidantes and hiking companions, Bishops Treinen and Skylstad, as well as Archbishop Levada, the newly installed prelate in Portland and former CDF secretary to Ratzinger. Treinen and Skylstad spent much of their time vouching for Hunthausen's orthodoxy and loyalty to the Holy See. Skylstad told the commission that the regional bishops should have been consulted earlier, since they might have helped achieve a solution that would have avoided the Vatican's harsh investigation.

Treinen argued that Rome's disciplining of the archbishop was ill conceived and counter-productive. He later wrote a column for the *Idaho Register*, his diocesan newspaper, explaining how it was possible to support both Hunthausen and the Holy Father. An irritated Cardinal Gantin, head of the Vatican Congregation for Bishops, saw the column and told Treinen that he was wrong. Such dual loyalty was not possible.

On Friday evening and Saturday, the commission members interviewed Hunthausen's priest consulters and department heads. The atmosphere was cordial and casual, with the three prelates dressed in shirtsleeves. O'Connor sprawled out with his leg thrown over the arm of the sofa. Quinn sat upright with a thin smile. Bernardin looked pensive.

Father Jaeger, the director of seminarians, was amazed that they asked him no questions about priest formation, which was a big issue in the Ratzinger letter. Instead the three prelates concentrated on coming up with a fix for the Hunthausen affair. They needed a face-saving solution for Rome.

Father McDermott, the director of administration, was asked the same questions tossed at Jaeger and the other archdiocesan leaders: What's the situation in Seattle? What could improve it? Should the archbishop resign? Should Wuerl stay? Should we send in a different auxiliary?

The commission soon realized that Hunthausen's full authority should be restored and Wuerl should be reassigned. Yet it knew that Rome would insist on appointing someone else to keep an eye on the archbishop. If that appointment was handled poorly, Hunthausen might resign, giving the impression that Rome had forced out the popular archbishop and creating more turmoil in the U.S. church.

As the three prelates struggled for a solution, Father Ryan was called back for a second interview. The archbishop's right-hand man told them that Hunthausen and Wuerl had fundamentally different visions of the church and, no matter how kind and respectful they were to each other, joint governance was simply not possible. O'Connor launched into a series of "what if" questions, proposing possible scenarios for resolving the crisis. He asked Ryan to recommend possible candidates for an auxiliary bishop to replace Wuerl.

Ryan, McDermott, Jaeger, and the other archdiocesan leaders returned to Seattle feeling that the commission had given them an honest and fair hearing. They thought they had effectively rebutted and reversed what had been a negative view of the local church. They envisioned the commission recommending a solution favorable to Hunthausen and the archdiocese. They would be sorely disappointed.

A week later, on March 12, 1987, Hunthausen and Wuerl met with the commission and the papal nuncio at Bernardin's historic brick mansion in Chicago. Afterward, the three commission members went to Rome, ostensibly to help prepare the pope for his visit to the United States in September. John Paul surely asked them for an update on the Hunthausen affair. In late March, Bernardin and Quinn met with Archbishop Hickey, the apostolic visitator, and Quinn on his own met with Archbishop Hurley, Hunthausen's episcopal advisor, and with Bishop Michael Kenny, Hunthausen's Region 12 colleague. On April 8, the full commission reconvened with Hunthausen alone at Bernardin's Chicago residence. The commission had access to what their subsequent report described as "voluminous documentation," all of which was made available to both Hunthausen and Wuerl.

Hunthausen compared the Chicago meetings to his initial meeting with the commission in Dallas: going over the same old stuff. Sometimes the three prelates agreed with Hunthausen's pastoral decisions and said they would have done things the same way. Other times they suggested alternatives. But mostly the four middle-aged men engaged in friendly conversation as they sat around Bernardin's living room and concentrated on finding a solution.

"They were realists, trying to figure out a way to get off the bubble, to make it all appear like a win-win," Hunthausen said. "We'd talk for several hours and then have dinner together at Bernardin's place and discuss other matters."

As they had done in Menlo Park, the commission members, particularly Bernardin, posed various scenarios to see if they might be acceptable to Hunthausen. Bernardin knew what would be acceptable to Rome. The conversation was candid and blunt. In search of a compromise, Bernardin asked Hunthausen: Would you resign if we do this? What would change your mind? Where is the middle ground?

At the April 8 meeting, the commission proposed to Hunthausen that he accept a coadjutor archbishop who would replace Wuerl. The coadjutor, who by definition would succeed the archbishop, would have responsibility for the problem areas listed in the Ratzinger letter but final authority would revert to Hunthausen. Moreover, Hunthausen would be permitted to suggest and approve the three candidates from whom Rome would choose the coadjutor.

In so many words, the commission members were telling Hunthausen that his ecclesiology—his understanding of the nature of the church—was flawed. Consequently, an administrative partner with sound ecclesiology was needed to help him rectify the Archdiocese of Seattle. They assured him that they found him faithful to church teaching and lauded his ability to balance compassion with church law. However, they added, some archdiocesan priests and leaders who admired his compassion did not give sufficient weight to the demands of church doctrine and practice. As a result, they concluded, "a climate of permissiveness" had developed within the local church. Consequently, it was not just a matter of correcting specific pastoral errors, they said. The archdiocese required a major makeover. As they put it in their final report, "it is the overall attitudinal 'climate' or psychological and ecclesiological orientation of the archdiocese" that must be changed. In short, Hunthausen's model of church, based on his understanding of Vatican II, was found sadly wanting.

The archbishop reacted to the commission's findings and recommendations in stunned disbelief. Appointing a coadjutor archbishop clearly said that Rome had no confidence in him. It was a continuation of Wuerl's special faculties by another, subtler means. Moreover, there was the commission's harsh judgment of the archdiocese as an aberrant, permissive place where pastors and administrators made up their own rules and did their own thing.

Defeated and depressed, Hunthausen left the Chicago meeting giving no indication of whether he would accept a coadjutor or the verdict on the archdiocese. He phoned Ryan to tell him what the chancellor described "as outrageous and incredible news." Back in Seattle the next day, Hunthausen talked further with Ryan and then the two of them phoned Hurley seeking his advice. Hunthausen was inclined to reject the deal, which meant the Vatican would likely force him from office.

Meanwhile Bernardin and Quinn made overtures to Ryan. They hoped the archbishop's loyal and trusted confidante would use his considerable persuasive powers to convince his boss to accept the deal. Quinn phoned Ryan on his private line and asked him to come to San Francisco for a confidential conversation about the archbishop's future. Ryan first consulted with Hunthausen and then headed to the airport.

In San Francisco, he and Quinn spent an afternoon and evening in candid dialogue. Ryan spoke his mind. There was nothing unorthodox about Hunthausen or the Archdiocese of Seattle, he insisted. This notion of flawed ecclesiology was crazy. Imposing a coadjutor when the archbishop was perfectly healthy in mind and body and well short of retirement age was nuts. Ryan flew back to Seattle that night, unsettled and angry. Over the course of their time together, he felt Quinn had tried to co-opt him.

Ryan told Hunthausen about his disturbing conversation with Quinn and then decided to phone Bernardin, whom he respected as the most understanding of the three commission members. Bernardin invited him to come to Chicago to talk about the commission's proposal.

So on Tuesday of Holy Week, Ryan flew to the Windy City to engage the cardinal in an exceptionally forthright conversation. "I pulled no punches and spared no feelings," Ryan recalled. "I made it clear that the proposal spelled disaster, I thought, for our church and reflected a total misreading of the situation."

Ryan described the Seattle situation as a "tar baby" in which each of the outside interveners—Hickey, Laghi, Wuerl, and now the three commissioners—got tarred, mired, and damaged because they didn't understand or respect Hunthausen and the local church. Imposing a coadjutor, he said, risked more of the same.

Bernardin listened attentively, took notes, and let Ryan talk until he ran out of things to say. Ryan asked the cardinal if he could ever envision a situation in which he might tell Rome that it was dead wrong about Hunthausen.

The cardinal sighed. His answer was careful, nuanced, and theoretical —an elliptical "maybe."

Ryan, who was fond of the empathetic Bernardin, told the cardinal that he had once dreamed of being a bishop. Now he realized, because he had stuck with Hunthausen, such dreams were dashed forever.

"Mike," Bernardin replied sadly, "enjoy what you have. When you get this far up the ladder, you're no longer free."

Ryan returned to Seattle to face a plethora of press inquiries seeking the archbishop's comment on a story in the *National Catholic Register* that claimed the Vatican would force Hunthausen into early retirement. The story, attributed to a "highly placed," unnamed Vatican official, said Rome hoped to "defuse tensions" and "bring a measure of peace to Seattle" before the pope's fall visit to the United States. The *Register* said Hunthausen's retirement would come "after a face-saving grace period during which the archbishop would be officially restored to full episcopal powers." The story also reported that Rome would transfer Wuerl and appoint a coadjutor archbishop.

Ryan was charged to respond to the *Register* story, which he knew was true with the exception of the forced retirement claim. And he wondered about that. Had someone higher up than Bernardin, O'Connor, and Quinn exacted an additional demand? The *Register*, a conservative newspaper based in Los Angeles and long critical of Hunthausen's ministry, was well connected in Rome. It had revealed Wuerl's special faculties a month before the archbishop's announcement of them.

In a public letter to the priests of western Washington, Ryan ignored the newspaper's report of a Vatican plan to transfer Wuerl and

appoint a coadjutor. Instead, he stoutly disputed the *Register's* assertion that Hunthausen would be forced to retire. He denounced the
claim as incorrect, unfounded speculation. At age sixty-five, the archbishop was in good health and ten years shy of the Vatican's mandatory retirement age for bishops.

"I can assure you that the archbishop has not been asked to retire
or resign, nor are any 'deals' being made in that direction," Ryan
wrote the priests. He added that the archbishop's discussion with the
Vatican-appointed commission was continuing.

While Ryan handled inquiries at the chancery, Hunthausen was
outside the Navy submarine base at Bangor. Fourteen Trident protesters had just been arrested for trying to block a train carrying nuclear
missile motors. Speaking at the Ground Zero Center for Non-Violent
Action, the archbishop praised the protesters' willingness to suffer
"pain and anguish" for the cause of peace.

The anti-Trident demonstration was a welcome distraction for
Hunthausen, who in the midst of Holy Week felt like he was on his
own road to Calvary. Burdened, beaten down, afflicted by self-doubt,
he retreated deeper into prayer, asking God to show him the way, to
guide him forward for the good of all his people. His brother bishops
appeared powerless to help him. And now the commission demanded
a settlement that deeply troubled him. In good conscience could he
accept a coadjutor whose very presence would seem to say that the
church in western Washington had failed badly and still needed serious fixing? Could the deal work if his full authority was restored and
the coadjutor functioned as a true colleague with a Vatican II vision
of church? Or would the arrangement prove to be as unworkable as
the one he now had with Bishop Wuerl?

If he refused the deal, he would be forced to resign. Certainly,
that had consequences for the good of the church. Yet, if he accepted
the deal, that also had consequences for the good of the church.

The three-member commission was also in a tight spot. If it resolved the Hunthausen affair, it furthered the hope that the U.S. bishops' conference could manage internal church affairs. If the commission
failed, it demonstrated that the bishops had little effective authority and
ought to leave all serious matters to Rome. If the commission bungled
it badly, the U.S. church would have a public relations disaster on its
hands just as John Paul was preparing to head for America.

On Easter Monday, Hunthausen convened a meeting of Ryan and his
priest consulters, the men who had met with the commission in Menlo
Park, to share the commission's assessment and recommendations. The

document, under pontifical seal and awaiting Hunthausen's signature, was hard-nosed and biting, the language largely reflective of the unsympathetic O'Connor. The New York cardinal wanted Hunthausen to confess his sins, bow to Vatican authority, and let Rome help him clean up the mess he'd made.

Hunthausen's advisors were dumbfounded. The commission's assessment of the state of the archdiocese seemed to have come out of the blue. There had been little hint of such criticism during their pleasant and relaxed conversations in Menlo Park.

"We thought this was crazy," recalled Father McDermott, who, along with Ryan, drafted a response for the archbishop. "It was if they thought there was something in the soil of Seattle that allowed all sorts of weeds to grow up. So we wrote back and said: 'You're wrong.'"

The archbishop's response, directed to Bernardin as the commission's de facto chair, rejected the characterization of "a climate of permissiveness" in the archdiocese, called appointment of a coadjutor a "punitive" and "seriously flawed" compromise, and questioned whether the Vatican would really give him a strong hand in choosing a compatible coadjutor. The seven-page letter, dated April 22, 1987, had a suspicious, truculent tone that sounded more like Ryan than Hunthausen. The archbishop refused to accept the commission's findings and recommendations and asked it to reconsider. The best solution, he wrote, would be to restore his full authority, reassign Bishop Wuerl, and allow a suitable time period for the archdiocese to address the Holy See's concerns with the help of outside evaluation and oversight.

He left the door open for further negotiation, however, by saying that he would reluctantly accept a coadjutor if Rome would let him select the three nominees for the position as Bernardin had proposed in Chicago. Otherwise, he wanted to discuss the whole matter directly with the Holy Father.

Meanwhile Father Ryan and four other priests mobilized a clergy response on the archbishop's behalf, hoping to prod the commission toward a settlement more favorable to Hunthausen. Ryan drafted a strongly worded statement calling for an immediate and unconditional restoration of Hunthausen's authority without any further Vatican intervention. The statement, signed by an overwhelming majority of the nearly four hundred priests in western Washington, described the archbishop as faithful, orthodox, and "a compassionate, appropriately firm and loving shepherd after the model of the Good Shepherd." Impugning the archbishop, the statement contended, impugned the ministry of the priests under his authority.

The following day the women religious of the archdiocese issued their own statement rejecting the Vatican's allegations of Hunthausen's wrongdoing. The nuns contended that the real reason for Rome's intervention was "the archbishop's strong and visible stand on Vatican II issues such as peace, the rights of women and minorities, and liturgical renewal." The statement was soon signed by 342 of the approximately 500 nuns in the archdiocese.

The chancery directors, the deacons, and the lay ministers weighed in with similar statements. At their annual meeting in St. Paul, Minnesota, the National Federation of Priests' Councils approved a resolution asking for full restoration of Hunthausen's authority and changes in Vatican disciplinary procedures. Delegates to the nation's largest priest organization passed the resolution 121 to 3.

Meanwhile the commission continued to negotiate with the archbishop over the exact terms of the settlement. Even the unflappable Bernardin, legendary for achieving agreements that nobody liked but all would support, was losing patience and hope. The overtures to Father Ryan had only stiffened Seattle's resistance. A milder second draft of the commission's report failed to mollify Hunthausen and his staff. By the end of April, with pressure growing for a settlement, the commission and the archbishop were at an impasse.

Then Hunthausen made a peace gesture. Although he had been burned by Rome's unilateral assignment of Wuerl with his special faculties, he decided that he would test Bernardin's offer regarding a coadjutor. He proposed three bishops as his choices: Kenny, his fellow peace activist; Hurley, his episcopal advisor; and Skylstad, his hiking companion. The commission eliminated Kenny as too much like Hunthausen and crossed off Hurley because a move from archbishop of Anchorage to coadjutor of Seattle would seem to be a demotion. That left Skylstad.

But Laghi, who as nuncio would forward the names for final selection by the pope, demanded more than one candidate. Consequently, Bernardin asked Hunthausen if the commission could submit the name of Thomas J. Murphy, bishop of Great Falls–Billings, Montana, along with Skylstad's. Bernardin knew the fifty-four-year-old Murphy as a moderate, sensible priest and theologian, an Irish-American from Chicago whose good humor and political savvy pleased most of the people most of the time. Hunthausen couldn't claim to know Murphy beyond the casual friendship they had struck up at Region 12 bishops' meetings. Yet overall his feelings were positive. So, despite some hesitation, he consented to Bernardin's request. Now the commission had two nominees for John Paul II to consider as coadjutor archbishop of Seattle: Skylstad and Murphy.

Skylstad, who was elected president of the U.S. bishops' conference in 2004, knew that there was no way he was going to Seattle in 1987. "My name was on the list as a space filler," he said. "There wouldn't have been a ghost of a chance. Everybody knew that I was a close friend with Dutch."

Hunthausen grew increasingly downcast and dejected as crunch time approached. He'd found it virtually impossible to hear God's small, still voice amid the din of warring statements and media reports.

At one point, Tom Fox, editor of the *National Catholic Reporter*, phoned Ryan and asked if he could talk to the archbishop. "I don't want to interview him," said Fox, who knew that the archbishop was not taking press calls. "I want to suggest some possible ways of considering what this means for the church."

Hunthausen, who liked and respected Fox, reluctantly agreed to take the call. The archbishop and the NCR editor talked for a long time. Fox argued that Hunthausen could better serve the church and the vision of the Council if he accepted the coadjutor deal and stayed in office. Surely, he argued, Hunthausen could be more effective as an active archbishop than a retired one commenting from the sidelines.

The archbishop thanked Fox for his counsel, said he'd pray over it, and hung up the phone. He weighed the arguments for and against the commission's report, for and against a coadjutor, and for and against resigning as archbishop. As he teetered back and forth, something happened. With the help of the Holy Spirit, he found a way forward.

The next day, Hunthausen told Bernardin that, for fear of causing an even greater rift in the church, he would sign the commission's report. On May 7, 1987, he and Bernardin reached a settlement that the three-member commission would take to Rome for the pope's approval. Hunthausen said that while he did not agree with some important aspects of the commission's assessment, he would accept the proposed solution. He committed himself to addressing the issues identified by the Vatican. Moreover, he would welcome the coadjutor whom the Holy See appointed and expected it to be one of the two bishops that he had recommended. He agreed to a continuation of the Vatican commission for a period of time and considered its procedures "to be fundamentally just, open, appropriate, and carried out with integrity." Finally, he consented to forgo a meeting with the pope until after the entire affair was resolved.

Hunthausen's acceptance of the compromise agreement cheered the commission but disappointed many of his staff and supporters who saw it as a Vatican victory and a Hunthausen defeat. But the archbishop did not think in such terms. The "good of the church" was not achieved on a battlefield.

Cardinal O'Connor, elated by Hunthausen's acceptance of the commission's deal, described the signing as one of the happiest moments of his life. Others were decidedly less pleased. Sister Chauncey Boyle, president of the archdiocesan Sisters' Council, grudgingly called the settlement "the best we could get."

Sometime later, Sister Joyce Cox, whom Hunthausen had named vice chancellor and vicar for religious women, asked him: "Do you still love the church?"

"Of course, I do," Hunthausen replied. "Never forget that the greatest of all theologies is the theology of struggle."

That was his answer. Cox, a warm, gregarious Montanan who astonished her Mormon family by becoming a nun, puzzled over his response. She took him to mean that struggle and suffering were as much a part of the human condition in the church as any place else. He could no more stop loving the church because of its failings than he could stop loving his family or God. The Body of Christ is bigger than all the sinners it contains.

On May 19, 1987, Bernardin, O'Connor, and Quinn presented the signed agreement to Pope John Paul II and Cardinals Ratzinger, Gantin, and Agostino Casaroli, the Vatican secretary of state. Despite assurances to Hunthausen that they would argue strenuously in support of Skylstad as coadjutor, there was only one name put forth in the report: Bishop Thomas J. Murphy.

Even then, Gantin wasn't so sure about Murphy. "We will begin our investigation of him," he told the others, meaning that the Vatican would solicit character references and consult further with other bishops about Murphy.

O'Connor interrupted. "There's no time for that," he said. "The appointment has to be made now."

Gantin objected. So O'Connor appealed directly to John Paul who sided with him and overruled the head of the Congregation for Bishops.

"We'll forgo the usual investigation," the pope said.

With Murphy's appointment as coadjutor now fast-tracked, Gantin, Ratzinger, and Casaroli signed off on the commission's recommendations. Ratzinger, whose infamous letter of September 30, 1985, took up nearly half of the final document, initialed the agreement with little enthusiasm. John Paul, on the other hand, affirmed the work of the commission and gratefully accepted the settlement.

On the following Saturday evening, Archbishop Laghi phoned Murphy in Billings, Montana, to tell him that the pope was appointing him coadjutor archbishop of Seattle. Murphy told Laghi that he could not accept until he had spoken directly with Hunthausen. He wasn't going to allow himself to be forced on the archbishop like Wuerl had been. Murphy phoned Hunthausen, who welcomed and congratulated him, and the deal was done. The Seattle archbishop told Murphy that he would look forward to seeing him at a celebration for retired Bishop Eldon Schuster in Great Falls three days later.

When Hunthausen walked into the reception for Schuster, he knew immediately that word of Murphy's appointment was out. Media from as far away as New York had descended on the celebration. The regional bishops and diocesan priests were buzzing with the news that Murphy was going to Seattle. Schuster, who had not been informed, at first wondered why, after years of quiet service in the Montana hinterlands, he was getting so much press attention. Meanwhile, Murphy's housekeeper, besieged by press calls to his home, was indignant.

"We are celebrating the jubilee of Bishop Schuster," she told one reporter, "so I don't know where Bishop Murphy is, what he is doing, or what is going on in his life. We're here for the other man!"

Somehow Murphy and Hunthausen slipped quietly out of the reception in Great Falls and prepared to face the press the following day in Seattle. On the afternoon of May 27, 1987, they sat side by side in the chancery conference room as the archbishop introduced Murphy. Bishop Wuerl, now in limbo, was nowhere to be seen. The archdiocesan public affairs department had a prepared text announcing the Holy Father's appointment of Murphy along with the commission's full report including the Ratzinger letter.

An imposing figure with a slight paunch, thin lips, pale blue eyes, and a large head topped with an unruly mane of white hair, Murphy was all smiles, laughter, and enthusiasm. Given to superlatives, he talked of God's providence as "amazing," "incredible," and "unbelievable." In marked contrast to his buttoned-down predecessor, Murphy wore his priestly garb indifferently, his Roman collar partly undone, his black clerical shirt stuffed carelessly into his trousers.

The newly appointed coadjutor arrived with an impressive curriculum vitae. Ordained to the priesthood for the Archdiocese of Chicago in 1958, he had served as pastor in several Chicago parishes, completed a doctorate in theology, headed the archdiocesan Priest Senate, served as rector of St. Mary of the Lake Seminary, and, after his appointment as bishop of eastern Montana in 1978, chaired the U.S. bishops' committee on priestly life and ministry. He had served on the committee on doctrine and would soon become a member of the conference's powerful executive committee, its key ruling body.

Murphy had a reputation for bringing people together and finding the safe middle ground. He was a moderate, a realist, and decidedly risk averse. Father Andrew Greeley, the author, researcher, and columnist, regarded Murphy as a good friend and a progressive. And, indeed, the ultraorthodox *Wanderer,* thoroughly disappointed with his appointment, described him as "a termite in the barque of St. Peter." Murphy himself categorically rejected political or partisan labels. "When you classify something," he said, "you make it dead."

Murphy was indeed a savvy operator. Unlike the guileless Hunthausen, he was adept at side-stepping tough questions, parrying sharp inquiries with humor, poetry, and a disarming laugh that told the interviewer: I'm not going there. He soon proved to be equally adept at knowing if, when, and how to engage the Vatican.

On that May afternoon, the two archbishops sat all smiles before reporters, photographers, and television lights. Murphy's white hair fell over his forehead and perspiration glistened on his brow. Hunthausen, holding a copy of his prepared statement, thanked the Vatican commission, praised Bishop Wuerl, and hailed Murphy as "a friend and trusted coworker."

Hunthausen made it clear that his full authority had been restored and Murphy had no special faculties. He conceded that it was unusual to have a coadjutor when the incumbent archbishop was healthy and short of retirement age. Yet, he added, Rome had given its assurances that he had final say-so and responsibility. He candidly noted that he disagreed with some major aspects of the commission's report, notably its characterization of him enabling "a climate of permissiveness" in the local church.

"Maybe permissiveness is another way of expressing a concern about the degree of sharing which I have found important in my ministry," he conjectured.

The archbishop said he and Murphy, under the commission's continued guidance, would work with archdiocesan priests, staff, and consultative bodies to resolve the concerns of the Ratzinger letter.

Asked if changes had already been effected as a result of Bishop Wuerl's eighteen months on the job, Hunthausen hesitated.

"I'm searching my mind to come up with something that would be significant," he replied. "We started a process but we got bogged down terribly when we discovered that misunderstanding around special faculties and we never did recover from that. So we found it difficult to discover what steps to take."

Two days after Murphy's press debut at the chancery, Hunthausen introduced him to the priests of the archdiocese at an emotional closed-door meeting and Mass at St. Francis of Assisi Church in Burien, just south of Seattle. The 125 priests at the meeting were eager to take Murphy's measure but they also wanted to talk about the commission's assessment of "a climate of permissiveness." They felt misunderstood and maligned. And many were suspicious.

One priest pointedly asked Murphy if Rome had sent him to Seattle with special faculties. Murphy repeated what he had told the press: Hunthausen was the final authority and he was here to serve him. In fact, he noted, he had had no contact with the Vatican until Laghi had called him in Great Falls the previous Saturday.

Deflating a tense situation with humor, Murphy told the priests that his nephew was puzzled by his new job title. "Uncle," the boy asked, "what does it mean to be a co-agitator?"

Murphy, like Hunthausen, asked the priests to put the Vatican report behind them and move on. He told them that he had heard great things about their work. In fact, under Hunthausen's leadership, the archdiocese had realized impressive gains in church observance and contributions. Mass attendance, infant baptisms, and adult conversions exceeded the national average by more than twenty percentage points. Giving to the annual Catholic appeal rivaled far bigger and wealthier dioceses.

The priests liked what they saw and heard in Murphy, describing him afterward as open, personable, energetic, and optimistic.

Bishop Wuerl joined Hunthausen in celebrating the Mass that followed the meeting. In delivering the homily, the archbishop looked directly at Wuerl and apologized.

"I firmly believe that no one has suffered more through all this than you," he said, as Wuerl's eyes grew wide and his face went red. "I'm so sorry for the experience you've had here. In any way that I have failed you, I ask for your forgiveness."

Some of the priests were flabbergasted. Did he really need to apologize?

A week later, on Sunday, June 7, Bishop Wuerl celebrated his final Mass in the archdiocese, a joyful affair at the parish he knew best, Holy Rosary in West Seattle. The church was full with more than six hundred people, many of whom fancied the young bishop as their kind of Catholic and told him so at a reception afterward. Hunthausen was also there to wish him well.

Father Mallahan, the silver-tongued pastor, summed up Wuerl's challenging year and a half in Seattle. "You came to us as a newly ordained bishop," he said, "and you leave very well-seasoned."

Wuerl flew home to Pittsburgh where nine months later he was named the city's new bishop. With Seattle behind him, he conceded that the power-sharing arrangement with Hunthausen had indeed been "unworkable." Moreover, he added, little had been done to address what he called Rome's legitimate concerns.

Hunthausen was in Pittsburgh for Wuerl's installation at St. Paul's Cathedral on March 25, 1988, as were six hundred priests, sixty-six archbishops and bishops, and three cardinals. After the communion service, the garrulous Cardinal O'Connor bounded to the pulpit to deliver an impromptu accolade.

"We know that during a period of his life, Bishop Wuerl was tested by a form of suffering that only almighty God and one other man would know because that other man suffered with him," O'Connor said, his voice wavering. "We have two men here who went through a period of intense pain, two men who were purified by that pain, two men whose commitment to the priesthood and the church never wavered. It is a great tribute to Bishop Wuerl but an even greater tribute to the honor, the unity, and the fraternity among bishops that we have here today Archbishop Raymond Hunthausen."

The crowd of clergy rose to its feet and applauded. Hunthausen, a wry smile on his face, stood and waved.

Under the terms of the settlement, the commission continued to oversee the archdiocese. In mid-July, the two Seattle archbishops were at Bernardin's residence in Chicago to talk with the commission members. That discussion led to Hunthausen's decision to give Murphy responsibility—although not ultimate authority—for the marriage tribunal, liturgy, public affairs, matters involving church law, and the Washington State Catholic Conference. Thus Murphy had hands-on accountability for most of the areas for which Wuerl had been responsible earlier.

The commission met privately with Hunthausen and Murphy on a quarterly basis for nearly two more years. They met in Chicago, Seattle, or at the annual meetings of the U.S. bishops' conference. O'Connor and Quinn were sometimes absent due to illness or personal leave. But Bernardin was always there, doing his utmost to keep Rome at arm's length and Hunthausen and Murphy on the same page.

When they couldn't agree, both archbishops phoned Bernardin. They liked and respected the cardinal, who seemed to have an inexhaustible patience and an unshaken belief in the power of prayer.

"I always trusted Cardinal Bernardin," Hunthausen recalled. "He was very concerned about me, about Murf, and about the church. And he tried to balance all those things."

When Pope John Paul II visited the United States in September 1987, the U.S. bishops called on Bernardin to make the first of four presentations to the pope on the state of the American church. On this trip, unlike his 1979 visit, John Paul came ready to listen albeit in the form of "structured dialogues" wherein the participants delivered prepared speeches to each other. The pope had advance copies of the speakers' texts while they had no knowledge of what his response would be until they heard it.

On the morning of September 15, 1987, the pope had a closed-door session with some three hundred U.S. bishops at the minor seminary adjacent to the historic San Fernando Mission in Los Angeles. The distress caused by the Hunthausen affair, though ostensibly resolved with the appointment of Murphy, hung over the meeting like a dark cloud. The bishops were pleased that three of their members had achieved a compromise solution acceptable to both Hunthausen and Rome. But the long ordeal had made them wary and distrustful of the Vatican, fearful that their critics had more influence in Rome than they did.

Hunthausen and Murphy were among the bishops whom the pope greeted one by one after morning prayers in the old mission church. Then Bernardin rose to speak. It fell to him, past president of the bishops' conference, chair of the committee on the peace pastoral, and mediator extraordinaire on the Hunthausen affair, to talk about the U.S. church's relationship with the Vatican. He began by affirming the deep faith of American Catholics and their acceptance of "the church as described in the conciliar documents of Vatican II."

American society, he explained to John Paul, prizes the freedom to speak one's mind. As a result, Bernardin suggested, Americans "react negatively when they are told that they must do something, even though in their hearts they may know they should do it." Consequently, he continued, when Rome unilaterally reaffirms traditional church teaching, an adversarial atmosphere can develop that makes genuine dialogue almost impossible. Invoking Vatican II's call for shared responsibility, Bernardin called for a collegial church in which bishops could talk with Rome "in complete candor, without fear." Avoiding mention of any of the painful issues dividing the church, he implied that true collegiality would allow for adaptation and development of doctrine and ministry.

Archbishop Quinn spoke next. He noted Vatican II's call to interpret church teaching in light of the "signs of the times." The American church faces the challenges of increased divorce and broken homes, rising affluence and education, advances in medical and scientific technology, changing sexual mores, and expectations of full equality for women, he told John Paul. "Moral theology must respond to these new human realities," said Quinn, adding that "the old remedies" simply don't suffice.

Archbishop Weakland followed Quinn. The Milwaukee archbishop told the Holy Father that educated American Catholics are more inclined to be convinced by reason than by authority. "An authoritarian style is counterproductive," he said.

Archbishop Daniel Pilarcyzk, of Cincinnati, closed the bishops' presentations by telling John Paul that the church's sacramental life was suffering for lack of priests. Celibacy, he implied, was a huge obstacle.

The bishops had spoken. Now it was the Holy Father's turn. Because the bishops' had submitted their texts in advance, John Paul had his arguments well marshaled over twenty-three pages of text, the longest speech of his entire trip. He knocked the Vatican II underpinnings out from under their addresses by criticizing the post-conciliar church for over-emphasizing the horizontal over the hierarchical dimension of the church. The divine order of church government, he said, is posited on "the Roman pontiff as its visible head and perpetual source of unity."

Rejecting Quinn's argument for putting new wine in new wineskins, the pope said true faith requires full acceptance of the unchanging word of God as defined by the teaching authority of the church. There is no such thing as legitimate dissent or pick-and-choose selection of doctrine, he said. In fact, cafeteria Catholics are in grave moral error and ought not receive the sacraments until they get right with the church. Rather than accommodate doctrine to American culture, John Paul said, the church needs to teach doctrine more effectively. Bishops, he noted, best serve the church by "preaching and teaching the word of God with fidelity to the truth." The pontiff closed his lengthy address with a few warnings, one of them a reminder of the church's teaching on the immorality of homosexual acts.

Archbishops Hunthausen and Murphy returned to Seattle conscious of the renewed weight of the Vatican's authority on their shoulders. John Paul heard but had not heeded the bishops' call for a Vatican II church that shares responsibility and recognizes that doctrine evolves as God's creation unfolds. After the pontiff's long talk in Los Angeles, Archbishop Pilarcyzk, the incoming conference president, was left to do damage control with the press. He conceded that the pope had told the bishops to teach hard truths no matter what the consequences.

"The purpose of the church is not to have lots of people in it," explained Pilarcyzk, anticipating what a future Pope Benedict would say. "The purpose is to teach the teachings of Christ."

As Archbishops Hunthausen and Murphy prepared for their December 1988 *ad limina* visit with the Holy Father, they hoped he would finally end the commission's oversight and return the archdiocese to normalcy. The two Seattle archbishops, carrying their documentation with them, arrived in Rome with appointments scheduled first with the pope and then with Cardinals Ratzinger and Gantin.

John Paul received them separately in his study in the papal living quarters overlooking St. Peter's Square. Hunthausen's fifteen-minute conversation with the pontiff was more personal than business. They talked in broad terms about the church and avoided the issues that had brought Rome's wrath down on Seattle. Hunthausen knew that Ratzinger and Gantin would handle those, then review them afterward with John Paul, who would make the final decision on his fate.

On Saturday morning, December 3, 1988, Hunthausen and Murphy walked from their lodgings at the North American College to their meeting with the two cardinals in Gantin's office at the Congregation for Bishops. As they traversed Rome's cobble-stoned streets, Hunthausen had a heart-to-heart with Murphy.

"Murf, I have no idea what's going to happen here," he said, "but I want you to know how grateful I am to you. I know this impossible arrangement wears very heavily on both of us. And once this is over, I think it's terribly important that we move with some haste toward my resignation and your full stature as the archbishop. It's the only way that makes sense."

Startled, Murphy became standoffish. "On, no," he protested. "I wouldn't want that to happen until you are at least seventy."

Murphy never mentioned Hunthausen's resignation again. But his suggestion of age seventy—Hunthausen was sixty-seven at the time—lodged in Hunthausen's mind.

As the two archbishops entered Gantin's office, Hunthausen uttered a silent prayer. "Lord, I don't care to go into this," he said to himself, "but come along. I know you're here."

Ratzinger, Gantin, and their respective secretaries were waiting for them. Gantin welcomed them and explained the purpose of the meeting. He then deferred to Ratzinger to review the lengthy list assembled by Murphy of what the archdiocese had done to resolve the Vatican's concerns. The one-hour meeting was cordial and perfunctory. There was no debate on any of the issues; the purpose was to achieve clarity, end the matter, and move on.

The prelates sat around a polished mahogany table with Ratzinger seated between Hunthausen and Murphy and Gantin and the two secretaries across from them. As the meeting came to a close, Ratzinger's secretary, Archbishop and later Cardinal Alberto Bovone interrupted to pose a question.

"Your Excellency," he asked Hunthausen, "now that we are at this point and looking back, wouldn't you agree that you were very wrong from the beginning?"

Hunthausen was astounded and suddenly very angry. What did they want from him? Was he to confess to sins that in good conscience he had not committed?

"Your Excellency," he responded coldly. "I have no such feeling. I would have done what I have always done. What I did at the time, I did out of pastoral motivation and I did the best I knew how under the circumstances."

Ratzinger abruptly intervened, ending the exchange. "It's over now," he said. "That's enough. It's done."

Ratzinger and Gantin gave no indication of what they would recommend to the pope. They would talk with the Holy Father, they told the two Seattle archbishops, and, in due time, advise them of John Paul's decision.

Hunthausen and Murphy had been invited to concelebrate Mass with the pope the following Tuesday morning, the last day of their Rome visit, and have breakfast with him afterward. The Mass invitation was also extended to several priests and a couple of dozen laypeople including James Michener, the best-selling American author, and Stan Musial, the great St. Louis baseball player. Musial joked, "I'm entitled to be here because I'm a Cardinal."

As the invitees mingled in the large antechamber outside the doors of the pope's chapel, Michener introduced himself to Hunthausen and drew a quick lesson from the archbishop's presence.

"You took some hard knocks, were humiliated in public, practically defrocked," he said to Hunthausen, "and today I meet you here at dawn. Clearly the Holy Father has invited you to Rome and now you're to help him officiate at his private Mass. How much more can he do to heal the breach?"

Hunthausen volunteered that John Paul had also invited Murphy and him to breakfast after Mass. Like Michener, Hunthausen concluded that the pope's gesture was an olive branch and a sign that the ordeal was finally over. He, Murphy, and the priests put on their vestments and then joined the pope and the others for Mass in the chapel, whose white marble walls were set off by a pair of Michelangelo murals depicting the crucifixion of St. Peter and the conversion of St. Paul. Hunthausen stood at the altar to the pope's immediate right.

At the Eucharist, the Holy Father, assisted by Hunthausen and Murphy, distributed communion to the congregation. He placed the consecrated host directly into the reverently cupped hands of Michener. Writing about it afterward, the author, a Quaker, reported that he was deeply moved to receive Roman Catholic communion for the first time in his life. And from no less than the pope!

With Mass concluded, the pope greeted his guests one by one and then crossed the room to throw his arm over Hunthausen's shoulders and lead him and Murphy into his private dining room. The breakfast conversation was light and pleasant with no mention of what had so disturbed the Vatican. Within half an hour, Hunthausen and Murphy were in a cab on the way to the airport and their flight back to Seattle.

Murphy asked Hunthausen if he had noticed that the Holy Father had given communion to Michener.

"You're kidding," said Hunthausen, who began to chuckle.

"Murf," he said, "it seems we ought to turn this cab around right now, head back to Ratzinger's office, and demand a visitation of the Holy See."

Upon his return to Seattle, Hunthausen provided the Catholics of western Washington with a copy of the report that he and Murphy had given Ratzinger and Gantin. The report listed how the archdiocese had responded to the twelve issues of concern listed in the original Ratzinger letter of September 30, 1985. Hunthausen noted that on the "vast majority of issues" no new pastoral practices would be put into effect. Rather there may be a "clearer formulation of pastoral practice" as a result of developments in church teaching and revisions in canon law.

What? After five and a half years of Vatican investigation and intervention, it all boiled down to providing a better explanation?

Hunthausen's critics were outraged, objecting that the archbishop had changed practically nothing and had no intention of doing so. They complained that he continued to pander to homosexuals; to tolerate liturgical abuses; to encourage advocates of women's ordination; to offer church shelter to illegal immigrants; to abide contraception, easy annulments, and civil disobedience; and to write toothless guidelines that had tricked Rome into thinking he had taken action.

"There's quite a difference between a guideline and a directive," groused John Krueger, a Marine Corps veteran and a member of the Sons of St. Peter Coalition, a new anti-Hunthausen group. The group published a thirty-eight-page, heavily footnoted "white paper" detailing the archbishop's alleged abuses with particular emphasis on failure to follow church teaching on homosexuality.

In his letter to the faithful, Hunthausen insisted that the archdiocese had been "faithful to the teaching and discipline of the universal church." He explained that he and Murphy had advised the pope and the curia that some Catholics, unwilling or unable to accept the post–Vatican II church, would continue to complain to Rome. Nonetheless, with the final decision now in John Paul's hands, he hoped the Vatican would soon declare the visitation over and done once and for all.

Three months later Hunthausen and Murphy were again in Rome, this time for an unusual four-day meeting of the thirty-five American archbishops, the curia, and the pope. The American hierarchy had proposed the meeting in 1986 in hopes of resolving tensions between the U.S. church and the Vatican in large part because of Rome's stripping of Hunthausen's authority. The pope, twenty-five members of the curia including Ratzinger and Gantin, and the U.S. archbishops gathered behind closed doors in the Vatican's Old Synod Hall for morning and evening sessions from March 8 through 11, 1989.

Hunthausen and Murphy were impressed by how intently John Paul listened to the presentations. At one point, the pope joked that he had been instructed to keep quiet and listen. There was little danger that he would hear what he didn't want to hear. The curia had prepared the agenda, focusing on the performance of the U.S. church and ignoring its own shortcomings. Consequently, the talks concentrated on Vatican concerns such as the need for U.S. bishops to rein in discordant theologians, adhere to church rules on confession, increase vocations to the priesthood, improve faith formation in Catholic schools, and clamp down on marriage tribunals perceived as lax in granting annulments. The negative influence of "radical feminism" was repeatedly decried, even by the Americans.

Cardinal Ratzinger declared that bishops functioning in the secular, materialistic culture of the United States must be "martyrs" who court unpopularity and suffer for the truth.

As the meeting wore on, Hunthausen became more anxious and depressed. In his breast pocket was the text of the remarks that he had planned to make at the opportune moment. The text was based on what he and Murphy had heard from archdiocesan priests when they had gathered for a Day of Prayer in anticipation of the meeting in Rome. The two questions that day were: What gives life to your ministry? And what are the negatives in your ministry? The ensuing discussion was so honest and powerful that Hunthausen asked Father Raschko, the archdiocesan theologian, to take notes. Later he, Raschko, and Father Ryan turned the notes into a statement that the archbishop would take to the meeting with the curia and the pope.

The statement dealt with the painful church issues that the Vatican meeting was ignoring: birth control, the role of women in the church, priestly celibacy, the treatment of former priests, church teaching on homosexuality, the appointment of bishops, and the Vatican II vision of a compassionate, collegial church.

Hunthausen shared the statement with Murphy and, once in Rome, with Archbishops Hurley and Weakland. They didn't discourage him from reading it to John Paul and the curia, but they implied that it was episcopal suicide.

"I had a great hesitancy about it," Hunthausen recalled. "I hadn't heard anything from the other archbishops that was anything akin to what I was about to say. As a matter of fact, I heard the opposite."

As the last day of the meeting approached, Hunthausen prayed over it. "I made up my mind," he said. "I just said I'm going to do it no matter what happens."

Hunthausen steeled himself to read his statement right after the coffee break on the concluding Saturday morning. But as the pope, the curia, and the archbishops broke for coffee, an ashen-faced Murphy approached and pulled Hunthausen aside. Laghi had just given him a letter, signed by Cardinal Gantin, formally declaring an end to the visitation.

"You won't believe it," Murphy groaned.

The letter, addressed to both archbishops, ended the visitation by giving Murphy final and absolute authority in all the areas that Rome had found Hunthausen wanting.

"I feel used," moaned Murphy, who was quite upset and deeply hurt. "This is not the way we've been playing this. This is not the way we've understood it and this letter is outrageous."

"Has Bernardin seen this letter?" Hunthausen asked.

"I don't know," Murphy replied.

The Seattle archbishops immediately sought out Bernardin, who read Gantin's letter and was furious. "Damn it," he exclaimed, "they'll never learn. This is absolutely off the wall."

Seizing the letter, Bernardin said, "Let me talk to Laghi." And off he marched to confront the nuncio.

As the meeting resumed, Hunthausen felt like the floor had fallen out from underneath him. First the visitation, then the humiliating removal of his authority and the denigration of the archdiocese, followed by the restoration of his powers, and now what? Humiliation again? How many more years could this go on?

He was so unnerved by the letter that his courage failed him. Once back in the meeting hall, he lacked the gumption to ask for the floor and read his statement. Instead he kept quiet.

"I couldn't bring myself to do it," he said years later. "I've had mixed feelings ever since like it was a missed opportunity. It leaves me with regret. It also leaves me with a sense that maybe this was the work of the Spirit and it was not meant to be."

Following the Saturday morning session, the U.S. archbishops and the members of the curia had a closing lunch with the Holy Father in a long, narrow dining hall. John Paul made some impromptu remarks about how grateful he was for the strength of the faith and the church in America. Then he walked down the aisle, shaking the prelates' hands. When he reached Hunthausen, he grasped his hand, again put an arm around his shoulder, and told him, "I'm so happy you're here."

It was a warm greeting that Hunthausen chose to interpret not as an apology but as an acknowledgment that he had suffered. It was clearly a gesture that went well beyond shaking hands.

Despite John Paul's gesture, the Vatican had not yet formally ended the visitation nor returned the archdiocese to normalcy. After being confronted by Bernardin, Laghi told Hunthausen and Murphy that he would work it out with them when they were together in Boise in early April 1989. The three archbishops would be in Idaho for the installation of the bishop succeeding Bishop Treinen, Hunthausen's old friend from Vatican II days.

Meanwhile, the coadjutor arrangement, now approaching its second year, was weighing heavily on Murphy. As coadjutor archbishop, he would automatically succeed Hunthausen when the latter retired or died. Hence he would build on—or take apart—whatever sort of church Hunthausen left behind. All new bosses have to deal with what their predecessors have done. But in this case, the old boss remained on the scene, fully in charge, while the new boss stood in the wings waiting for up to ten years to do it his way.

Murphy was expected to support Hunthausen's vision of church no matter how much it differed from his own or how much he thought it differed from Rome's. From the very beginning, the two archbishops understood this tension and discussed it often.

"My deepest desire and prayer was that the two of us not destroy one another," Hunthausen said. "Murf shared how hard it was to have a conviction that did not jive with mine. And, yet, he always supported my role as the ordinary and supported my decisions."

Hunthausen and Murphy went back and forth on issues such as ministry to homosexuals, the role of women and laypeople, correct church teaching in schools and faith programs, and many others. When they could not reach agreement, Murphy bit his lip, kept quiet, and let Hunthausen proceed.

But the clumsy arrangement drained both men, especially Murphy. The coadjutor archbishop, who could be joyful and ecstatic, could also fall into deep and depressive funks that he was incapable of masking. When he realized that Laghi was finally going to sign the official document that would close the Vatican investigation, he saw an opportunity to escape.

Murphy told Hunthausen that he planned to ask Laghi for a transfer to some other diocese. The Seattle arrangement had become impossible for him. The two archbishops simply had different agendas and different ways of operating. Moreover, Murphy argued, with Rome's tacit acceptance that the archdiocese was meeting the requirements of the Ratzinger letter, wasn't his purpose for being in Seattle fulfilled? Hadn't the two of them demonstrated to the public and their superiors that the archdiocese was healthy and moving in the right direction?

"Murf, Murf," Hunthausen replied, "they won't let you do this. You have my sympathy but they won't let you do this. They're not going to leave me alone. And they aren't going to go through the same travail and turmoil in trying to assign somebody else. It's for me to get out, Murf, not you. Because we're trapped, Murf, we're trapped."

Murphy persisted; he desperately wanted out. Hunthausen suggested that he talk to Bernardin before going to Laghi. Murphy asked Hunthausen to prepare the ground for him by phoning the cardinal first. Hunthausen agreed and, after repeated attempts, managed to reach Bernardin early in the morning in Chicago and tell him of Murphy's request.

The master mediator was not pleased. "Ahh," he said. "He can't do that. He simply can't do that. That's impossible."

Bernardin called Murphy immediately. By the time the coadjutor archbishop of Seattle arrived in Boise on the Sunday of the new bishop's installation, it was obvious that Bernardin had held his feet to the fire. Stiff-lipped and taciturn, Murphy acknowledged to Hunthausen that he had had a conversation with Bernardin but was unwilling to talk about it.

That afternoon, Hunthausen, Murphy, and Laghi met in the nuncio's Boise hotel room to draft the statement that would officially end the visitation while affirming the existing arrangement of archbishop and coadjutor. It was a brief meeting, focused on the statement. Murphy, playing editor, chopped Laghi's convoluted three pages down to two paragraphs. The key sentence awkwardly read that the two archbishops "will continue to address the issues which have been of concern to the church in the Archdiocese of Seattle by implementing the changes in the pastoral care of the archdiocese which have already been initiated." The three-member Vatican commission was disbanded.

In a subsequent interview with *The Progress*, Hunthausen explained that any changes made in the local church as a result of the Vatican's concerns had already been made. He didn't anticipate any more. As for his personal plans, he said he was in excellent health and had no intention of retiring. When that day came, Coadjutor Archbishop Murphy would succeed him as planned.

The Progress also interviewed Murphy, who denied rumors of another assignment or a promotion to someplace else. "I hope to live and die in western Washington," he said.

The Archdiocese of Seattle settled into a state of normalcy, or as normal as a local church can be when it has two archbishops—one in power, and the other waiting to be empowered.

One day Archbishop Hunthausen received an unusual letter postmarked from Rome, an aerogramme handwritten on flimsy paper, folded over and sealed. The letter was from Archbishop Jean Jadot, the previous papal delegate to the United States, now living in near obscurity in his native Belgium. Over the years, Hunthausen and Jadot had maintained a warm friendship. Hunthausen had visited him in Rome during his 1978 and 1983 *ad limina* visits and they talked openly. But the two had not seen each other since Jadot's retirement from a minor Vatican office in 1984.

Jadot's letter was in reaction to what he had learned subsequently about the Vatican's machinations in the Seattle affair—its condemnation of Hunthausen's ministry, its dismissal of his credibility, its attempt to impose an auxiliary bishop with special powers, then a coadjutor archbishop, and all the interminable back and forth.

"I'm just so sorry that all this has happened to you," Jadot wrote. "I was never told about it."

Sister Joyce Cox, who as vice chancellor also assisted Hunthausen with his correspondence, watched as the archbishop read the letter, then put it down. He got up from his desk, walked over to the office window, and gazed off into some distant space. A heavy silence settled over him as if a wave of emotion was quietly building that might break and sweep him away.

Sensing his strong feelings, Cox asked, "Archbishop, do you want to talk about this?"

A far-off look in his eye, Hunthausen sighed and said, "No." He thought of the former papal delegate, the humble, Vatican II–believing Belgian responsible for his appointment as archbishop, and how he had been discarded and shunted aside.

Staring into some great beyond, Hunthausen said, "Jadot was a fine man."

12

FAREWELL

There's only one evil in the world, fear.
There's only one good in the world, love.
—Anthony de Mello

A much-reproduced photo that first appeared on the front-page of *The Progress* shows Coadjutor Archbishop Murphy and Archbishop Hunthausen, both dressed in full episcopal regalia, in a warm embrace on the sunny steps of St. James Cathedral. The bear hug suggested that their symbiotic working relationship would last until Hunthausen's mandatory retirement at age seventy-five. The reality, however, was more complex.

Hunthausen compared their joint effort to govern the archdiocese to "two guys trying to drive the same car." While Hunthausen was in the driver's seat, he felt duty bound to consult Murphy at every turn. After all, someday Murphy himself would be the driver. If Hunthausen made a wrong turn, Murphy would have to pay for it.

Plus there was a third, virtual driver who could pull either of their drivers' licenses at any time—the Vatican. Murphy, in particular, was acutely conscious of the third driver. By circumstance and temperament he worried and fretted over what Hunthausen might do that could cause consternation in Rome. He agonized over ex-priests doing volunteer work in parishes, over what theology the Jesuits were teaching at Seattle University, over the dialogue with gays who rejected church teaching on homosexuality, and over the open discussion on issues the Vatican had ruled closed, such as priestly celibacy and the ordination of women and married men.

If the light was generally green for Hunthausen, it was always amber for Murphy. No matter how often or how long the two of them talked together, Murphy wanted Hunthausen's foot close to the brake.

One time at the archbishops' regular weekly meeting with the chancery directors the conversation wandered into the subject of women's ordination. It was particularly candid and blunt. Dennis O'Leary, a married layman who served as director of chancery services, remarked that the secular world regarded the church's ban on women priests in much the same way as it regarded the Ku Klux Klan's bigotry against blacks.

Murphy looked dolefully at O'Leary and pleaded, "What do you want? Are you asking Archbishop Hunthausen and me to be martyrs?"

"Well, yes," O'Leary replied.

Hunthausen was as weary and worn down by the power-sharing arrangement as was Murphy. When he came through the chancery garage in the morning, he'd make note of whether Murphy's car was parked in the space reserved for the "Coadjutor Archbishop." He realized one day that he always felt better when it wasn't.

I walked into this awkward situation when I joined the chancery staff as public affairs director in November 1989. I soon found myself going back and forth between the offices of the two archbishops trying to get a decision on some communications or media matter. Each archbishop would typically ask me, "Have you talked to the archbishop? What does he think?"

One day, tired of shuttling back and forth, I asked Murphy in an exasperated tone, "Don't you two talk to each other?"

"We do," Murphy replied, sighing, "all the time, but it's impossible to talk about everything."

Hunthausen was reluctant to make big decisions without Murphy's agreement. On smaller matters, he was fine with deferring to his coadjutor. But it was often difficult to know whether an issue was big or small.

Sister Joyce Cox, the vice chancellor, sometimes stood in the passageway between the open doors of their two offices and asked, "Who's making the decision today?"

The particularly vexing issues involved the concerns spelled out in the Ratzinger letter. Per their arrangement, Murphy took the lead not only in addressing them but, perhaps more important, in demonstrating to the Vatican how the archdiocese had addressed them. Nicknamed "The White Tornado" for his shock of white hair and indefatigable energy, the coadjutor overwhelmed Rome with paperwork.

"He knocked himself out in providing documentation upon documentation to try to bring an end to the visitation," recalled Hunthausen, smiling at the memory. "He just wrote and wrote. I don't think he gave them any more information than they had before. But it certainly gave the impression that we were taking it all very seriously. It sort of blew them out of the water."

Complying with the Ratzinger letter, the archdiocese made the specific changes demanded by Rome: First confession now preceded first communion. Laicized priests did not serve in ministerial or teaching roles. General absolution was forbidden. So was intercommunion with Protestants. The marriage tribunal was strengthened, etcetera.

What was harder to change was what the commission had called "the overall attitudinal climate of permissiveness."

"How do you get a handle on something like that," mused Hunthausen, adding that even if such a climate existed, how would he change it? "It's not like changing a tire."

While Murphy concentrated on addressing the Ratzinger concerns, Hunthausen continued to speak out on justice and peace issues. Both archbishops emphasized the church's commitment to life. Joined by thousands of Catholics and other pro-lifers, they prayed on the steps of the state Legislative Building in Olympia at the annual March for Life in January. They campaigned against state ballot measures that would have expanded abortion rights and permitted physician-assisted suicide. And, in their homilies in parishes throughout western Washington, they borrowed Bernardin's language and spoke of a Catholic faith that embraces a "consistent ethic of life" from womb to tomb.

The peripatetic Murphy crammed his schedule with confirmations, youth retreats, faith formation events, bishops' conference committees, and fundraising galas. He put special emphasis on recruiting men for priesthood and began a vigorous vocations drive.

Hunthausen was undeterred by the lingering suspicion that his peace activities were the real cause of the Vatican investigation. He continued to participate in anti-nuke protests at the gates of the Trident submarine base and to advocate for unilateral disarmament. He told the national Pax Christi meeting in Chicago in 1987 that the bishops needed to reevaluate their justification of the morality of nuclear deterrence. Citing the Reagan administration's new Strategic Defense Initiative ("Star Wars"), he said, "the nuclear arms race has accelerated in outer space, under the oceans, and across the world" since publication of the bishops' 1983 peace pastoral. The "expansion of this evil," he noted, took place under the bishops' conditioned acceptance of nuclear deterrence.

In addresses on college campuses around the state, Hunthausen praised the administration's tentative agreement with the Soviet Union to reduce medium-range ballistic missiles but bemoaned the simultaneous development of the next generation of nuclear weapons. Are we simply dumping obsolete weapons to build yet more lethal ones? he asked. True peace, he said, is built not on weapons but on the Gospel values of justice, repentance, nonviolence, and reconciliation.

The archbishop's application of Gospel values to nuclear weapons still failed to convince some audiences, even Christian ones. The board of regents at Pacific Lutheran University rejected a unanimous vote by the school's faculty to award Hunthausen an honorary doctorate. Ironically, the archbishop had first attracted international media attention by announcing his tax protest against nuclear arms in a speech at PLU. Hunthausen shrugged off the insult.

Some months later he was wandering through the church facilities at a small parish in the San Juan Islands. He happened across a display of wall portraits assembled by the church youth group. The wording above the images proclaimed: "People Who Struggled for Social Justice." There were pictures of Jesus, Mahatma Gandhi, Martin Luther King Jr., and then him—Hunthausen. Beneath his picture was an explanation: "Denied an honorary doctorate."

Sometimes Hunthausen showed up at peace events, unannounced and perfectly content to be part of the crowd. On Palm Sunday 1988, he walked quietly with more than two hundred other Christians for four hours down Seattle streets to pray for world peace. In February 1989, he joined hundreds of other clergy, nuns, and laity for an Ash Wednesday prayer service northwest of Las Vegas at the Nevada Test Site, the country's only atomic-bomb testing range. All the while, he continued to divert half of his federal income taxes to charitable causes. The IRS sent him delinquent tax notifications and periodically garnished part of his salary.

His nonviolent advocacy included welcoming Salvadoran and Guatemalan refugees who found sanctuary in local churches after fleeing war and persecution in their homelands. Offering sanctuary, he noted, raised the question of U.S. complicity in arming the forces that had caused them to flee, namely, contra rebels in Nicaragua and corrupt governments that killed their own people.

With the end of the Reagan administration in 1988 and the collapse of the Soviet Union in 1989, the international picture changed dramatically. The U.S. Congress banned military aid to the Nicaraguan contras and armed conflict in Central America subsided. The Berlin Wall came down, and the Cold War was over. The peril of a nuclear doomsday that had so gripped an anxious and apprehensive world receded. Trident submarines with their ability to unleash a global Armageddon continued to roam the seas, but their likely target and enemy number one, the USSR, had vanished.

While the threat of nuclear war diminished, conventional war continued. In August 1990, Iraqi dictator Saddam Hussein sent his troops into neighboring Kuwait and seized the oil-rich sheikdom. International condemnation ensued, followed by economic sanctions and the creation of an invading force under U.S. leadership. President George H. W. Bush gave the Iraqis a deadline of January 15, 1991, to withdraw.

On the Monday evening before the war deadline, thirty thousand people clogged the streets of Seattle for a silent candlelight peace procession from St. James Cathedral to St. Mark's Episcopal Cathedral two miles away. Press reports described it as the biggest peace demonstration in Seattle since the end of the Second World War. Many of the demonstrators were mothers and fathers, pushing children in strollers or pulling them in wagons. Hunthausen, his voice amplified on outdoor speakers for those in the streets, prayed as he lit the first candle in the darkened sanctuary of St. James. And the procession began.

Nonetheless, the war came. U.S. and allied warplanes attacked Saddam Hussein's troops in Kuwait and bombed military targets in Iraq. Iraq launched SCUD missiles at Israel. Retreating Iraqi troops blew up Kuwaiti oil wells. In western Washington, Archbishops Hunthausen and Murphy asked pastors to keep their church doors open so people could come inside for prayer and consolation.

Some demonstrators, however, were not about to be consoled. On the evening of January 16, the day the war began, Seattle Mayor Norm Rice summoned Hunthausen and a few other prominent peace activists to city hall for an emergency meeting with him and Police Chief Patrick Fitzsimmons. Rice, an affable African American opposed to the war, was apprehensive. More than a thousand protesters, their ranks swollen with anarchists and troublemakers, were about to descend upon the Federal Building for an impromptu rally and demonstration. They were carrying anti-war banners and shouting "No Blood for Oil." More worrisome to the mayor and the police chief were those who were chanting, "Shut the City Down." They feared that the mob would trash storefronts, hurl stones and bottles at police, and force a violent confrontation in the middle of Second Avenue.

Rice and Fitzsimmons had decided to keep the police in the wings lest an overwhelming show of mounted and shielded cops further aggravate the situation. Now they were asking religious leaders and peace activists to pacify the multitude. An impromptu stage had been set up on the plaza in front of the Federal Building. Would Hunthausen and some of the others please speak to the crowd?

The archbishop, sitting next to Fitzsimmons, a Catholic, silently nodded. The others also agreed. With no time to be lost, the group rose to its feet and quickly walked the three blocks to the Federal

Building. Rice mounted the stage and spoke first. When he told the restless, angry crowd that everyone has the right to go to work or school without disruption, they booed. It was not going well.

Sister Kathleen Pruitt, an outspoken peace activist and a Sister of St. Joseph of Peace, made some headway with the crowd as did a couple of other civic leaders. But they failed to move the menacing gang who wanted to shut the city down.

Finally, Rice pushed Hunthausen forward. Removing his flat wool cap and squaring his raincoat against a bitter wind, the archbishop took the microphone and paused. The mayor had not introduced him.

"I'm Ray Hunthausen," he said, occasioning an outburst of applause and a knowing look of comprehension from the crowd. "And I'll be brief. We need to admit that in each of us there is some violence. We need to make sure we do not become part of what we are here to protest."

He said little more than that. By acknowledging the violence within himself and the violence within the crowd, he made peace. No one else spoke. Someone played a guitar and sang. A few people chanted peace slogans. And then the crowd, no longer threatening, drifted off into the night.

The Ratzinger letter's explicit instruction to the archdiocese to withdraw all support from any group that did not "unequivocally accept" church teaching on "the intrinsic evil of homosexual activity" put pressure on Hunthausen to do something about Dignity. The Catholic gay group continued to meet and sponsor weekly Masses at St. Joseph Church, the Jesuit parish on Seattle's Capitol Hill. Bishop Wuerl, exercising his special faculties, had discussed the matter with the Dignity board and the priests who celebrated the Masses, but was reassigned before taking any action. Now it was in Hunthausen's lap.

The Dignity issue was not unique to Seattle. Across the country, bishops were either kicking the Catholic gay group off church property or trying to come up with alternatives. Hunthausen noted that the Ratzinger letter also encouraged development of "a compassionate ministry to homosexual persons." At the height of the AIDS epidemic, he reasoned, what could be more pressing?

He and Murphy began meeting with the Dignity's Seattle leadership to discuss how the archdiocese could minister in a pastorally sensitive way to the gay community. Meanwhile Dignity had refined its statement of position and purpose, placing it squarely at odds with church teaching. At its 1987 convention in Miami, it declared: "We affirm that gay and lesbian people can express their sexuality physically in a unitive manner that is loving, life-giving, and life affirming."

Pat Roche, the Seattle banker and former seminarian who later served as Dignity's national president, recalled how he and other members struggled to reconcile their gay and Catholic identities. As master of ceremonies at the 1983 Dignity Convention in Seattle, Roche had introduced Hunthausen's videotaped welcome at the cathedral Mass. At that time, the group had had no official position on church teaching regarding gay sex. But the Ratzinger letter had forced them to write one.

A thoughtful, well-spoken man who had realized he was gay at age twelve, Roche recalled the moment in Miami when a Dignity delegate stood up and said, "If we won't honor our own relationships, who will?" An eerie silence descended. When the discussion resumed, the tone had changed. An overwhelming majority approved the new position statement and called for a reexamination of church teaching on homosexuality.

Roche, Ed Elliott, president of Dignity's Seattle chapter, and Cathy Cruikshank, its vice president, met with Hunthausen and Murphy to find a pastoral solution that would respect the conscience of Dignity members *and* church teaching. The archbishops did not want to take over the Dignity Mass without the group's support.

The intense meetings continued over several months as Dignity members told the archbishops their own stories of trying to square their sexuality with their spirituality. Meanwhile, Hunthausen's critics, knowing the Vatican was watching, mounted demonstrations and complained to the media that the archbishop was thumbing his nose at Rome. The Sons of St. Peter Coalition held a vigil on the chancery steps demanding that Hunthausen shut down the Dignity Mass. The group's spokesperson, conflating homosexuality with pedophilia, attacked the archbishop for giving comfort to sodomites and perverts.

Ultimately, Hunthausen proposed to do what Bernardin had just done in Chicago. The archdiocese would establish its own ministry to gay and lesbian Catholics and give this new ministry responsibility for what had been Dignity's Sunday evening Mass at St. Joseph's.

Dignity was divided on the proposal. Elliott argued they should accept the plan because, among other things, Hunthausen was the best bishop advocate that gays and lesbians had. Cruikshank argued they should reject it because it tacitly implied that homosexuals had no right to loving, committed relationships. Roche recalled how they had agonized over how to maintain their integrity as Catholics *and* homosexuals without blowing the community apart.

In the end, the Dignity board decided to take no position on the proposal and leave it up to members whether they would attend the archdiocesan Mass.

On July 10, 1988, the priests who had served the Seattle chapter celebrated Dignity's last Mass at St. Joseph's. The gay Seattle Men's Chorus sang "We Are a Family." Dignity's officers ceremoniously returned the church keys they had used to set up for the Mass. And, after the closing prayer, priests, gays, lesbians, and their friends, many of them in tears, followed the processional crucifix out of the nave and into the evening air. Two Sundays later Hunthausen celebrated the new archdiocesan gay Mass.

Dignity moved to Central Lutheran Church where it met monthly but never again sponsored a Mass. About half its membership continued to worship at St. Joseph's where the number of gay Mass-goers gradually increased. But others departed, some of them abandoning the church altogether. A sorrowful Cruikshank said she could not worship in a community whose leadership condemned her and her long-time partner as morally disordered sinners.

Roche described the Seattle solution as the most compassionate compromise achieved anywhere in the nation. "It was successful," he said, "because of the willingness of people on both sides to put community above doctrine. We valued family first."

In the spirit of family, Roche, his partner Wayne, Elliott, and a lesbian couple had Hunthausen to dinner in the couple's home after the Dignity matter was resolved. The archbishop was open and relaxed, seemingly void of judgment, Roche recalled. "He was very warm to Wayne, asking how we had met and got together. Yet here we were—'practicing homosexuals.'"

As Dignity's national president, Roche tried to move the organization beyond the preoccupation with gay sex and engage the church hierarchy on issues such as AIDS ministry, civil rights legislation, prejudice, and hate crimes. With a helpful letter of introduction and support from Hunthausen, he contacted Archbishop Daniel Pilarcyzk, the conference president, and asked for a dialogue. Pilarcyzk arranged for Roche to meet with Msgr. Robert Lynch, who as the conference secretary was the chief administrative officer. Lynch received Roche well and promised a subsequent meeting with Pilarcyzk. But despite follow-up calls and letters from Roche, the meeting never happened.

Pilarcyzk eventually wrote to Roche, advising him that a meeting would be unproductive. After all, church teaching on homosexuality was clear, he wrote. There was nothing more to be said.

No issue has done more damage to the image and credibility of the Roman Catholic Church in modern times than its failure to address the sexual abuse committed by its clergy. Bishops covered up the crimes of pedophile priests, disregarded and dismissed the victims, and quietly moved offenders from one unsuspecting parish to another.

The Archdiocese of Seattle was no exception. In 2003, at the height of the clergy sex abuse scandal, the archdiocese revealed that forty-seven priests who had served in western Washington since the 1950s had been accused of sexual abuse of children. That same year it settled a sex abuse lawsuit for nearly $8 million with fifteen men who were molested as boys by Father James McGreal, a serial pedophile. Meanwhile, sex abuse lawsuits and settlements were bankrupting other dioceses, including the neighboring jurisdictions of Portland and Spokane, as well as the Oregon Province of the Jesuits. In Boston, denial, wrongdoing, and cover-ups cost Cardinal Law his job as well as $85 million in church and insurance funds paid to 552 victims of clergy sex abuse.

A big difference between Seattle and Boston was Hunthausen. When complaints about McGreal first came to his attention in 1977, Hunthausen sent him off for treatment. Like other bishops and society at large, he regarded sexual attraction to children as a psychological deviancy that could be treated and eliminated. Consequently, when Hunthausen got more complaints about McGreal, he sent him off for treatment again. Over McGreal's forty years in the archdiocese, the pedophile priest cycled through several parishes, two hospitals, and multiple treatments. Court papers in the settlement alleged that he plied boys with altar wine, showed them pornography, and kissed, fondled, and had sex with them. His victims ranged in age from nine to twelve and, in some cases, the abuse lasted for years. Yet he was never arrested or charged with a crime.

In 1985, Hunthausen asked the King County Prosecutor's Office to investigate the incidents documented in McGreal's personnel file with an eye toward filing charges. The office determined that the allegations were too old for criminal prosecution; the statute of limitations had run out. The archbishop also dug into other priest personnel files with "new eyes," turning over those that raised concerns to the state attorney general's office for review. While no priests were prosecuted as a result of the review, the archbishop forced several into early retirement and barred them from further ministry.

At the same time, Hunthausen enlisted mental health and law enforcement experts to help the archdiocese draft new guidelines on sexual abuse by clergy. Under his direction, the archdiocese created an independent review panel to evaluate "special cases" that came to its attention. The original panel, split evenly between Catholics and non-Catholics, included the director of Harborview Hospital's Center for Sexual Assault and Traumatic Stress. Subsequent panels had a former U.S. attorney, a county prosecutor, a psychologist, and an expert in church law. Archdiocesan policy required immediate reporting to authorities of credible sexual abuse claims, suspension of the accused pending an investigation, and a compassionate outreach to and care for victims. If the accusations were substantiated, the priest was subject to prosecution. Proven pedophiles were removed from priesthood.

The Seattle policy was subsequently adopted as the gold standard by other dioceses, including Bernardin's Chicago. Jason Berry, the journalist and author credited with sounding the alarm on the sexual abuse scandal in the U.S. Catholic Church, described Seattle's policy as "pioneering."

"Hunthausen was really the first archbishop to deal with this problem publicly," Berry told the *Seattle Times* in 2002. "The fact that Hunthausen spoke out and was so forthright—you cannot underestimate that."

After turning over McGreal's file to the authorities, Hunthausen ordered the priest to go for long-term treatment at the Paraclete Center in New Mexico. On his return a year later, the archbishop, acting on the advice of the treatment center, assigned McGreal to a parish where he was supervised by the pastor. What Hunthausen didn't know was that treatment at the Paraclete Center frequently failed and that one of the priests at the parish to which he sent McGreal was also a pedophile. In 1988, Father Paul Conn, assistant pastor of Queen of Angels Church in Port Angeles, was charged, convicted, and sent to prison for molesting six altar boys.

Sister Joyce Cox, the archbishop's point person on sexual abuse cases, cannot forget the meeting that she, Father George Thomas, the new chancellor, and Hunthausen had with the abused boys and their parents. They drove to Port Angeles, sat in a circle in a church meeting room, and let everyone say whatever needed to be said. There was anger, there were tears, recrimination, outrage, hurt, and grief. How could children entrusted to the care of the church be violated like this?

"It was such a bad scene, so hard, with those little boys sitting there alongside their parents," Cox recalled.

There were no words to assuage the pain of what had happened. Hunthausen listened so sorrowfully and so long that Cox wondered if they'd miss the last ferry back to Seattle. When there was no more to be said, Hunthausen apologized for his failure to prevent what had happened. He told the parents the archdiocese would pay for counseling for them and their children. And he prayed that someday they would experience God's healing love. Soon after, he visited Conn, an inmate at the Twin Rivers Corrections Center, and told him that, no matter how repentant he was, he would never be a priest again.

McGreal, meanwhile, was placed as a retired but still active priest under the supervision of Father Joe Kramis, the well-regarded pastor at St. Theresa Parish in the Seattle suburb of Federal Way. Only Kramis and selected parish staff members knew of McGreal's history of child sex abuse. Hunthausen decided that all should know.

In a May 26, 1988, letter to all pastors in the archdiocese, he identified McGreal as having had a long history of child molestation. He instructed pastors to read his letter from the pulpit and advised them of the procedure for caring for any child-abuse victims who might come forward. He explained that he had named McGreal and would name other priest pedophiles if he knew of them in an effort "to break the cycle of silence that perpetuates abuse."

The archdiocese removed McGreal from St. Theresa's, placed him on permanent inactive status, and sent him to a locked priest retirement home in Missouri. The Vatican finally suspended him in 2004 and he died in 2011.

In 2002, the U.S. bishops, reeling from the sex abuse scandal, readjusted the line between forgiveness for penitent priests and justice for their victims. They embraced a "zero tolerance" policy that required dismissal of any priest who molested even one child one time. As a result, priests who had engaged in any sex act with a minor, including inappropriate touching or fondling, were permanently removed from ministry.

Among them was Father David Jaeger, who had directed the Catholic Youth Organization and headed the vocations office and the archdiocesan AIDS ministry. Jaeger, who had also demonstrated with Hunthausen at Bangor, was devoted to the archbishop and committed to his vision of church. But as a naïve and sexually confused seminarian twenty-five years earlier, he had fondled several teenage boys. He insisted it never happened again and therapists believed him. Following extensive treatment, which included monitoring and lie detector tests, psychologists concluded that Jaeger posed no further danger to children. Nonetheless, under "zero tolerance," he was out.

Hunthausen could not fathom how such a smart, sensitive, and talented individual like Jaeger had failed to understand sexual boundaries. The archbishop put victims first but he also believed in forgiveness. He never imagined that "zero tolerance" would ensnare Jaeger and others who did not seem to be dangerous serial pedophiles like McGreal or Conn. But how is one to know? How does the church keep kids safe?

Under the policy put in practice by Hunthausen in 1986, the archdiocese received virtually no new allegations of sexual abuse of children by its clergy. It did, however, have to deal with numerous abuse allegations from earlier years, some of them dating back to the 1950s.

In 1989, Archbishop Hunthausen named a married woman with two children to be the spiritual leader of St. Patrick Church in Seattle. As "parochial minister," Victoria Reis would preach, visit the sick, counsel the suffering, preside at communion services, and bear responsibility for the parish's spiritual growth, religious education, staff, budget, and buildings. Visiting priests would celebrate the Mass and perform the sacraments.

Reis, who had a doctorate in theology and a decade of experience in church pastoral work, was the first wife and mother to be a parochial minister in the archdiocese. But she was not the first parochial minister. Hunthausen had also appointed seven nuns and a deacon to lead parishes around western Washington. In about 70 of the nation's 185 dioceses, other bishops were copying him, naming women religious and laypeople to head parishes, typically when priests were not available.

The 1983 Code of Canon Law allowed for such a practice although it was conceived as an emergency measure that would not be employed if there were sufficient priests. At the time of Reis's appointment, the Seattle archdiocese predicted that over the next decade the number of priests would decline 20 percent while the number of registered Catholics would increase 20 percent. As a result, more parishes would be without resident priests.

Hunthausen wanted to keep healthy, viable parishes open even if they didn't have priests to staff them. One way was to hire more lay staff. The archdiocese counted more than five hundred career lay ministers, a remarkable total compared to other dioceses. Appointing parochial ministers and other lay leaders to positions traditionally occupied by clerics helped compensate for the priest shortage. But in Hunthausen's mind, it rightly asked lay Catholics to share responsibility for the church. It also empowered women, since the overwhelming number of lay leaders and parochial minister candidates were female.

As Hunthausen was appointing laywomen to leadership positions, the U.S. bishops' conference was drafting a pastoral letter on women in the church and society. In doing so, it was struggling with the same issue that had bedeviled the archbishop when he wrote his own pastoral letter on women in 1980: How do you make women equal partners in the church when you shut them out of the priesthood and deny them the top jobs?

Or, as Hunthausen succinctly put it, "How are you going to denounce the sin of sexism when the church is sexist?"

Nonetheless, the six-member panel of bishops charged with writing the letter tried mightily. It gathered comments from more than seventy-five thousand people across the nation to complete its first draft in 1988. The document affirmed the equality of men and women and condemned sexism as a moral and social evil. It deplored violence against women, the high rates of poverty among single mothers, and gender discrimination in the workplace. It faltered, however, when it sought to address internal church issues. While it endorsed broadening non-sacramental opportunities for women, it affirmed the church's traditional teaching prohibiting artificial contraception and barring women from priesthood.

The pastoral went through four drafts, each time becoming more guarded and dogmatic as the result of Vatican interference. At their annual fall meeting in 1992, the bishops failed to reach a two-thirds majority vote on the fourth and final draft, marking the first time they had not achieved consensus on a major policy statement.

Archbishops Hunthausen and Murphy dutifully conducted "listening sessions" around the archdiocese to solicit comments after the first draft was released in the spring of 1988 and again after the second draft was released two years later. Local reaction mirrored the division the bishops would experience in later abandoning the pastoral altogether. Nearly one thousand Catholics, most of them women, showed up at listening sessions purposely staged in Bellevue, Centralia, and Everett, all cities where traditional views were likely to be stronger. In Bellevue, where dissident parishioners had hired a detective in an attempt to out their pastor, the feedback included personal attacks on Hunthausen and rants about heresy and radical feminism. The two archbishops sat grim-faced through the barrage.

In each locale, Hunthausen made a special effort to talk with his most virulent critics. In Centralia, he sat next to Erven Park, editor of the libelous *Catholic Truth,* and introduced himself to Danny Barrett, head of Catholics Against Marxist Theology. In Everett, he tried to make contact with Gary Bullert, a former Catholic high school teacher who had self-published a contemptuous book on the archbishop. Bullert turned his back on him.

The common denominator at the listening sessions was the view that the women's pastoral should be scrapped. The traditionalists contended that it was unnecessary; church teaching on the issue was clear. The reformers asserted that the pastoral was hypocritical; despite the lofty language about "the full personhood of women," it did not confront the church's sexism.

In the midst of the contentious debate around the pastoral, Hunthausen decided to push the women's issue. In April 1990, he announced that he was suspending training for future deacons in the archdiocese until the role of women in the church was more adequately addressed. The permanent diaconate, an early church office revived by Vatican II, is an ordained ministry limited to men. Deacons can administer some of the sacraments performed by priests, including baptism and matrimony. They can be married and most are. Their wives receive deacon training along with them, but when the time comes to be ordained, the spouses step aside.

Hunthausen's decision to suspend deacon training was influenced by what he had heard at the listening sessions on the women's pastoral. In fact, he had promised earlier that the archdiocese would start a new deacon class. But as he heard women speak of how unappreciated and undervalued they felt in the church, he changed his mind. He knew that deciding against deacons and for women would cost him with deacons and with pastors who depended on their help. Some ninety deacons were serving in parishes in western Washington while nearly nine thousand served the church nationwide.

In his letter to deacons and priests, the archbishop explained that while canon law required him to have a formation program for priests, a deacon program was optional. He said he had to weigh the local church's need for sacramental help provided by deacons against the restrictions that women faced in ministry.

"There were genuine values on both sides," he wrote. "In the end I decided as I did primarily because I believe that the women's question is now the priority question for a church that preaches justice." The formation of a new deacon class, he added, would reinforce "the sexism already operative in the church."

Halting a diaconate program to call attention to sexism in the church was a first. As anticipated, Hunthausen's decision got mixed reviews. The chair of the Archdiocesan Women's Commission hailed it as a "wonderful move" against the exclusion of women from ministerial roles.

Some priests, however, were critical. They understood Hunthausen's desire to send a message to Rome about excluding women from ministry, but why target deacons? "Why shoot ourselves in the foot?" asked a pastor who depended on deacons to help him meet ministry needs in the San Juan Islands.

Hunthausen's decision on deacons brought into sharp relief the two-headed governance of the archdiocese. It was the archbishop's decision to make, but Coadjutor Archbishop Murphy struggled mightily with it. The deacons' issue dramatized their ongoing differences and highlighted their challenging working relationship.

In January 1991, Hunthausen asked Father Michael McDermott, his confidante and the archdiocesan director of ministry, to help him draft two letters. The first was addressed to Cardinal Ratzinger. It said that while Hunthausen, then sixty-nine, considered himself in good health and sound mind and very capable of continuing in office until age seventy-five, he planned to resign "for the good of the church."

The second letter, addressed "Dear Tom," was to Murphy. It said that Hunthausen had no intention of resigning and, in fact, planned to serve as archbishop until seventy-five. It praised Murphy as a fine man devoted to the church and the archdiocese, but then noted that the two of them had very different styles and very different priorities that prevented effective leadership. Furthermore, their collegial style of decision-making was simply not working. When they differed on issues, the letter said, nothing happened. Consequently, Hunthausen was informing Murphy that, while consultation would continue, he would be making more decisions that Murphy was unlikely to support. For at least the next six years, the letter suggested, Hunthausen would drive the car by himself.

Over the next several months, Hunthausen kept both letters close at hand but ultimately he sent neither of them. He couldn't decide. Should he go? Or should he stay? Resigning in good health would look like he had been forced out which could upset the archdiocese and damage Murphy. Staying on continued to make it unbearable for Murphy who had already begged for reassignment.

By the spring of 1991, the archdiocese had begun several long-range projects. It was conducting a comprehensive evaluation of its Catholic school system; it had launched a multi-million dollar renovation of St. James Cathedral; and it was implementing its program to keep all viable parishes open despite a shortage of priests. Hunthausen began to question whether he should oversee these long-range efforts when he knew that Murphy would have to implement them.

"I shouldn't be building a house that I'm not going to live in," he said.

After what he described as "long and prayerful deliberation," Hunthausen decided to submit his resignation to Pope John Paul II, effective August 21, 1991, the date of his seventieth birthday. He was doing so, he said, "for the good of the church." The Vatican received the letter and accepted his resignation immediately.

Hunthausen publicly announced his resignation at the annual June retreat of archdiocesan priests in the coastal resort community of Ocean Shores. He told his colleagues that his decision to step down was his alone.

"Yes, I'm hurting," he acknowledged, "but I feel in the depth of my soul I'm at peace."

He explained that he had intended to stay on until age seventy-five but changed his mind when he felt the Lord wanted something else of him. Recalling his episcopal motto—"Thy Will Be Done"—he said he trusted that he was doing God's will. He encouraged the priests, sitting in stunned silence, some wiping tears from their eyes, to do what God asks of them: Love God, love your people, and tell them God loves them.

When he finished speaking, the entire gathering of clergy rose to its feet and applauded long and hard. The heartfelt applause continued until Hunthausen, embarrassed by the display of affection, walked away from the podium.

On the warm balmy evening of August 12, 1991, after sixteen years of leading the church in western Washington, Hunthausen gave his last homily as archbishop of Seattle. A crowd of more than one thousand admirers packed St. James Cathedral to hear his farewell remarks and queued up outdoors afterward to offer him a handshake, a hug, or a few words of appreciation.

Speaking from the pulpit, Hunthausen described himself and his motivation. "I have never seen myself as a go-getter, an initiator, or a visionary," he said. "Instead, I have come to view myself as someone who was invited to be a leader. Invited to join a struggle to be faithful to the Gospel."

He explained how Vatican II had resonated deeply with his hopes for a church that would transform lives and the world. He left the Council "born again," convinced that we are all "People of God" called to "share responsibility" in building the kingdom of God in this world, not the next. Those are the values, he said, by which he had tried to guide his ministry.

The Council had taught him, he said, that the church is *semper reformanda*, always in need of reform. That means continuing to examine our hearts and minds as we seek to understand God's will for us today.

"Are we a church that includes gays, welcomes the divorced and separated, offers equal opportunity to women?" Hunthausen asked. "Have we really made a preferential option for the poor? How willing are we to dialogue with those troubled by what we teach or how we act? Are we good stewards of what God has given us?"

"Whether it be the Gulf War, sexual morality, nuclear disarmament, respect for life, this is God's world," he said. "So I try to find a way to let God come into it and live with me and among us. That's really what I think prayer is—letting God live among us."

"My friends," Hunthausen concluded, "to have shared this journey with so many of you has been such a blessing in my life.... May the Lord Jesus continue to guide and direct the journey we all share. May the power of His Spirit be yours in all you do and may you know the presence of God's joy, peace, and love in your life always."

AFTERWORD

When Archbishop Hunthausen announced his resignation, a front-page editorial in the *National Catholic Reporter* urged him to speak out on the issues of the day "guided only by fidelity to Gospel and conscience." The Catholic weekly imagined Hunthausen as a modern Isaiah, "a U.S. archbishop with little left to lose," able to call the church back to the vision of Vatican II.

But Hunthausen didn't see himself that way. Yes, he followed his conscience in trying to follow the Gospel. But in retirement he wasn't going to grandstand for church reform. What could he possibly say that would make a difference? Plus, it could be problematic and divisive. He knew that Rome wanted him gone and that in many dioceses he was regarded as persona non grata.

God, he decided, wanted something different now. He began a period of self-imposed quiet and reflection with limited pastoral duties. He declined virtually all invitations to speak at conferences, universities, forums, and other public gatherings. He refused to do media interviews, even interviews with the Catholic press. He didn't go to meetings and went out of his way to stay invisible.

Gradually he gravitated toward retreat work, helping others experience God's love in their lives through meditation and prayer. In early 1993, he moved out of the cathedral rectory in Seattle and returned to his native Montana. There he resumed his ministry of spiritual direction, guiding priests, nuns, and laypeople on their own faith journeys. He talked often about the need for forgiveness, about how resentments against others interfere with prayer and distract us from God's unconditional love.

Paraphrasing Anthony de Mello, he said, "The three most difficult things in life are returning love for hate, including the excluded, and admitting that you are wrong." If we can acknowledge our resentments and confess our culpability, he said, we can achieve an authentic and fulfilling prayer life.

Hunthausen told stories—the Gospel's and his own—to make his points. The story of the leper in the Gospel of Mark (1:40–45) was especially meaningful to him.

"I have down times, times in which I ask: 'What's it all about, Lord?'" he said, "and the spirit prompts me to reflect on the leper. I need to come before the Lord and, like the leper, ask to be cured. To say, 'Touch me, Lord.'"

Often he illustrated his point about dependence on God's love by telling a family story. For example, one Thanksgiving, the Hunthausen clan had grown so large with nieces, nephews, grandnieces, and grand-nephews that no one's house could accommodate the big holiday dinner. So they rented the fire hall in East Helena. After the celebration, the families doubled and tripled up to overnight in the homes of those who lived in the Helena area. The archbishop and his sister Edna were up early the next morning to make coffee when they heard the patter of little feet enter the kitchen. Here was their three-year-old grandniece, Brianne.

The little girl sat down with them at the kitchen table. She jabbered away about this and that until a thought suddenly seized her. She got down from the table and announced that she was going downstairs to find her daddy.

"Why don't you stay here with us and let your daddy sleep?" the archbishop suggested.

Brianne's face clouded up. Her hands closed into tight little fists.

"He's mine," she declared, "and I need him."

The archbishop and his sister looked at each other and both thought of God. And how desperately we need God.

"Unless you can be touched by the love of God, nothing is going to happen in your life," Hunthausen told those seeking God. "Faith is the willingness to say 'yes' to God's love. It's the acceptance of God's love. God accepts me as I am. God loves me as I am. God can't do anything else but love me."

In 1997, Archbishop Murphy died of a brain hemorrhage after being diagnosed with leukemia. He was just sixty-four. With Murphy's death the archdiocese began rewriting Hunthausen's legacy, reducing his official history to a tax protest and an unexplained Vatican investigation. Excised from ecclesial memory was the Vatican II bishop who had welcomed the "People of God" as full partners in governing the church and in building Christ's kingdom on earth. Hunthausen's issues—putting reliance in God rather than nuclear weapons; welcoming women, gays, the divorced, and the alienated into the life of the church; and working with other faiths for the common good—were not high on the agendas of the next archbishops of Seattle.

In fact, the "Restoration" had begun under Murphy. The hyperactive archbishop was outspoken on labor, poverty, and life issues. He gave special emphasis to youth, ethnic minorities, and people struggling in coastal lumber towns. But on internal church matters, Murphy either stood still or turned back the clock. He appointed no laypeople as parochial ministers. He resumed the deacon-training program. He saw to it that former priests kept their distance from Catholic schools and parish ministry despite an acute shortage of ordained clergy.

His successor, Archbishop Alexander J. Brunett, came to Seattle after three years as bishop of Helena. A Detroit native who had spent his seminary years in Rome, Brunett had a reputation as an ecumenical and interfaith expert and participated in national dialogues with Jewish, Islamic, and Orthodox leaders. In western Washington, however, he withdrew the archdiocese from membership in the Washington Association of Churches and ignored the Church Council of Greater Seattle. He abandoned the ecumenical Church Advocacy Day in Olympia, replacing it with a Catholic Advocacy Day that excluded the Protestants. He had perhaps his biggest splash in the local press when he condemned proposed county zoning regulations that would have limited the size of new buildings, including churches, in rural areas. He called it a "religious liberty" issue. Dedicated, argumentative, and controlling, Brunett incurred the wrath of victims' advocates when he rejected the recommendation of the independent review panel and refused to release the names of thirty-six dead, departed, or elderly priests accused of having sexually abused children.

Over the Murphy and Brunett years, the archdiocesan Pastoral Council, the Priest Senate, the Women's Commission, the Justice and Peace Office and other collaborative bodies created by Hunthausen withered and died away. Also dead was the archdiocesan ministry to gay and lesbian Catholics. It was replaced by Courage, a national Catholic group whose primary mission is to help gays be celibate.

Archbishop J. Peter Sartain, previously bishop in Little Rock, Arkansas, and Joliet, Illinois, succeeded Brunett upon the latter's retirement in 2010. Smart, genial, and also Roman-educated, Sartain concentrated on deepening the faith life of his flock while defending traditional Catholic teaching. In 2012, he testified before the state legislature in opposition to a bill that would legalize same-sex marriage. When lawmakers passed it anyway, he urged parishes to collect signatures in support of a referendum to repeal the new law. The referendum was defeated. Two years later, he backed the firing of the vice principal at Eastside Catholic High School for marrying another man.

In 2012, Pope Benedict XVI gave Sartain the unenviable task of overseeing the Leadership Conference of Women Religious, the nation's umbrella group of American nuns. Cardinal William Levada, Ratzinger's successor as CDF prefect, had accused the LCWR of espousing radical feminism and straying from church teaching on issues such as homosexuality, contraception, and an all-male priesthood.

Sartain had a five-year mandate to review and change the group's laws, programs, and practices so as to correct those elements judged incompatible with the Catholic faith.

Meanwhile the U.S. Conference of Catholic Bishops, packed with John Paul II and Benedict XVI look-alikes, obsessed over same-sex marriage, abortion, and birth control. "Religious liberty" became synonymous with opposition to the contraceptive mandate in the federal health care act. With the U.S. economy experiencing the worst recession since the Great Depression, the bishops had little to say about the poor, the unemployed, or the growing concentration of wealth at the top. Long gone were the cogent pastoral letters of the 1980s, with their moral critiques of nuclear weapons and laissez faire capitalism. Instead the bishops fulminated about errant theologians, wayward nuns, and cafeteria Catholics.

Whether the bishops will continue on the same path became uncertain with the unexpected resignation of Benedict and the surprise election of Pope Francis in 2013. After thirty-five years of a single, binding interpretation of church doctrine along with dictatorial enforcement of Vatican discipline, the Restoration appeared to be over. While not eschewing the past, Francis launched the barque of St. Peter on a different course with a different style of being church.

From its opening moments, his papacy has communicated the Catholic faith more by gesture than by word. Francis moved from the papal apartments to a room in a nearby guesthouse. He exchanged the Mercedes limousine for an old Renault sedan. He invited the homeless to dine with him at the Vatican. And he reenacted the Holy Thursday ritual by washing the feet of twelve prison inmates, including two Muslims and two women.

When asked by a reporter about the status of gay priests, he dumbfounded the world with his reply: "Who am I to judge?"

With that single comment, Francis backed away from the judgmental and moralizing manner of his predecessors. He bemoaned the church's preoccupation with abortion, gay marriage, and artificial contraception. He said those issues had distracted the church from its more fundamental mission of proclaiming God's merciful love for all, especially the poor and suffering.

In his apostolic exhortation, *Evangelii Gaudium* ("The Joy of the Gospel"), Francis wrote that the church must heal wounds and warm the hearts of the faithful. "Prescriptive, distant, and abstract" teaching doesn't do it, he said, insisting that the church needs to be close, tender, and caring. He called for a "conversion of the papacy," a decentralization of the curia, and a return of authority—even authority on doctrine—to national bishops' conferences. The reforms of Vatican II, which he regarded as halted halfway, should unfold in their entirety.

Francis objected to mean-spirited forces within the church that conduct "veritable witch hunts" and cautioned against "ostentatious preoccupation" with liturgy and doctrine. He criticized the clericalism of arrogant, pretentious priests and bishops who lust for power and privilege. Bishops, he said, should be patient, humble, gentle pastors with a great sense of joy they can share with others.

Hunthausen drew comfort from Pope Francis's vision for the church. He was cheered by the Holy Father's affirmation of the "People of God," of an inclusive, caring church that engages the world and makes space for listening, dialogue, and even disagreement.

"Francis is doing the things I tried to do," the archbishop told me, suggesting perhaps that his own long exile was coming to a close.

We had this conversation in a Helena nursing home where Hunthausen, ninety-two, was recovering from a stroke. Over the previous few years, he had gradually lost use of his limbs. He got around first with a cane, then a walker, and now a wheelchair. His active ministry was over. His disability had forced him to give up golf, driving, and the family outings at Moose Lake and Legendary Lodge. Now the family came to him, especially his brother, Jack, who visited daily and would take him home to the house they shared once he was released from the nursing facility.

When I visited him that hot July day in 2013, Hunthausen was sitting upright in a stuffed reclining chair, wearing a short-sleeve blue shirt, brown trousers, and black priest shoes. His complexion was pasty white; his breath short. He looked weak and a bit disheveled, his remaining white hair indifferently pushed back from his forehead. He required help eating, dressing, and using the bathroom.

"We begin and end life the same way," he observed. "In diapers and having to be fed. It's a great lesson in humility."

The two of us reminisced about our time together at the chancery in Seattle, about mutual friends who had come and gone, and about my only visit to Moose Lake twenty years earlier. Hunthausen chuckled, recalling the remark I had made after using what he called "the biffy."

"Archbishop," I said at the time, "that must be the only outhouse in the world with copies of *Commonweal* and *The Tablet*." The two publications are highbrow Catholic weeklies.

After an hour of conversation, Hunthausen began to weary. I realized it was time for me to go. I gave him a copy of Henri Nouwen's little book, *Our Greatest Gift: A Meditation on Dying and Caring*, but, as I suspected, he was already familiar with it. I asked him if he was ready to die.

He would go when God was ready to take him, he replied. Despite his physical limitations, he said he wasn't depressed, bored, or frustrated. He could still read, albeit with difficulty, closing his right eye so he could see the words with his left. Mostly he was happy to pass the day in prayer and contemplation, enjoying his memories.

"I've had a good life," he told me. "And I'm very thankful for that."

Surely, I said, you must have some regrets.

Sighing, he paused and then replied that he had at least one. He wished that he had engaged Pope John Paul II and Cardinal Ratzinger in a more extended, more heartfelt conversation about the church. He wanted them to understand that he and so many others had such high hopes for the open, inclusive, collegial, and engaged church envisioned by Vatican II. And then those hopes were dashed. Why? he wanted to ask. Why?

"Now," Hunthausen said, "I'll have that conversation in the next life."

I told him that he had been a significant person in my life, a model and mentor for following the Gospel. I got teary-eyed. I grasped his right hand and shook it with both my hands.

"Thank you," I said. "Thank you very much."

Shakily, he raised his right arm from the recliner, made a wobbly sign of the cross, and blessed me in the name of the Father, the Son, and the Holy Spirit.

As I rose to depart, he handed me a prayer card of Thomas Merton's "Thoughts in Solitude." Merton's invocation was a favorite of his, one he had shared with many others:

My Lord God, I have no idea where I am going. I do not see the road ahead of me. I cannot know for certain where it will end. Nor do I really know myself, and the fact that I think that I am following your will does not mean that I am actually doing so.

But I believe that the desire to please you does in fact please you. And I hope that I will never do anything apart from that desire.

And I know that if I do this you will lead me by the right road though I may know nothing about it. Therefore I will trust you always though I may seem to be lost and in the shadow of death.

I will not fear, for you are ever with me, and will never leave me to face my perils alone.

ACKNOWLEDGMENTS

The raw material for this book would still be languishing on a twenty-five-year-old Macintosh computer in the crawl space above the carport if it weren't for Pope Francis. It was Francis' surprise election in 2013 that motivated me to revisit an abandoned project—a biography of Archbishop Raymond G. Hunthausen, whom I believe was the epitome of the pastoral, Vatican II bishop the church so desperately needs today. The kind of bishop that Francis wants and the people of God deserve.

Telling Hunthausen's story more than twenty years after I conducted most of the interviews with him, his siblings, friends, and colleagues means thanking some people who are no longer with us. I am very grateful to the priests, bishops, childhood friends, and others who kindly gave me their time but will not see the fruit of my labor. May eternal light shine upon them.

A very special thanks to the archbishop, his brothers Tony, Jack, and Art, his sisters, Marie, Edna, and Jeanne, and their spouses and children who welcomed me into their homes and spoke openly from their hearts.

Hunthausen's colleagues, his fellow bishops, priests, religious women, and laypeople who served with him in Helena and Seattle were very willing to share their experience of him. I thank them for their time and their memories. Their names and their recollections of the archbishop appear throughout the text.

I am especially grateful to Father Michael G. Ryan, the former archdiocesan chancellor, who kept files, a journal, and meticulous notes from his years of serving as Hunthausen's right-hand man and confidante. Ryan kindly shared much of this material with me.

I am also grateful to Sister Joyce Cox, BVM, the ecumenical and interfaith officer for the Archdiocese of Seattle and former vice chancellor, for her encouragement and her continual reminder to "tell the stories."

Another source of inspiration was Frank Fromherz, who wrote a doctoral dissertation about Hunthausen in 1990 and was convinced that someone must write a book. I was also motivated by the examples of Peter Lewis, Steve Sanger, and Dean Owen, friends and journalists of a certain age, who impressed upon me that it is never too late to write a book.

301

In researching the story of the archbishop's life, I am indebted to Greg Magnoni and Vee Harris, of the Seattle archdiocesan public affairs office, who provided me with bound copies of *The Progress*; to Seth Dalby, archdiocesan director of archives and records management; to Father John Robertson, the chancellor in Helena, who gave me access to the diocesan archives; to Michael Brown, the communications director and archivist of the Diocese of Boise, for providing access to the unpublished journals of Bishop Nicolas E. Walsh; and to John Driscoll, a former colonel at the Pentagon and ex-Montana legislator, for his extensive investigative work into the connections between the Vatican and the Reagan administration.

I also benefited from newspaper files and other archival materials housed at the Seattle Public Library in downtown Seattle, the Carroll College Library in Helena, the Museum of History and Industry in Seattle, and the Pacific Northwest Regional Newspaper Collection in the Allen Library at the University of Washington.

As for the actual writing of the book, I am especially thankful for the advice of two long-time friends and my sister, all accomplished and published authors. O. Casey Corr emphasized finding a theme that builds tension and makes an argument. Tim Egan stressed the importance of using the most compelling material and weaving a narrative. My sister, Genevieve McCoy, urged me to apply fiction techniques in crafting a non-fiction story and helped me write a book proposal. Egan and Father Patrick Howell, SJ, an author and Hunthausen friend, kindly critiqued and improved the proposal.

As for editing, I owe special appreciation to Robert Ellsberg, the publisher and editor-in-chief of Orbis Books, for his enthusiastic support and his wise counsel on restructuring the manuscript; to Celine Allen, who copyedited the text with the astute eyes of a diligent reader; and to George Murphy, an old friend and a committed, Vatican II Catholic, whose knowledge and love of the church, the archdiocese, and the Christian faith was invaluable. George kindly read first drafts of all chapters and was candid and specific in providing feedback.

Throughout the book project, I was nourished and cheered by those Catholics who continue to believe that our church is capable of authentic and compelling witness to the Gospel. Aside from those already mentioned, I think of old friends, Tom Bianchi, David Giusti, Geoff Stamper, Jessie Dye, and Tony Cole.

Finally, I want to acknowledge the two women to whom this book is dedicated: my late mother, Marian E. McCoy, who gave me the gift of her Catholic faith; and my wife, Karen C. McCoy, who has given me her love and her conviction of God's unconditional love.

SOURCES

Chapter 1: Trident

Description of anti-Trident rally at Point Julia: *Seattle Times*, Aug. 9, 1982; *Seattle Post-Intelligencer* (*Seattle P-I*), Aug. 8, 9, 1982; *The Catholic Northwest Progress* (*The Progress*), Aug. 12, 1982.

Description of Point Julia, Klallam Reservation, from author visit, Sept. 4, 2013.

Securing reservation for rally from author interview with Jim Douglass, July 25, 1992.

Raymond G. Hunthausen, "Remarks on the Officers and Crew of the Ohio," *Origins* 12, no. 13 (Aug. 9, 1982).

Hunthausen reflections on peace rally from author interview, Feb. 28, 1992.

Community support for the Trident from Brian Casserly, "Confronting the U.S. Navy at Bangor, 1973–1982," *Pacific Northwest Quarterly* (Summer 2004): 130–38; *The Progress*, Aug. 26, 1982; *Seattle P-I*, Aug. 12, 1982.

Information on religious leaders' boat from *Seattle P-I*, Aug. 7, 1982; Hunthausen interview, Feb. 28, 1992; author interviews with Rev. Jim Halfaker, Sept. 17, 2013; Rev. Loren Arnett, Sept. 17, 2013.

Description of a nuclear attack from "Consequences of Nuclear War," a film on website of Ground Zero Center for Nonviolent Action, www.gzcenter.org; Jonathan Schell, "The Fate of the Earth," *The New Yorker* (Feb. 1982).

Militarization of western Washington from Frank A. Fromherz, "Archbishop Raymond Hunthausen's Thought and Practice in Society and Church: A Socio-Historical and Ethical Case Study of Nonviolence," PhD dissertation, Graduate Theological Union, Berkeley, CA, 1990, 4; Casserly, "Confronting the U.S. Navy," 133.

U.S. submarine warfare history and Trident information from author visit to Naval Undersea Museum, Keyport, WA, Sept. 4, 2013; "Ohio Class Submarine," military. discovery. com/.../videos/ohio-class-submarine.htm; "Trident Missile Submarine," www.tv.com/shows/history-alive/trident-missile-submarine; "Trident Facts and Figures—Physicians for Social Responsibility," Washington chapter, psr.org/chapters/Washington/energy-and-peace/trident.html.

Information on Jim Douglass from author interview, July 25, 1992; Hunthausen interview, Feb. 28, 1992; *Honolulu Star Bulletin*, April 20, 1968, May 7, 1968; Ronald G. Musto, *The Catholic Peace Tradition* (New York: Peace Books, 2002), 252–53; George Weigel, *Tranquillitas Ordinis: The Present Failure and Future Promise of American Catholic Thought on War and Peace* (New York: Oxford University Press, 1987), 170–73; Fromherz, "Archbishop Raymond Hunthausen's Thought and Practice," 25.

Background on Pacific Life Community from Douglass interview, July 25, 1992; Matt Dundas, "Post-Vietnam: Non-Violence at Bangor," Anti-Nuclear Special Section, Pacific Northwest Labor and Civil Rights Projects, University of Washington, 2008; website of Ground Zero Center for Nonviolent Action, www.gzcenter.org.

Illegitimacy of nuclear weapons from Rev. Richard McSorley, SJ, "It's a Sin to Build a Nuclear Weapon," US Catholic (Oct. 1976).

Jim Douglass letter from jail. The Progress, Dec. 24, 1976.

On Ground Zero and demonstrations from Douglass interview, July 25, 1992; Hunthausen interview, Feb. 28, 1992; The Progress, May 26, 1978, Nov. 2, 1979; Robert B. Scripko, "A Moral Agent: Bishop as Leader," PhD dissertation, Gonzaga University, 1992, 154.

Reaction to Hunthausen's nuclear stand from Seattle Times, May 18, 1977, and The Progress, May 19, 1978.

On debate over nuclear deterrence and unilateral disarmament from Hunthausen interview, Feb. 28, 1992; Douglass interview, July 25, 1992; author interview with Rev. Peter Chirico, SS, July 24, 1992.

Retreat at Ground Zero from Weigel, Tranquillitas Ordinis, 170–71; Douglass interview, July 25, 1992; Hunthausen interview, Feb. 28, 1992.

Tax resistance speech at PLU from author interviews with Hunthausen, Feb. 28, 1992; Douglass, July 25, 1992; Halfaker, Sept. 17, 2013; Arnett, Sept. 17, 2013; and Rev. Michael G. Ryan, Nov. 23, 1992.

Chapter 2: Tax Protest

Tax resistance speech at PLU from Raymond G. Hunthausen, "Faith and Disarmament," Origins 11, no. 7 (July 2, 1981).

Reaction to tax resistance speech from Seattle P-I, June 17, 18, 19, 20, 1981; The Progress, June 18, 25, 1981, Sept. 3, 1981. Also from microfilm ND1 and ND2 files containing copies of letters to Hunthausen on nuclear disarmament, Archdiocese of Seattle Archives; Hunthausen interview, Feb. 28, 1992.

Bishop Matthiesen and other peace bishops from Weigel, Tranquillitas Ordinis, 263; Hunthausen interview, Feb. 28, 1992; Douglass interview, July 25, 1992; Fromherz, "Archbishop Raymond Hunthausen's Thought and Practice," 198.

Announcement of tax protest from The Progress, Jan. 28, 1981, Seattle Times, June 17, 1981.

Speech at Notre Dame from The Progress, Feb. 4, 1982.

Panel discussion on nuclear weapons at Berkeley from Robert McAfee Brown, Reflections Over the Long Haul: A Memoir (Louisville, KY: Westminster John Knox Press, 2005), 144.

Bethlehem Peace Pilgrimage from Seattle Times, April 7, 10, 1982; regarding federal court case, The Progress, July 15, 1982; Target Seattle, Seattle Times, July 17, 1982.

Ash Wednesday homily from Seattle Times, June 20, 1982.

Background and speech of Navy Secretary John Lehman Jr., from Gregory L. Vistica,

Fall From Glory: The Men Who Sank the U.S. Navy (New York: Touchstone, 1997), 151–52; John Lehman, "The Immorality of Unilateral Disarmament," *Origins* 11, no. 42 (April 1, 1982); *Seattle P-I,* March 8, 9, 1982; *Seattle Times,* March 8, 1982.

Office visit of Vice Admiral J. D. Williams from author interviews with Hunthausen, Feb. 28, 1992; Ryan, Nov. 23, 1992; and Williams, Sept. 26, 2013.

Phone call from Edward Rowny from Ryan interview, Nov. 23, 1992.

Attempted lunch with labor secretary and schoolchildren story from author interview with Rev. Matthew Naumes, Oct. 14, 1992.

Peace blockade against the Trident from *Seattle Times,* Aug. 1, 11, 12, 1982; *Seattle P-I,* Aug. 13, 1982; Dundas, "Post-Vietnam: Non-Violence at Bangor,"; Paul Rogat Loeb, *Hope in Hard Times: America's Peace Movement and the Reagan Era* (Lexington, MA: Lexington Books, D. C. Heath, 1987); "Interview with Kim Wahl, Peace Blockader," by Matt Dundas and Steve Beba, Antiwar and Radical History Project, Pacific Northwest Labor and Civil Rights Projects, University of Washington, 2008; Douglass interview, July 25, 1992

U.S. Catholic bishops' pastoral letter on peace from Hunthausen interview, Feb. 28, 1992; Douglass interview, July 25, 1992; *Seattle Times,* May 1, 3, 4, 6, 7, 1983; Jim Castelli, *The Bishops and the Bomb* (Garden City, NY: Image Books, 1983); Weigel, *Tranquillitas Ordinis,* 257–85; Gerard F. Powers, "The U.S. Bishops and War since the Peace Pastoral," *U.S. Catholic Historian* 27, no. 2 (Spring 2009): 73–96; Luke Hansen, S.J., "The Challenge of Peace Today," *America* (May 3, 2013), http://america-magazine.org/content/all-things/challenge-peace-today.

Bishops' presentations at November 1982 meeting: Hunthausen interview, Feb. 28, 1992; Castelli, *The Bishops and the Bomb,* 113–17; "Presentations of Five Bishops on Proposed War and Peace Pastoral," *Origins* 12, no. 25 (Dec. 2, 1982).

Vatican intervention from Weigel, *Tranquillitas Ordinis,* 275–80; Castelli, *The Bishops and the Bomb,* 130–39; Penny Lernoux, *People of God: The Struggle for World Catholicism* (New York: Penguin Books, 1989), 189–92.

Description of Pio Laghi from Hunthausen interview, Feb. 28, 1992; Ryan interview, Nov. 23, 1992; Lernoux, *People of God,* 68–72.

Chapter 3: Montana Youth

Description and history of Anaconda from author visits on July 17–18, 1993, and July 10, 2013; Laurie Mercier, *Anaconda: Labor, Community, and Culture in Montana's Smelter City* (Urbana: University of Illinois Press, 2001), 10, 78, 128; author interviews with Hunthausen family members; Rev. Jack Morris, SJ, March 17, 1993; Rev. Peter Byrne, MM, Feb. 25, 1993; Al Murray, June 15, 1992.

Information on Anthony and Edna Tuchscherer Hunthausen from author interviews with Rev. Raymond Hunthausen, Feb. 13, 14, 15, 1992; Tony Hunthausen and Marie Hunthausen Walsh, July 16, 1993; Sister Edna Ruth Hunthausen, July 20, 1993; Rev. Jack Hunthausen, July 30, 1993; Art Hunthausen, June 16, 1992; Jeanne Hunthausen Stergar, July 16, 1993, July 10, 2013.

Description of Hunthausen home from author visits, July 16, 1993, July 10, 2013.

Dutch Hunthausen's childhood from above interviews with Hunthausen, other family members, Morris, Murray, Dr. Ed Dolan, and Owen Greenough, Nov. 6, 1992; *The Progress*, Oct. 1, 1987, 10; Hunthausen interview in *Ground Zero* newsletter, Summer 1987.

Accounts of Dutch Hunthausen's social life from above interviews with Hunthausen, family members, Dolan, Greenough, Byrne, and Murray.

The "personality rating" from John Mark Semmens, "A Man Called Dutch: The Lasting Impact of Archbishop Raymond G. Hunthausen on Carroll College," PhD dissertation, Carroll College, 2008.

The road trip to Los Angeles from above author interviews with Hunthausen and Greenough.

Beginnings of Carroll College from Semmens, "A Man Called Dutch," chapters 1, 12.

Coach Simonich and Hunthausen as athlete at Carroll from Hunthausen interview, Feb. 15, 1992; *The Helena Record Herald*, Sept. 6, 1939, Oct. 17, 1939, Sept. 11, 12, and 27, 1940, Oct. 2, 10, and 29, 1940, Nov. 23, 1940; *The Prospector*, Carroll College student paper, Nov. 30, 1939, Nov. 27, 1940, Feb. 27, 1941, Sept. 30, 1942.

Student life at Carroll College, 1939–43, from Hunthausen interview, Feb. 15, 1992; *The Prospector*, April 26, 1940, Sept. 30, 1942; the *Record Herald*, Oct. 8, 1939, Oct. 13, 1940, Dec. 15, 1940.

Hunthausen's fascination with flying from Hunthausen interview, Feb. 15, 1992.

Background on Rev. Bernard Topel from author interviews with Hunthausen, Feb. 15, 1992; Rev. Emmett Kelly, July 23, 1993; Bishop William Skylstad, March 26, 1993; Guido Bugni, June 15, 1992; and Sister Edna Hunthausen, July 20, 1993; *Time* magazine, Nov. 13, 1968; the *Walla Walla Union-Bulletin*, Oct. 14, 1977.

Junior-Senior Dinner Dance from Hunthausen, Feb. 15, 1992; *The Prospector*, April 24, 1942

Making the decision for priesthood from Hunthausen interview, Feb. 15, 1992; Dolan interview, Nov. 6, 1992.

Anthony Hunthausen letter to Ray Hunthausen, Dec. 15, 1945.

The 1943 Carroll College graduation exercises from *The Prospector*, March 26, April 30, and May 21, 1943.

Carroll's war preparations, *The Prospector*, Oct. 30, 1942, Aug. 20, 1943.

Background on St. Edward's Seminary from www.stjames-cathedral.org/pubs/midst/10Feb/archives.htm; *Catalog, St. Edward's Seminary, 1931–1945, 378.797 Ed 9G.*

Seminary life from author interviews with Hunthausen, Feb. 15, 1992; Rev. Joseph Oblinger, July 19, 1993; Rev. Bernard Sullivan, July 15, 1993; *The Harvester*, St. Edward's Seminary quarterly, Spring–Summer 1944 and Summer 1946.

Reaction to A-bomb from author interview with Hunthausen, Feb. 28, 1992; Pacific Magazine, *Seattle Times*, June 20, 1982; Hunthausen address at PLU, "Faith and Disarmament," *Origins* 11, no. 7 (July 2, 1981).

Ordination to priesthood from Hunthausen interview, Feb. 15, 1992; Semmens, "A Man Called Dutch," chapter 3; Dolan interview, Nov. 6, 1992; Sister Edna Hunthausen interview, July 20, 1993.

Chapter 4: Priest, Coach, and College President

About Bishop Gilmore from *The Hilltopper*, Carroll College yearbook, 1947, 1962; *The Prospector*, April 8, 1962; and Kelly interview, July 23, 1993.

Gilmore letter assigning Hunthausen to Carroll from Hunthausen interview, Feb. 15, 1992, and Semmens, "A Man Called Dutch," chapter 3.

Hunthausen academic background from Hunthausen interview, Feb. 15, 1992.

Statistics on faculty numbers at Carroll in 1950s from Semmens, "A Man Called Dutch," chapter 4.

Carroll College culture and dorm life in St. Charles Hall in the 1950s from Hunthausen interview, Feb. 15, 1992; and author interviews with Guido Bugni, June 15, 1992; Rev. Humphrey Courtney, June 17, 1992; Rev. Joseph Harrington, June 16, 1992; Rev. William Greytak, June 17, 1992.

Background on Coach John Gagliardi from *New York Times*, Nov. 19, 2012; *The Prospector*, Nov. 30, 1951, March 5, 1953; Catholic News Service, Oct. 20, 1993.

Building of new football field from interviews with Hunthausen, Feb. 15, 1992; Bugni, June 15, 1992.

Story of Montana Western basketball game from Hunthausen interview, Feb. 15, 1992.

Story of South Dakota Mines football game from interviews with Hunthausen, Feb. 15, 1992; Bugni, June 15, 1992; *The Prospector*, Oct. 23,1953.

Story of Carroll vs. Grizzly Cubs basketball games from Hunthausen interview, Feb. 15, 1992; *Helena Independent Record*, Feb. 7 and 13, 1954.

Deaths of "Doc" Neuman and Msgr. Kavanagh from Hunthausen interview, Feb. 18, 1992; *The Prospector*, April 10, 1957.

Hunthausen homily at Mass of the Holy Spirit from *The Prospector*, Oct. 11, 1957.

Hunthausen building and beautification campaign at Carroll from Hunthausen interview, Feb. 18, 1992; *Independent Record*, May 23, 1957; *The Prospector*, Oct. 11, 1957; Semmens, "A Man Called Dutch," chapter 3; *The Hilltopper*, 1963.

Senator Mansfield visit and wrestling match with Jim Stanaway from Bugni interview, June 15, 1992, and Hunthausen interview, Nov. 19, 2015.

Quotes and material about Al Murray from interview with Murray, June 15, 1992.

Description of Carroll rules after co-eds arrive from Hunthausen interview, Feb. 18, 1992; Harrington interview, June 16, 1992; Greytak interview, June 17, 1992; Bugni interview, June 15, 1992.

On Gilmore seeking an auxiliary from Kelly interview, July 23, 1993

Background on Gilmore's death from interviews with Hunthausen, Feb. 18, 1992; Kelly, July 23, 1993; Oblinger, July 19, 1993; *The Prospector*, April 8, 1962.

Hunthausen's appointment as bishop from Hunthausen interview, Feb. 18, 1992; Greytak interview, June 17, 1992; *Independent Record*, July 11, 1962.

Background on Archbishop Vagnozzi from interviews with Hunthausen, June 28, 1990, Feb. 18, 1992; Robert Blair Kaiser, *Inside the Council* (London: Burns & Oates, 1963), 150–51, 214).

Dr. Ed Dolan at the consecration Mass from interview with Dolan on Nov. 6, 1992.

Chapter 5: Vatican II

Hunthausen's seat at Council from interview with Hunthausen, Feb. 18, 1992.

Summary of Council purpose, achievements, and opening event from: Remi De Roo, *Chronicles of a Vatican II Bishop* (Toronto: Novalis, 2012); Edward P. Hahnenberg, *A Concise Guide to the Documents of Vatican II* (Cincinnati, OH: Franciscan Media, 2007); Gary MacEoin, *What Happened at Rome? The Council and Its Implications for the Modern World* (New York: Echo Books, 1967); John W. O'Malley, *What Happened at Vatican II* (Cambridge, MA: Harvard University Press, 2008), 306–7; Xavier Rynne, *Vatican Council II* (Maryknoll, NY: Orbis Books, 1999); Robert E. Tracy, *American Bishop at the Vatican Council* (New York: McGraw-Hill, 1966).

Bishop Sheen invitation to Gilmore from Kelly interview, July 23, 1993.

Dinner with Anceschis, driving a VW Beetle in Rome from Hunthausen interview, Feb. 18, 1992; Raymond G. Hunthausen, "We Need a Miracle—Expect One: Reminiscences on Vatican II and My Life as a Bishop," *Seattle Theology and Ministry Review* 3 (2003): 6–13; Hunthausen, "Vatican II: Forty Years Later," *In Your Midst*, a journal for St. James Cathedral Parish, Seattle, March 2006.

Curial opposition to the Council from Rynne, *Vatican Council II*, 3.

Papal opposition to modernity from O'Malley, *What Happened at Vatican II*, 58–59, 70.

John XIII's address to the Council from Rynne, *Vatican Council II*; O'Malley, *What Happened at Vatican II*; Tracy, *American Bishop at the Vatican Council*.

Liénart's intervention, the traditionalists, Ottaviani's silencing, and the reformers from Rynne, *Vatican Council II*; O'Malley, *What Happened at Vatican II*; Tracy, *American Bishop at the Vatican Council*; MacEoin, *What Happened at Rome?* and Christopher Hollis, *The Achievements of Vatican II* (New York: Hawthorn Books, 1967).

Pope John's reaction to first business session from Tracy, *American Bishop at the Vatican Council*, 32.

Quotes from Ottaviani on being an old soldier from MacEoin, *What Happened at Rome?* 166; and on planning a revolution from O'Malley, *What Happened at Vatican II*, 68.

Hunthausen reaction to first session from interview with Hunthausen, Feb. 18, 1992.

The daily Mass at the Council and Ethiopian rite from DeRoo, *Chronicles of a Vatican II Bishop*; Tracy, *American Bishop at the Vatican Council*; Rynne, *Vatican Council II*; and Hunthausen interview, Feb. 18, 1992.

Anecdote on incomprehensible Latin from Tracy, *American Bishop at the Vatican Council*, 46.

Use of Latin at Council from Tracy, *American Bishop at the Vatican Council*; Rynne, *Vatican Council II*; O'Malley, *What Happened at Vatican II*.

Hunthausen's afternoons, evenings, and reflections at the Council from Hunthausen interview, Feb. 18, 1982; Tracy, *American Bishop at the Vatican Council*; and author interviews with Bishops George Speltz and Sylvester Treinen, Aug. 24, 1992.

Anecdote about Bishop Speltz' tape recorder from Hunthausen, *Seattle Theology and Ministry Review* 3 (2003): 6–13; Speltz interview, Aug. 24, 1992.

Archbishop Connolly remarks from the Council floor from Rynne, *Vatican Council II*, 527.

Cardinal McIntyre's comment on the Mass from Rynne, *Vatican Council II*, 72.

Religious liberty issue informed by Rynne, *Vatican Council II*; O'Malley, *What Happened at Vatican II*; Hahnenberg, *A Concise Guide to the Documents of Vatican II*; Tracy, *American Bishop at the Vatican Council*; MacEoin, *What Happened at Rome?* and Hunthausen interview, Feb. 18, 1992.

Quote from Ottaviani on war from O'Malley, *What Happened at Vatican II*, 264.

Archbishop Hannan's intervention on nuclear weapons informed by Rynne, *Vatican Council II*; O'Malley, *What Happened at Vatican II*; Tracy, *American Bishop at the Vatican Council*; and MacEoin, *What Happened at Rome?*

Hunthausen thoughts on *Gaudium et Spes* from interview with Hunthausen, Feb. 18, 1992.

Background on Augustinians and Thomists from O'Malley, *What Happened at Vatican II*; and Massimo Faggioli, *Vatican II: The Battle for Meaning* (New York: Paulist Press, 2012).

Paul VI at Council from O'Malley, *What Happened at Vatican II*; Rynne, *Vatican Council II*; and Robert McClory, *Turning Point: The Inside Story of the Papal Birth Control Commission and How* Humanae Vitae *Changed the Life of Patty Crowley and the Future of the Church* (New York: Crossroad, 1995).

Quote on Paul VI and the synod from O'Malley, *What Happened at Vatican II*, 252.

Conclusion of the Council from O'Malley, *What Happened at Vatican II*, 289; Rynne, *Vatican Council II*; and Tracy, *American Bishop at the Vatican Council*.

Hunthausen closing comments from interview with Hunthausen, Feb. 18, 1992.

Chapter 6: Bishop of Helena

Hunthausen's letters on the Council in *Montana Catholic Register* (the *Register*), Dec. 3, 24, 1965.

Hunthausen on Rev. Godfrey Diekmann from interview with Hunthausen, Feb. 18, 1992.

Hunthausen on the laity, the *Register*, May 22, 1964, Sept. 9, 1966, Sept. 1, 1967.

Priest Senate from interview with Hunthausen, Feb. 18, 1992; Oblinger interview, July 19, 1993; the *Register*, Oct. 21, 1966, March 21, Nov. 21, 1969, Jan. 23, 1970, Feb. 18, May 4, 1972.

Diocesan Pastoral Council from interview with Hunthausen, Feb. 18, 1992; the *Register*, March 7, 1969, July 10, 24, 1970; Aug. 7, 1970

Diocesan survey from Hunthausen, Feb. 18, 1992; Oblinger interview, July 19, 1993; the *Register*, Aug. 29, 1969; *The WestMont Word*, Aug. 13, 1972.

Background on Rev. James Provost from *New York Times*, Aug. 29, 1986; Hunthausen interview, Feb. 18, 1992; author interviews with Rev. Tom Haffey, July 20, 1993; Rev. Sarsfield O'Sullivan, July 19, 1993.

Meetings of Region 12 bishops from interview with Hunthausen, Feb. 18, 1992; the

Register, July 16, Sept. 10, 1971, Feb. 11, 18, March 3, 1972, May 3, 1973, March 28, July 18, Dec. 12, 1974; *Seattle Times*, Sept. 1, 4, 1971, Feb. 26, 1972.

Montana abortion bill defeated, the *Register,* Oct. 2, Dec. 11, 1970, Feb. 5, 12, 1971, Feb. 1, 1973.

About Project Equality, the *Register,* Oct. 15, 1971.

About Native Americans, the *Register, ,* April 19, 1973; *The WestMont Word*, March 20, 1975.

Joint ecumenical service in Butte, the *Register*, April 19, 1968; Episcopal bishop, the *Register,* Sept. 17, 1968; Montana Association of Churches, the *Register,* Oct. 17, 1969; *The WestMont Word*, Dec. 14, 1972.

Priest Senate statements on MX missile and FBI File, the *Register,* May 16, 1969, March 20, 1970; *The Progress,* Oct. 1, 1987.

Story of Msgr. Michael English and the altar, author interviews with Jack Hunthausen, July 30, 1993; Oblinger, July 13, 1993; and Sullivan, July 15, 1993.

Story of Msgr. Edward Gilmore and the altar, Oblinger interview, July 13, 1993.

Quote about Hunthausen's listening skills from author interview with Rev. Emmett O'Neill, July 22, 1993.

Letter to Mrs. A. B. Chenovick of April 6, 1970, from Diocese of Helena Archives.

Story of neurotic, vicious lady from O'Sullivan interview, July 19, 1993.

Comments on drinking priests and pedophilia from Hunthausen interview, Feb. 18, 1992; Haffey interview, July 20, 1993; O'Sullivan interview, July 19, 1993; and Oblinger interview, July 13, 1993

Bankruptcy filing by Diocese of Helena from the *Montana Standard,* Feb. 1, 2014.

Statistics on students, lay and women religious teachers in Helena Diocese from the *Register*, March 13, 1964; Jan. 17, Feb. 29, 1969,

School costs and closures from author interviews with Hunthausen, Feb. 18, 1992; Jack Hunthausen, July 30, 1993; Greytak, June 17, 1992; the *Register*, March 3, 1967.

Comment from Msgr. Edward Gilmore on Butte schools from the *Register*, Oct. 11, 1968.

No state aid for Catholic education, the *Register*, Feb. 14, 1969.

Sacrificial giving plan, the *Register*, Sept. 10, 1965; Feb. 10, 1967; Oblinger interview, July 19, 1993.

Fundraising in southern California, USC–Notre Dame football game, and Benjamin Swig story from Hunthausen interview, June 7, 1992.

Correspondence from Gov. Edmund "Pat" Brown and Benjamin Swig from file box labeled "Lay Friends Outside Diocese to 1972 RGH Personal," Helena diocesan archives.

School consolidation and closure in Butte and Helena from interviews with Hunthausen , Feb. 18, 1992; Jack Hunthausen, July 30, 1993; Oblinger. July 19, 1993; the *Register*, March 14, May 9, 1969.

School closures in Anaconda, the *Register*, Sept. 17, 1969; Jan. 21 and Dec. 28, 1972; Jan. 18, 1973; Feb. 22, 1973; *The Westmont Word*, Feb. 22 and May 31, 1973.

Graduation address by Rev. Bill Stanaway, *The Westmont Word*, May 31, 1973.

On Hunthausen and the Guatemala mission, interview with Hunthausen, Feb. 18, 29, 1992; the *Register*, May 17, July 12, 1963; March 27, 1964; April 1, 1966.

On 1980 trip to Peru from interview with Byrne, Feb. 25, 1993.

Hunthausen letter to Sheila McShane of March 21, 1974, Helena diocesan archives.

Statistics on number of priests ordained in western Montana by Hunthausen, Helena diocesan archives.

Quotes from Hunthausen on priests leaving, from interview with Hunthausen, Feb. 18, 1992.

Background on Michael Miles from Hunthausen interview, Feb. 18, 1992; Michael Miles, *Love Is Always* (New York: Avon Books, 1986), quote from p. 118.

Comments on Michael Miles from interviews with O'Sullivan, July 19, 1993; O'Neill, July 22, 1993; and Oblinger, July 13, 1993.

Hunthausen's skiing and golfing from interview with Kelly, July 23, 1993.

Skiing anecdote about Charlie from interview with O'Neill, July 22, 1993.

Pilgrimage to St. Mary's Peak, the *Register*, Aug. 5. 1966.

Horse packing in the Bob Marshall Wilderness from Hunthausen interview, Oct. 22, 1992.

Correspondence with wrangler Pat Timmons, file box labeled "Lay Friends in Diocese to 1972," Helena diocesan archives.

Hunthausen's appointment to Seattle, Hunthausen interview, Feb. 18, 1992.

On Archbishop Jean Jadot, *National Catholic Reporter*, Jan. 21, 2009; *New York Times*, Jan. 22, 2009.

Jadot's questionnaire from Thomas Reese, "The Selection of Bishops," *America* (Aug. 25, 1984): 65–72.

Bishop profile sought by Seattle priests from Scripko, "A Moral Agent," 58.

Chapter 7: Archbishop of Seattle

Installation ceremony at Seattle Center Arena from author interviews with Hunthausen, Feb. 27, May 12, 1992; Rev. David Jaeger, Sept. 21, 1992; Haffey, July 20, 1993; *Seattle Times*, May 23, 1975; *The Progress*, May 16, 30, 1975.

Unchurched Washington State from: http://usatoday30.usatoday.com/life/2002/2002-03-07-church-free.htm.

Early Catholic history in western Washington and first bishops from Patricia O'Connell Killen (edited by Christine M. Taylor), *Abundance of Grace: The History of the Archdiocese of Seattle, 1850–2000* (Archdiocese of Seattle, 2000); Wilfred P. Schoenberg, *A History of the Catholic Church in the Pacific Northwest, 1743–1983* (Washington, DC: Pastoral Press, 1987).

Phone anecdote about Bishop Shaughnessy from author interview with Rev. William Gallagher, Sept. 27, 1994.

About Archbishop Connolly from Killen, *Abundance of Grace*; *New York Times*, April 20, 1991; author interviews with Maury Sheridan, Feb. 17, 1993; Rev. Mike McDermott, July 16, 1992; Rev. Loren Arnett, Sept. 17, 2013; Jaeger, Sept. 21, 1992; and Ryan, Sept. 6, 1992.

Connolly and Mike McKay's wedding from author interview with McKay, Sept. 30, 1994.

Connolly and Gov. Albert D. Rosellini from http://m.columbian.com/news/2013/jun/13/fbi-files-show-disdain-for-former-washington-gov-r/.

Hunthausen contrasted to Connolly from author interviews with John Pinette, Feb. 11, 1993; Jaeger, Sept. 21, 1992.

Hunthausen management style from author interviews with Don Espen, March 11, 1993; Sheridan, Feb, 17, 1993; McDermott, July 16, 1992; Jaeger, Sept. 21, 1992; and Hunthausen, Feb. 27, 1992.

Story of boy with the tin plate from Hunthausen interview, Oct. 12, 1992.

Bicentennial Project and Call to Action from *New York Times*, Oct. 22, 1976, June 16, 1977; *The Progress*, Feb. 6, Oct. 29, Nov. 5, 1976, Sept. 19, 1975, March 18, 1977; Hunthausen interview, Feb. 28, 1992.

National Opinion Research Center data on Catholic participation and belief from *New York Times*, June 16, 1977.

Reform and action plans in Seattle archdiocese from *Seattle Times*, Nov. 10, 1979; *The Progress*, March 18, June 17, 1977; Hunthausen interview, Feb. 28, 1992; McDermott interview, July 16, 1992.

Reilly meeting and working with Hunthausen from author interviews with Rev. Larry Reilly, Sept. 4, 1992; Hunthausen, Feb. 29, 1992.

Ryan meeting and working with Hunthausen on seminary issue from Ryan interview, Sept. 6, 1992; Hunthausen interview, Feb. 27, 1992.

Closing of the seminary from *The Progress*, Jan. 21, 1977, Jan. 12, 1979; interviews with Skylstad, March 26, 1993; Jaeger, Sept. 21, 1992; Pinette, Feb. 11, 1993.

Archdiocesan priestly formation program from *The Progress*, Jan. 21, April 22, 1977; Ryan interview, Sept. 6, 1992.

Background on Bishop Walsh from Schoenberg, *A History of the Catholic Church in the Pacific Northwest*; interviews with Hunthausen, Feb. 27, 1992; Pinette, Feb, 11, 1993.

George Kotolaris story from *Seattle Times*, Sept. 18, 1987, March 29, 1990; *The Progress*, April 5, 1990; Hunthausen interview, Jan. 11, 1991.

Hunthausen dream and "wow" experience in Canadian Rockies from interviews with Hunthausen, July 18, 1993; Sister Edna Hunthausen, July 20, 1993.

Statement on "The Morality of Being a Single Issue Person," from *The Progress*, July 4, 1980.

Hunthausen protest at Everett abortion clinic from *The Progress*, Nov. 24, 1983.

Hunthausen break with Protestant clerics on abortion aid ban from *Seattle P-I*, Oct. 24, 1984.

Hunthausen on abortion and Catholic conscience, *Seattle P-I*, Oct. 27, 1984.

Abortion and the United Way decision from Hunthausen interviews, April 24, May 12, 1992; *Seattle P-I*, Oct. 27, 1984; *The Progress*, Oct. 1, 1976, Oct. 6, 13, 1988; *Seattle Times*, Oct. 5, Nov. 4, 1988.

Archdiocesan interaction with Planned Parenthood from Reilly interview, Sept. 4, 1992; Chirico interview, July 24, 1992.

Pastoral letter on women from interviews with Hunthausen, Feb. 27, 28, 1992; Skylstad, March 26, 1993; Sister Diana Bader, October 1992; *The Progress*, Oct. 2, 16, 23, 1980.

Story on Andrew Prouty from Marnie Beattie-Prouty: *Sweet Burdens on My Heart* (Paradiso, 1995), quote from p. 388.

Text of Vatican document *Persona Humana* at: http://www.vatican.va/roman_curia/congregations/cfaith/documents/rc_con_cfaith_doc_19751229_persona-humana_en.html.

Hunthausen on homosexuality, from interview with Hunthausen, Feb. 29, 1992.

Establishing Dignity in the Seattle archdiocese from *The Progress*, March 10, 1978; Gary L. Atkins, *Gay Seattle: Stories of Exile and Belonging* (Seattle: University of Washington Press, 2003), 272–75, 279.

Quote from Pat Roche of Dignity from author interview with Roche, Sept. 9, 1992.

Hunthausen letter opposing discrimination against gays, *The Progress*, July 1, 1977.

Hunthausen endorsement of Gay Pride Week, Atkins, *Gay Seattle*, 282.

Letters to *The Progress* on gay rights, *The Progress*, July 8, 15, 1977.

Series on "The Homosexual and the Church," *The Progress*, March 3, 10, 17, 1978.

"The Prejudice against Homosexuals and the Ministry of the Church," a WSCC document, from *The Progress*, June 16, 1983.

Hunthausen meeting with the Dorian Society, Atkins, *Gay Seattle*, 284.

Hunthausen meetings with Dignity members and consultation on Dignity Mass from interviews with Hunthausen, Feb. 29, 1992; Sheridan, Feb. 17, 1993; Roche, Sept. 9, 1992.

Hunthausen comments on homosexuality and videotaped remarks to Dignity members from *The Progress*, Sept. 1, 8, 1983.

Protests and ad against Dignity from *Seattle Times*, Sept. 3, 1983; *The Progress*, Sept. 8, 1983.

Chapter 8: The Visitation

Background on Archbishop Hickey from interview with Hickey, Nov. 2, 1983; *Washington Post*, Oct. 25, 2004; *The Independent*, Oct. 28, 2004.

Hunthausen's efforts to understand the visitation from interviews with author, March 4, April 23, 1992; Hunthausen letter to Archbishop Laghi, May 27, 1983; Laghi letter to Hunthausen, June 24, 1983.

Hunthausen conversations with Hickey, Skylstad, Jack Hunthausen, and Edna Hunthausen from author interviews with Hunthausen, March 4, 1992; Skylstad, March 26, 1993; Edna Hunthausen, July 20, 1993.

Hunthausen meeting in Chicago with Hickey from Hunthausen interview, March 4, 1992; *Seattle Times*, July 12, 1980.

Background on *The Wanderer*, www.thewandererpress.com, and Catholics United for the Faith, www.cuf.org; *The Progress*, Nov. 29, 1984.

On Erven Park and Danny Barrett from *The Progress*, Nov. 29, 1984; *Seattle P-I*, Nov. 4, 8, 1983; *Seattle Times*, Nov. 8, 1983; *National Catholic Reporter*, Oct. 3, 1986.

Interview with the Rev. William Ogden from *Seattle P-I*, Nov. 5, 1983.

Frank Morriss address at Seattle University from taped recording of his presentation, Aug. 8, 1983.

Chirico's explanation of Catholic teaching from Chirico interview, July 24, 1992; *Seattle P-I*, Nov. 5, 1983

Hunthausen's meetings with Bishop Levada, Cardinals Baggio and Ratzinger, and Pope John Paul II in Rome in September 1983 from Hunthausen interviews, April 23, May 31, 1990, March 4, 1992; *Memoirs/Reflections*, No. 1041, unpublished writings of Bishop Nicolas E. Walsh, Catholic Diocese of Boise Archives.

Background on Cardinal Baggio, http://www.independent.co.uk/news/people/obituary-cardinal-sebastiano-baggio-1499403.html.

Comment from Archbishop Weakland from Hunthausen interview, March 4, 1992; author interview with Weakland, May 14, 1992.

John Paul II's address to bishops at September 1983 *ad limina* visit from *Origins* 13, no. 14 (Sept. 15, 1983).

Bishop Kenny's and Hunthausen's exchanges with John Paul II from Hunthausen interviews, April 23, 1990, March 1, 1995.

Hunthausen and Hickey announcements of the visitation from *Origins* 13, no. 22 (Nov. 10, 1983).

Hickey arrival in Seattle witnessed by author; *The Progress*, Nov. 3, 1983; *Seattle P-I*, Nov. 3, 1983; *Seattle Times*, Nov. 3, 4, 1984.

Hickey's visitation interview with Hunthausen from Hunthausen interview, March 7, 1992.

Information on Hickey interviews with Hunthausen critics from *The Progress*, Nov. 29, 1984; *Seattle P-I*, Nov. 4, 8, 1983.

Laghi's comment on "mean-spirited criticism" from his letter to Hunthausen, Nov. 14, 1985, *Origins* 15, no. 8.

Hickey interviews with Rev. Ed Holen and Naumes from Naumes interview, Oct. 14, 1992.

Information on Hickey interviews from author interviews with Bader, October 1992; Jaeger, Sept. 21, 1992; Chirico, July 24, 1992; McDermott, July 16, 1992; Michael Reichert, May 3, 1996; Ryan, Sept. 6, 1992; and Reilly, Sept. 24, 1992, April 7, 2013.

Hickey's comments on leaving Seattle from *Seattle P-I*, Nov. 9, 1983; *Seattle Times*, Nov. 9, 1983.

Letter of Dec. 12, 1983 from Ratzinger to Hunthausen ending Hickey's visitation from *The Progress*, Jan. 26, 1984.

Letter of Jan. 26, 1984 from Ratzinger to Hunthausen regarding Vatican concerns from private files of Rev. Michael G. Ryan.

Hunthausen's meeting with Ratzinger in Dallas in February 1984 and imprimatur for *Sexual Morality* from Hunthausen, March 7, 1992.

Anecdote of Hunthausen conversation with Walsh at Carroll College from Walsh *Memoir/Reflections*, No. 1051.

Laghi's proposal of a coadjutor bishop with special faculties from Laghi letter of Oct. 1, 1984 to Hunthausen and Hunthausen's letter of response of Oct. 14, 1984 from Ryan files.

Hunthausen's heart attack and recovery from Hunthausen interview, June 7, 1992, and author interview with Marianne Coté, June 12, 2013.

Laghi's admission that the Hunthausen matter was out of his hands and regional bishops' reaction from Walsh *Memoirs/Reflections*, No. 1094.

Laghi's request for auxiliary bishops for Seattle in his letter of April 19, 1985 to Hunthausen from Ryan files.

Ryan's meeting with Laghi in New York City and dining with Wuerl from Ryan interview, Sept. 6, 1992.

Wuerl's appointment from Hunthausen interview, March 7, 1992; Laghi letter of July 9, 1985 to Hunthausen insisting on special faculties for Wuerl from Ryan files.

Hunthausen, Hurley, and Ryan meeting in Spokane, drafting of Hunthausen response to Laghi rejecting special faculties, and Hunthausen refusal to meet Wuerl from Hunthausen interview, March 7, 1992; Ryan interview, Sept. 6, 1992; and Hunthausen letter of July 15, 1985 to Laghi from Ryan files.

Hunthausen and Hurley meetings with Rev. James A. Coriden and with Laghi and Hickey at nunciature from Hunthausen interview, March 7, 1992.

Laghi letter to Hunthausen of Oct. 7, 1985 giving primary responsibility in five ministry areas to Wuerl from Ryan files.

The Ratzinger letter to Hunthausen of Sept. 30, 1985 listing Vatican concerns from *Origins* 17, no. 3 (June 4, 1987).

Hunthausen reaction to Ratzinger letter from interviews with Hunthausen March 7, April 24, 1992.

Hunthausen rejecting special faculties for Wuerl in Oct. 23, 1985 letter to Laghi from Ryan files.

Background on Hunthausen meeting with Wuerl in Washington, DC, in November 1985 from Hunthausen interview, March 7, 1992.

Laghi letter of Nov. 14, 1985 closing the Vatican investigation and Hunthausen letter of Nov. 26, 1985 expressing gratitude from *The Progress*, Nov. 28, 1985.

Hunthausen agreement to compromise on special faculties from his letter to Laghi of Dec. 2, 1985 in Ryan files; Ryan interview, Sept. 6, 1992; *Origins* 16, no. 21 (Nov. 6, 1986).

Ryan trip of November 1985 to Pittsburgh from Ryan interview, Sept. 6, 1992.

Reaction to Wuerl appointment from *The Progress*, Jan. 9, Feb. 6, 1986; *Seattle*

Times, Dec. 4, 1985; Walsh *Reflections/Memoirs*, No. 1123; *National Catholic Reporter*, Dec. 13, 1985.

Bishop Wuerl's ordination, banquet, and papal audience in Rome from *The Progress*, Jan. 9, 1986; "Wuerl Episcopal Ordination" video, Jan. 6, 1986, Vatican television; Pinette interview, Feb. 11, 1993

Hunthausen meeting with Gantin from Hunthausen interviews, March 7, April 23, 1992; Gantin obituary, *Catholic News Service*, May 14, 2008.

Hunthausen reading aloud the Ratzinger letter from Hunthausen interview, April 23, 1992; *The Progress*, May 15, 1986.

Wuerl's first days in Seattle from *The Progress*, Jan. 30, Feb. 6, 1986; Hunthausen, April 24, 1992; Pinette interview, Feb. 11, 1993; McDermott interview, July 16, 1992; *Seattle P-I*, Feb. 1, 1986; *Seattle Times*, Feb. 1, 1986.

Background on gay rights legislation from *Seattle Times*, March 18, 1986.

Disagreement over final authority on gay rights issue from author interviews with Don Hopps, Jan. 3, 1992; Hunthausen, March 7, 1992; Ryan, Sept. 6, 1992; McDermott, July 16, 1992.

Chapter 9: The Explanation

Anecdote on Vatican making its point from Msgr. George A. Kelly, *Battle for the American Church Revisited* (San Francisco: Ignatius Press, 1995), 91.

Background on Pope John Paul II from George Weigel, *Witness to Hope* (New York: HarperCollins, 1999) and *The End and the Beginning* (New York: Doubleday, 2010); Penny Lernoux, *People of God* (New York: Penguin Books, 1989); Kenneth A. Briggs, *Holy Siege: The Year that Shook Catholic America* (New York: HarperCollins, 1992); John Wilkins, "The Odd Couple: Canonizing John XXIII and John Paul II," *Commonweal*, March 31, 2014; and http://www.nationalcatholicreporter.org/update/conclave/jp_obit_main.htm.

Background on Cardinal Joseph Ratzinger from Lernoux, *People of God*; John L. Allen Jr., *Pope Benedict XVI: A Biography of Joseph Ratzinger* (New York: Continuum, 2000), 23, 31, 49, 117; Matthew Fox, *The Pope's War* (New York: Sterling Ethos, 2011), 17-18.

Comment from Archbishop Jadot on John Paul II's appointments as bishops from Thomas J. Reese, *Archbishop: Inside the Power Structure of the American Catholic Church* (New York: Harper & Row, 1989), 93.

Quote from Ratzinger on North America from http://www.catholicscholars.org/PDF-Files/v8n2mar1985.pdf.

Signing of U.S.–Vatican diplomatic relations from research by John B. Driscoll available at www.stewardmagazine.com and Confidential Memorandum from Robert C. McFarlane to President Reagan regarding meeting with Vatican Secretary of State Cardinal Casaroli, November 22, 1983, Reagan Presidential Archives.

On William A. Wilson from Lernoux, *People of God*, 72; *National Catholic Reporter*, Oct. 21, 1983.

The Vatican–U.S. alliance from *Catholic News Service*, Nov. 17, 2004; Carl Bernstein, "The Holy Alliance: Ronald Reagan and John Paul II," *Time*, Feb. 24, 1992.

Reagan national security directives on destabilizing USSR and weapons buildup from http://www.fas.org/irp/offdocs/nsdd/nsdd-32.pdf; http://www.fas.org/irp/offdocs/nsdd/nsdd-75.pdf.

Acknowledgment of receiving U.S. confidential report from personal letter of Archbishop Laghi to William Clark, February 9, 1983, Bishops' Letters—October 1982 (4), Box 90745, Richard C. Morris File, Ronald Reagan Library.

Ambassador Wilson's list of troublesome bishops from Reese, *Archbishop,* 12.

Reagan officials' meeting with the bishops from Jim Castelli, *The Bishops and the Bomb* (Garden City, NY: Image Books, 1983); letter from Defense Secretary Weinberger, *New York Times,* Oct. 4, 1982; letter from William P. Clark to Archbishop Bernardin, Nov. 16, 1982, http://www.nuclearfiles.org/menu/key-issues/ethics/issues/eligious/clark-archbishop-bernadin_print.htm.

Information on U.S. bishops' executives meeting at Vatican and third draft of pastoral from Lernoux, *People of God,* 43–44; Castelli, *The Bishops and the Bomb,* 156.

Background on Reagan administration acceptance of peace pastoral from *New York Times,* April 7, 1983; Lernoux, *People of God,* 71.

Ratzinger quotations on bishops' conferences from Cardinal Joseph Ratzinger with Vittorio Messori, *The Ratzinger Report* (San Francisco: Ignatius Press, 1985), 59-60.

Division and confusion in U.S. church from Msgr. George A. Kelly, *The Crisis of Authority, John Paul II and the American Bishops* (Chicago: Regnery Gateway, 1982), 46.

Ratzinger citation on homosexuality from *The Ratzinger Report,* 87.

Vatican doctrine on homosexuality issued by the Congregation for the Doctrine of the Faith, "On the Pastoral Care of Homosexual Persons," *Origins* 16, no. 22 (Nov. 13, 1986).

Pope Benedict and homosexuality from John Thavis, *The Vatican Diaries* (New York: Penguin, 2013), 264–68.

On Rev. Enrique Rueda, his links with Reagan backers, including William Wilson, from Allen, *Pope Benedict XVI,* 154; Lernoux, *People of God,* 175–76; Wilson telex to Michael Hornblower, Sept. 23, 1982, Special Collections Archives, Georgetown University; Enrique Rueda, *The Homosexual Network, Private Lives and Public Policy* (Old Greenwich, CT: Devin Adair, 1982); and research by Driscoll at www.stewardmagazine.com.

Wilson meeting with Ratzinger from telex dated March 22, 1983 by Hornblower to Wilson, Wilson correspondence, Special Collections Archives, Georgetown University.

Information on Bishop Sullivan, including his biography, the investigation and the letters to Bishops Malone and Hunthausen from Phyllis Theroux, *The Good Bishop* (Maryknoll, NY: Orbis Books, 2013); on his peace stand from "The Bishops and the Bomb," a Dutch television show broadcast April 11, 1982; Castelli, *The Bishops and the Bomb,* 53; *Seattle Times,* Nov. 5, 1983; on special faculties awarded Auxiliary Bishop Foley from Theroux, *The Good Bishop;* author interviews with Sullivan and Steve Neill, associate editor of *The Catholic Virginian,* Nov. 4, 1993.

Chapter 10: The Humiliation

Culture clash between Hunthausen's and Wuerl's views of the church from McDermott interview, July 16, 1992; Bader interview, October 1992; Espen interview, March 11, 1993; author interview with Patrick Sursely, Aug. 12, 1993; Naumes interview, Oct. 14, 1992; Pinette interview, Feb. 11, 1993.

Hunthausen remarks and reception at April 1986 meeting of National Federation of Priests' Councils (NFPC), *Seattle Times*, April 19, 1986.

Vatican letter of reprimand received by Bishop Murphy regarding NFPC award from author interview with Murphy, Dec. 18, 1992.

Hunthausen conversation with Archbishop Laghi at bishops' meeting at Collegeville from Hunthausen, April 23, 1992

Hunthausen and other reaction to Michael Miles's book from Hunthausen interview, Feb. 21, 1992; *Origins* 16, no. 10 (Aug. 14, 1986).

Hunthausen conversation with Wuerl and letter from Cardinal Gantin from Hunthausen interview, April 23, 1992.

Hunthausen's disclosure of Wuerl's special faculties from VCM 735, video of Hunthausen, Wuerl press conference on Sept. 4, 1986, and VCM 693, video of "Real to Reel" television program of Sept. 13, 1986, Public Affairs Department, Archdiocese of Seattle; *The Progress*, Sept. 11, 1986.

Reaction to Wuerl's special faculties from *Seattle Times*, Sept. 5, 1986.

Rev. Theodore Hesburgh letter of Sept. 8, 1986 to Hunthausen from Ryan files.

Information on Concerned Catholics from *Seattle Times*, Sept. 6, 1986; author interviews with Sister Carol Ann McMullen, Oct. 21, 1992; Jaeger interview, Oct. 2, 1992.

Meeting of Hunthausen and Wuerl with archdiocesan priests at St. Thomas Center on Sept. 12, 1986 from *The Progress*, Sept. 18, 1986; Naumes interview, Oct. 14, 1992; Hunthausen interview, April 24, 1992; Ryan interview, Sept. 6, 1992.

Wuerl letter to archdiocesan priests from *Origins* 16, no. 17 (Oct. 9, 1986); *The Progress*, Sept. 25, 1986.

Concerned Catholics petition from *Seattle P-I*, Sept. 19, 1986.

Installation of Bishop Levada and meeting of Pacific Northwest bishops in Portland from *Seattle Times*, Sept. 27, 1986; *The Progress*, Sept. 25, 1986; *National Catholic Reporter*, Oct. 3, 1986; Skylstad interview, March 26, 1993; Treinen interview, Aug. 24, 1992.

Meeting of Hunthausen and Wuerl with priests and archdiocesan leaders at St. Thomas Center on Sept. 26, 1986 from *The Progress*, Oct. 2, 16, 1986; Walsh *Memoirs/ Reflections*, including "Agenda, Notes and Statements from Archdiocesan Meeting of Archbishop, Bishop, Presbyterate, Consultative Bodies, Central Agency Managers," Sept. 26, 1986; McDermott interview, July 16, 1992; Jaeger interview, Sept. 21, 1992; *National Catholic Reporter*, Oct. 10, 1986; author interview with Cindy Wooden, Sept. 30, 1993.

Convocation at Kennedy High School from *Seattle Times*, Nov. 3, 1986; *Seattle P-I*, Nov. 3, 1986.

Letters from Concerned Catholics and women religious in support of Hunthausen from *Seattle Times*, Nov. 4, 1986; *Seattle P-I*, Nov. 5, 1986.

Rev. Dale Turner op-ed on Hunthausen from *Seattle Times*, Sept. 27, 1986.

National reaction to Seattle situation from *Seattle Times*, Oct. 12, 1986; *The Progress*, Oct. 16, 1986; *National Catholic Reporter*, Oct. 3, 1986; Lernoux, *People of God*, 219.

Hunthausen family letter to bishops from *The Progress*, Oct. 23, 1986; Edna Hunthausen, July 20, 1993; Jack Hunthausen, July 30, 1993; Marie Hunthausen, July 16, 1993.

Anecdote about Hunthausen's mother and the pope from Hunthausen interview, May 21, 1992.

Hunthausen letter to western Washington Catholics from *The Progress*, Oct. 16, 1986.

Bishop Gumbleton cancelling a Seattle appearance from *Seattle Times*, Nov. 1, 1986.

Hunthausen at funeral of Bishop Topel from *National Catholic Reporter*, Nov. 7, 1986.

Hunthausen's initial reaction to Vatican chronology from Hunthausen interview, April 24, 1992.

The Vatican "Chronology of Recent Events in the Archdiocese of Seattle" from *Origins* 16, no. 21 (Nov. 11, 1986).

Hunthausen response to Vatican chronology from *Origins* 16, no. 23, (Nov. 20, 1986).

Walsh's trip to Rome from his *Memoirs/Reflections*, No. 1000.004, Dec. 16, 1986; his letters to Pope John Paul II, dated Nov. 4, 1986, Oct. 20–27, 1986, Diocese of Boise Archives.

Drafting of Hunthausen's address to the U.S. bishops from Ryan interview, Sept. 11, 1995; Skylstad interview, March 26, 1993; Hunthausen interview, April 24, 1992.

Opening address of Bishop Malone to U.S. bishops' conference from *National Catholic Reporter*, Nov. 21, 1986.

Laghi's address to U.S. bishops' conference from *National Catholic Reporter*, Nov. 10, 21, 1986; Briggs, *Holy Siege*, 85.

Anecdotes on what Hunthausen should tell bishops from Ryan interview, Sept. 11, 1995; Hunthausen interview, April 24, 1992; Speltz interview, Aug. 24, 1992.

Demonstrators at U.S. bishops' conference meeting from *Seattle Times*, Nov. 11, 1986; *New York Times*, Nov. 13, 1986.

Story about sitting next to Hunthausen from author interview with Bishop Ken Untener, June 9, 1992.

Hunthausen address at the U.S. bishops' conference from *Origins* 16, no. 23 (Nov. 20, 1986); Hunthausen interview, April 24, 1992; Briggs, *Holy Siege*, 88–93; Walsh, *Memoirs/Reflections*, No. 1000.006, Dec. 17, 1986.

Statement by Malone, Hunthausen's and other bishops' comments from the floor from Briggs, *Holy Siege*, 86–87, 93–94; unpublished notes of Bishop Raymond A. Lucker from the executive sessions of the U.S. bishops' conference, Nov. 11, 12, 1986; *Origins* 16, no. 23 (Nov. 20, 1986).

Hunthausen reaction at Region 12 bishops' meeting in Washington from Walsh, *Memoirs/Reflections*, No. 1000.006, Dec. 17, 1986.

Remarks by Bishop Kenny from *New York Times*, Nov. 13, 1986.

About the nunciature reception from Hunthausen interview, April 24, 1992.

Hunthausen reception at SeaTac airport from *Seattle P-I*, Nov. 14, 1986.

Hunthausen press conference in Seattle on Nov. 14, 1986 from *Seattle Times*, Nov. 15, 1986; *New York Times*, Nov. 14, 1986; VCM 703, videotape of the Nov. 14, 1986 press conference, Public Affairs Department, Archdiocese of Seattle.

Background on chancery environment from Reilly interview, Sept. 24, 1992; Pinette interview, Feb. 11, 1993.

Attempted chancery reconciliation service from Coté interview, June 12, 2013.

Prayer services for church in western Washington from *The Progress*, Dec. 11, 1986.

Hunthausen's prostate surgery from *The Progress*, Dec. 18, 1986; Hunthausen interview, April 12, 1992; VL 697, video of press conference with Ryan and Dr. Jerry Minzell, Dec. 17, 1986, Public Affairs Department, Archdiocese of Seattle.

Telegram from Pope John Paul II from Ryan interview, Sept. 11, 1995.

Chapter 11: The Coadjutor Compromise

Announcement of Vatican commission and its initial meeting in Dallas from *New York Times*, Jan. 30, 1987, and Hunthausen interview, April 24, 1992.

Reilly's encounter with Cardinal O'Connor from Reilly interview, April 7, 2013.

Commission meeting in Menlo Park from Ryan interview, Sept. 11, 1995; Skylstad interview, March 26, 1993; Treinen interview, Aug. 24, 1992; Jaeger interview, Sept. 21, 1992; McDermott interview, July 16, 1992.

Commission meetings of March 12 and April 8, 1987 in Chicago from Hunthausen interview, April 24, 1992.

Commission's report on Archdiocese of Seattle from *Origins* 17, no. 3 (June 4, 1987).

Archbishop Quinn's and Cardinal Bernardin's overtures to Ryan from Ryan interview, Sept. 11, 1995.

Archdiocesan reaction to Hunthausen retirement story in *National Catholic Register* from Ryan interview, Sept. 11, 1995; *Seattle P-I*, April 15, 16, 1987; Briggs, *Holy Siege*, 285.

Hunthausen at anti-Trident protest at Bangor from *Seattle Times*, April 16, 1987.

Hunthausen response to the commission's report from McDermott interview, July 16, 1992; Hunthausen letter to Bernardin of April 22, 1987 from Ryan's files.

Response of priests, nuns, lay Catholics to the commission's report from *The Progress*, April 23, 30, May 7, 21, 1987; *Seattle P-I*, April 21, 22, 1987; *Seattle Times*, April 26, May 15, 1987.

Background on nominees for coadjutor archbishop from Hunthausen interviews, April 24, May 21, 1992; Skylstad interview, March 16, 1993; and Briggs, *Holy Siege*, 337–38.

Hunthausen conversation with Fox from Hunthausen interview, May 21, 1992; Ryan interview, Sept. 11, 1995.

Reaction to Hunthausen's acceptance of commission's settlement from Ryan interview, Sept. 11, 1995; *Seattle Times*, May 27, 1987.

Hunthausen comments on theology of struggle from author interview with Sister Joyce Cox, BVM, July 5, 2013.

Background on the selection of Bishop Murphy as coadjutor from Murphy interview, Dec. 18, 1992; Ryan interview, Sept. 11, 1995; Briggs, *Holy Siege*, 341.

Revelation of Murphy's appointment in Great Falls from Murphy interview, Dec. 18, 1992; Walsh *Memoirs/Reflections*, No. 1000.022, July 6, 1987.

Background on Murphy and introductory press conference from *The Progress*, May 28, 1987; *Seattle Times*, May 28, 1987; author interview with Rev. Andrew Greeley, Nov. 20, 1989; VC 788, VC 778, videotapes of press conferences of Archbishops Hunthausen and Murphy, May 27 and July 15, 1987, Public Affairs Department, Archdiocese of Seattle.

Introduction of Murphy to archdiocesan priests from *Seattle Times*, May 30, 1987; Jaeger interview, Sept. 21, 1992.

Statistics on church observance and giving in the Seattle archdiocese from *Seattle P-I*, April 16, 1987.

Wuerl farewell at Holy Rosary Church from *Seattle P-I*, June 8, 1987; *Seattle Times*, June 8, 1987.

Installation of Bishop Wuerl in Pittsburgh from *Seattle Times*, March 26, 1988; VC 855, videotape of Wuerl installation in Pittsburgh, March 25, 1988, Public Affairs Department, Archdiocese of Seattle.

Hunthausen-Murphy working relationship from Hunthausen interview, May 21, 1992; Cox interview, July 5, 2013.

Presentations of U.S. bishops to Pope John Paul II in Los Angeles from Briggs, *Holy Siege*, 535–43.

Ad limina visit to Rome in December 1988 from Hunthausen interview, May 21, 1992; *The Progress*, Dec. 8, 1988; *Seattle Times*, Dec. 7, 1988.

Mass and breakfast with John Paul II from Hunthausen interview, May 21, 1992; James Michener, *Pilgrimage, A Memoir of Poland and Rome* (Emmaus, PA: Rodale Press, 1990), 91–93.

Hunthausen letter on archdiocesan response to Vatican concerns and reaction from *The Progress*, Dec. 22, 1988; VLM 0909, videotape of Hunthausen and Murphy press conference, Dec. 7, 1988, Public Affairs Department, Archdiocese of Seattle; *Seattle Times*, Dec. 25, 1988.

Remarks by John Paul II and Cardinal Ratzinger at March 1989 meeting with U.S. archbishops from *Origins* 18, no. 41 (March 23, 1989); *The Progress*, March 16, 1989; *New York Times*, March 12, 1989.

Hunthausen, his planned remarks, reaction to Gantin letter at the U.S. archbishops' meeting with pope and curia from Hunthausen interview, April 23, 1992.

Murphy wanting reassignment from Hunthausen interview, May 29, 1992.

Hunthausen's and Murphy's reactions to announcement ending the visitation from *The Progress*, April 13, 1989.

Story of letter from Archbishop Jean Jadot to Hunthausen from Cox interview, July 5, 2013.

Chapter 12: Farewell

Hunthausen's working relationship with Murphy from Hunthausen interview, May 21, 1992; Cox interview, July 5, 2013.

Quote from Hunthausen on the climate of permissiveness from *National Catholic Reporter*, June 3, 1988.

Hunthausen remarks to Pax Christi meeting from *Seattle Times*, Aug. 1, 1987; *National Catholic Reporter*, Aug. 14, 1987.

Hunthausen speeches on college campuses from *Seattle Times*, Nov. 9, 1987, March 7, 1988.

Denial of honorary doctorate from *The Progress*, May 16, 1991; Hunthausen interview, June 7, 1992.

Palm Sunday and Ash Wednesday peace events from *Seattle Times*, March 28, 1988, Feb. 3, 1989.

Hunthausen at peace events against the Gulf War from *The Progress*, Jan. 3, 17, 24, 1991; *Seattle Times*, Jan. 11, 1991; author's presence at those events.

Dignity 1987 statement of purpose from http://www.dignityusa.org/node/979.

Dignity's conversations with Hunthausen and Murphy from Roche interview, Sept. 9, 1992; *The Progress*, July 7, 1988; *Seattle Times*, June 30, July 16, Aug. 9, 1988.

Roche's efforts to speak with U.S. bishops' leadership from Roche interview, Sept. 9, 1992; *The Progress*, April 26, 1990.

McGreal and the magnitude of clergy sex abuse scandal in Seattle from *Seattle Times*, May 26, 1988, May 17, 2002, Sept. 12, 2003, Aug. 28, 2011; *Seattle P-I*, Sept 12, 2003.

Quote from Jason Berry on Hunthausen publicizing sexual abuse from *Seattle Times*, May 17, 2002.

Conn pedophile case from *Seattle Times*, May 3, 1988, May 18, 2002; *Seattle P-I*, Sept. 5, 2003; Cox interview, July 5, 2013; *The Progress*, Nov. 24, 1988.

Development of clergy sexual abuse policy in Seattle archdiocese from *The Progress*, June 23, 1988, March 8, 1990; *Seattle Times*, May 17, 2002.

Jaeger sex abuse case from *Seattle Times*, Sept. 1, 2002.

Appointment of women as parochial ministers from *Seattle Times*, May 17, 1987, Nov. 18, 1989, June 7, 1990; *Seattle P-I*, June 7, 1990.

U.S. bishops' pastoral letter on women from Hunthausen interview, April 15, 1992; *New York Times*, Nov. 19, 1992; Briggs, *Holy Siege*, 469–72, 574–75.

"Listening sessions" on women's pastoral in Seattle archdiocese from *The Progress*, April 12, July 5, 1990.

Suspension of deacon program from Hunthausen interview, Feb. 27, 1992; *The Progress*, March 8, 15, April 19, 1990.

Anecdote about Murphy and martyrdom from Dennis O'Leary interview, July 7, 1992.

Hunthausen's draft letters of resigning and not resigning from Hunthausen interview, Feb. 5, 1991.

Hunthausen announcement of resignation at Ocean Shores from *Seattle P-I*, June 19, 1991; *Seattle Times*, June 19, 1991; *The Progress*, June 20, 1991; Byrne interview, Feb. 25, 1993.

Hunthausen farewell address from *Origins* 21, no. 14 (Sept. 12, 1991).

Afterword

Editorial urging Hunthausen to speak out from *National Catholic Reporter*, July 5, 1991.

Hunthausen's post-retirement life from Hunthausen interviews, May 29, Oct. 12, 1992, July 17, 1993; Ryan interview, Jan. 8, 1993; Greytak interview, June 17, 1992.

Hunthausen's spiritual direction work from Hunthausen interviews, April 15, Oct. 12, 1992; Untener interview, June 9, 1992; *Origins* 25, no. 35 (Feb. 22, 1996).

Hunthausen's remarks on God's love, anecdote about grandniece from his presentation to staff at Catholic Community Services of Western Washington on May 2, 1996; Hunthausen interview, May 29, 1992.

Background on Archbishop Brunett from *Seattle P-I*, Oct. 11, 2004.

Background on Archbishop Sartain from http://en.wikipedia.org/wiki/J._Peter_Sartain; *Seattle Times*, Aug. 4, 2012, Jan. 16, 2014.

Background on Pope Francis from "Pope Francis: The Exclusive Interview," *America*, Sept. 30, 2013; James Carroll, "Who Am I To Judge?" *New Yorker*, Dec. 23 and 30, 2013; *The Economist*, March 8, 2014; *National Catholic Reporter*, July 3, 28, 2013; Massimo Faggioli, "The Italian Job," *Commonweal*, Aug. 15, 2014.

BIBLIOGRAPHY

Allen, John L., Jr. *Pope Benedict XVI: A Biography of Joseph Ratzinger.* New York: Continuum, 2000.

Atkins, Gary L. *Gay Seattle: Stories of Exile and Belonging.* Seattle: University of Washington Press, 2003.

Beattie-Prouty, Marnie. *Sweet Burdens on My Heart.* Paradiso, 1995.

Bernardin, Joseph L. *The Gift of Peace.* Chicago: Loyola Press, 1997.

Bernstein, Carl. "The Holy Alliance: Ronald Reagan and John Paul II." *Time.* February 24, 1992.

Bokenkotter, Thomas. *Essential Catholicism.* Garden City, NY: Doubleday, 1985.

Briggs, Kenneth A. *Holy Siege: The Year that Shook Catholic America.* New York: HarperCollins, 1992.

Brown, Robert McAfee. *Reflections Over the Long Haul: A Memoir.* Louisville, KY: Westminster John Knox Press, 2005.

Casserly, Brian. "Confronting the U.S. Navy at Bangor, 1973–1982." *Pacific Northwest Quarterly*, Summer 2004.

Castelli, Jim. *The Bishops and the Bomb.* Garden City, NY: Image Books, 1983.

De Mello, Anthony, SJ, *Awareness.* New York: Image Books, 1992.

DeRoo, Remi. *Chronicles of a Vatican II Bishop.* Toronto: Novalis, 2012.

Douglass, James W. *The Nonviolent Cross: A Theology of Revolution and Peace.* New York: Macmillan, 1968.

———. *Resistance and Contemplation: The Way of Liberation.* New York: Dell, 1972.

Dundas, Matt, "Post-Vietnam: Non-Violence at Bangor." Anti-Nuclear Special Section, *Pacific Northwest Labor and Civil Rights Projects.* University of Washington, 2008.

Faggioli, Massimo. *Vatican II: The Battle for Meaning.* New York: Paulist Press, 2012.

Fox, Matthew. *The Pope's War.* New York: Sterling Ethos, 2011.

Fromherz, Frank A. "Archbishop Raymond Hunthausen's Thought and Practice in Society and Church: A Socio-Historical & Ethical Case Study of Nonviolence." PhD dissertation, Graduate Theological Union, Berkeley, CA 1990.

Hahnenberg, Edward P. *A Concise Guide to the Documents of Vatican II.* Cincinnati, OH: Franciscan Media, 2007.

Hollis, Christopher, *The Achievements of Vatican II*. New York: Hawthorn Books, 1967.

Hunthausen, Raymond G., "We Need a Miracle—Expect One: Reminiscences on Vatican II and My Life as a Bishop," *Seattle Theology and Ministry Review,* Vol. 3, 2003.

Kaiser, Robert Blair. *Inside the Council*. London: Burns & Oates, 1963.

Keane, Philip S., SS. *Sexual Morality: A Catholic Perspective*. New York: Paulist Press, 1977.

Kelly, Msgr. George A., *Battle for the American Church Revisited*. San Francisco: Ignatius Press, 1995.

————. *The Crisis of Authority, John Paul II and the American Bishops*. Chicago: Regnery Gateway, 1982.

Kennedy, Eugene. *Tomorrow's Catholics, Yesterday's Church, The Two Cultures of American Catholicism*. New York: Harper & Row, 1988.

Killen, Patricia O'Connell. *Abundance of Grace: The History of the Archdiocese of Seattle, 1850–2000*. Archdiocese of Seattle, 2000.

Lader, Lawrence. *Politics, Power and the Church*. New York: Macmillan, 1987.

Lehman, John. "The Immorality of Unilateral Disarmament." *Origins*, Vol. 11, No. 42, April 1, 1982.

Loeb, Paul Rogat. *Hope in Hard Times: America's Peace Movement and the Reagan Era*. Lexington, MA: Lexington Books, D. C. Heath, 1987.

Lernoux, Penny. *People of God: The Struggle for World Catholicism*. New York: Penguin Books, 1989.

MacEoin, Gary. *What Happened at Rome? The Council and Its Implications for the Modern World*. New York: Echo Books, 1967.

McClory, Robert. *Turning Point: The Inside Story of the Papal Birth Control Commission and How Humanae Vitae Changed the Life of Patty Crowley and the Future of the Church*. New York: Crossroad, 1995.

McCormick, Richard A., SJ. *Corrective Vision: Explorations in Moral Theology*. Kansas City: Sheed & Ward, 1994.

McSorley, Richard, SJ. "It's a Sin to Build a Nuclear Weapon." *U.S. Catholic*, October 1976.

Mercier, Laurie. *Anaconda: Labor, Community, and Culture in Montana's Smelter City*. Urbana and Chicago: University of Illinois Press, 2001.

Michener, James A. *Pilgrimage: A Memoir of Poland and Rome*. Emmaus, PA, 1990.

Miles, Michael. *Love is Always*. New York: Avon Books, 1986.

Muggeridge, Anne Roche. *The Desolate City: Revolution in the Catholic Church*. San Francisco: Harper & Row, 1986.

Musto, Ronald G. *The Catholic Peace Tradition*. New York: Peace Books, 2002.

O'Malley, John W. *What Happened at Vatican II*. Cambridge, MA: Harvard University Press, 2008.

Quinn, John R. *The Reform of the Papacy*. New York: Crossroad Publishing, 1999.

Ratzinger, Cardinal Joseph, with Vittorio Messori. *The Ratzinger Report*. San Francisco: Ignatius Press, 1985.

Reese, Thomas J. *Archbishop: Inside the Power Structure of the American Catholic Church*. New York: Harper & Row, 1989.

Rueda, Enrique. *The Homosexual Network, Private Lives and Public Policy*. Old Greenwich, CT: Devin Adair, 1982.

Rynne, Xavier. *Vatican Council II*. Maryknoll, NY: Orbis Books, 1999.

Schell, Jonathan. "The Fate of the Earth." *The New Yorker*, February 1982.

Semmens, John Mark. "A Man Called Dutch: The Lasting Impact of Archbishop Raymond G. Hunthausen on Carroll College." PhD dissertation, Carroll College, 2008.

Schoenberg, Wilfred P., SJ. *A History of the Catholic Church in the Pacific Northwest, 1743–1983*. Washington, DC: Pastoral Press, 1987.

Scripko, Robert B. "A Moral Agent: Bishop as Leader." Phd dissertation, Gonzaga University, 1992.

Thavis, John. *The Vatican Diaries*. New York: Penguin, 2013.

Theroux, Phyllis. *The Good Bishop*. Maryknoll, NY: Orbis Books, 2013.

Thomas, Gordon and Max Morgan-Witts. *The Year of Armageddon: The Pope and the Bomb*. London: Panther Books, 1985.

Tracy, Robert E. *American Bishop at the Vatican Council*. New York: McGraw-Hill, 1966.

Van Breemen, Peter G., SJ. *As Bread That is Broken*. Denville, NJ: Dimension Books, 1973.

Vistica, Gregory L. *Fall From Glory: The Men Who Sank the U.S. Navy*. New York: Touchstone, 1997.

Walsh, Nicolas E.. *Memoirs/Reflections*, unpublished writings, Catholic Diocese of Boise Archives.

Weigel, George. *Witness to Hope*. New York: HarperCollins, 1999

——. *The End and the Beginning*. New York: Doubleday, 2010.

——. *Tranquillitas Ordinis: The Present Failure and Future Promise of American Catholic Thought on War and Peace*. New York: Oxford University Press, 1987.

INDEX